Data Structures in Depth Using C++

Mahmmoud Mahdi

Data Structures in Depth Using C++

A Comprehensive Guide to Data Structure Implementation and Optimization in C++

Apress®

Mahmmoud Mahdi
Zagazig, Egypt

ISBN-13(pbk): 979-8-8688-0801-2   ISBN-13(electronic): 979-8-8688-0802-9
https://doi.org/10.1007/979-8-8688-0802-9

© Mahmmoud Mahdi 2025

This work is subject to copyright. All rights are reserved by the Publisher, whether the whole or part of the material is concerned, specifically the rights of translation, reprinting, reuse of illustrations, recitation, broadcasting, reproduction on microfilms or in any other physical way, and transmission or information storage and retrieval, electronic adaptation, computer software, or by similar or dissimilar methodology now known or hereafter developed.

Trademarked names, logos, and images may appear in this book. Rather than use a trademark symbol with every occurrence of a trademarked name, logo, or image we use the names, logos, and images only in an editorial fashion and to the benefit of the trademark owner, with no intention of infringement of the trademark.

The use in this publication of trade names, trademarks, service marks, and similar terms, even if they are not identified as such, is not to be taken as an expression of opinion as to whether or not they are subject to proprietary rights.

While the advice and information in this book are believed to be true and accurate at the date of publication, neither the authors nor the editors nor the publisher can accept any legal responsibility for any errors or omissions that may be made. The publisher makes no warranty, express or implied, with respect to the material contained herein.

Managing Director, Apress Media LLC: Welmoed Spahr
Acquisitions Editor: Melissa Duffy
Development Editor: James Markham
Coordinating Editor: Gryffin Winkler

Cover designed by eStudioCalamar

Cover image by Mahmmoud Mahdi

Distributed to the book trade worldwide by Apress Media, LLC, 1 New York Plaza, New York, NY 10004, U.S.A. Phone 1-800-SPRINGER, fax (201) 348-4505, e-mail orders-ny@springer-sbm.com, or visit www.springeronline.com. Apress Media, LLC is a California LLC and the sole member (owner) is Springer Science + Business Media Finance Inc (SSBM Finance Inc). SSBM Finance Inc is a **Delaware** corporation.

For information on translations, please e-mail booktranslations@springernature.com; for reprint, paperback, or audio rights, please e-mail bookpermissions@springernature.com.

Apress titles may be purchased in bulk for academic, corporate, or promotional use. eBook versions and licenses are also available for most titles. For more information, reference our Print and eBook Bulk Sales web page at http://www.apress.com/bulk-sales.

Any source code or other supplementary material referenced by the author in this book is available to readers on GitHub (https://github.com/Apress). For more detailed information, please visit https://www.apress.com/gp/services/source-code.

If disposing of this product, please recycle the paper.

To my dear father, may God forgive him.

Contents

About the Author xv

About the Technical Reviewer xvii

Acknowledgments xix

Introduction xxi

Acronyms xxv

1 Introduction 1

1.1 Introduction — 2
1.1.1 What Are Data Structures and Algorithms? 2
1.1.2 Interplay Between Data Structures and Algorithms 2
1.1.3 The Significance of Data Structures 3
1.1.4 Selecting the Appropriate Data Structure 4

1.2 Types of Data Structures — 5

1.3 Fundamentals of Algorithms — 6
1.3.1 Distinguishing Programming and Algorithmic Problems 6
1.3.2 Algorithm Design Strategies 7
1.3.3 Common Algorithmic Problem Types 8

1.4 Analyzing Algorithm Efficiency — 8
1.4.1 Understanding Algorithm Analysis 8

1.4.2	Evaluating Algorithms	9
1.4.3	Analyzing Time Efficiency	9
1.4.4	Understanding Growth Orders	9
1.4.5	Evaluating Algorithm Performance	10
1.4.6	Asymptotic Growth Orders	10

1.5 Summary — 11

Problems — 11

2 Primary Building Blocks — 15

2.1 Principles of Software Design — 16

2.2 Data Structure Interfaces — 16

2.2.1	Benefits of Using Interfaces	16
2.2.2	Interface vs. Implementation	17
2.2.3	Interface Example	18

2.3 Templates — 19

2.3.1	Templates and Type Abstraction	19
2.3.2	Template Usage in Practical Scenarios	19
2.3.3	Templates in Interface Design	20
2.3.4	Considerations and Best Practices	20

2.4 Core Data Structure and Interfaces — 21

2.4.1	List Data Structure	21
2.4.2	Sets Data Structure	24

2.5 Advanced Data Structure Interfaces — 26

2.5.1	Tree Data Structure	26

2.6 Summary — 30

Problems — 31

3 Arrays and Dynamic Arrays — 33

3.1 Arrays and Pointers — 34

3.1.1	Arrays	34
3.1.2	Pointers to Arrays	36
3.1.3	Stack vs. Heap Arrays	36
3.1.4	Performance Analysis	37
3.1.5	Advantages and Limitations	40

3.2 Dynamic Arrays — 41

3.2.1	Resizable Array	41
3.2.2	Advantages and Limitations	41

3.2.3	Dynamic Array Implementation	42
3.2.4	Resizing Operation	47

3.3 Optimization — 48
3.3.1	An Optimized Copy	48
3.3.2	Optimized Dynamic Array Operations	48

3.4 Summary — 50

Problems — 50

4 Linked List — 57

4.1 Introduction to Linked Pointers — 58
4.1.1	Pointers to Objects	58
4.1.2	Creating Linked Objects	60
4.1.3	Memory Management	62
4.1.4	Why Pointers Matter in Linked Lists	63

4.2 A Singly-Linked List (SLList) — 63
4.2.1	Anatomy of a Singly-Linked List	63
4.2.2	Creating a Singly-Linked List Without Tail	64
4.2.3	Creating a Singly-Linked List with a Tail	71
4.2.4	Accessing Elements	78
4.2.5	Traversing	79

4.3 A Doubly-Linked List (DLList) — 80
4.3.1	Anatomy of a Doubly-Linked List	80
4.3.2	A Circular Doubly-Linked List with Dummy Node	80
4.3.3	Implementing Operations	82
4.3.4	Insert and Remove	85
4.3.5	Accessing Elements	89
4.3.6	Traversing	89

4.4 Performance Analysis — 90
4.4.1	Linked Lists vs. Arrays	90
4.4.2	Linked List Performance Comparison	91
4.4.3	Best Practices and Common Use Cases	92

4.5 Summary — 93

Problems — 95

5 Stack and Queue — 99

5.1 Stack — 100
5.1.1	Introduction to Stack	100
5.1.2	Array-Based Stack	100

5.1.3	Linked List Stack	102
5.2	**Queue (Single-Ended Queue)**	**103**
5.2.1	Introduction to Queue	103
5.2.2	Array-Based Queue	103
5.2.3	Linked List Queue	113
5.3	**Deque (Double-Ended Queue)**	**114**
5.3.1	Introduction to Deque	114
5.3.2	Array-Based Deque	115
5.3.3	Linked List Deque	119
5.4	**Performance Analysis**	**121**
5.4.1	Stack Performance Analysis	121
5.4.2	Queue Performance Analysis	121
5.4.3	Deque Performance Analysis	121
5.4.4	Choosing the Right Data Structure	121
5.5	**Summary**	**122**
	Problems	**122**

6 Hash Tables 129

6.1	**Hashing Introduction**	**130**
6.1.1	Array vs. Linked List	130
6.1.2	Introducing Hash Tables	130
6.1.3	Applications of Hashing	131
6.1.4	Usage Example: Management and Analysis of Access Logs	131
6.2	**Hash Functions**	**133**
6.2.1	Use of Hash Functions	133
6.2.2	Multiplicative Hash Function	133
6.2.3	Generating Hash Codes for Various Data Types	135
6.2.4	Collisions	139
6.3	**Hash Table Techniques**	**140**
6.3.1	Chaining	140
6.3.2	Open Addressing	141
6.3.3	Performance Analysis	144
6.4	**Hash Table Implementation**	**147**
6.4.1	Chaining	147
6.4.2	Linear Probing	150
6.4.3	Hash Table Performance Comparison	158
6.5	**Summary**	**159**
	Problems	**159**

7 Trees ... 165

7.1 Binary Trees — 166
- 7.1.1 Introduction to Binary Trees ... 166
- 7.1.2 Properties of Binary Trees ... 166
- 7.1.3 Types of Binary Trees ... 166
- 7.1.4 Representation of Binary Trees ... 168
- 7.1.5 Computing Size, Height, and Depth ... 171
- 7.1.6 Destroying a Binary Tree ... 173
- 7.1.7 Binary Tree Traversal Methods ... 174
- 7.1.8 Implementation of Traversal Techniques ... 175
- 7.1.9 Traversing Binary Trees – Examples ... 177
- 7.1.10 Comparison of Tree Traversal Methods ... 179

7.2 Binary Search Trees (BSTs) — 179
- 7.2.1 Introduction to Binary Search Trees ... 179
- 7.2.2 Properties of Binary Search Trees ... 180
- 7.2.3 Basic Operations in BST ... 180
- 7.2.4 Performance Analysis ... 186
- 7.2.5 Class Implementation of BST ... 186
- 7.2.6 Summary ... 187

7.3 Balanced Binary Trees — 187
- 7.3.1 Unbalanced Binary Search Trees ... 187
- 7.3.2 Self-Balancing Binary Search Trees ... 188

7.4 AVL Trees — 190
- 7.4.1 Introduction to AVL Trees ... 190
- 7.4.2 AVL Property ... 190
- 7.4.3 Balanced and Unbalanced AVL Trees ... 191
- 7.4.4 Rotations in AVL Trees ... 191
- 7.4.5 Implementation of AVL Tree ... 196
- 7.4.6 Performance Analysis ... 201

7.5 Summary — 201

Problems — 203

8 Graphs ... 207

8.1 Introduction to Graphs — 208
- 8.1.1 What Is a Graph? ... 208
- 8.1.2 Graph Terminology ... 209
- 8.1.3 Types of Graphs ... 209
- 8.1.4 Examples and Applications ... 211
- 8.1.5 Difference Between Graph and Tree ... 212

8.2 Graph Representations — 212
- 8.2.1 Basic Graph Operations — 212
- 8.2.2 Abstract Interface for Graph Class — 213
- 8.2.3 Adjacency Matrix — 217
- 8.2.4 Adjacency List — 227
- 8.2.5 Other Representations — 236
- 8.2.6 Conclusion — 236

8.3 Graph Traversals and Advanced Operations — 236
- 8.3.1 Depth-First Traversal (DFS) — 236
- 8.3.2 Breadth-First Traversal (BFS) — 238
- 8.3.3 Advanced Graph Operations — 240
- 8.3.4 Graph Traversal Class Updates — 242

8.4 Performance Considerations — 243
- 8.4.1 Time Complexity of Graph Operations — 243
- 8.4.2 Space Complexity — 243
- 8.4.3 Choosing the Right Representation — 244

8.5 Summary — 244

Problems — 246

9 Specialized Data Structures and Techniques — 249

9.1 Introduction — 250

9.2 Heaps — 250
- 9.2.1 Introduction to Heaps — 250
- 9.2.2 Binary Heaps — 253
- 9.2.3 Optimizing Binary Heap Operations — 263
- 9.2.4 Customizing Binary Heaps with HeapType — 264

9.3 Priority Queues — 267
- 9.3.1 Introduction to Priority Queues — 267
- 9.3.2 Implementing a Priority Queue with a Heap — 267
- 9.3.3 Priority Queue Operations — 269
- 9.3.4 Performance Analysis — 271

9.4 Maps — 272
- 9.4.1 Introduction to Maps — 272
- 9.4.2 Key-Value Pairs — 272
- 9.4.3 Map Structure — 273
- 9.4.4 Implementing a Map — 273

9.5 A Space-Efficient Linked List — 279
- 9.5.1 Structure of a Space-Efficient Linked List — 279

9.5.2	Node Definition	281
9.5.3	Implementation of Space-Efficient Linked List	282
9.5.4	Performance Analysis	293
9.5.5	Advantages and Trade-Offs	293

9.6 Skip Lists — 294

9.6.1	Introduction to Skip Lists	294
9.6.2	Skip List Structure and Rules	294
9.6.3	Node Structure Definition	296
9.6.4	Skip List Class Definition	296
9.6.5	Implementing Operations	297
9.6.6	Performance Analysis	305

9.7 Summary — 306

Problems — 307

10 Applications and Real-World Examples — 311

10.1 Task Scheduling System — 312

10.1.1	Solution and Analysis	312
10.1.2	Implementation	314
10.1.3	Method Implementations	316
10.1.4	Example Scenario	321
10.1.5	Performance Analysis	322
10.1.6	Optimization	323

10.2 Social Network Friend Recommendations — 324

10.2.1	Solution and Analysis	324
10.2.2	Implementation	326
10.2.3	Method Implementations	327
10.2.4	Example Scenario	335
10.2.5	Performance Analysis	336
10.2.6	Optimization	337

10.3 Library Management System — 338

10.3.1	Solution and Analysis	339
10.3.2	Implementation	339
10.3.3	Method Implementations	343
10.3.4	Example Scenario	350
10.3.5	Performance Analysis	351
10.3.6	Optimization	352

10.4	**Summary**	**352**
10.5	**Book Summary**	**352**
	Problems	**353**

Index 357

About the Author

Mahmmoud A. Mahdi, Ph.D., is a seasoned computer science professional with extensive experience in academia, research, and software development since 2005. His expertise spans machine learning, natural language processing, and programming, with a strong emphasis on C++. Over the course of his career, he has developed enterprise-grade solutions, led pioneering projects in big data analytics and Arabic natural language processing, and designed a custom compiler for robotic simulation that serves as both a technical innovation and an educational tool.

He has a profound focus on algorithm design and analysis, tackling complex computational challenges with innovative solutions. His research interests, published in leading journals and conferences, reflect his dedication to advancing the fields of computational research and scalable systems.

As an experienced educator, Dr. Mahdi has designed and delivered courses on data structures, algorithms, machine learning, and software testing, emphasizing the practical application of theoretical concepts. His book, *Data Structures in Depth Using C++*, reflects his decades of teaching, research, and hands-on experience, providing readers with a seamless integration of foundational knowledge and real-world insights.

Beyond his academic and research endeavors, Dr. Mahdi is dedicated to fostering innovation, collaboration, and excellence in programming and software development. He continues to inspire the next generation of technologists, equipping them to bridge the gap between theory and practice and drive progress in the field of computer science.

About the Technical Reviewer

Wael Said received his M.Sc. degree in Computer Science from Helwan University in 2004 and his Ph.D. degree in Computer Science in 2011 from Technical University Darmstadt. He is Associate Professor in the Department of Computer Science, Faculty of Computers and Informatics, at Zagazig University and currently is Assistant Professor in the Department of Computer Science, College of Computer Science and Engineering, Taibah University, Saudi Arabia. His research interests are in the areas of machine and deep learning, text and data mining, data analysis and data science, cloud and mobile computing, information and database security, as well as cryptography and cryptanalysis.

Acknowledgments

The journey of writing this book has been a rewarding and enlightening experience, and it would not have been possible without the support and encouragement of many individuals who contributed in various ways.

I would like to express my deepest gratitude to my family for their unconditional love, patience, and support. Your encouragement has been my greatest motivation throughout this process, and I am forever grateful for your belief in me.

A special thanks to Dr. Wael Said, whose insightful reviews and constructive feedback greatly enriched the quality of this book. Your expertise and guidance were invaluable in refining the content and ensuring its accuracy.

A special acknowledgment goes to my outstanding student, Fatma Omara, whose meticulous revisions and thoughtful suggestions greatly improved the clarity and coherence of the material. I am also deeply thankful to Menna Jaheen for her creative contributions to the book's visual appeal, particularly her work on the engaging cartoon graphics. I would also like to extend my heartfelt appreciation to the team at Apress. Managing Director, Welmoed Spahr, Acquisitions Editor, Melissa Duffy, Development Editor, James Markham, and Coordinating Editor, Gryffin Winkler, your professionalism, dedication, and attention to detail were instrumental in bringing this book to life. I am deeply thankful for your guidance and support throughout the publishing process.

Finally, I wish to thank you, the reader, for choosing this book. I hope it serves as a valuable resource on your journey to mastering data structures and algorithms in C++. Your enthusiasm for learning inspires the creation of works like this, and I am honored to be a part of your educational journey.

Thank you all for your support.

Introduction

Welcome to *Data Structures in Depth Using C++*, a comprehensive guide designed to help you master the fundamental and advanced concepts of data structures and algorithms. This book is your gateway to understanding how to efficiently organize, manage, and manipulate data to solve complex computational problems. Whether you are a student, educator, or professional, this book will equip you with the knowledge and skills to implement and optimize data structures using C++, one of the most powerful and widely used programming languages in the software industry.

The content below already serves as the introduction, addressing what the book is about, its target audience, the structure, and learning outcomes. It includes:

Who This Book Is For
Structure of the Book
Learning Outcomes

Who This Book Is For

This book is intended for **students**, **educators**, and **professionals** alike who wish to deepen their understanding of data structures and algorithms using C++. Whether you're a beginner looking to get started with the basics or an experienced developer aiming to refine your skills, this book offers something valuable for every reader. The content is particularly suited for those preparing for technical interviews, academic examinations, or looking to enhance their problem-solving abilities in software development.

Structure of the Book

The book is structured to take the reader on a journey from the basic concepts to the more advanced topics in data structures. Each chapter follows a structured approach:

- **Introduction:** Each chapter begins with an overview of the data structure, including its definition, characteristics, and common use cases.
- **Implementation:** This section provides a step-by-step guide to implementing the data structure using C++. The code examples are thoroughly explained, ensuring that readers understand every line of code.
- **Performance Analysis and Optimization:** This section analyzes the efficiency of the data structures and explores techniques to optimize their performance.
- **Exercises:** To reinforce learning, each chapter concludes with a set of exercises, ranging from basic to challenging, designed to test the reader's understanding and encourage further exploration.

The chapters are organized as follows:

- **Chapter 1: Introduction** – Covers the fundamentals of data structures and algorithms, their significance, and the interplay between them
- **Chapter 2: Primary Building Blocks** – Discusses the principles of software design, data structure interfaces, and the use of templates
- **Chapter 3: Arrays and Dynamic Arrays** – Focuses on array structures, including static and dynamic arrays, their implementation, and optimization techniques
- **Chapter 4: Linked List** – Explores singly- and doubly-linked lists, their memory management, and performance analysis
- **Chapter 5: Stack and Queue** – Introduces stack and queue structures, including array-based and linked list implementations, and their performance considerations
- **Chapter 6: Hash Tables** – Discusses hashing techniques, hash functions, and hash table implementation strategies
- **Chapter 7: Trees** – Delves into binary trees, binary search trees, and AVL trees, covering their properties, operations, and performance analysis
- **Chapter 8: Graphs** – Covers graph theory, graph representations, and advanced operations like traversals and graph algorithms
- **Chapter 9: Specialized Data Structures and Techniques** – Introduces advanced data structures like heaps, skip lists, and space-efficient linked lists
- **Chapter 10: Applications and Real-World Examples** – Provides case studies and real-world examples that demonstrate the application of data structures in practical scenarios, such as task scheduling, social network analysis, and library management systems

By reading this book, you will:

- Gain a deep understanding of data structures and their implementation in C++
- Learn how to optimize data handling and storage for efficient software performance
- Develop the ability to solve complex programming problems using appropriate data structures
- Understand best practices in data structure design and performance analysis

How to Use This Book

Each chapter includes detailed explanations, code snippets, and exercises to reinforce learning. The code examples are designed to be run in a standard C++ development environment, and the exercises at the end of each chapter provide opportunities to test your understanding. Whether you are reading sequentially or jumping to specific topics, this book aims to provide both theoretical insights and practical skills. Use the exercises to practice and the case studies to see how these data structures are applied in real-world scenarios.

Final Remarks

Data Structures in Depth Using C++ is more than a textbook; it is a practical guide designed to help you transition from understanding basic concepts to mastering advanced data structures. The book encourages experimentation with code, exploration of exercises, and deeper engagement with C++ programming. By the end, you will have built a strong foundation in data structures, preparing you for advanced studies or professional development in computer science.

Enjoy your journey into the world of data structures with C++!

Acronyms

ADT	Abstract Data Type
API	Application Programming Interface
ASCII	American Standard Code for Information Interchange
AVL	Adelson-Velsky and Landis
BFS	Breadth-First Search
BST	Binary Search Tree
DLList	Doubly-Linked List
DFS	Depth-First Search
FIFO	First In, First Out
GUI	Graphical User Interface
IDE	Integrated Development Environment
LIFO	Last In, First Out
LR	Left Rotation
LRR	Left-Right Rotation
OOP	Object-Oriented Programming
RLR	Right-Left Rotation
RR	Right Rotation
SEList	Space-Efficient List
SLList	Singly-Linked List
UML	Unified Modeling Language

1. Introduction

Objectives

In this chapter, I will introduce you to the world of data structures and algorithms, laying the foundation for understanding how these elements are pivotal in crafting efficient software solutions. Together, we will explore

- The **basic concepts** of data structures and how they are utilized to organize and store data efficiently
- The **distinction between data structures and algorithms**, illustrating their interdependence and individual roles in problem-solving
- **Core algorithms** and their functioning, setting the stage for deeper dives into algorithmic strategies and complexities
- **Algorithm analysis and design techniques**, including an introduction to complexity analysis, to equip you with the skills necessary to evaluate and choose the right algorithmic approach

By the end of this chapter, you will have a solid understanding of the foundational concepts of data structures and algorithms, preparing you to delve deeper into more complex structures and computational strategies in the subsequent chapters.

1.1 Introduction

In this section, I'll introduce you to the core concepts of data structures and algorithms, the fundamental elements in computer science and software engineering. We'll explore what data structures and algorithms are, their interplay, and why understanding this relationship is critical for creating efficient and effective software solutions.

1.1.1 What Are Data Structures and Algorithms?

Data structures are essential constructs that organize and store data within a computer's memory. They form the backbone of effective software development, enabling efficient data management to facilitate easy access, modification, and maintenance. Unlike file organization, which arranges data on disk storage, or data warehousing and databases, which are designed for large-scale data storage and retrieval across multiple platforms, data structures are primarily concerned with the optimization of performance and efficiency for specific algorithmic requirements in real-time processing environments. The design and selection of data structures are critical, focusing on leveraging the characteristics of memory usage to enhance application performance.

An **algorithm** is a finite sequence of well-defined, computer-implementable instructions, typically used to solve a class of problems or to perform a computation. Algorithms are essential for specifying how tasks are executed and in what order. They take one or more inputs, process them through a series of steps, and produce an output or a solution to the problem.

1.1.2 Interplay Between Data Structures and Algorithms

Data structures are the building blocks of algorithms, and the choice of a data structure can significantly impact the performance of an algorithm. In some cases, using the wrong data structure can make an algorithm unusable.

The relationship between data structures and algorithms can be likened to a "well-oiled machine": *data structures* provide the framework or the infrastructure, much like the gears and cogs in a machine, while *algorithms* act like the engine that drives these components to solve problems efficiently (see Figure 1.1). This synergy ensures that the overall system (or the solution developed) operates smoothly and effectively, maximizing performance and minimizing resource usage.

Illustrating the Relationship

Imagine a scenario where workers (representing data structures) are tasked with organizing and storing boxes in a warehouse. Alongside, a spider handler (symbolizing an algorithm) navigates through the warehouse, solving problems and collaborating with workers to optimize the arrangement and retrieval of boxes.

1.1 Introduction

Figure 1.1: Illustration of a spider handler (algorithm) solving problems and collaborating with workers (data structures) to efficiently organize and access data

Data structures and algorithms complement each other, with the efficacy of data handling and processing relying on their synergistic relationship.

Refer to Table 1.1 for a side-by-side comparison of algorithms and data structures, which will help you understand their unique characteristics and how they complement each other in the realm of computing.

1.1.3 The Significance of Data Structures

Data structures play an indispensable role in computer science and software development, transcending simply data storage to encompass efficient organization and management of data. These structures are crucial for enabling quick data access and manipulation, thereby forming the bedrock upon which algorithms operate. This, in turn, significantly influences the performance and scalability of software solutions.

The significance of data structures manifests in three key areas:

- **Enable Efficient Data Storage and Retrieval:** Data structures allow data to be stored in a way that enables fast retrieval. This is essential for managing and accessing information effectively.
- **Facilitate Algorithm Design:** Efficient data structures are the foundation of many algorithms. They allow one to design and implement algorithms that perform tasks more quickly and with fewer resources.
- **Key to Solving Complex Problems:** Many real-world problems require complex data manipulation. Effective data structures provide the tools to solve these problems efficiently.

Table 1.1: Comparison Between Algorithms and Data Structures

Aspect	Algorithm	Data Structure
Definition	A step-by-step procedure or formula for solving a problem	A particular way of organizing and storing data in a computer so that it can be accessed and modified efficiently
Purpose	To outline the process of solving a specific problem or performing a computation	To efficiently manage and organize data to enhance the performance of algorithms
Focus	Process and steps to achieve a task or solve a problem	Organization, management, and storage of data
Examples	Sorting algorithms (quick sort, merge sort), search algorithms (binary search, linear search)	Arrays, linked lists, trees, hash tables, stacks, queues
Operations	Executed to perform a task like searching, sorting, processing information	Include operations like insertion, deletion, traversal, and accessing data
Performance Measure	Time complexity and space complexity (efficiency of the algorithm)	Time complexity of operations (how quickly data can be accessed or modified)

1.1.4 Selecting the Appropriate Data Structure

Choosing the right data structure is a decision that can greatly influence the efficiency of your software. We will discuss the key factors to consider when selecting a data structure, ensuring you make informed decisions that enhance your application's performance and manageability.

There are many different types of data structures, each with its strengths and weaknesses. Choosing the right data structure for a particular application requires careful consideration of the following factors:

- **Access Patterns:** How often will the data be accessed? Will it be accessed randomly, sequentially, or both?
- **Insertion and Deletion Frequency:** How often will new elements be added to the data structure? How often will elements be removed?
- **Memory Constraints:** How much memory is available to store the data?
- **Performance Requirements:** How important are fast access times? How important is it to have efficient insertion and deletion operations?

Understanding these considerations helps in developing software that is both efficient and effective, capable of solving complex problems with optimal resource utilization. Once a data structure is chosen, its implementation should be both efficient and easy to understand.

1.2 Types of Data Structures

Data structures are essential for organizing, managing, and storing data in a computer. They are categorized into primitive and composite types, each serving specific computational purposes.

As you can see in Figure 1.2, data structures are divided based on their complexity and the operations they support, ranging from simple primitive types to more complex composite structures.

Data structures can be categorized into several types depending on their characteristics and functionality. Below is a detailed examination of these types.

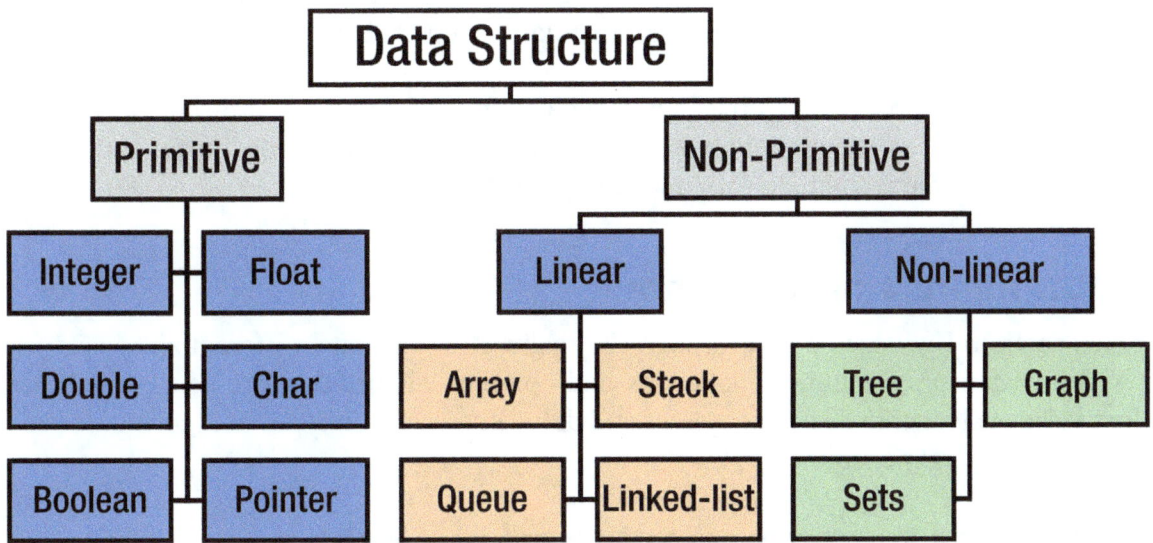

Figure 1.2: Types of data structures

Primitive Data Structures

In programming, you'll frequently encounter basic types essential for handling data. To give you a clear picture of these types, I've detailed them in Table 1.2, which includes examples to illustrate their practical applications.

Table 1.2: Examples of Primitive Data Structures in C++

Type	Use	Example
Integer	For whole numbers	`int age = 30`
Float	For single-precision floating numbers	`float temperature = 26.3f`
Double	For double-precision floating numbers	`double balance = 98765.43`
Char	For character representation	`char initial = 'A'`
Boolean	For true or false values	`bool isFullTime = true`
Pointer	For memory address referencing	`int* ptr = &age`

As you can see in Table 1.2, primitive data structures are the building blocks of data handling in programming, with each serving a specific and essential function in software development.

Composite Data Structures

Composite or non-primitive data structures build on the basics to enable more complex and efficient data organization. These structures can be broadly classified by their organization style:
- **Linear:** Data elements are stored in a sequential manner, facilitating ordered access. Common examples are arrays, stacks, queues, and linked lists.
- **Nonlinear:** Data elements are structured in a nonsequential arrangement, often to reflect hierarchical or interconnected relationships. This category includes trees, graphs, and sets.

Understanding the diverse types and functionalities of data structures allows you as a developer to choose the most suitable options to effectively address specific computational challenges and optimize the performance of applications.

1.3 Fundamentals of Algorithms

In this section, I will guide you through the realm of algorithms, differentiating between straightforward programming challenges and complex algorithmic problems. We'll explore various algorithm design strategies and delve into common types of algorithmic problems that you might encounter.

1.3.1 Distinguishing Programming and Algorithmic Problems

Let's begin by understanding the key differences between simple programming tasks and more complex algorithmic problems.

Simple Programming Problems

Simple programming tasks are often characterized by
- **Ease of Implementation:** Solutions are usually straightforward, requiring basic programming skills.
- **Direct Approach:** Problems can often be solved through a linear process or direct methods without the need for complex algorithms.
- **Limited Optimization:** These problems typically have a clear solution path, leaving little scope for significant performance improvements.

Examples:
- A script to calculate the sum of two numbers.
- A script to convert temperature from Celsius to Fahrenheit.
- Using a loop, print the first ten natural numbers.

1.3 Fundamentals of Algorithms

Algorithmic Problems

In contrast, algorithmic problems require a more in-depth approach:
- **Complex Solution Paths:** Finding a solution requires abstract thinking and strategic planning, often without a clear-cut path.
- **Execution Challenges:** Implementing solutions to these problems can be complex and requires advanced algorithmic strategies to optimize performance.
- **Optimization Opportunities:** There is a significant scope to improve solutions, enhance efficiency, and reduce resource consumption.
- **Algorithm Development:** Such problems may necessitate the development of bespoke algorithms or the innovative adaptation of existing ones.
- **Efficiency Analysis:** A key element is the evaluation and enhancement of the algorithm's efficiency to guarantee its scalability and performance.

Examples:
- Design an algorithm to sort a large dataset efficiently.
- Find the shortest path in a graph, such as querying the quickest route between two cities.

Given the importance of each difference, you can use the best method for such a problem, whether a simple programming task or a complex algorithmic challenge.

1.3.2 Algorithm Design Strategies

Developing effective algorithms is essential to solving challenging problems. Here are some of the basic strategies:
- **Brute Force:** Finding the best solution to the problem by testing all possible solutions
- **Divide and Conquer:** Breaking down the original problem into smaller subproblems until they can be solved, then merging the solutions
- **Greedy Method:** Choosing the best choice available at each step, aiming to find the best or a near-optimal solution
- **Dynamic Programming:** Solving overlapping subproblems once and reusing their solutions
- **Iterative Enhancement:** Gradually improving an available solution through repeated changes
- **Backtracking:** Exploring all potential solutions systematically and discarding paths that fail to meet the criteria
- **Branch and Bound:** Systematically exploring subproblems to find the optimal solution while pruning non-promising paths
- **Randomized Algorithms:** Using randomness in decision-making to simplify and speed up complex problems
- **Heuristic Algorithms:** Employing practical methods that may not guarantee an optimal solution but provide acceptable outcomes

These strategies are not stand-alone and can be combined to create efficient algorithms for solving complex computational problems. For example, dynamic programming can complement divide and conquer techniques, or heuristics can be used to improve greedy methods.

When choosing an algorithm design strategy, several factors should be considered:
- **Problem Nature:** The inherent characteristics and constraints of the problem
- **Solution Requirements:** The desired accuracy and optimality of the solution
- **Computational Resources:** The available time and memory for executing the algorithm
- **Scalability:** The algorithm's ability to handle increasing input sizes efficiently
- **Ease of Implementation:** The complexity of implementing the algorithm and the possibility of errors

By carefully evaluating these factors, you can choose the strategy or combination of strategies that is most appropriate to effectively meet the computational challenge at hand.

1.3.3 Common Algorithmic Problem Types

An understanding of different algorithmic problems is crucial for applying the appropriate algorithmic strategy. Here are some common types:
- **Sorting:** Organizing data in a specified order, such as numerical or alphabetical
- **Searching:** Identifying the existence or position of an element within a data structure
- **String Manipulation:** Performing operations on strings, such as matching, searching, and transformation
- **Graph Theory:** Solving problems involving nodes and the connections between them
- **Combinatorial Logic:** Dealing with the selection and arrangement of items from a set based on specified rules
- **Geometrical Computation:** Addressing issues related to spatial figures, measurements, and properties
- **Numerical Analysis:** Engaging in methods and operations involving numerical calculations

1.4 Analyzing Algorithm Efficiency

In this section, I will introduce you to the concept of algorithm analysis, where we delve into understanding how algorithms perform in terms of resource usage, specifically time and space. Let's explore how to evaluate and choose the most efficient algorithm for a given problem.

1.4.1 Understanding Algorithm Analysis

Algorithm analysis is the process of evaluating algorithms based on their resource consumption, focusing on time and space requirements. The goal here is to select the most efficient algorithm for our needs, ensuring optimal performance in our applications.

1.4 Analyzing Algorithm Efficiency

1.4.2 Evaluating Algorithms

When we talk about evaluating an algorithm, two primary aspects come into play:
1. **Time Efficiency:** This refers to how quickly an algorithm can solve the given problem.
2. **Space Efficiency:** This concerns the amount of memory required by the algorithm to execute.

Beyond performance, we also look into potential for enhancement:
1. **Lower Bounds:** What are the theoretical limitations on an algorithm's efficiency for this problem?
2. **Optimality:** Is there a possibility to devise an algorithm that surpasses current time and space efficiencies?

1.4.3 Analyzing Time Efficiency

In our journey to understand algorithms, it's crucial to delve into how time efficiency is evaluated. Let me guide you through this process, focusing on the basic operations and their impact on the algorithm's running time.

Calculating Running Time

The running time $T(n)$ of a program that implements an algorithm can be estimated using the formula:

$$T(n) \approx c_{op} \times C(n) \tag{1.1}$$

Here's what each term in Equation 1.1 represents:
- c_{op}: The time taken by the basic operation of the algorithm
- $C(n)$: The count of how often this basic operation is executed for an input size n

This calculation is pivotal as it helps us understand the time it takes for an algorithm to run and allows us to gauge its efficiency effectively.

1.4.4 Understanding Growth Orders

Growth order is a framework that helps us articulate how an algorithm's time complexity escalates with increasing input size. It's about comprehending the scalability of algorithms and their behaviors in extensive problem contexts.

Key considerations in growth order include
- The scalability of algorithm performance on enhanced hardware or with larger input sizes
- The implications of increasing the problem size on the algorithm's execution time

Recognizing these factors is essential in identifying the primary elements that influence algorithm efficiency, which is crucial for real-world applications.

1.4.5 Evaluating Algorithm Performance

To gain a well-rounded understanding of an algorithm's performance, we explore it under different conditions:

- **Worst-Case** ($C_{worst}(n)$): This scenario assesses the maximum resource usage across all possible inputs of size n.
- **Best-Case** ($C_{best}(n)$): Conversely, this scenario evaluates the minimum resource usage for any input of size n.
- **Average-Case** ($C_{avg}(n)$): This considers the expected resource usage across a spectrum of inputs of size n.

These perspectives offer a comprehensive view of an algorithm's efficiency and are instrumental in crafting robust and scalable algorithmic solutions.

1.4.6 Asymptotic Growth Orders

We use asymptotic notations such as $O(g(n))$, $\Theta(g(n))$, and $\Omega(g(n))$ to generalize the growth patterns of algorithms, focusing on the leading factors that affect their scalability with large inputs. These notations are indispensable for contrasting different algorithms and understanding their relative efficiencies.

Asymptotic Efficiency Classes

The concept of asymptotic efficiency classes categorizes algorithms based on their growth behavior, shedding light on their scalability. Table 1.3 outlines these classes, offering a glance at how different algorithms perform as their input size expands.

Table 1.3: Summary of Asymptotic Efficiency Classes

Class	Name	Examples
1	Constant	Operations with fixed execution time
$\log n$	Logarithmic	Searching in a sorted array
n	Linear	Traversing an array or list
$n \log n$	Linearithmic	Merge sort or heap sort
n^2	Quadratic	Nested loops on two-dimensional array
n^3	Cubic	Nested loops on three-dimensional array
2^n	Exponential	Solving subsets or combinations
$n!$	Factorial	Determining all permutations

In essence, understanding the asymptotic growth orders and efficiency classes is crucial for predicting how an algorithm will perform, especially as we deal with increasingly large datasets or complex problem domains.

1.5 Summary

In this chapter, I introduced you to the basics of data structures and algorithms, crucial for building efficient software. We explored what data structures are and how they help in organizing data, alongside the concept of algorithms as processes for solving problems.

The relationship between data structures and algorithms was highlighted, showing how the choice of data structure can affect the efficiency of an algorithm. We looked at different types of problems and how various algorithmic approaches address them, setting the foundation for more advanced topics to come.

We also touched on the importance of algorithm analysis and different strategies used in algorithm design, preparing you for deeper discussions in the following chapters. Moving forward to the next chapter, we will delve into the foundations of data structure design. You will uncover the principles guiding the design of robust and efficient data structures, such as modularity, encapsulation, and abstraction.

Problems

Discussion

Understanding Data Structures and Algorithms

1. Define an algorithm and explain its key characteristics. Provide an example of a real-world problem that can be solved using an algorithm.
2. Distinguish between simple programming problems and algorithm problems. Describe the characteristics of each and give an example of a problem for each category.
3. Discuss the importance of recognizing the distinctions between simple programming problems and algorithm problems when approaching problem solving. How can understanding these distinctions improve problem-solving strategies?
4. Categorize the following problems into the appropriate problem types:
    - Sorting a list of names
    - Finding the shortest path in a network
    - Checking if a given string is a palindrome
    - Determining the prime factors of a number

   Justify your categorization.

Analyzing Algorithm Efficiency

1. What is the primary objective of algorithm analysis, and why is it essential in the field of computer science?
2. Explain the distinction between time efficiency and space efficiency in algorithm analysis. Provide examples to illustrate each concept.
3. Describe the importance of lower bounds and optimality in algorithm analysis. How do they relate to evaluating algorithm performance?

4. What are the two main approaches to evaluating algorithms and how do they differ? Provide scenarios in which each approach is particularly useful.
5. Arrange the following classes of algorithms in ascending order of their growth rates, from the lowest growth rate to the highest:
    - $O(\sqrt{n})$
    - $O(n)$
    - $O(2n)$
    - $O(n^2)$
    - $O(\log n)$
    - $O(n \log n)$
    - $O(2^n)$

Multiple Choice Questions

1. Which of the following data structures is linear?
    (a) Tree
    (b) Graph
    (c) Stack
    (d) Set
2. What is the purpose of the Big-O notation in algorithm analysis?
    (a) To represent the best-case scenario
    (b) To indicate the exact running time of an algorithm
    (c) To describe the upper bound on the growth rate of an algorithm
    (d) To measure the space complexity of an algorithm
3. In the context of algorithm efficiency, what does $O(N^2)$ represent?
    (a) Linear time complexity
    (b) Quadratic time complexity
    (c) Logarithmic time complexity
    (d) Constant time complexity
4. In the context of algorithmic complexity, what does "space complexity" refer to?
    (a) The amount of memory an algorithm uses
    (b) The number of operations an algorithm performs
    (c) The time it takes for an algorithm to execute
    (d) The size of the input data
5. Which of the following is an example of an algorithm with exponential time complexity?
    (a) $O(N^2)$
    (b) $O(2^N)$
    (c) $O(\log N)$
    (d) $O(N \log N)$

1.5 Summary

6. What is the primary purpose of analyzing the time complexity of algorithms?
   (a) To determine the amount of memory used by an algorithm
   (b) To compare the performance of different algorithms
   (c) To measure the speed of an algorithm on a specific machine
   (d) To identify the best-case scenario for an algorithm's execution time
7. What is the significance of algorithm analysis in the context of data structures?
   (a) To design algorithms for data manipulation
   (b) To evaluate the efficiency of algorithms in terms of time and space
   (c) To implement data structures in a programming language
   (d) To analyze the theoretical properties of data structures
8. What does "order of growth" refer to in the analysis of algorithm efficiency?
   (a) The actual running time of an algorithm
   (b) The space complexity of an algorithm
   (c) The rate at which the algorithm's performance grows with input size
   (d) The number of operations performed by the algorithm
9. In the context of algorithm efficiency analysis, what do best-case, average-case, and worst-case scenarios represent?
   (a) Different types of algorithms
   (b) Different input scenarios that affect algorithm performance
   (c) Various stages of algorithm execution
   (d) Different measures of space complexity
10. Why is the understanding of asymptotic order of growth important in algorithm analysis?
    (a) To measure the actual running time of an algorithm
    (b) To compare the efficiency of different algorithms
    (c) To focus on the dominant term that determines algorithm performance with large inputs
    (d) To analyze the best-case scenario of algorithm execution
11. What is the primary importance of data structures in computer science?
    (a) To determine the time complexity of algorithms
    (b) To analyze the space efficiency of algorithms
    (c) To organize and manage data for efficient access and modification
    (d) To evaluate the worst-case scenario of algorithm execution
12. What is the primary purpose of theoretical analysis of time efficiency in algorithm design?
    (a) To determine the best-case scenario
    (b) To evaluate the worst-case scenario
    (c) To understand the mathematical properties of algorithm performance
    (d) To analyze the time complexity under different input scenarios

13. When analyzing the order of growth in algorithm efficiency, why is it important to consider the asymptotic order of growth rather than the exact running time?
    (a) Asymptotic analysis provides a more accurate representation of real-world performance.
    (b) Asymptotic analysis focuses on the dominant term that determines performance with large inputs.
    (c) Exact running time is difficult to calculate in most cases.
    (d) Exact running time is only relevant for small input sizes.
14. In the context of data structures, why is understanding the best-case, average-case, and worst-case scenarios important for algorithm analysis?
    (a) To identify the most common use case for the data structure
    (b) To analyze the time and space complexity of algorithms under different conditions
    (c) To determine the types of data structures suitable for a specific problem
    (d) To evaluate the speed of data structure operations in a controlled environment

2. Primary Building Blocks

Objectives

In this chapter, I will guide you through the foundational principles of data structure design and the essential interfaces that facilitate efficient and effective data management. Here are the key objectives we aim to achieve:

- **Explore Design Principles:** Understand the core principles of software design, such as modularity, encapsulation, and abstraction, and their impact on data structure development.
- **Discover Data Structure Interfaces:** Learn about the significance of interfaces in data structures, focusing on how they abstract the functionality and provide a blueprint for implementation.
- **Implement Core Interfaces:** Delve into the `IList` and `ISet` interfaces, understanding their operations, usage, and how they enforce a structured approach to data management.
- **Advanced Structure Interfaces:** Investigate the `ITree` interface, exploring how trees organize and manage hierarchical data efficiently.

By the end of this chapter, you should have a comprehensive understanding of the principles that guide the design of efficient data structures and the interfaces that form the backbone of these structures.

2.1 Principles of Software Design

In software development, design principles are fundamental to constructing robust, maintainable, and scalable systems. These guidelines shape the architectural and operational framework, ensuring the software's functionality, efficiency, and adaptability:

- **Cohesion and Coupling:** I emphasize designing with high cohesion within components and loose coupling between them to simplify management and enhance scalability.
- **Abstraction and Encapsulation:** Abstraction reduces complexity by revealing only the necessary operations, while encapsulation safeguards the internal state of components, thus promoting integrity and security.
- **Separation of Concerns:** By decomposing the system into distinct, functional sections, complexity is reduced, enabling focused improvement and clearer understanding of each part.
- **Design Patterns:** Utilizing established design patterns offers efficient solutions to common design challenges, providing structured templates for system architecture.

These principles are essential for developing software that is not only functional but also efficient and manageable over time.

The development of an efficient data structure library relies on a solid grasp of object-oriented programming (OOP) concepts. OOP provides a robust framework, emphasizing code reusability, maintainability, and scalability – qualities particularly advantageous in the realm of data structures where functions often share commonalities.

2.2 Data Structure Interfaces

Data structure interfaces define standardized operations across various data structures, bridging the gap between a data structure's capabilities and an algorithm's requirements:

- **Consistency:** Interfaces guarantee uniform access and manipulation across different data structures, enhancing system coherence.
- **Interoperability:** By enabling various data structures to be used interchangeably, interfaces promote flexibility in algorithm design.

2.2.1 Benefits of Using Interfaces

Employing interfaces in data structure design offers significant benefits:

- **Abstraction:** Interfaces separate operational definitions from their implementations, focusing on available operations rather than their internal mechanics.
- **Reusability:** Through interface standardization, various implementations of the same data structure can be interchanged seamlessly, simplifying code adaptation and enhancement.

2.2 Data Structure Interfaces

- **Testability:** Defined interfaces facilitate straightforward testing by enabling the creation of tests that specifically target the operations of the interface.

Interfaces play a key role in the development of extensible and maintainable software architectures, streamlining the management, testing, and evolution of data structures.

2.2.2 Interface vs. Implementation

In the context of data structures, understanding the roles of interfaces is crucial. Distinguishing between interface and implementation is key in software design:

- The **interface** acts as a contract outlining accessible operations, dictating how the functionalities of a data structure or component are presented and used within the system.
- The **implementation** involves the specific logic and data management that execute these operations, adaptable without impacting the predefined interface.

This distinction significantly enhances the software's adaptability and maintainability, allowing for modifications in the implementation without disrupting the system's interface interactions.

Figure 2.1: Illustration of different worker characters in a store, each organizing boxes in unique ways, representing the concept of data storage interfaces (how data should be stored) and implementations (the actual method of storing). This analogy helps to understand that while the interface (the storage requirement) remains constant, the implementation (how the workers store the boxes) can vary

As illustrated in Figure 2.1, the workers depict various implementation strategies of a storage interface. Each worker handles the boxes differently, symbolizing the flexibility in implementing the data storage methods while adhering to the specified storage interface. This reflects the principle that different implementations can fulfill the requirements of a single interface, highlighting the separation between what needs to be done and how it can be done.

2.2.3 Interface Example

To deepen our understanding of interfaces, let us explore the `IExecuter` interface, which represents a task execution contract:

```cpp
class IExecuter {
public:
    virtual void execute() = 0;
};
```

IExecuter Interface Definition

This interface requires an `execute()` method, embodying a single responsibility: to execute an action.

Interface and Virtual Functions

The use of the `virtual` keyword in C++ signifies that the method `execute()` is meant to be overridden in derived classes. This is a fundamental aspect of interfaces in C++: they define a set of virtual functions without providing their implementations.

Pure Virtual Functions

A function declared as `virtual ... = 0` is known as a *pure virtual function*. This declaration makes the class abstract, meaning that it cannot be instantiated directly. In our `IExecuter` interface, the `execute()` method is a pure virtual function, indicating that any concrete class that implements this interface must provide its own implementation of the `execute()` method.

Now, let us examine how different classes can implement this interface to fulfill specific roles. When classes like `LogExecuter` and `CalExecuter` implement the `IExecuter` interface, they provide specific behaviors for the `execute()` method, tailored to their respective functionalities:

```cpp
class LogExecuter : public IExecuter {
public:
    void execute() override {
        std::cout << "Logging an action..." ;
    }
};

class CalExecuter : public IExecuter {
public:
    void execute() override {
        std::cout << "Performing a calculation..." ;
    }
};
```

Implementations of IExecuter Interface

The `IExecuter` interface and its implementations by classes like `LogExecuter` and `CalExecuter` demonstrate the practical application of interfaces, virtual functions, and pure virtual functions in C++. This architecture facilitates polymorphic behavior and abstraction, which are cornerstones of effective object-oriented design and software engineering principles.

2.3 Templates

In this section, we will explore the concept of templates in C++, a fundamental feature that facilitates generic programming. Templates allow you to define functions and classes with placeholder types, making it possible to create flexible and reusable data structures and algorithms. This section will cover the basics of templates, their role in type abstraction, and their benefits in software design.

2.3.1 Templates and Type Abstraction

Templates in C++ provide a mechanism for type abstraction, allowing the creation of generic and reusable code components. This feature aligns with the principle of abstraction in software design, as it lets you define a template for a data structure or algorithm without specifying the exact data type. This abstraction leads to several important capabilities, which can be utilized in different ways:

- **Generic Data Structures:** With templates, you can design data structures that are type independent, such as lists, trees, and graphs, which can then be instantiated with any data type.
- **Compile-Time Polymorphism:** Templates enable compile-time polymorphism, allowing functions and classes to operate with different data types without sacrificing performance.

The use of templates directly contributes to the reusability and flexibility of code, key aspects of efficient software design:

- **Code Reusability:** Templates allow for the writing of a single generic code segment that can be reused with different data types, reducing code duplication and errors.
- **Design Flexibility:** They provide the flexibility to create data structures and algorithms that can be adapted to various needs and data types without changing the underlying codebase.

2.3.2 Template Usage in Practical Scenarios

Templates are not just theoretical constructs; they have practical applications in everyday programming tasks. For instance, consider a generic function to swap two values:

```
1 template<typename T>
2 void Swap(T& a, T& b) {
3     T temp = a;
4     a = b;
```

```
5     b = temp;
6 }
```
Generic Swap Function in C++

This `Swap` function exemplifies how templates can be used to create flexible and reusable code segments that can operate on a wide range of data types.

Consider a generic C++ template for a simple Node class, which is a building block for many data structures like linked lists and trees:

```
1 template<typename T>
2 class Node {
3 public:
4     T data;
5     Node* next;
6 };
```
Template for a Generic Node Class

This `Node` class uses templates to allow for storage of any data type, making it a versatile component in various data structures. Here, T represents the data type stored in each node, and `next` points to the subsequent node in the structure, illustrating a basic linked list node.

Templates, as demonstrated in the `Node` class, provide the flexibility to work with different data types, facilitating the creation of generic and reusable data structures. They embody the concept of type abstraction and compile-time polymorphism, essential for efficient and scalable software design.

2.3.3 Templates in Interface Design

In the context of data structure interfaces, C++ templates play a crucial role in defining flexible and robust interfaces. Specifically, templates offer the following benefits:
- **Interface Standardization:** Templates contribute to the standardization of interfaces, enabling the consistent definition of operations across diverse data structures.
- **Efficient Implementation:** By facilitating type-safe implementations at compile time, templates help in creating efficient and error-free data structures.

2.3.4 Considerations and Best Practices

While leveraging the power of templates, it is vital to follow best practices to maximize their benefits and minimize potential drawbacks, such as
- Avoid overengineering: Use templates judiciously to keep the codebase simple and maintainable.
- Optimize for readability and maintenance: Ensure that template use does not obscure the code's logic and intent.

Some best practices include

2.4 Core Data Structure and Interfaces

- Use templates only when necessary, and prefer non-template versions for simple cases.
- Keep template implementations concise and well documented.
- Consider the impact of templates on compile time and executable size, especially in large projects.

2.4 Core Data Structure and Interfaces

In this section, we explore the foundational interfaces that define the operations of core data structures, such as Lists and Sets, which are essential in computer science and software development.

2.4.1 List Data Structure

Before delving into the specifics of the `IList` interface, it is essential to comprehend the List as a fundamental data structure in computer science. A List is an ordered collection of elements, where each element can be accessed and manipulated based on its position within the collection.

Lists are characterized by the following properties:
- **Ordered Collection:** The elements in a List are arranged in a specific sequence, allowing for ordered data manipulation and retrieval.
- **Dynamic Size:** Lists are dynamic and can grow or shrink, accommodating the addition and removal of elements.
- **Element Access:** Lists provide the ability to access, insert, and remove elements at specific positions, facilitating versatile data management.

Understanding these characteristics of Lists lays the foundation for exploring how they are represented and managed through interfaces in software development.

Figure 2.2 depicts the conceptual model of a List, illustrating how elements are indexed and arranged.

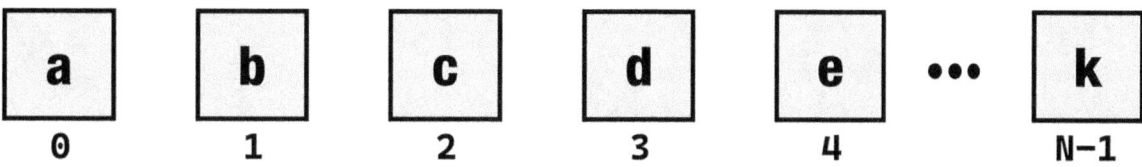

Figure 2.2: Conceptual illustration of a List: a sequence indexed by $0, 1, 2, \ldots, n-1$

List Interface: `IList`

The `IList` abstract template class represents a list of elements of type `T`. It provides a set of abstract member functions for accessing, modifying, and managing the elements of the list. The concrete subclasses of `IList` must implement these abstract member functions to provide the actual implementation of the list operations.

In Figure 2.3, we unravel the `IList` interface further, demonstrating fundamental operations such as `topFront`, `topBack`, `pushFront`, `pushBack`, `popFront`, `popBack`, `insertAt`, and `removeAt`.

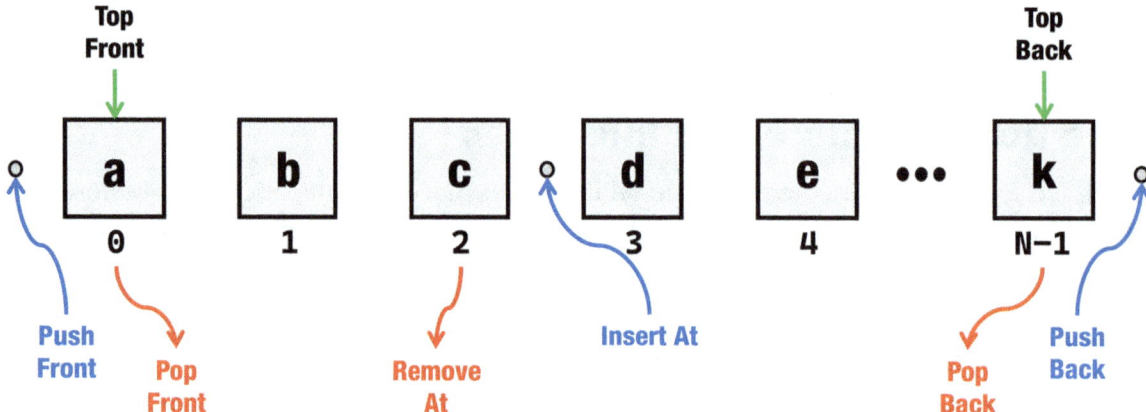

Figure 2.3: Operational visualization of an `IList`, highlighting essential methods

The code block below defines the `IList` interface template:

```
1  template <typename T>
2  class IList {
3  public:
4     IList() : size(0) {}
5  
6     virtual size_t getSize() const {
7        return size;
8     }
9     virtual bool isEmpty() const {
10       return size == 0;
11    }
12 
13    virtual void clear() = 0;
14    virtual void print() const = 0;
15 
16    virtual T& get(size_t index) = 0;
17    virtual void set(size_t index, const T item) = 0;
18    virtual T& operator[](size_t index) = 0;
19    virtual int indexOf(const T item) const = 0;
20 
21    virtual void insertAt(size_t index, const T item) = 0;
22    virtual void removeAt(size_t index) = 0;
23    virtual void pushFront(const T item) = 0;
24    virtual void pushBack(const T item) = 0;
25    virtual T popFront() = 0;
```

2.4 Core Data Structure and Interfaces

```
26    virtual T popBack() = 0;
27    virtual T topFront() const = 0;
28    virtual T topBack() const = 0;
29
30 protected:
31    size_t size;
32 };
```

IList Abstract Interface Definition

The class has the following abstract member functions:
- `getSize()`: Retrieves the number of elements currently stored in the list
- `isEmpty()`: Returns `true` if the list is empty and `false` otherwise
- `clear()`: Removes all elements from the list and resets its size to zero
- `print()`: Prints the elements of the list
- `get(size_t index)`: Returns the element at the specified position in the list
- `set(size_t index, const T item)`: Sets the value of the element at the specified position to the specified element
- `operator[](size_t index)`: Returns a reference to the element at the specified index
- `indexOf(const T item)`: Returns the position of the first occurrence of the specified element in the list or −1 if the element is not present
- `insertAt(size_t index, const T item)`: Inserts the specified element into the list at the specified position
- `removeAt(size_t index)`: Removes the element at the specified position from the list
- `pushFront(const T item)`: Adds the specified element to the front of the list
- `pushBack(const T item)`: Adds the specified element to the end of the list
- `popFront()`: Removes and returns the element from the front of the list
- `popBack()`: Removes and returns the element from the end of the list
- `topFront()`: Returns the element at the front of the list without removing it
- `topBack()`: Returns the element at the back of the list without removing it

Figure 2.4 is a UML class diagram that presents the relationship and structure of the `IList` interface.

The `IList` interface provides a comprehensive set of operations for managing lists, enabling developers to build various data structures and algorithms with ease. Concrete subclasses of `IList` can specialize the interface to suit specific needs while adhering to the fundamental principles of ordered list management.

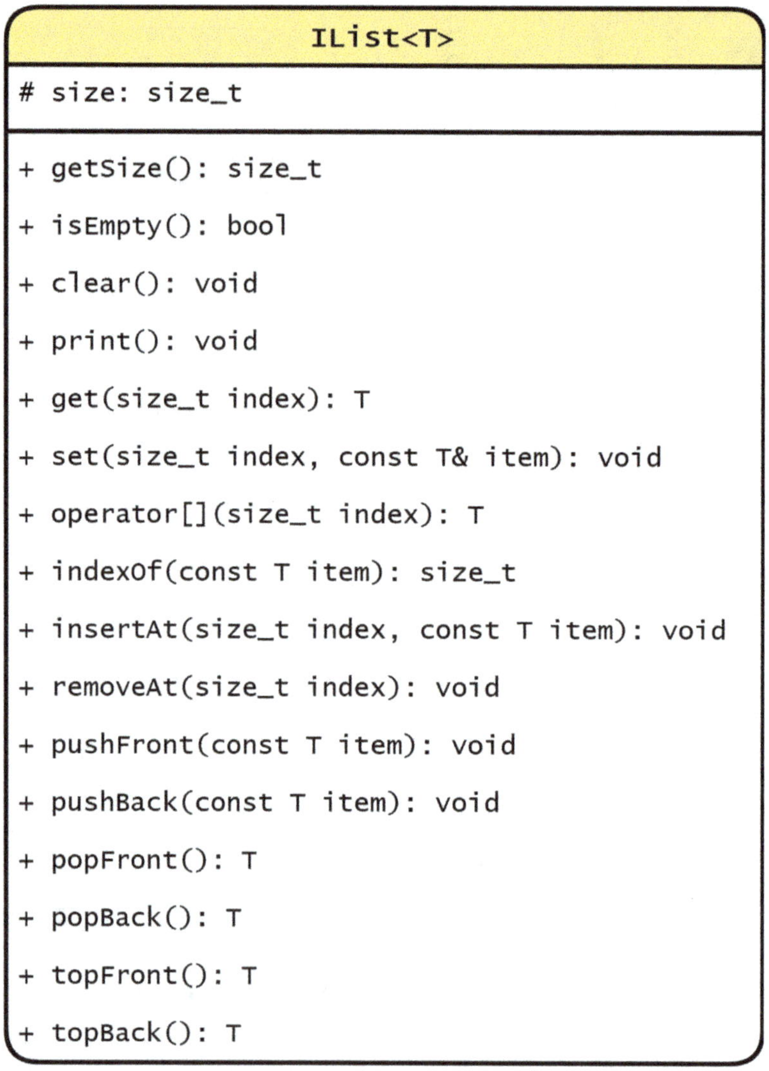

```
┌─────────────────────────────────────────┐
│              IList<T>                   │
├─────────────────────────────────────────┤
│ # size: size_t                          │
├─────────────────────────────────────────┤
│ + getSize(): size_t                     │
│ + isEmpty(): bool                       │
│ + clear(): void                         │
│ + print(): void                         │
│ + get(size_t index): T                  │
│ + set(size_t index, const T& item): void│
│ + operator[](size_t index): T           │
│ + indexOf(const T item): size_t         │
│ + insertAt(size_t index, const T item): void │
│ + removeAt(size_t index): void          │
│ + pushFront(const T item): void         │
│ + pushBack(const T item): void          │
│ + popFront(): T                         │
│ + popBack(): T                          │
│ + topFront(): T                         │
│ + topBack(): T                          │
└─────────────────────────────────────────┘
```

Figure 2.4: The `IList` UML class diagram showing the interface's blueprint

2.4.2 Sets Data Structure

Sets, in computer science, represent a collection of unique elements, where each element occurs only once. Unlike arrays or lists where order and element duplication are significant, Sets focus on the presence or absence of values, making them ideal for operations involving uniqueness and membership determination.

Characteristics of Sets include

- **Uniqueness:** Sets do not allow duplicate elements, ensuring that each element in the set is distinct.
- **Unordered:** The elements in a set do not have a defined order, which differentiates sets from sequence-based data structures like arrays or lists.
- **Efficient Membership Checking:** Sets provide efficient operations to check whether an element is present, making them ideal for applications like data deduplication, membership testing, and set-based operations (union, intersection, difference).

2.4 Core Data Structure and Interfaces

Figure 2.5 provides an illustration of key operations on an `ISet`, showcasing operations such as `add` and `remove`.

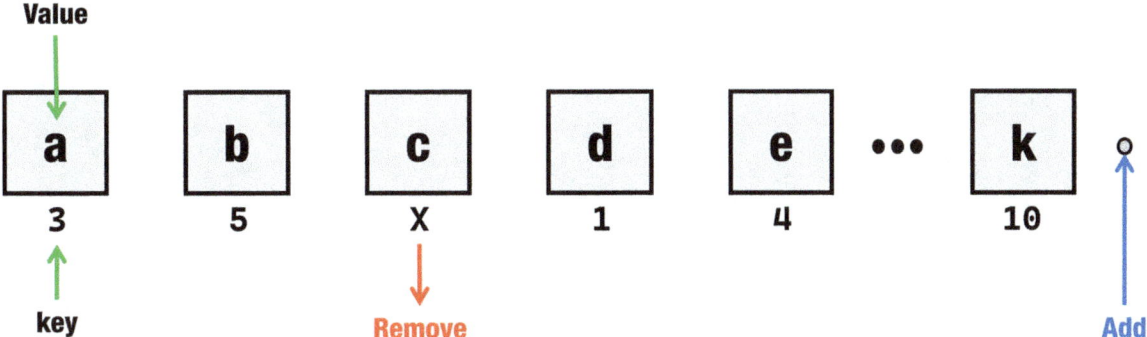

Figure 2.5: Key operations on a Set, illustrating the process of adding and removing elements

Sets Interface: `ISet`

The `ISet` interface abstracts the functionality of a mathematical set into a series of operations that can be performed on any set data structure.

This interface defines the essential operations for managing a set, including adding and removing elements, checking for their existence, and determining the set's size.

The `ISet` interface provides a concise set of operations for managing unordered sets, enabling developers to implement and utilize various algorithms and data structures efficiently.

Essential Operations

The `ISet` interface mandates the implementation of fundamental set operations, facilitating the essential characteristics of Sets:

- **Addition and Removal:** These operations modify the Set's contents, adhering to the uniqueness property.
- **Membership Testing:** Determines if an element is part of the Set, enabling efficient lookup.
- **Size and Clear:** Provide information about the Set's size and allow for resetting its contents.

The code block below defines the `ISet` interface template, laying out the contractual methods that a concrete set implementation must fulfill:

```cpp
template <typename T>
class ISet {
public:
    ISet() : size(0) {}

```

```cpp
 6    virtual size_t getSize() const {
 7      return size;
 8    }
 9    virtual bool isEmpty() const {
10      return size == 0;
11    }
12
13    virtual void clear() = 0;
14    virtual void print() const = 0;
15
16    virtual bool add(const T) = 0;
17    virtual bool remove(const T) = 0;
18    virtual bool contains(const T) const = 0;
19
20 protected:
21    size_t size;
22 };
```
ISet Abstract Interface Definition

Outlined below are the core operations defined in the `ISet` interface:
- `getSize()`: Retrieves the number of elements currently stored in the set
- `isEmpty()`: Returns `true` if the set is empty and `false` otherwise
- `clear()`: Removes all elements from the set and resets its size to zero
- `print()`: Prints the elements of the set
- `add(x)`: Adds the element x to the set if not already present. Returns `true` if x was added to the set and `false` otherwise
- `remove(x)`: Removes the element x from the set. Returns `true` if x was removed from the set and `false` otherwise
- `contains(x)`: Asserts the presence or absence of the element x in the set

Complementing the operational definitions, Figure 2.6 presents the `ISet` UML class diagram, which encapsulates the interface's structure and provides insights into its integration with implementing classes.

2.5 Advanced Data Structure Interfaces

After exploring the core interfaces, we delve into more complex data structures, focusing on hierarchical and linked structures.

2.5.1 Tree Data Structure

Trees are a fundamental data structure in computer science, used to represent hierarchical relationships and structures. Trees are essential in representing hierarchical data, such as file systems, organizational structures, and decision processes. Unlike arrays and linked

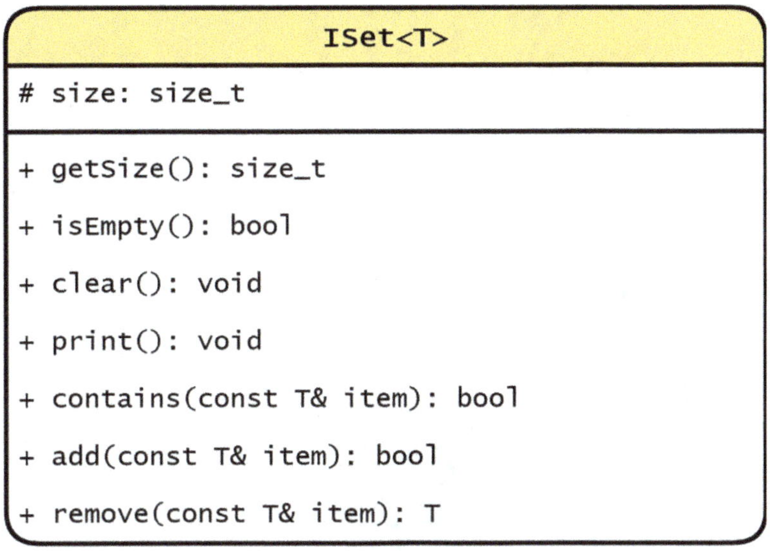

2.5 Advanced Data Structure Interfaces

```
┌─────────────────────────────────────────┐
│               ISet<T>                   │
├─────────────────────────────────────────┤
│ # size: size_t                          │
├─────────────────────────────────────────┤
│ + getSize(): size_t                     │
│ + isEmpty(): bool                       │
│ + clear(): void                         │
│ + print(): void                         │
│ + contains(const T& item): bool         │
│ + add(const T& item): bool              │
│ + remove(const T& item): T              │
└─────────────────────────────────────────┘
```

Figure 2.6: The `ISet` UML class diagram showing the interface's blueprint

lists, which are linear, trees are hierarchical and branch out in multiple directions. A tree consists of nodes connected by edges, and it has a unique starting node called the root.

As illustrated in Figure 2.7, a typical tree structure consists of several key components such as the root, nodes, edges, and leaves.

Understanding these fundamental aspects of Trees is vital for comprehending their role in organizing and storing data in a hierarchical manner.

Tree Terminology

Characteristics of Trees include
- **Node:** The fundamental unit of a tree, containing data and links to other nodes
- **Edge:** The connection between two nodes
- **Root:** The topmost node of a tree, with no parent
- **Leaf:** A node with no children
- **Depth:** The length of the path from the root to the node
- **Height:** The length of the longest path from the node to a leaf
- **Subtree:** A tree formed by a node and all its descendants
- **Internal Node:** A node with at least one child

Types of Trees

Trees come in various forms, each serving specific purposes in computer science:
- **General Trees:** Trees where nodes can have any number of children, useful in representing non-binary hierarchical structures
- **Binary Trees:** Trees where each node has at most two children, commonly used in sorting and searching algorithms
- **Balanced Trees:** Trees that maintain a low height even as they grow, critical to optimizing search operations in large datasets

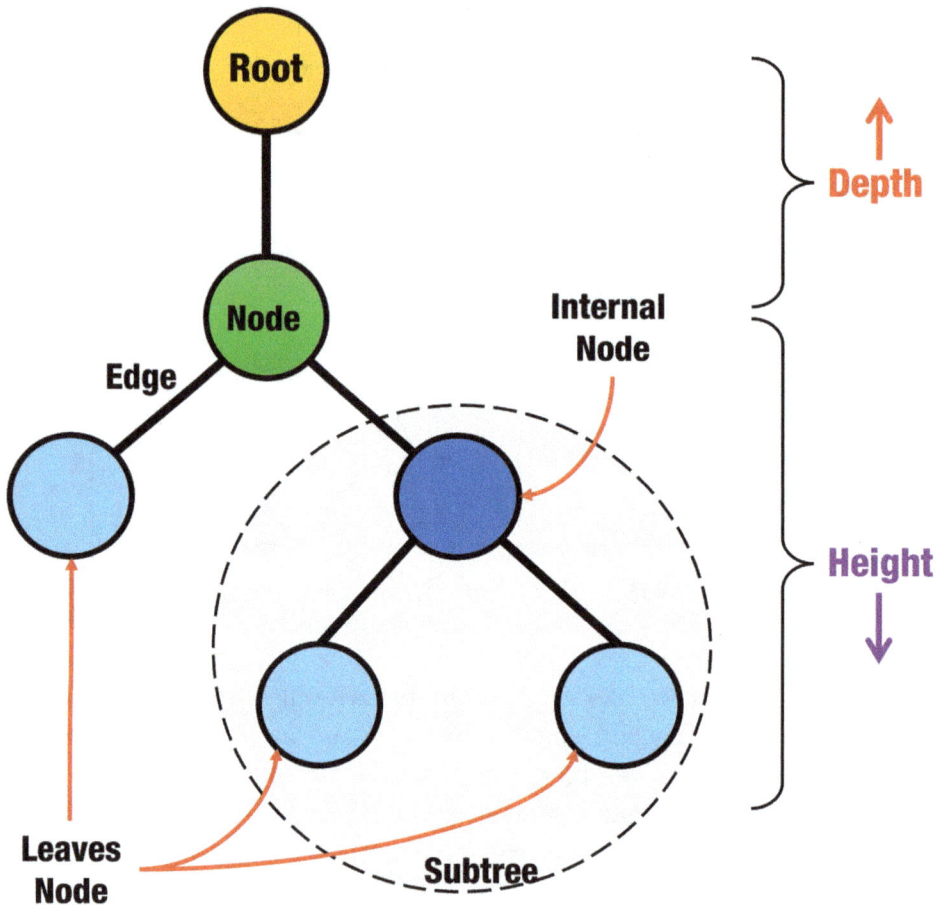

Figure 2.7: Illustration of tree structure and terminology

- **Binary Search Trees:** A specialized binary tree in which nodes are organized in an ordered manner, facilitating efficient searching, insertion, and deletion
- **AVL Trees, Red-Black Trees:** Examples of self-balancing binary search trees, ensuring that the tree remains efficient for operations regardless of the data inserted
- **Other Tree Types:** Additional types such as Trie, Segment Tree, or B-tree, each having unique characteristics and applications

Tree Interface: `ITree`

The `ITree` interface abstracts the concept of a tree into a series of operations that can be performed on any tree data structure, ensuring a standardized way of interacting with and managing hierarchical data.

This interface defines essential operations for tree manipulation, including node addition and removal, tree traversal, and search functionalities.

2.5 Advanced Data Structure Interfaces

- **Node Addition and Removal:** Functions like `insert()` and `remove()` facilitate the dynamic structure of the tree, allowing nodes to be added or removed.
- **Traversal Operations:** Methods such as `traverse()` enable the examination of all nodes in the tree, following specific orders like pre-order, in-order, or post-order.
- **Search and Query:** Operations like `find()` and `getSize()` are used to locate nodes and determine the tree's properties, respectively.
- **Clear Operation:** The `clear()` method allows for the complete removal of all nodes from the tree, effectively resetting it.

These operations are critical for managing and interacting with tree data structures, allowing for flexible implementation while maintaining the fundamental characteristics of a tree.

Here is a template declaration for the `ITree` interface, which outlines the basic structure and essential operations of a tree:

```cpp
template <typename N, typename T>
class ITree {

public:
    virtual ~ITree() {}
    ITree() {}

    virtual size_t depth(N* node) const = 0;
    virtual size_t height() const = 0;
    virtual size_t height(N* node) const = 0;

    virtual size_t getSize() const = 0;
    virtual size_t getSize(N* node) const = 0;

    virtual N* getRoot() const = 0;

    virtual bool insert(const T) = 0;
    virtual bool remove(const T) = 0;
    virtual N* find(const T) const = 0;
    virtual void traverse() const = 0;
    virtual void clear() = 0;
};
```

ITree Abstract Interface Definition

Outlined below are the core operations defined in the `ITree` interface:
- `getRoot()`: Retrieves the root node of the tree
- `insert(const T value)`: Inserts a node with the specified value into the tree, returning `true` if successful
- `remove(const T value)`: Removes the node with the specified value from the tree, returning `true` if successful
- `find(const T value)`: Searches for a node with the specified value and returns it
- `traverse()`: Performs a traversal of the tree, such as pre-order, in-order, post-order, or level-order, and applies a function or action to each node
- `getSize()`: Returns the total number of nodes in the tree
- `getSize(N* node)`: Returns the number of nodes in the subtree rooted at the specified node
- `isEmpty()`: Indicates whether the tree is empty (i.e., contains no nodes)
- `depth(N* node)`: Calculates the depth of a specified node in the tree
- `height()`: Determines the height of the tree, defined as the length of the longest path from the root to a leaf
- `height(N* node)`: Determines the height of the specified node
- `clear()`: Removes all nodes from the tree, effectively resetting it to an empty state

Complementing the operational definitions, Figure 2.8 presents the `ITree` UML class diagram.

In this interface, `Node<T>` represents a generic node in the tree, which contains data of type `T`. The `ITree` interface provides a foundation for implementing various types of tree, such as binary trees, AVL trees, or B-trees, offering a standardized approach to tree operations and management.

2.6 Summary

In this chapter, we explored the foundational principles of data structure design, beginning with essential software design principles and progressing to the details of data structure interfaces. We highlighted the importance of templates in C++ for crafting generic and reusable components, enabling the development of flexible data structures such as lists and sets.

We examined the core data structure interfaces, focusing on the mechanics and applications of `IList` and `ISet`. This was followed by a discussion on advanced data structure interfaces, particularly the `ITree` interface, which underscored the dynamic nature of hierarchical data management.

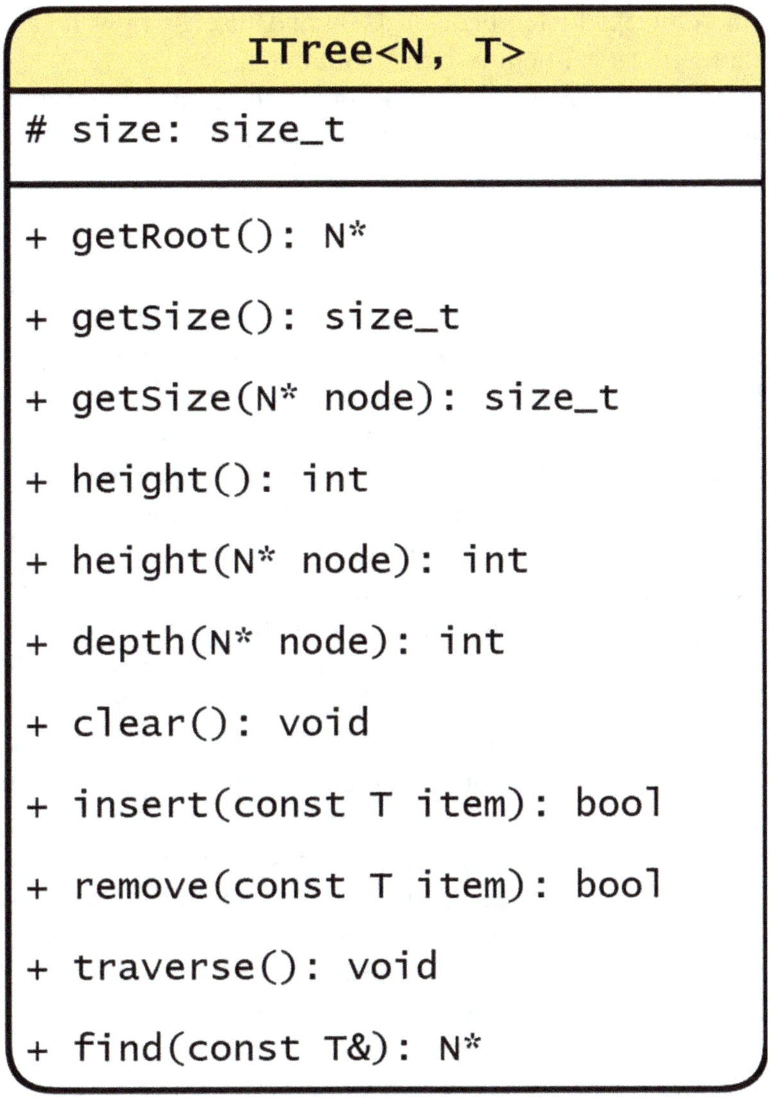

2.6 Summary

```
┌─────────────────────────────────┐
│         ITree<N, T>             │
├─────────────────────────────────┤
│ # size: size_t                  │
├─────────────────────────────────┤
│ + getRoot(): N*                 │
│ + getSize(): size_t             │
│ + getSize(N* node): size_t      │
│ + height(): int                 │
│ + height(N* node): int          │
│ + depth(N* node): int           │
│ + clear(): void                 │
│ + insert(const T item): bool    │
│ + remove(const T item): bool    │
│ + traverse(): void              │
│ + find(const T&): N*            │
└─────────────────────────────────┘
```

Figure 2.8: The `ITree` UML class diagram showing the interface's blueprint

By encapsulating the principles, interfaces, and practical implementations of data structures, this chapter lays the groundwork for a more detailed exploration of each data structure in the subsequent chapters. This foundational knowledge equips you with the understanding needed to utilize and adapt these structures in various software design contexts.

Problems

Discussion

1. What is the primary purpose of using data structure interfaces, and how do they contribute to software design?

2. Explain the concept of template in C++ and discuss how it facilitates generic programming in data structure implementation.
3. How can the principles of software design such as encapsulation and abstraction be applied in the context of data structure interfaces?

Multiple Choice Questions
1. Which of the following best describes the purpose of data structure interfaces?
    (a) To provide specific implementation details of data structures
    (b) To define a set of operations that can be performed on a data structure
    (c) To increase the computational complexity of data structures
    (d) To serve as the actual storage mechanism for data elements
2. What does the principle of abstraction in software design primarily focus on?
    (a) Removing all details from a class to make it abstract
    (b) Providing a simple interface to complex underlying structures
    (c) Encouraging direct interaction with the data structure's internals
    (d) Ensuring that all data structures are concrete and well-defined
3. In the context of C++ templates, what is template specialization?
    (a) Creating a unique template that cannot be reused
    (b) Adapting a generic template to serve a specific type more efficiently
    (c) Removing all templates from the code to reduce complexity
    (d) Copying the same template multiple times for different data types
4. Which of the following is true about the `ISet` interface in data structure design?
    (a) It allows duplicate elements in the set.
    (b) It orders elements based on their insertion sequence.
    (c) It ensures that each element in the set is unique.
    (d) It only supports numeric data types.
5. What is the primary benefit of using templates in data structure design?
    (a) To reduce the execution time of the program
    (b) To increase the size of the compiled binary
    (c) To provide type independence and reusability in code
    (d) To eliminate the need for virtual functions in classes

3. Arrays and Dynamic Arrays

Objectives

In this chapter, I will guide you through the essential topics of pointers and arrays in C++. You will discover the pivotal roles these structures play in memory management and data manipulation. Here are the key objectives we will cover:

- **Pointer Review:** I will review the fundamental concept of pointers in C++, emphasizing their importance in memory management and data manipulation.
- **Array Features and Disadvantages:** You will learn the features of arrays as data structures and understand their advantages and disadvantages, especially in terms of memory usage and runtime performance. We will also look into their operational costs in different scenarios.
- **Dynamic Array Operations:** I will explain the operations associated with dynamic arrays, such as insertion, deletion, and access. You will understand how dynamic arrays resize to accommodate growing data.
- **Resize Implementation:** You will study the details of how dynamic arrays are resized, including strategies to minimize data copying and optimize the resizing process.

3.1 Arrays and Pointers

In this section, you will learn about **arrays** and **pointers**, two fundamental concepts in programming. **Arrays** are *ordered collections of elements of the same data type*, allowing for efficient storage and access of multiple values. **Pointers**, on the other hand, are variables that *store memory addresses* and are crucial for memory management and data manipulation.

3.1.1 Arrays

An **array** is a structured collection of elements, each of the same data type, allocated in a contiguous block of memory. The consistent size of elements and their sequential arrangement allow for efficient indexing and access using a simple mathematical calculation. We represent arrays visually to enhance understanding; Figure 3.1 depicts an array's structure, and Figure 3.2 shows the array's allocation in memory, particularly within a program's stack space.

> The **stack space** is a region of memory that stores temporary variables created by each function (including `main`) during program execution. In contrast, the **heap space** is used for dynamic memory allocation, where blocks of memory can be allocated and freed in an arbitrary order, offering more flexibility than the stack.

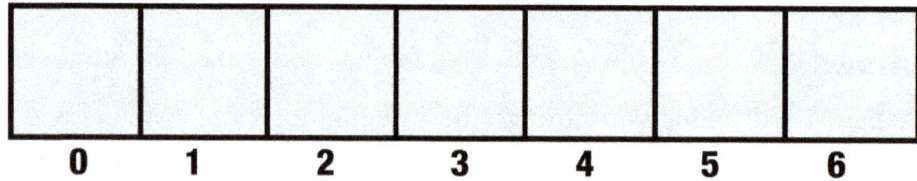

Figure 3.1: A simple array representation

In Figure 3.2, you can see how an array with seven elements is placed in the stack segment of memory. The starting memory address for this array is indicated as `0x01155f`. The contiguity principle of arrays means that the subsequent elements are sequentially stored at addresses immediately following the first, facilitating rapid access and calculation of any element's position.

Static Arrays

Static arrays are defined with a specific size at compile time. Here's how you can declare a static array in C++:

```cpp
// Declaration of a static array
int array[10000];
```
Static Array Declaration Example

3.1 Arrays and Pointers

These arrays have a fixed size and are allocated on the **stack**. They are limited by the available stack size, making them suitable for smaller-sized arrays.

Dynamically Allocated Arrays

Dynamically allocated arrays, on the other hand, are created at runtime and offer more flexibility in terms of memory management. Here is how you can dynamically allocate an array in C++:

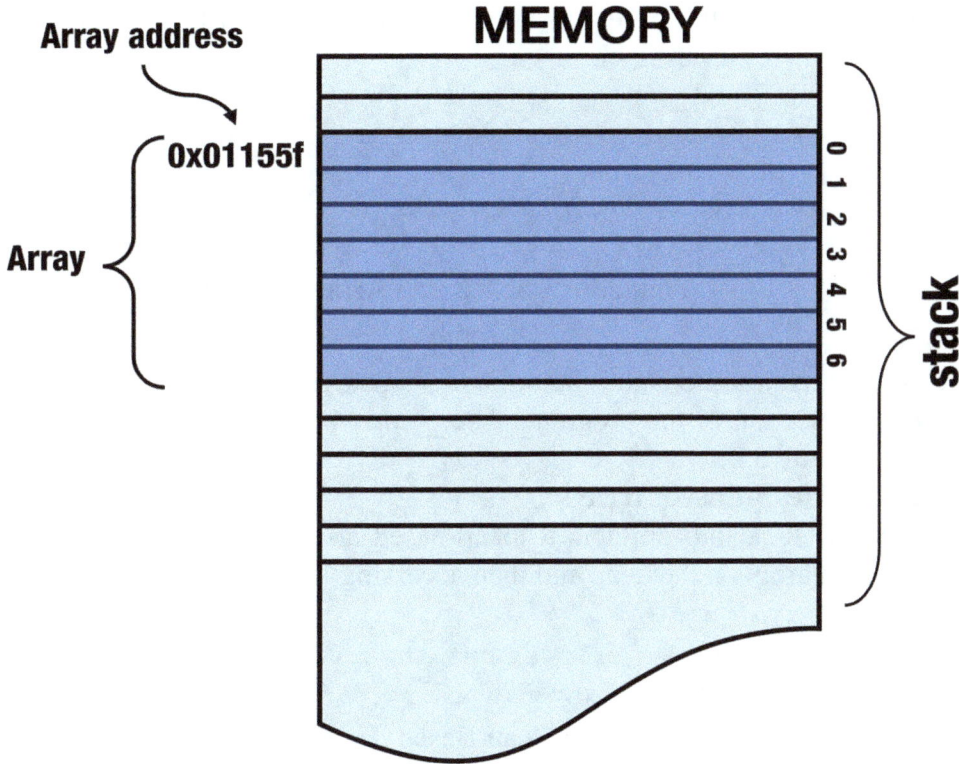

Figure 3.2: Visualization of an array within the stack segment of program memory, starting at address `0x01155f`

```
// Dynamically allocate an array
int *array = new int[size];
```
Dynamically Allocated Array Example

Unlike static arrays, dynamically allocated arrays reside on the **heap**. This allows for dynamic memory allocation and the ability to adjust the array size during the execution of the program, free from the limitations of the stack size.

3.1.2 Pointers to Arrays

Pointers provide a powerful way to access and manipulate arrays in C++. There are primarily two types of arrays you'll work with:

1. **Pointers to Stack-Based Arrays**
   Let's start with a simple example of a pointer to a stack-based array. This approach involves declaring an array that resides on the stack and then using a pointer to access this array.
   Consider the following example where a pointer is used to access a stack-based array:

   ```cpp
   // Declaring a stack-based array
   int stackArray[7];
   // Creating a pointer to the array
   int* stackArrayPointer = stackArray;
   ```
   Pointer to Stack-Based Array Example

   The array `stackArray` and the pointer `stackArrayPointer` are both stored in the stack section of the program. The pointer holds the address of the array, as shown in Figure 3.3.

2. **Pointers to Heap-Based Arrays**
   We will now look into pointers to heap-based arrays, which involve dynamically allocating an array on the heap and then accessing it through a pointer.

   ```cpp
   // Dynamically allocating an array on the heap
   int* heapArray = new int[7];
   ```
   Pointer to Heap-Based Array Example

   In this case, `heapArray` is a pointer to an array that is allocated on the heap using `new`. This approach is suitable for arrays whose size may need to be adjusted during runtime or that must persist beyond the lifespan of a single function.
   As shown in Figure 3.4, the array is allocated on the heap, while the pointer that references this array is stored on the stack.

3.1.3 Stack vs. Heap Arrays

Let us delve into the differences between stack-based and heap-based arrays to understand their distinct characteristics and when to use each type. Table 3.1 provides a comparison of these two array types.

This table highlights the key differences between stack-based and heap-based arrays, illustrating their strengths and limitations to help you make informed decisions in your programming projects.

3.1 Arrays and Pointers

Stack-Based Array

Stack-based arrays are stored directly in stack memory, as shown in Figure 3.3. These arrays are particularly useful for managing local variables and function call management. They are confined to the function scope, with memory automatically managed (allocated and deallocated) as the function is called and returns. This automatic management leads to fast access times due to the stack's nature.

Heap-Based Array

Conversely, heap-based arrays reside in the heap memory, as shown in Figure 3.4. These arrays require manual management for allocation and deallocation, typically using `new` and `delete`. While they offer flexibility and the ability to extend the scope beyond a single function or block, the trade-off is a slightly slower access speed due to the overhead of dynamic allocation.

Table 3.1: Comparison Between Stack-Based and Heap-Allocated Arrays

Aspect	Stack-Based Array	Heap-Based Array
Memory Location	Resides on the stack, ideal for function call management and local variables	Resides on the heap, suitable for dynamic memory allocation
Memory Management	Automatically allocated and deallocated with the function's scope	Requires explicit allocation and deallocation, typically using `new` and `delete`
Scope	Limited to the function's scope where it is declared	Extends beyond the function's scope, accessible throughout the program
Size	Fixed size determined at compile time	Flexible size, can be modified at runtime
Access Speed	Generally faster, due to the nature of stack allocation	May be slower due to the overhead of dynamic memory management

3.1.4 Performance Analysis

In this subsection, you will learn how quickly common operations on arrays can be performed. Direct access to an array element is a straightforward operation, involving only the calculation of the element's memory address. This is typically a single-step process, with the access time mainly dependent on how quickly the address can be calculated. Let's look at the equation that represents this calculation in Equation 3.1:

$$\text{Access Address} = \text{Array Address} + (\text{Element Size} \times \text{Index}) \qquad (3.1)$$

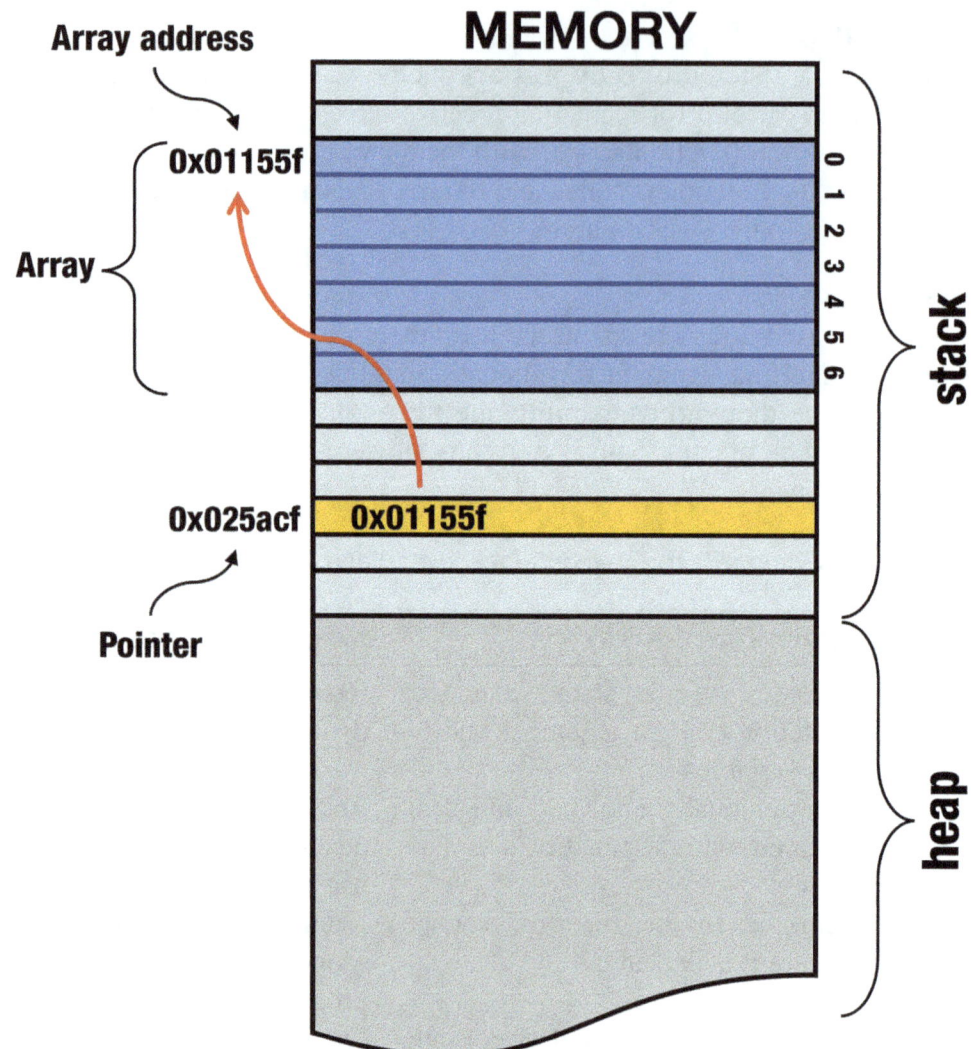

Figure 3.3: An array allocated on the stack at address `0x01155f`, with a pointer located at address `0x025acf` referencing it. Both the array and pointer are stored within the program's stack

Let us break down each component in Equation 3.1:
- **Access Address:** The memory address where the desired element is located.
- **Array Address:** The address of the first element in the array.
- **Element Size:** The size of each element of the array, determined by the data type. For instance, if the array is of type `int` and each `int` occupies 4 bytes, then the element size would be 4 bytes.
- **Index:** The position of the desired element within the array, starting from 0.

This formula demonstrates that the time to access an element is primarily determined by how quickly the access address can be calculated, which is a fast and efficient process.

3.1 Arrays and Pointers

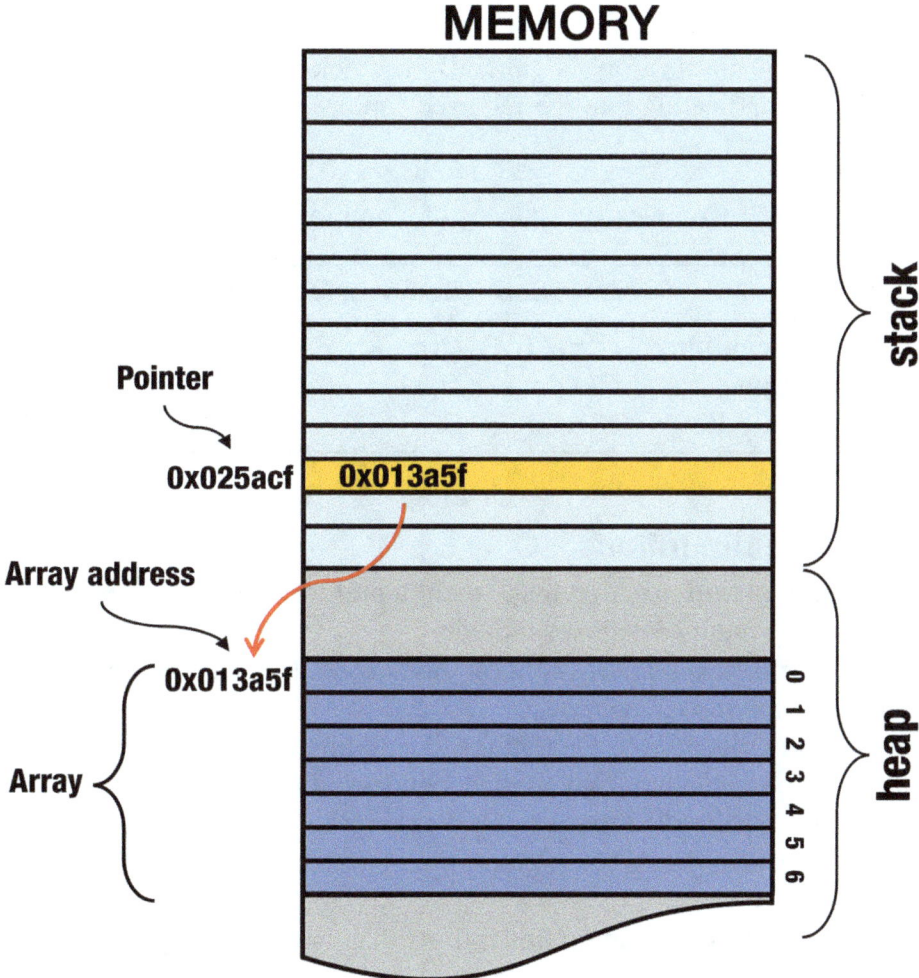

Figure 3.4: An array allocated on the heap at address `0x013a5f`, with a pointer located on the stack at address `0x025acf` storing the array's address

Complexity Analysis

Let's take a closer look at the time complexities for common array operations, which reflect their efficiency. Table 3.2 summarizes these complexities, excluding the time it might take to resize the array.

Insertion and Removal

The duration to insert or remove elements within an array depends on the position of the operation. Inserting or removing elements at the beginning or in the middle requires time proportional to the number of subsequent elements to shift, denoted as $O(n - i)$, where i is the operation's index. This means the operation time increases with the number of elements to be moved. Conversely, inserting or removing elements at the array's end is much quicker, occurring in constant time, represented as $O(1)$.

Modification

Modifying an element in an array is generally a quick operation, with a constant time complexity of $O(1)$, indicating that the required time remains the same regardless of the size of the array.

Table 3.2: Complexity Analysis of Common Array Operations

	Insertion	Removal	Modification
Beginning	$O(n-i)$	$O(n-i)$	$O(1)$
End	$O(1)$	$O(1)$	$O(1)$
Middle	$O(n-i)$	$O(n-i)$	$O(1)$

3.1.5 Advantages and Limitations

Arrays offer several **advantages** that make them a preferred choice for efficient and effective data storage. The main advantages include

- **Constant-Time Access:** Arrays allow fast access to elements, providing constant-time retrieval for any element.
- **Efficient End Operations:** Operations like adding or removing elements at the end of an array are efficient, as they are independent of the array's overall size.
- **Linear-Time Arbitrary Operations:** Performing operations at arbitrary positions within an array takes linear time, proportional to the number of elements to be shifted or processed.

However, arrays also have certain **limitations** that can impact their efficiency and flexibility. The main limitations include

- **Insertion and Removal Complexity:** Inserting or removing elements, particularly in the middle of an array, often requires shifting many elements, with the time complexity depending on the array's size and the operation's position.
- **Fixed Capacity:** Arrays have a predetermined capacity. Exceeding this capacity necessitates allocating a new array and copying the existing elements, which can be resource-intensive and time-consuming.

While arrays are known for their speed and efficiency in direct access and end operations, they present challenges in insertions, deletions, and resizing. These characteristics underscore the importance of choosing the right data structure based on the specific needs of your application. In the following sections, we will explore dynamic arrays, which address some of the limitations of traditional arrays by offering flexible resizing capabilities and potentially more efficient management of insertions and deletions.

3.2 Dynamic Arrays

3.2.1 Resizable Array

One major **limitation** of static arrays is their fixed size. For example, declaring a static array with a large predetermined size might look like this:

```
int array[1000000000];
```
Static Array Declaration Example

While static arrays are useful, they can be impractical if the maximum needed size is unknown. A **partial solution** is the use of dynamic memory allocation:

```
int *array = new int[size];
```
Dynamic Memory Allocation Example

However, this approach has its own problem. You might not always know the maximum size you'll need when allocating an array.

The solution to this problem lies in **dynamic arrays** (resizable arrays). These are arrays whose size can be adjusted dynamically based on your needs. The fundamental idea is to store a pointer to a dynamically allocated array and replace it with a newly-allocated array when needed.

3.2.2 Advantages and Limitations

Dynamic arrays present several benefits over static arrays, particularly regarding memory efficiency and flexibility. However, they also have their limitations.

Advantages
- **Efficient Memory Usage:** Dynamic arrays allocate memory only as needed, which makes them more memory-efficient compared to static arrays, where a large amount of memory may be allocated regardless of actual usage.
- **Adaptability:** They can resize during runtime, offering flexibility when the number of elements is unknown or variable. This ability to grow or shrink helps optimize memory usage.
- **Constant-Time Access:** Dynamic arrays retain the benefit of constant-time access to elements, akin to static arrays, making element retrieval fast and efficient.

Limitations
- **Resizing Overhead:** They may require frequent memory reallocation to grow or shrink, involving copying elements to a new array, which can be a resource-intensive operation, particularly for large arrays.

- **Insertion and Removal Complexity:** Like static arrays, dynamic arrays can incur performance penalties for insertions and removals in the middle of the array due to the need to shift elements, affecting efficiency based on the array's size and operation location.

In conclusion, dynamic arrays provide a flexible and memory-efficient solution for data storage when the amount of data varies. However, they introduce complexities such as resizing overhead and potential inefficiencies in mid-array insertions or removals.

3.2.3 Dynamic Array Implementation

Dynamic arrays are a cornerstone of efficient data handling in programming, typically implemented using pointers and allowing for memory reallocation as needed. In this section, we delve into the design of a dynamic array class, highlighting the critical methods and attributes essential for its functionality.

Dynamic Array Interface

For the implementation, we introduce the `DynamicArray` class, which extends the `IList`. This class is characterized by key data members essential for dynamic array operation:

- `arr`: A pointer to the dynamically allocated storage area for the array elements
- `capacity`: Represents the total available space in the array, indicating how many elements it can hold before needing to resize
- `size`: Tracks the current number of elements in the array, which is inherited from the `IList` interface

Below is the interface of the `DynamicArray` class, which outlines its structure and core functionalities. The accompanying UML class diagram in Figure 3.5 provides a visual representation of the relationship between `DynamicArray` and the `IList` interface.

```cpp
template <typename T>
class DynamicArray : public IList<T> {
public:
    // Default constructor
    DynamicArray() : IList<T>(),
        arr(new T[getDefaultCapacity()]),
        capacity(getDefaultCapacity()) {}

    // Constructor with specified capacity
    DynamicArray(size_t capacityValue)
        : IList<T>(),
          arr(new T[capacityValue]),
          capacity(capacityValue) {}

    // Constructor with capacity and initial value
    DynamicArray(size_t capacityValue,
            const T initialValue)
```

3.2 Dynamic Arrays

```cpp
18          : IList<T>(),
19            arr(new T[capacityValue]),
20            capacity(capacityValue)
21      {
22          for (size_t i = 0; i < capacityValue; ++i) {
23              arr[i] = initialValue;
24          }
25          size = capacityValue;
26      }
27
28      // Destructor
29      virtual ~DynamicArray(){
30          delete [] arr;
31      }
32
33      // Copy constructor
34      DynamicArray(const DynamicArray<T>& other);
35
36      // Interface Methods
37      virtual void resize();
38      DynamicArray& operator=(const DynamicArray<T>& other);
39
40      // Accessor for capacity
41      virtual size_t getCapacity() const {
42          return capacity;
43      }
44
45      // IList Interface Methods
46      virtual void insertAt(size_t index, const T item);
47      virtual void removeAt(size_t index);
48      virtual void pushFront(const T item);
49      virtual void pushBack(const T item);
50      virtual T popFront();
51      virtual T popBack();
52      virtual void clear();
53      virtual void print() const;
54      // ... Other Abstract Interface methods
55
56  protected:
57      T* arr;              // Pointer to array data
58      size_t capacity;     // Total capacity of the array
59
60      // To allow derived classes to change default capacity
61      virtual size_t getDefaultCapacity() const {
62          return 8;
```

```
63    }
64
65        // Inherited members to use directly
66        using IList<T>::size;
67  };
```

DynamicArray Class Interface

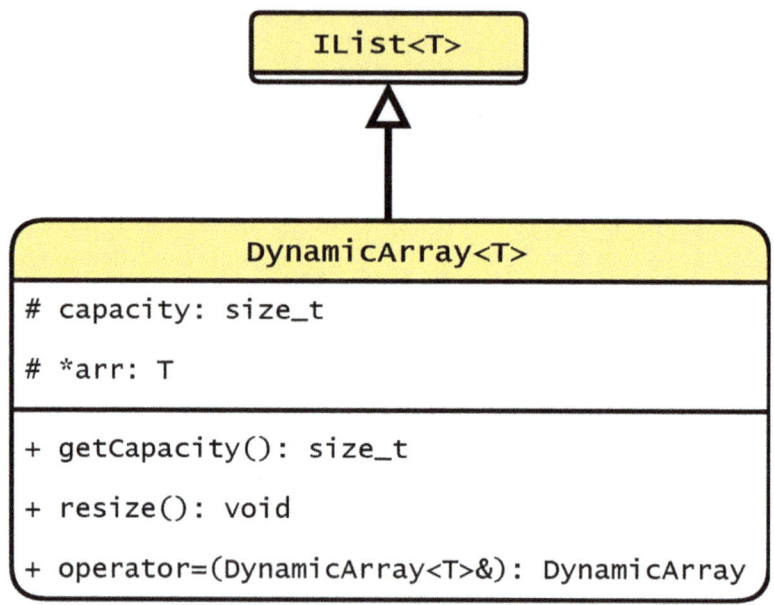

Figure 3.5: The `DynamicArray` UML class diagram details the composition of the dynamic array class and its relationship with the `IList` interface

The `DynamicArray` comprehensively defines the essential methods and attributes for creating, manipulating, and managing dynamic arrays. The class facilitates dynamic resizing, element access, and various operations to add and remove elements.

Array Operations
Accessing Elements
The `get` function allows you to access elements in the dynamic array by index. It checks that the provided index is within a valid range and returns a reference to the element at that index.

```
1 template <typename T>
2 T& DynamicArray<T>::get(size_t i) {
3     assert(i >= 0 && i < size);
4     return arr[i];
5 }
```

get Function: Access Array Element by Index

3.2 Dynamic Arrays

The `set` function is used to modify elements in the dynamic array by providing an index and a new value. It verifies that the specified index is within bounds and then updates the element at that index with the provided value.

```cpp
template <typename T>
void DynamicArray<T>::set(size_t i, const T item) {
    assert(i >= 0 && i < size);
    arr[i] = item;
}
```

`set` Function: Update Array Element by Index

Accessing Elements Using `operator[]`

You can also access and modify elements in the dynamic array using the `operator[]`.

```cpp
template <typename T>
T& DynamicArray<T>::operator[](size_t i) {
    return arr[i];
}
```

`operator[]` Overload: Array Access and Modification

Using `operator[]` provides a more concise way of getting and setting elements within the dynamic array. Make sure the index is within the valid range to avoid errors.

Insertion and Removal

The `insertAt` function adds an element at a specified location in the dynamic array. It checks if the array is at full capacity and resizes it if necessary. It shifts elements to make room for the new element and then assigns the new value to the specified index. Finally, it increments the array's size.

```cpp
template <typename T>
void DynamicArray<T>::insertAt(size_t i, const T item) {
    assert(i >= 0 && i <= size);
    if (size == capacity)
        resize();
    for (size_t j = size; j > i; --j)
        arr[j] = arr[j - 1];
    arr[i] = item;
    ++size;
}
```

`insertAt` Function: Insert Element at Specific Index

The `removeAt` function deletes an element from the dynamic array based on the specified index. It verifies that the index is valid and then shifts elements to remove the selected item. If the array's size becomes significantly smaller than its capacity, it triggers a resizing operation to optimize memory usage.

```
1 template <typename T>
2 void DynamicArray<T>::removeAt(size_t i) {
3     assert(i >= 0 && i < size);
4     for (size_t j = i; j < size - 1; ++j)
5         arr[j] = arr[j + 1];
6     --size;
7     if (capacity >= 3 * size)
8         resize();
9 }
```

removeAt Function: Remove Element at Specific Index

Appending Elements

The `pushBack` function adds an element to the end of the dynamic array. It first checks if the array is at full capacity and triggers a resizing operation if needed. Then, it appends the new element to the end of the array and increments the array's size.

```
1 template <typename T>
2 void DynamicArray<T>::pushBack(const T item) {
3     if (size == capacity)
4         resize();
5     arr[size++] = item;
6 }
```

pushBack Function: Append Element to End of Array

Note: The following operations are easily sufficient to implement using `insertAt` and `removeAt`:
- pushFront(x) $\Rightarrow$ insertAt(0, x)
- popFront() $\Rightarrow$ removeAt(0)
- pushBack(x) $\Rightarrow$ insertAt(size, x)
- popBack() $\Rightarrow$ removeAt(size $-$ 1)

3.2 Dynamic Arrays

```cpp
template <typename T>
void DynamicArray<T>::pushBack(const T item) {
    insertAt(size, item);
}

template <typename T>
void DynamicArray<T>::pushFront(const T item) {
    insertAt(0, item);
}

template <typename T>
T DynamicArray<T>::popFront() {
    assert(size > 0);
    T& frontData = arr[0];
    removeAt(0);
    return frontData;
}

template <typename T>
T DynamicArray<T>::popBack() {
    assert(size > 0);
    T& backData = arr[size - 1];
    --size;
    return backData;
}
```

Push and Pop Operations in `DynamicArray`

3.2.4 Resizing Operation

Resize Rules

Dynamic arrays require resizing under specific conditions. The resizing operation is triggered by the following rules:
- **On Add:** If the current size of the array equals its capacity, just before inserting a new element
- **On Remove:** If the capacity of the array is greater than or equal to three times the current size of the array, right after removing an element

Resize Function

The resizing operation, performed by the `resize` function, ensures that the dynamic array can accommodate new elements without exceeding its capacity. The function doubles the current capacity of the array and copies the existing elements to the newly allocated memory space. Here is the code for the `resize` function:

```cpp
template <typename T>
void DynamicArray<T>::resize() {
    size_t new_capacity
        = std::max(2 * static_cast<int>(size), 2);
    T* brr = new T[new_capacity];
    for (size_t i = 0; i < size; i++)
        brr[i] = arr[i];
    delete[] arr;
    arr = brr;
    capacity = new_capacity;
}
```

`resize` Function: Adjust Capacity of DynamicArray

The `resize` function effectively manages the capacity of the dynamic array, ensuring it can adapt to changing data storage requirements.

3.3 Optimization

3.3.1 An Optimized Copy

Optimizing dynamic arrays involves making the data shifting and copying processes more efficient. Much of the work performed by dynamic arrays, particularly during **insertAt(i,x)**, **removeAt(i)**, and **resize()** operations, revolves around the shift and copying of data. Traditionally, these operations were implemented using **for** loops, but it turns out that many programming environments provide highly efficient functions for copying and moving blocks of data.

In C++, for instance, there is the `std::copy(a0, a1, b)` algorithm. This function is specifically designed for efficient data copying, often utilizing special machine instructions that outperform conventional **for** loop implementations.

3.3.2 Optimized Dynamic Array Operations

Optimization of dynamic arrays can significantly enhance their performance by replacing conventional `for` loops with more efficient data copying functions.

Resize

For resizing, we can replace manual element copying with the `std::copy` function for efficient data transfer:

3.3 Optimization

```
1  template <typename T>
2  void DynamicArray<T>::resize() {
3      size_t new_capacity
4          = std::max(2 * static_cast<int>(size), 2);
5      T* brr = new T[new_capacity];
6      std::copy(arr, arr + size, brr);
7      delete[] arr;
8      arr = brr;
9      capacity = new_capacity;
10 }
```

`resize` Function: Optimized Resizing of DynamicArray

Instead of manually copying data with a `for` loop, we employ the efficient `std::copy` function to move data from the old array to the new one.

Insert

Optimizing insertion involves using `std::copy_backward` to shift existing elements and create space for the new element:

```
1  template <typename T>
2  void DynamicArray<T>::insertAt(size_t i, const T item) {
3      assert(i >= 0 && i <= size);
4      if (size == capacity)
5          resize();
6      std::copy_backward(arr + i,
7                         arr + size,
8                         arr + size + 1);
9      arr[i] = item;
10     size++;
11 }
```

`insertAt` Function: Optimized Insertion in DynamicArray

Utilizing `std::copy_backward`, we efficiently shift elements to make room for the new value while optimizing the operation.

Remove

For removal, `std::copy` can be employed to efficiently condense the array after an element is taken out:

```
1  template <typename T>
2  void DynamicArray<T>::removeAt(size_t i) {
3      assert(i >= 0 && i < size);
```

```
4      std::copy(arr + i + 1,
5                arr + size,
6                arr + i);
7      --size;
8      if (capacity >= 3 * size)
9          resize();
10 }
```
`removeAt` Function: Optimized Removal from DynamicArray

We efficiently move the elements beyond the removed one using `std::copy`, ensuring an optimized removal process.

3.4 Summary

This chapter has explored the intricacies of arrays and dynamic arrays, highlighting their structure, usage, and optimization. Here are the key points we covered:
- Dynamic arrays overcome the limitations of static arrays by allowing **dynamic resizing**, adapting seamlessly to changing data storage needs.
- Operations on dynamic arrays are generally efficient, with append actions usually executing in constant time. However, occasional resizing may require $O(n)$ time complexity.
- Despite their adaptability, dynamic arrays can lead to some **wasted space**, but this is typically capped at half the array's capacity, ensuring memory efficiency.
- Through **optimization**, particularly in data copying and shifting, dynamic arrays become even more efficient and suited for various computational tasks.

As we have seen, dynamic arrays are foundational in managing collections of data, allowing for both flexibility and efficiency. Moving forward, we will delve into *linked lists* in the next chapter, exploring another fundamental data structure that offers different advantages and is particularly useful in scenarios where dynamic arrays may not be the most efficient choice.

Problems

Discussion
Understanding Arrays and Pointers
1. What is an array in programming, and how does it differ from a pointer?
2. Explain the characteristics of static arrays, including their declaration and memory location.

3. How are dynamically allocated arrays different from static arrays, and why are they more flexible?
4. What are the two primary ways to use pointers to access arrays, and how do they differ?

Comparative Analysis of Array Types
1. Compare stack-based arrays and heap-based arrays in terms of memory location, memory management, scope, size determination, and access speed. Discuss the strengths and limitations of each approach.
2. What is the primary limitation of static arrays, and can you provide an example that illustrates this limitation?
3. Why might dynamically allocated arrays be considered a partial solution to the limitation of static arrays, and what common issue is associated with this approach?
4. Explain the advantages of dynamic arrays over static arrays in terms of memory usage and adaptability.

Optimizing Dynamic Array Operations
1. What are the key operations in dynamic arrays that benefit from optimization, and why are they important?
2. How are data shifting and copying traditionally implemented in dynamic arrays, and what are the limitations of this approach?
3. Explain the advantages of using `std::copy` for data copying in dynamic arrays during the resizing operation.
4. How does the use of `std::copy_backward` improve the efficiency of the insert operation in dynamic arrays?

Multiple Choice Questions
1. What is an array?
   (a) An unordered collection of elements
   (b) An ordered collection of elements of the same data type
   (c) A variable that stores memory addresses
   (d) None of the above
2. What is a pointer?
   (a) A variable that stores memory addresses
   (b) A data type to represent real numbers
   (c) An ordered collection of elements of the same data type
   (d) None of the above
3. What is a dynamic array?
   (a) An array declared with a fixed size at compile time
   (b) An array that resides on the stack

(c) An array whose size can be dynamically adjusted based on needs
(d) An array that requires explicit deallocation using functions like new
4. What is the main limitation of static arrays addressed by dynamic arrays?
    (a) Constant-time access
    (b) Efficient memory usage
    (c) Fixed size
    (d) Stack-based allocation
5. What is the primary advantage of dynamic arrays over static arrays?
    (a) Efficient memory usage
    (b) Fixed size
    (c) Constant-time access
    (d) Adaptability to changing data size
6. What is the overhead associated with dynamic arrays?
    (a) Constant-time access
    (b) Memory wastage
    (c) Efficient memory usage
    (d) Resizing overhead
7. When do dynamic arrays require reallocation of memory?
    (a) Only when the program starts
    (b) Periodically, based on the program's execution time
    (c) When they need to expand or shrink
    (d) Never, as they have a fixed memory allocation
8. What is a disadvantage of dynamic arrays related to insertion and removal operations?
    (a) Constant-time access
    (b) Stack-based allocation
    (c) Shifting a significant number of elements during certain operations
    (d) Efficient memory usage
9. What is the primary reason for dynamic arrays having constant-time access?
    (a) Efficient memory usage.
    (b) Pre-allocated memory.
    (c) Periodic reallocation.
    (d) Array elements can be directly accessed regardless of their position within the array.
10. How do dynamic arrays compare to static arrays in terms of memory allocation?
    (a) Dynamic arrays pre-allocate memory.
    (b) Dynamic arrays have fixed memory allocation.
    (c) Dynamic arrays adjust their memory footprint dynamically based on needs.
    (d) Dynamic arrays always use more memory than needed.
11. How are dynamically allocated arrays created?
    (a) By using the `malloc` function.
    (b) By declaring with a fixed size at compile time.

3.4 Summary

      (c) By using the `new` operator during runtime.

      (d) Dynamically allocated arrays are not created.

12. Where does a stack-based array reside?
    - (a) On the heap.
    - (b) On the stack.
    - (c) In a global memory pool.
    - (d) Nowhere; stack-based arrays do not reside in memory.

13. How is the scope of a heap-allocated array different from a stack-based array?
    - (a) Heap-allocated arrays have a more limited scope.
    - (b) Heap-allocated arrays have a broader scope.
    - (c) Both have the same scope.
    - (d) Arrays don't have a scope.

14. What is the primary factor determining access time for array elements?
    - (a) The array's size
    - (b) The number of elements in the array
    - (c) The calculation of the access address
    - (d) The element's index in the array

15. What is a major advantage of arrays?
    - (a) Constant-time access to any element
    - (b) Efficient resizing operations
    - (c) Variable capacity
    - (d) Slow access speed

16. In the `DynamicArray` class, what does the `capacity` attribute represent?
    - (a) The current size of the array
    - (b) The maximum number of elements the array can hold
    - (c) The number of elements currently in the array
    - (d) The default capacity of the array

17. How does the `pushBack` operation differ from the `insertAt` operation in a dynamic array?
    - (a) `pushBack` adds an element to the beginning, while `insertAt` adds at the end.
    - (b) `pushBack` always triggers a resize, while `insertAt` may not.
    - (c) `insertAt` adds an element at a specified index, while `pushBack` adds at the end.
    - (d) There is no difference; they perform the same operation.

18. What is the purpose of the `setDefaultCapacity` function in the `DynamicArray` class?
    - (a) To set the default size of the array.
    - (b) To change the capacity of the array at runtime.
    - (c) To allow derived classes to change default capacity.
    - (d) There is no such function in the `DynamicArray` class.

19. When is the `resize` function triggered during array operations?
    (a) Only on adding elements.
    (b) Only on removing elements.
    (c) Both on adding and removing elements.
    (d) Never; the array size is fixed during initialization.
20. What is the role of the `assert` function in the `insertAt` method of the `DynamicArray` class?
    (a) To check for memory leaks
    (b) To ensure the array is not empty
    (c) To verify the validity of the index
    (d) To stop the execution of the program
21. In the `removeAt` method, why is the condition `capacity>=3*size` used for triggering a resize?
    (a) It ensures that resizing only occurs when the array is almost full.
    (b) It prevents resizing if the array is less than one-third full.
    (c) It guarantees that resizing happens when the array is significantly larger than needed.
    (d) It has no significance; the resizing always occurs.
22. What advantage does using `std::copy` provide in dynamic array operations compared to traditional `for` loops?
    (a) Improved readability of the code.
    (b) Faster and more efficient data copying.
    (c) Compatibility with all programming languages.
    (d) It allows for copying data in reverse order.

True/False Questions
1. Static arrays and dynamic arrays both have a fixed memory allocation.
2. The primary advantage of dynamic arrays over static arrays is efficient memory usage.
3. The scope of a heap-allocated array is more limited than that of a stack-based array.
4. Arrays do not have a scope; their elements can be accessed from any part of the program.
5. The `pushBack` operation always triggers a resize in a dynamic array.
6. The time complexity of the `insertAt` operation in a dynamic array is always $O(1)$.
7. The `resize` function in a dynamic array doubles the current capacity of the array each time it is called.
8. Dynamic arrays are more memory-efficient than linked lists when it comes to storage overhead.

3.4 Summary

9. The `popFront` operation in a dynamic array is equivalent to the `removeAt(0)` operation.
10. In a dynamic array, the time complexity of the `pushBack` operation is always equal to or better than the time complexity of the `insertAt` operation.

Challenge Questions

1. In a real-time system with strict memory constraints, you need a structure to store and frequently manipulate a collection of integers. Would you opt for a stack-based array or a heap-allocated array? Justify your choice based on memory management, access speed, and system flexibility.
2. **Optimizing:** Design a dynamic array that efficiently manages memory, particularly focusing on minimizing wasted space during resizing. How can you reduce memory overhead when elements are removed? Detail the design and implementation considerations.
3. **Advanced Resizing Strategy:** The typical resize function doubles the array's capacity, but what if we change this factor, say to tripling the capacity? Develop a resizing mechanism that alters the array size by a different factor and discuss the potential benefits or drawbacks of this method.
4. **Custom Copying Mechanism:** Beyond `std::copy`, investigate alternative techniques for copying data in dynamic arrays. Craft a custom function to copy elements and compare its performance and simplicity with standard library functions. What are the trade-offs involved in using a custom copying function vs. built-in ones?

4. Linked List

Objectives

In this chapter, I will guide you through the essential topics of linked lists in C++. You will discover the pivotal roles these structures play in data organization and manipulation. Here are the key objectives we will explore together:

1. **Linked Pointers:** Understand the concept of linked pointers and how they are used to connect elements in a linked list data structure.
2. **Singly-Linked List:** Implement and operate on a singly-linked list, including insertion, deletion, and traversal techniques.
3. **Doubly-Linked and Circular Linked Lists:** Recognize the advantages of doubly-linked lists over singly-linked lists, including bidirectional traversal and its impact on operations. Explore the concept, implementation, and practical use cases of circular linked lists.
4. **Performance Analysis:** Analyze the performance characteristics and trade-offs of different types of linked lists, and determine when to use each type according to specific requirements.

4.1 Introduction to Linked Pointers

Linked lists are a fundamental data structure in computer science and programming. They provide a flexible and efficient way to manage dynamic collections of elements. Each element, or node, contains a reference to the next node, creating a chain-like structure. This interconnected nature allows linked lists to excel in scenarios where elements need to be frequently inserted or removed, making them powerful tools for various applications.

Pointers play a fundamental role in programming and data structures, enabling us to establish relationships between data elements. This capability is important for creating complex structures, such as linked lists.

In this section, we will explore how pointers work with objects and how they are used in linked lists.

4.1.1 Pointers to Objects

Consider the following example using a simple structure:

```
struct Node {
    int x;
    int y;
};
```
Node Structure Definition

Creating Instances

You can create an instance of this structure or a pointer to an object of type `Node`:

```
Node obj;                  // Instance
Node *ptr = new Node;      // Pointer to an object
```
Creating an Instance and Pointer to a Node

Accessing Members

To access the `x` and `y` members from `ptr`, you can use the arrow operator or the traditional dereference operator:

```
// Using the arrow operator
ptr->x = 1000;
// OR, using the traditional dereference operator
(*ptr).x = 1000;
```
Accessing Members of a Node Using Pointers

4.1 Introduction to Linked Pointers

As shown in Figure 4.1, a pointer to an object can be used to store and access values. What if the object contains pointers? Consider the following structure:

```
struct Node {
    int x, y;
    int *pz;
};
```

Node Structure with an Internal Pointer

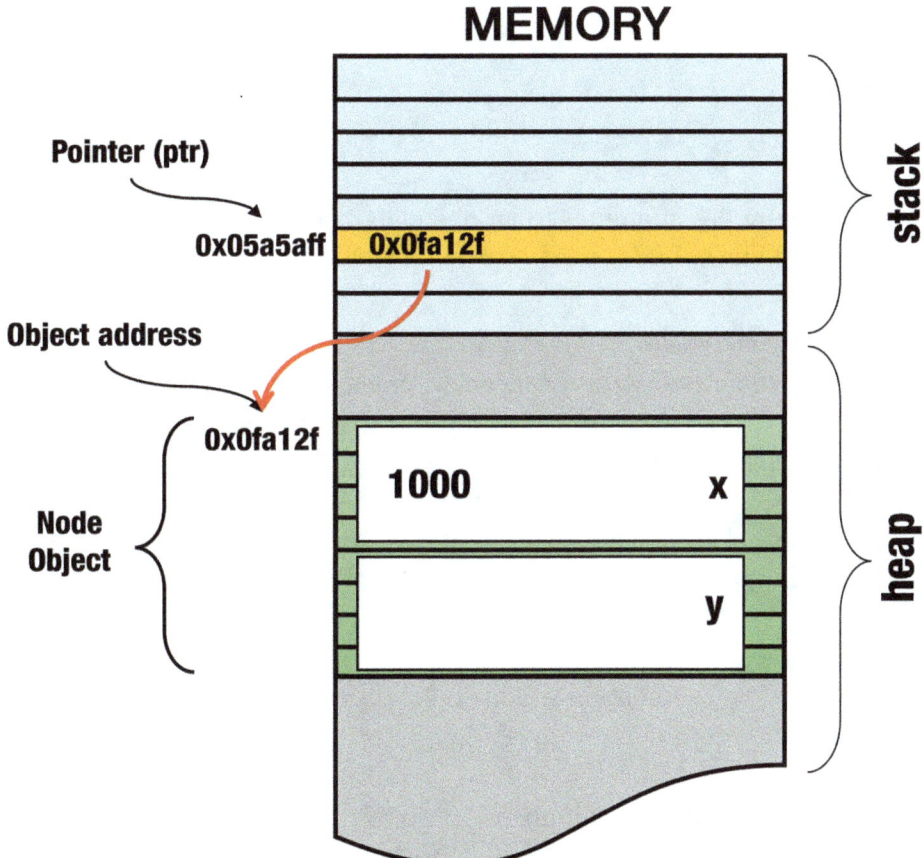

Figure 4.1: A pointer on the stack with address `0x05a5aff`, storing the start address of a new node allocated on heap memory with address `0x0fa12f`

Working with Pointers Inside Objects

To access the pointer inside the object and allocate memory for it:

```
Node *ptr = new Node;     // Pointer to the object
ptr->pz = new int;        // Access pointer inside object
```
Allocating Memory for a Pointer Inside a Node

Storing Values

To store a value in the allocated space:

```
// Storing the value 1000 in the allocated space
*(ptr->pz) = 1000;
```
Storing a Value in the Allocated Pointer

As shown in Figure 4.2, a pointer to an object can contain another pointer. Figure 4.3 provides a simplified view.

4.1.2 Creating Linked Objects

Now, consider the scenario where you need to create a list of objects of the same type connected together. To achieve this, store pointers of the same type inside the objects, allowing you to link the objects together in memory.

```
struct Node {
    int data;
    Node *next = nullptr;
};
```
Creating a Linked Node Structure

Ensure that the `next` pointer is initialized to `nullptr` when a `Node` object is created. This practice ensures a default state for the object.

In this structure, the `next` member is a pointer to the next node in the list. As shown in Figure 4.4, linked objects in memory use pointers.

Figure 4.5 provides a simplified view with traversal.

4.1 Introduction to Linked Pointers

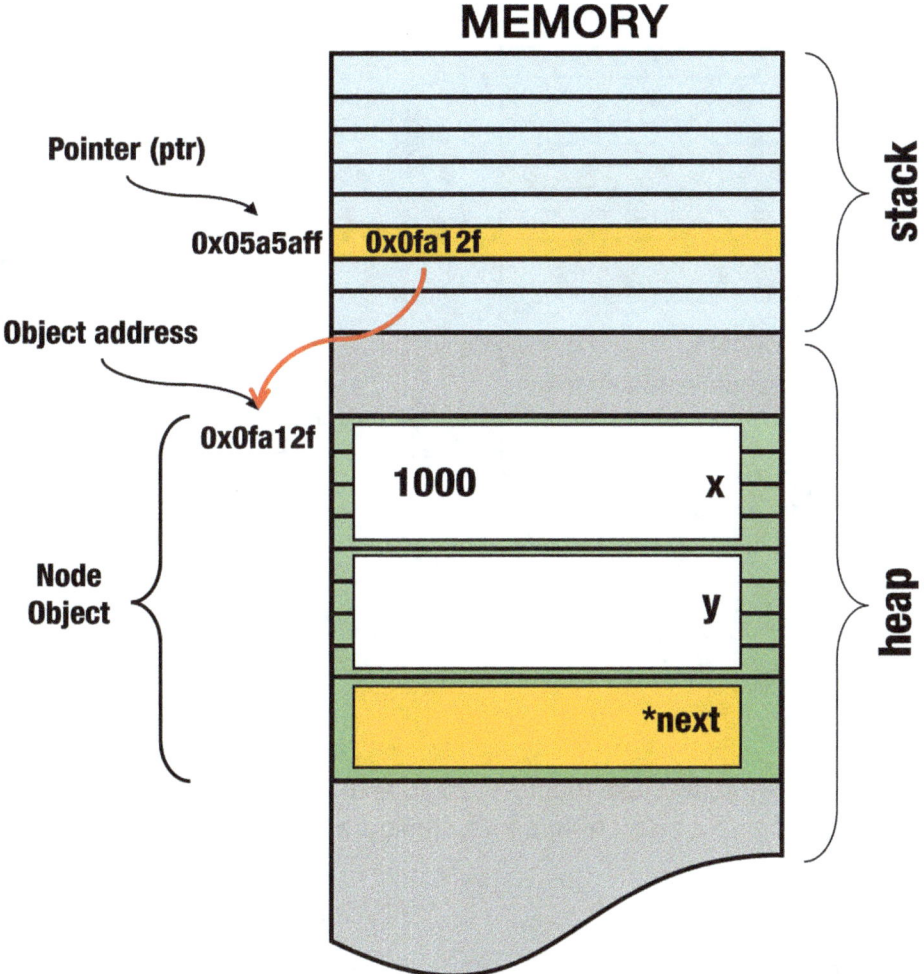

Figure 4.2: Pointer to an object containing an additional pointer member (*next) to allow linking to the next object

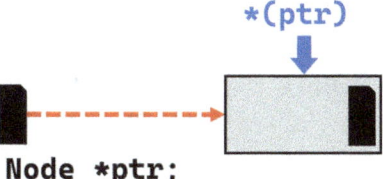

Figure 4.3: Simple representation of a pointer (ptr) pointing to a node, accessing it using *(ptr). The node is represented as a box with an arrow pointing to the next node

To access any node in this linked list, you start from the previous node.

```
// Pointer to the first node object
Node *ptr = new Node;
// Allocate a new node linked to the first node
ptr->next = new Node;
```

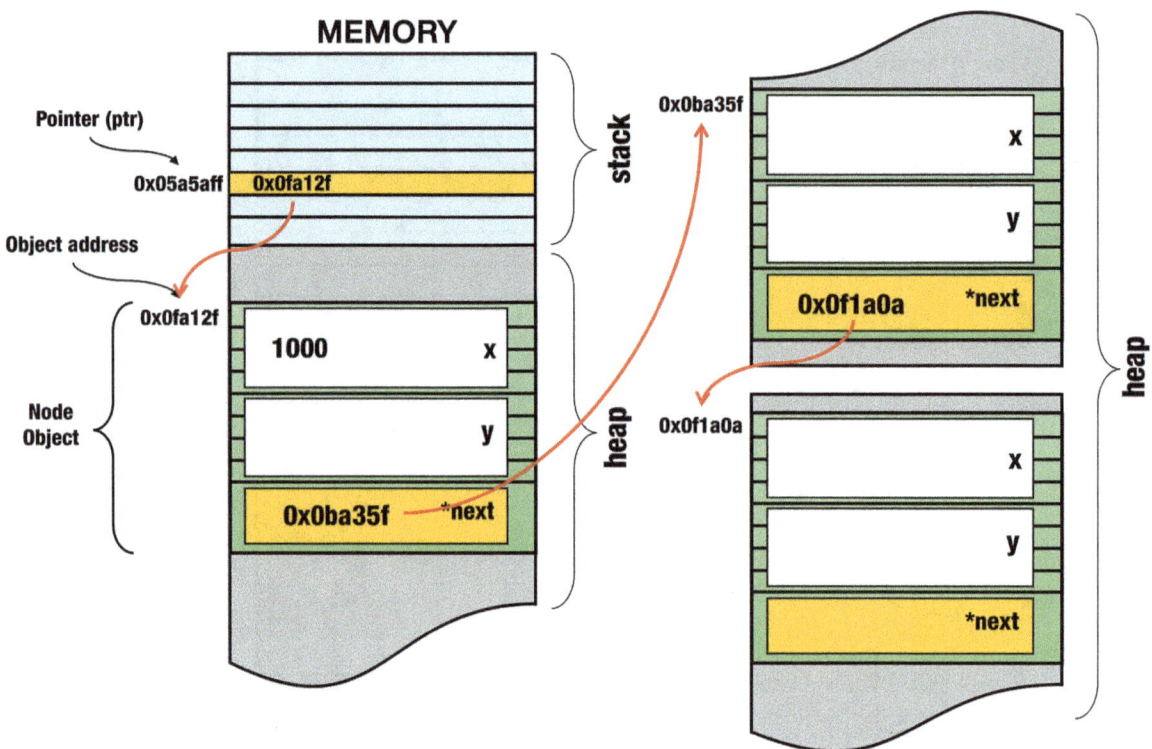

Figure 4.4: Linked objects in heap memory. Each node's *next pointer holds the address of the next node, creating a chain in memory, illustrating the dynamic linking of objects

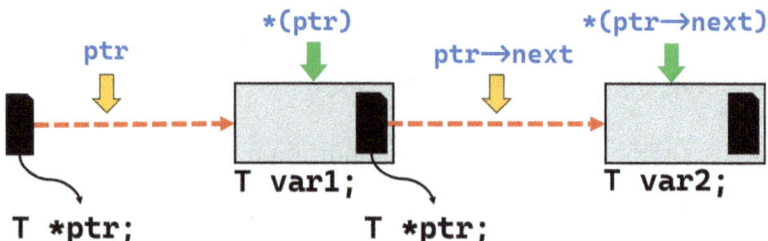

Figure 4.5: Simplified view of linked objects with traversal. Nodes are represented as boxes linked by arrows, showing the conceptual structure of linked lists

```
// Allocate a new node linked to the second node
ptr->next->next = new Node;
```
Creating Linked Nodes in a List

4.1.3 Memory Management

Memory management is a critical aspect of working with linked lists. As you create and manipulate nodes, it's essential to allocate and deallocate memory efficiently. Each node in a linked list is allocated on the heap to ensure dynamic growth and flexibility. However, it's equally important to release memory properly when nodes are removed to avoid memory leaks and maintain system resources.

4.1.4 Why Pointers Matter in Linked Lists

Pointers are fundamental to linked lists, as they enable the creation of a dynamic structure where each element (node) references the next one. This interconnected structure gives linked lists their name and power.

It is **important** to note that all nodes are created using pointers because they are stored in the **heap** (as opposed to the stack). Using the heap ensures that the data isn't automatically deleted when the scope ends. This allows linked lists to be dynamic and flexible, as they can grow or shrink as needed during program execution.

4.2 A Singly-Linked List (SLList)

In this section, I will guide you through the concept of singly-linked lists (SLLists), which are fundamental data structures. SLLists consist of nodes, each containing data and a reference to the next node, enabling dynamic collections that can efficiently grow or shrink.

4.2.1 Anatomy of a Singly-Linked List

A singly-linked list comprises nodes, with each node consisting of two key elements:
1. **Data:** This field holds the actual information or value associated with the node.
2. **Next Pointer:** This field is a reference to the next node, forming the linked structure. If a node is the last in the list, its next pointer is set to `nullptr`.

A node can be defined as follows:

```cpp
template <class T>
struct Node {
    T data;
    Node* next;

    Node() : next(nullptr) {}
    Node(const T& item) : data(item), next(nullptr) {}
};
```

Node Structure Definition for Singly-Linked List

In this definition, `data` represents the value stored in the node, and `next` is a pointer to the next node in the list, as illustrated in Figure 4.6.

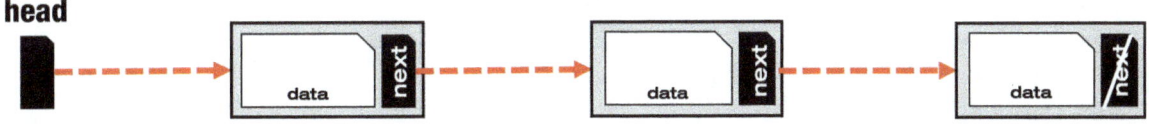

Figure 4.6: A simple view of a singly-linked list. The head points to the first node, and each node points to the next node in the sequence

Example: Creating a Singly-Linked List

To illustrate the creation of a singly-linked list, let's create a list of integers and add a few elements to it, as shown in Figure 4.7:

```
Node<int>* head = new Node<int>;
head->data = 1;

Node<int>* second = new Node<int>;
second->data = 2;
head->next = second;

Node<int>* third = new Node<int>;
third->data = 3;
second->next = third;
```

Creating a Singly-Linked List of `int` Nodes

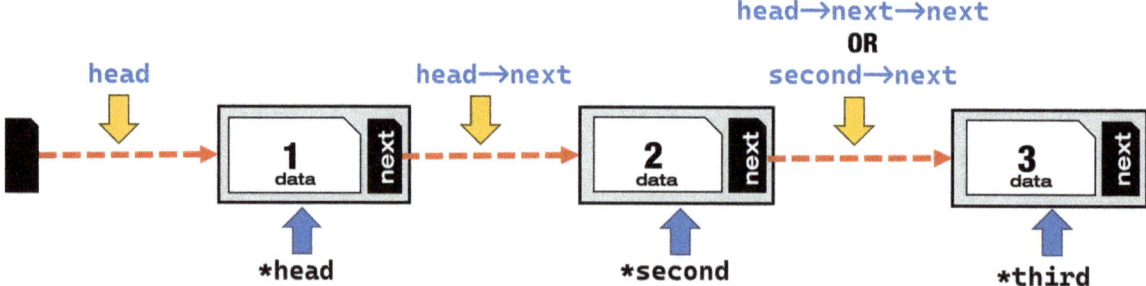

Figure 4.7: Example of a singly-linked list, illustrating the code and structure of a simple list with nodes linked sequentially

4.2.2 Creating a Singly-Linked List Without Tail

To implement a singly-linked list, we define a class called `SinglyLL` with the following essential data members:
- `head`: A pointer to the first node in the list (composed from `Node`)
- `size`: The number of nodes in the list (inherited from `IList`)

The interface code is presented below. Figure 4.8 illustrates the UML Class Diagram of `SinglyLL`, `Node`, and the `IList` interface.

```
1 template <typename T>
2 class SinglyLL : public IList<T> {
3 public:
4     SinglyLL() : IList<T>(),
5                  head(nullptr) {}
```

4.2 A Singly-Linked List (SLList)

```
 6
 7      virtual ~SinglyLL(){
 8          clear();
 9      }
10
11      // IList Interface Methods
12      virtual void pushFront(const T item);
13      virtual void pushBack(const T item);
14      virtual T popBack();
15      virtual T popFront();
16      // ..... Other Abstract Interface methods
17
18 protected:
19      Node<T>* head;
20
21      // Inherited members to use directly
22      using IList<T>::size;
23 };
```
SinglyLL Class Interface

This interface defines the core methods and attributes needed to work with a singly-linked list.

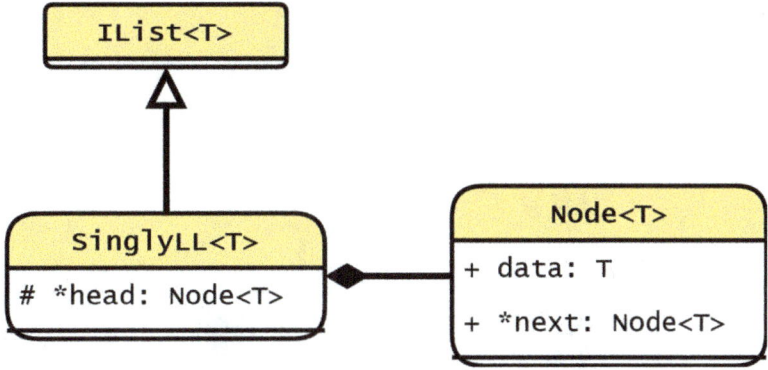

Figure 4.8: SinglyLL UML class diagram, showing the inheritance from IList<T> and composition with Node<T>

To create a singly-linked list, you typically start with a pointer to the head node, which is the first element in the list. Here's how you can initialize an empty list:

```
1 SinglyLL() : IList<T>(),
2              head(nullptr) {}
```
Initializing an Empty Singly-Linked List

PushFront and PushBack
PushFront

The `pushFront` function adds an element to the beginning of the linked list. It creates a new node, links it to the current head, and updates the head pointer to the new node. The time complexity of `pushFront` is $O(1)$ (see Figure 4.9).

```cpp
template <typename T>
void SinglyLL<T>::pushFront(const T item) {
    Node<T>* newNode = new Node<T>(item);

    // (1) Link the new node to the current head.
    newNode->next = head;

    // (2) Update the head pointer to the new node.
    head = newNode;

    ++size;
}
```

`pushFront` Function: Add Element to Front of List

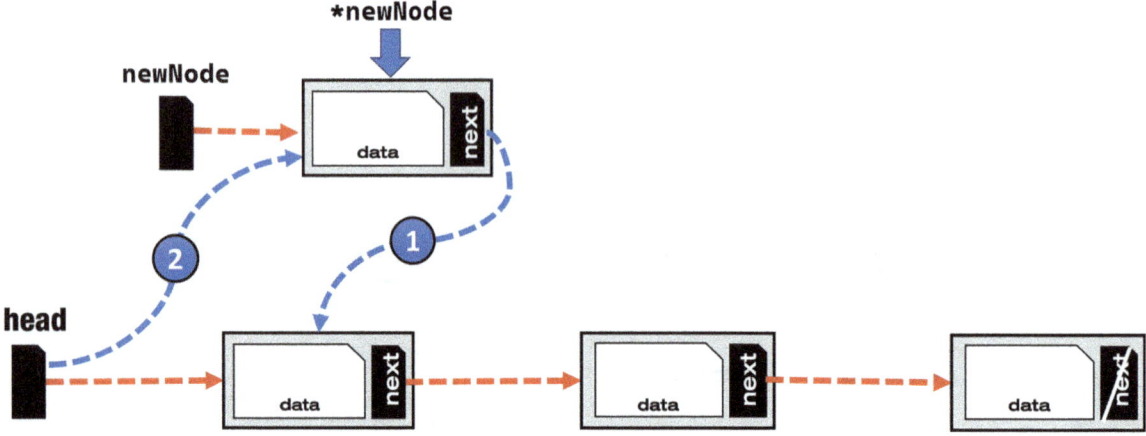

Figure 4.9: Visualizing the `pushFront` operation, showing steps to link a new node to the current head and update the head pointer

PushBack

The `pushBack` function adds an element to the end of the linked list. It iterates through the list to find the last node and appends the new element to it. Therefore, the time complexity of `pushBack` is $O(n)$, where n is the number of elements in the list.

4.2 A Singly-Linked List (SLList)

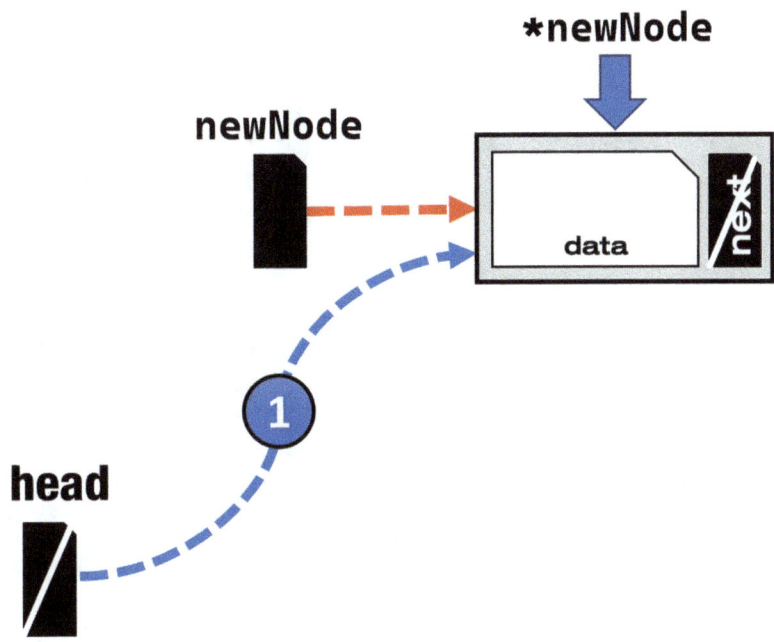

Figure 4.10: `PushBack` operation with no head. The new node is set as the head, illustrating the initial insertion into an empty list

When adding an element to the end of the linked list using `pushBack`, two scenarios may occur:
- **Case 1:** If there is no existing head, the new element becomes the first and only node in the list (Figure 4.10).
- **Case 2:** If there are existing nodes in the list, the new element is appended to the last node. This involves two steps (Figure 4.11):
    1. Seeking to the last node
    2. Appending the new element to the last node

```
1 template <typename T>
2 void SinglyLL<T>::pushBack(const T item) {
3     Node<T>* newNode = new Node<T>(item);
4
5     // CASE 1: If there is no head
6     if (!head) {
7         // (1) Set the new node as the head.
8         head = newNode;
9     }
10    // CASE 2: If there are existing nodes
11    else {
12        Node<T>* current = head;
13        // (1) Seek to the last node.
```

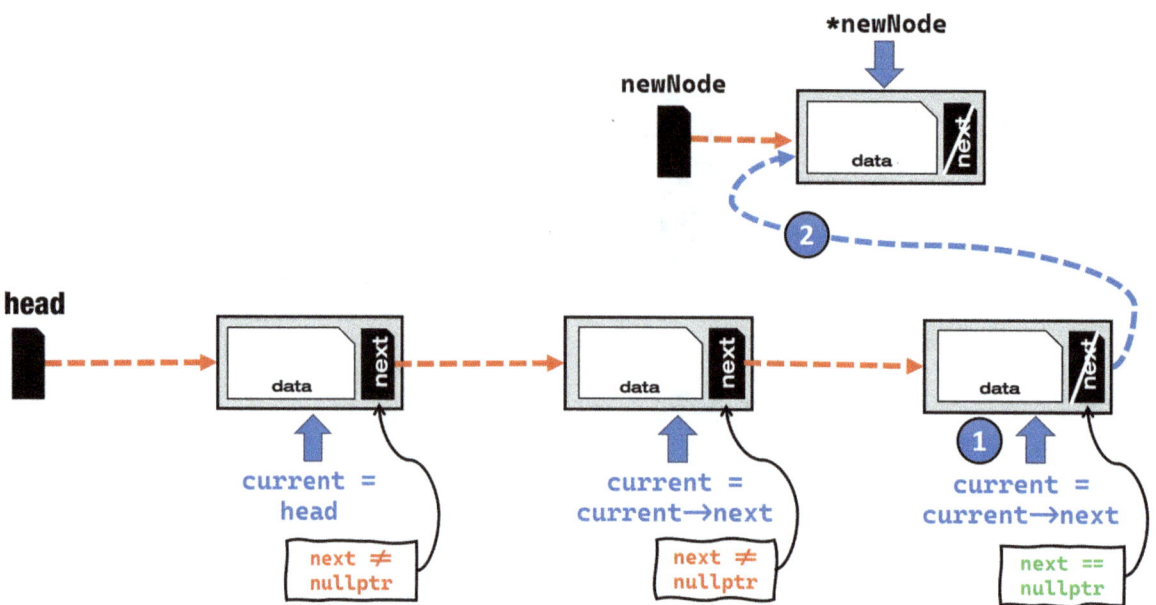

Figure 4.11: `PushBack` operation with existing nodes. The process shows locating the current last node and appending the new node to the end

```
14          while (current->next) {
15              current = current->next;
16          }
17          // (2) Append the new element to the last node.
18          current->next = newNode;
19      }
20      ++size;
```

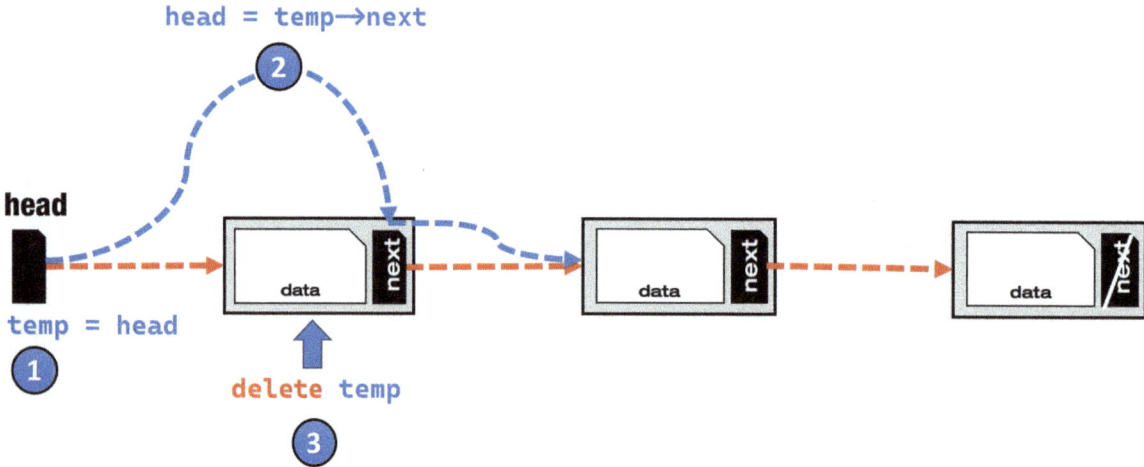

Figure 4.12: Visualizing the `popFront` operation, showing steps to update the head pointer and remove the first node from the list

```
21 }
```
pushBack Function: Add Element to End of List

PopFront and PopBack

PopFront

The `popFront` function removes the element from the beginning of the linked list. It updates the head pointer to the next node and deletes the old head (Figure 4.12). The time complexity of `popFront` is $O(1)$.

```
1  template <typename T>
2  T SinglyLL<T>::popFront() {
3      assert(head && size > 0);
4
5      // (1) Save a reference to the current head node.
6      Node<T>* temp = head;
7      // (2) Update the head pointer to the next node.
8      head = head->next;
9      T frontData = temp->data;
10     // (3) Delete the old head node.
11     delete temp;
12     --size;
13     return frontData;
14 }
```
popFront Function: Remove Element from Front of List

PopBack

The `popBack` function removes the element from the end of the linked list. It iterates through the list to find the second-to-last node, updates its next pointer to null, and deletes the last node.

When removing an element from the end of the linked list using `popBack`, two scenarios may occur:
- **Case 1:** If there's only one element (head) in the list (Figure 4.13), `popBack` removes this element, and the list becomes empty. This involves two steps:
    1. Deleting the head node (the only node in this case)
    2. Updating the head pointer to null, indicating an empty list
- **Case 2:** If there are multiple nodes in the list (Figure 4.14), `popBack` removes the last element while preserving the rest of the list's structure. This involves three steps:
    1. Traversing the list to locate the second-to-last node
    2. Deleting the last node
    3. Updating the second-to-last node's `next` pointer to null, indicating the new end of the list

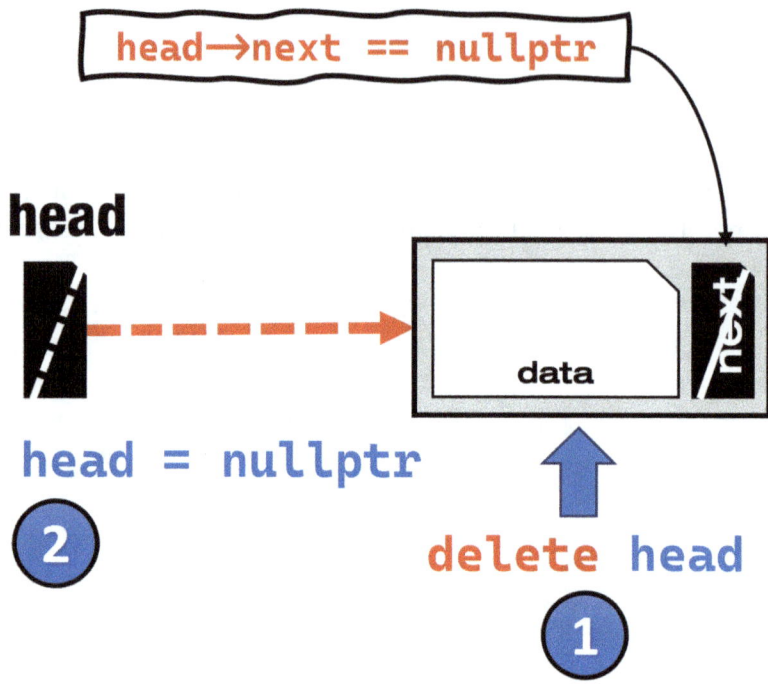

Figure 4.13: `PopBack` operation with only one head node. The process shows deleting the head node and setting the head pointer to `nullptr`

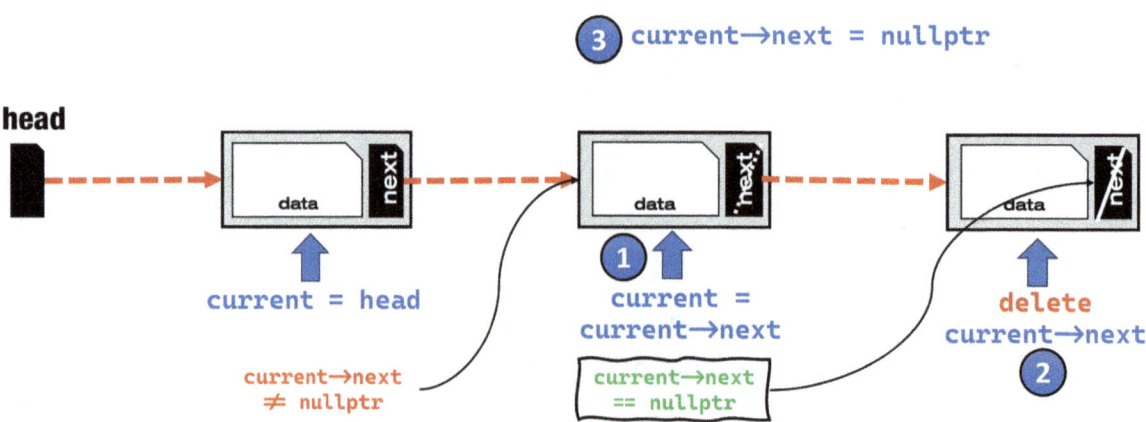

Figure 4.14: `PopBack` operation with existing nodes. The process shows traversing to the second-to-last node and updating the pointers to remove the last node

4.2 A Singly-Linked List (SLList)

```cpp
1  template <typename T>
2  T SinglyLL<T>::popBack() {
3      // Ensure the list is not empty
4      assert(head && size > 0);
5  
6      T backData;
7      // Case 1: If there's only one element in the list
8      if (head->next == nullptr) {
9          backData = head->data;
10         // (1) Delete the head node.
11         delete head;
12         // (2) Update the head pointer to null.
13         head = nullptr;
14     }
15     // Case 2: If there are multiple nodes in the list
16     else {
17         Node<T>* current = head;
18         // (1) Traverse to the second-to-last node.
19         while (current->next->next) {
20             current = current->next;
21         }
22         backData = current->next->data;
23  
24         // (2) Delete the last node.
25         delete current->next;
26         // (3) Update the node's 'next' pointer to null.
27         current->next = nullptr;
28     }
29     --size;
30     return backData;
31 }
```

popBack Function: Remove Element from End of List

4.2.3 Creating a Singly-Linked List with a Tail

In this section, I will introduce the concept of a tail pointer that points to the last node in the list (Figure 4.15). This enhancement simplifies and optimizes operations that involve the end of the list, such as appending elements.

To implement a singly-linked list with a tail, we inherit from the `SinglyLL` class and introduce an additional essential data member:

- `tail`: A pointer to the last node in the list (composed from `Node`)

The interface code is presented below. Figure 4.16 illustrates the UML class diagram of `SinglyLLTailed`, `Node`, and the `IList` interface.

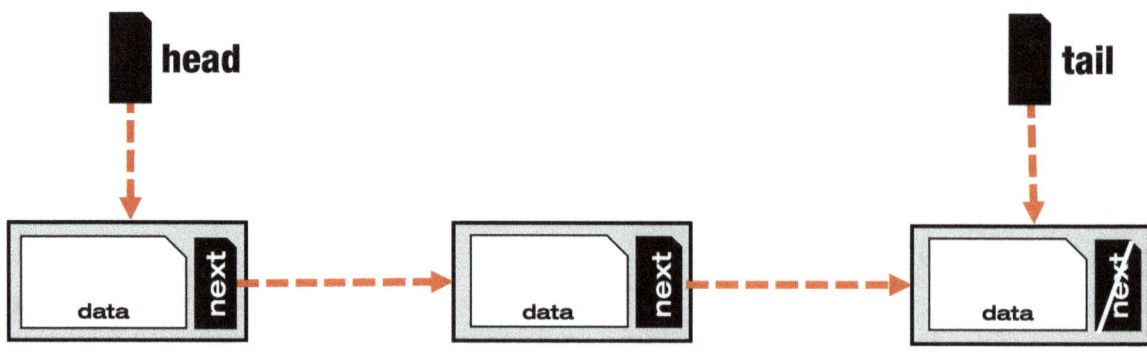

Figure 4.15: A simple view of a singly-linked list with a tail pointer. The head points to the first node, and the tail points to the last node

```cpp
template <typename T>
class SinglyLLTailed : public SinglyLL<T> {
public:
    SinglyLLTailed() : SinglyLL<T>(),
                       tail(nullptr) {}

    virtual ~SinglyLLTailed();

    // IList Interface Methods
    virtual void clear();
    virtual void pushBack(const T item);
    virtual void pushFront(const T item);
    virtual T popBack();
    virtual T popFront();
    virtual T topBack() const;

protected:
    Node<T>* tail;

    using SinglyLL<T>::size;
    using SinglyLL<T>::head;
};
```
`SinglyLLTailed` Class Interface

This updated interface now includes the `tail` pointer. Initialization of the list is performed as follows:

```cpp
SinglyLLTailed() : SinglyLL<T>(),
                   tail(nullptr) {}
```
Initializing a Singly-Linked List with a Tail

4.2 A Singly-Linked List (SLList)

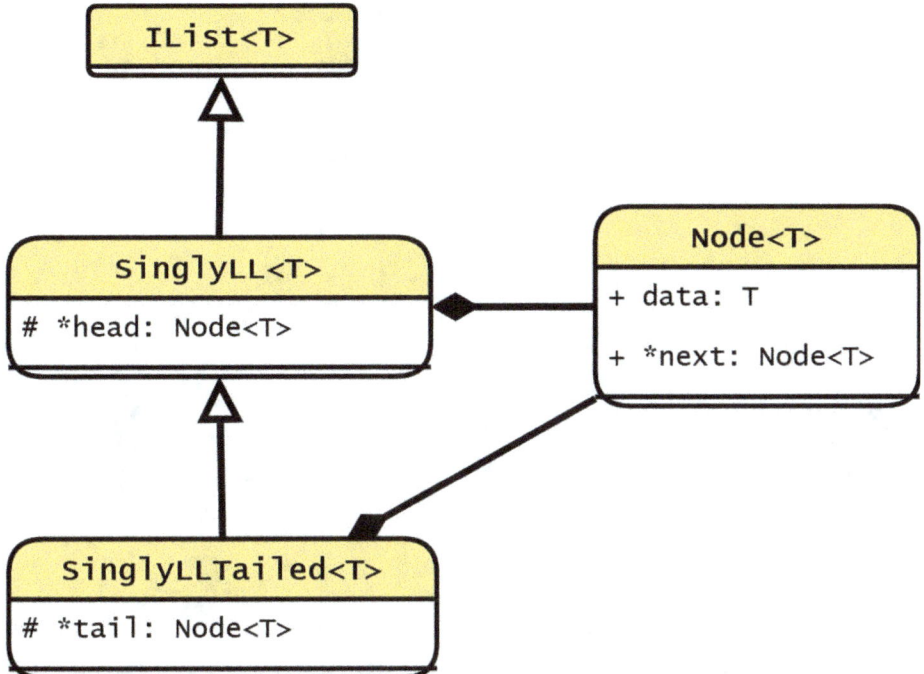

Figure 4.16: SinglyLLTailed UML class diagram, showing the inheritance from SinglyLL<T> and composition with Node<T>, highlighting the addition of a tail pointer

Enhancing with a Tail Pointer

Introducing the tail pointer significantly improves the efficiency of the pushBack operation, allowing for constant time ($O(1)$) insertion at the end of the linked list. The other fundamental operations, including pushFront, popFront, and popBack, remain unaffected and continue to operate in the same way as in linked lists without a tail pointer.

It's important to note that while the popBack operation does not directly rely on the tail pointer to find the second-to-last node in the list, it requires adjusting the tail pointer when removing the last element.

PushBack

The pushBack function adds an element to the end of the linked list in constant time, achieving a time complexity of $O(1)$.

When using pushBack to add an element to the end of the linked list, two scenarios may occur:
1. **Case 1: No Existing Head**: In this scenario, the new element becomes the first and only node in the list.
2. **Case 2: Existing Nodes** (see Figure 4.17): When there are already existing nodes in the list, the new element is appended to the last node using the following steps:
   (a) Updating the current tail's next pointer to point to the new element
   (b) Updating the tail pointer to the new node

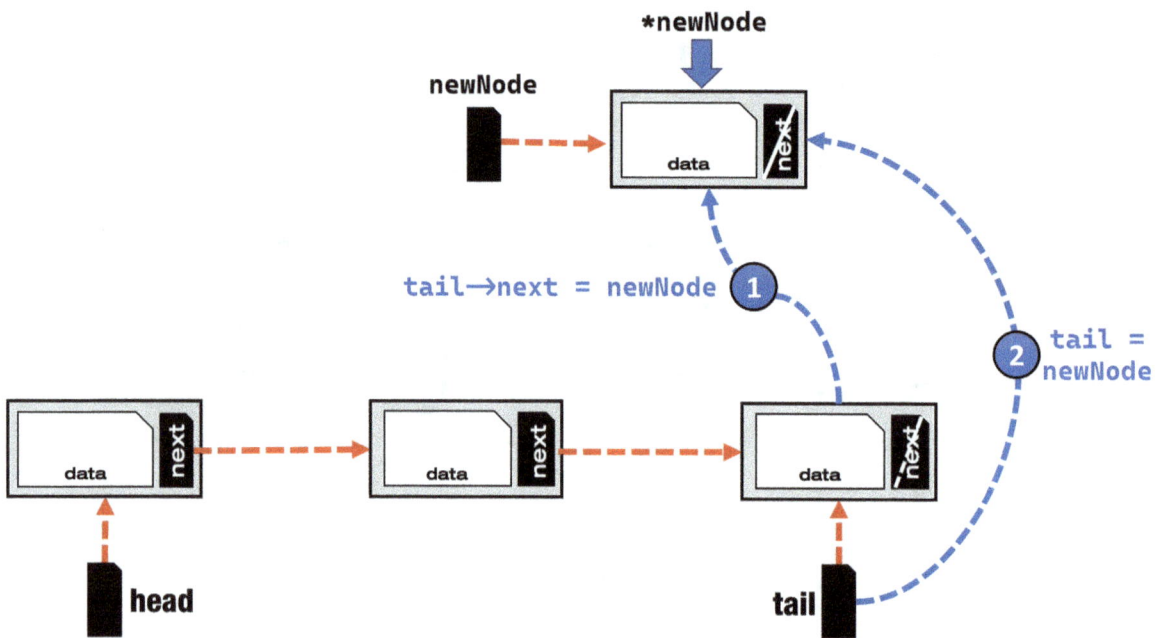

Figure 4.17: PushBack operation in `SinglyLLTailed` with existing nodes. The new node is linked to the end of the list, and the tail pointer is updated

```cpp
template <typename T>
void SinglyLLTailed<T>::pushBack(const T item) {
    Node<T>* newNode = new Node<T>(item);

    // Case 1: If there is no head
    if (!head) {
        // (1) Set the new node as the head.
        head = newNode;
        // (2) Set the new node as the tail.
        tail = newNode;
    }
    // Case 2: If there are existing nodes
    else {
        // (1) Append the new element to the current tail.
        tail->next = newNode;
        // (2) Update the tail to the new node.
        tail = newNode;
    }
    ++size;
}
```

pushBack Function: Add Element to End of List with Tail Pointer

4.2 A Singly-Linked List (SLList)

PopBack

The `popBack` operation is responsible for removing the last element in a linked list. When the last element is removed, it's important to update the tail pointer to maintain a reference to the new last node.

When using `popBack`, two scenarios may occur:
1. **Case 1: Only One Element (Head) Exists**: In this scenario, `popBack` removes the only element, and the list becomes empty.
2. **Case 2: Multiple Elements Exist**: In this scenario, `popBack` removes the last element, and the tail pointer is updated to the new last node.

```cpp
template <typename T>
T SinglyLLTailed<T>::popBack() {
    // Ensure the list is not empty
    assert(head && size > 0);

    T backData;

    // Case 1: If there's only one element in the list
    if (head->next == nullptr) {
        backData = head->data;
        // (1) Delete the head node.
        delete head;
        // (2) Update the head and tail pointers to null.
        head = tail = nullptr;
    }
    // Case 2: If there are multiple nodes in the list
    else {
        Node<T>* current = head;
        // (1) Traverse to the second-to-last node.
        while (current->next->next) {
            current = current->next;
        }
        backData = current->next->data;
        // (2) Delete the last node.
        delete current->next;
        // (3) Update the tail pointer to
        //     the second-to-last node.
        current->next = nullptr;
        tail = current;
    }
    --size;
    return backData;
}
```

`popBack` Function: Remove Element from End of List with Tail Pointer

Insertion and Removal
Insert

The `insertAt` function adds an element at a specified location in the linked list. It verifies that the index is valid and updates the node connections to accommodate the new element (see Figure 4.18). This function operates in $O(n)$ time complexity in the worst case.

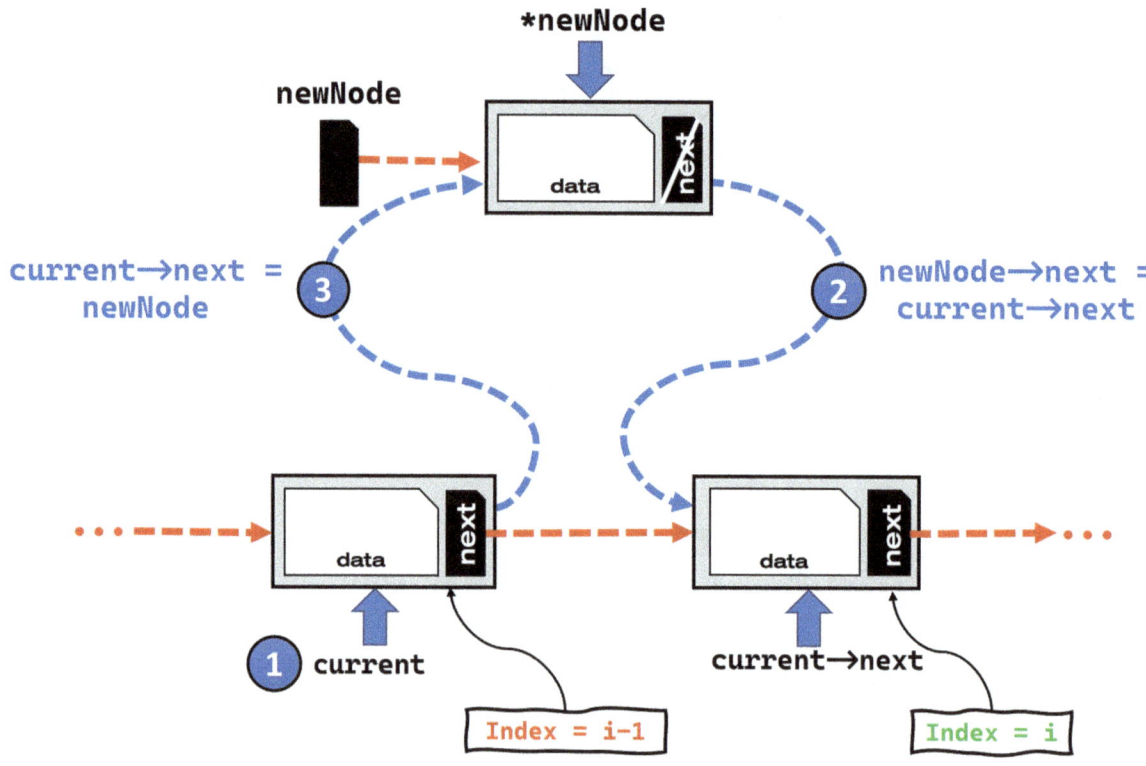

Figure 4.18: `InsertAt` operation with existing nodes. The new node is inserted within the sequence by updating pointers to link it correctly

```
1  template <typename T>
2  void SinglyLL<T>::insertAt(size_t index, const T item) {
3      // Check if the index is within valid range
4      assert(index >= 0 && index <= size);
5  
6      // Case 1: Inserting at the beginning of the list
7      if (index == 0) {
8          pushFront(item);
9      }
10     // Case 2: Inserting in the middle or end of the list
11     else {
12         Node<T>* newNode = new Node<T>(item);
13         Node<T>* current = head;
```

4.2 A Singly-Linked List (SLList)

```
14          // (1) Traverse to the node before the index
15          for (size_t i = 1; i < index; i++) {
16              current = current->next;
17          }
18          // (2) Update the new node's 'next'.
19          newNode->next = current->next;
20          // (3) Update the previous node's 'next'.
21          current->next = newNode;
22          ++size;
23      }
24 }
```

insertAt Function: Add Element at a Specific Index

Remove

The removeAt function deletes an element from the linked list based on the specified index. It checks if the index is valid and updates the node connections to remove the selected item (see Figure 4.19). The time complexity of removeAt is $O(n)$ in the worst case.

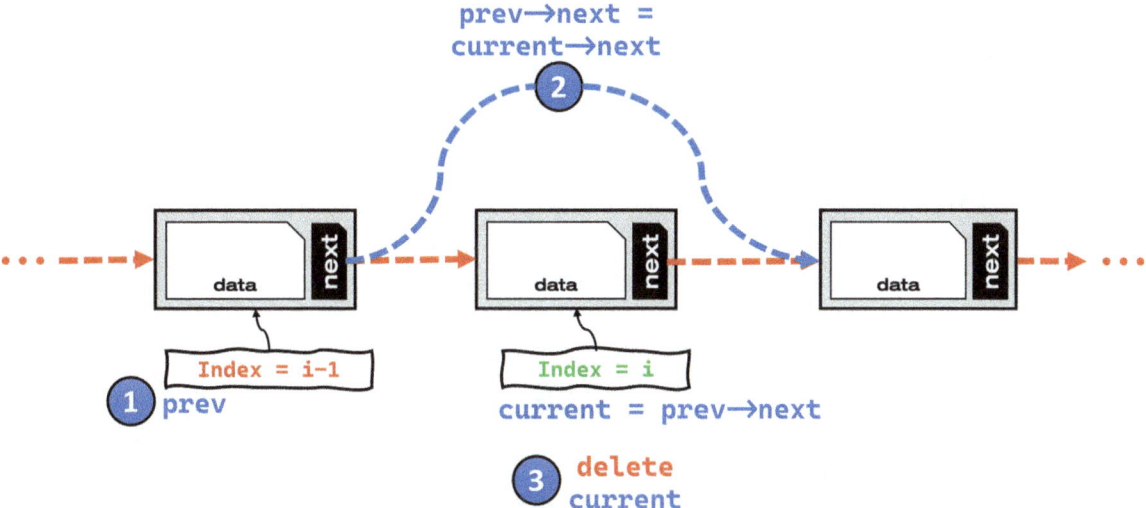

Figure 4.19: RemoveAt operation with existing nodes. The links are updated to exclude the current node, which is then removed from the list

```
1 template <typename T>
2 void SinglyLL<T>::removeAt(size_t index) {
3     // Check if the index is within valid range
4     assert(index >= 0 && index < size);
5
6     // Case 1: Removing the first element
```

```
 7      if (index == 0) {
 8          popFront();
 9      }
10      // Case 2: Removing from the middle or end of the list
11      else {
12          Node<T>* prev = head;
13          // (1) Traverse to the node before the
14          //     one to be removed
15          for (size_t i = 1; i < index; i++) {
16              prev = prev->next;
17          }
18          Node<T>* current = prev->next;
19          // (2) Update the previous node's `next`.
20          prev->next = current->next;
21          // (3) Delete the element at the specified index.
22          delete current;
23          --size;
24      }
25 }
```

removeAt Function: Remove Element at a Specific Index

4.2.4 Accessing Elements

You can also access and modify elements in the singly-linked list using the `operator[]` and the `get` function. The time complexity is $O(n)$ in the worst case.

```
 1 template <typename T>
 2 T& SinglyLL<T>::get(size_t index) {
 3     assert(index >= 0 && index < size);
 4     Node<T>* current = head;
 5     for (size_t i = 0; i < index; ++i) {
 6         current = current->next;
 7     }
 8     return current->data;
 9 }
10
11 template <typename T>
12 T& SinglyLL<T>::operator[](size_t i) {
13     return get(i);
14 }
```

Accessing Elements in a Singly-Linked List

4.2.5 Traversing

To interact with the elements within a singly-linked list, you need to traverse it from the head to the desired node. This process allows you to examine and print the contents of the list.

Printing the Singly-Linked List

A fundamental operation is to print the elements in the singly-linked list, providing a visual representation of its contents. The time complexity of the `print` function is $O(n)$.

```cpp
template <typename T>
void SinglyLL<T>::print() const {
    Node<T>* current = head;
    while (current) {
        std::cout << current->data << " ";
        current = current->next;
    }
    std::cout << std::endl;
}
```

`print` Function: Display Contents of the List

Destructor for Proper Memory Management

The destructor ensures that all allocated memory for the singly-linked list is properly released when the list goes out of scope or is explicitly destroyed, preventing memory leaks and promoting efficient resource management. The time complexity of the destructor is $O(n)$.

```cpp
template <typename T>
void SinglyLLTailed<T>::clear() {
    while (head != nullptr) {
        Node<T>* temp = head;
        head = head->next;
        delete temp;
    }
    // Release `tail` pointer.
    tail = nullptr;
}

template <typename T>
SinglyLLTailed<T>::~SinglyLLTailed() {
    clear();
}
```

`clear` and Destructor: Proper Memory Management

The `clear` method performs the same logic as your original destructor, cleaning up the list by deleting each node and releasing associated memory. By calling `clear` from the destructor, you ensure that the cleanup process is consistent, making your code more maintainable and reducing the chances of errors related to memory management.

4.3 A Doubly-Linked List (DLList)

A doubly-linked list (DLList) is similar to a singly-linked list (SLList) but with an added feature: each node in a DLList not only points to the next node in the sequence but also has a reference to the previous node in the list (Figure 4.20). This additional backward reference provides more flexibility and convenience when navigating the list.

4.3.1 Anatomy of a Doubly-Linked List

A doubly-linked list comprises nodes, with each node consisting of three key elements:
1. **Data:** This field holds the actual information or value associated with the node.
2. **Next Pointer:** This field is a reference to the next node in the sequence.
3. **Previous Pointer:** This field is a reference to the previous node in the sequence.

Here is a typical structure for a node in a DLList, defined as `DNode`:

```cpp
template <class T>
struct DNode : public Node<T> {
    DNode* prev;
    DNode* next;

    DNode() : Node<T>(),
              prev(nullptr), next(nullptr) {}
    DNode(const T& item) : Node<T>(item),
                           prev(nullptr), next(nullptr) {}
};
```

DNode Structure Definition for Doubly-Linked List

In this definition, `data` represents the value stored in the node, while `next` and `prev` are pointers to the next and previous nodes in the list, respectively, as illustrated in Figure 4.20.

This structure allows each node to maintain connections to both its successor and predecessor, creating a bidirectional linkage. This bidirectional connection enhances list navigation, making it easy to traverse the list in both directions.

4.3.2 A Circular Doubly-Linked List with Dummy Node

In SLLists, we encountered situations that required special consideration, such as removing the last element or adding an element to an empty list. Ensuring that the `head` and `tail` pointers are updated correctly in these scenarios can be complex. In DLLists, the number of such special cases increases, making efficient management of the list more challenging.

4.3 A Doubly-Linked List (DLList)

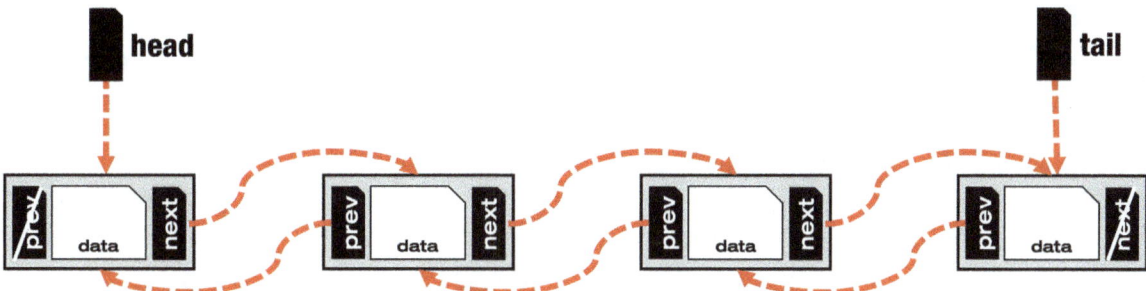

Figure 4.20: A simple view of a doubly-linked list. The head points to the first node, the tail points to the last node, and each node has next and prev pointers

To address these complexities and simplify DLList operations, a practical solution is to introduce a dummy node. This node does not contain any data but acts as a placeholder. It plays a pivotal role in simplifying list management by ensuring that there are no special cases. Each node in the DLList is linked (double-linked) in a cycle, as shown in Figure 4.21, where the dummy node acts as the node that follows the last node in the list and precedes the first node in the list. This methodology establishes a more uniform structure and eases the navigation of challenging scenarios within DLLists.

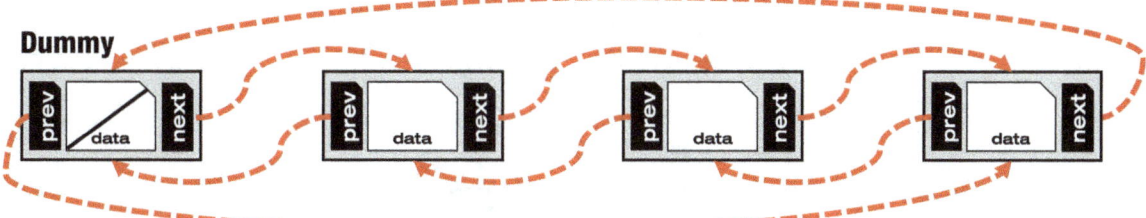

Figure 4.21: A simple view of a circular doubly-linked list with a dummy node. The dummy node links the first and last nodes, facilitating a continuous structure

Here, we define the circular DLList class that includes the dummy node (see Figure 4.22):

```
1 template <typename T>
2 class DLList : public IList<T> {
3 public:
4     DLList() : IList<T>() {
5         dummy = new DNode<T>();
6         dummy->next = dummy;
7         dummy->prev = dummy;
8     }
9
```

```
10      virtual ~DLList();
11
12      // IList Interface Methods
13      virtual void insertAt(size_t index, const T item);
14      virtual void removeAt(size_t index);
15      virtual void pushFront(const T item);
16      virtual void pushBack(const T item);
17      virtual T popFront();
18      virtual T popBack();
19      virtual T topFront() const;
20      virtual T topBack() const;
21
22      virtual void clear();
23      virtual void print() const;
24      // ..... Other Abstract Interface methods
25
26 private:
27      DNode<T>* dummy;
28
29      DNode<T>* jumpTo(size_t index) const;
30 };
```

DLList Class Interface with Dummy Node

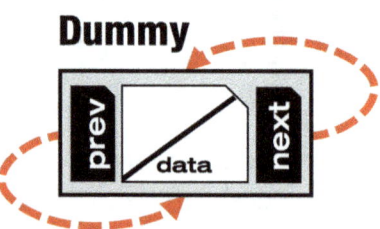

Figure 4.22: An empty circular DLList with only a dummy node, illustrating the initial state of the list

The class diagram (see Figure 4.23) illustrates the relationships and inheritance among Node, DNode, and DLList.

4.3.3 Implementing Operations
PushBack

The pushBack function adds an element to the end of the doubly-linked list. The time complexity of pushBack is $O(1)$.

```
1 template <typename T>
2 void DLList<T>::pushBack(const T item) {
```

4.3 A Doubly-Linked List (DLList)

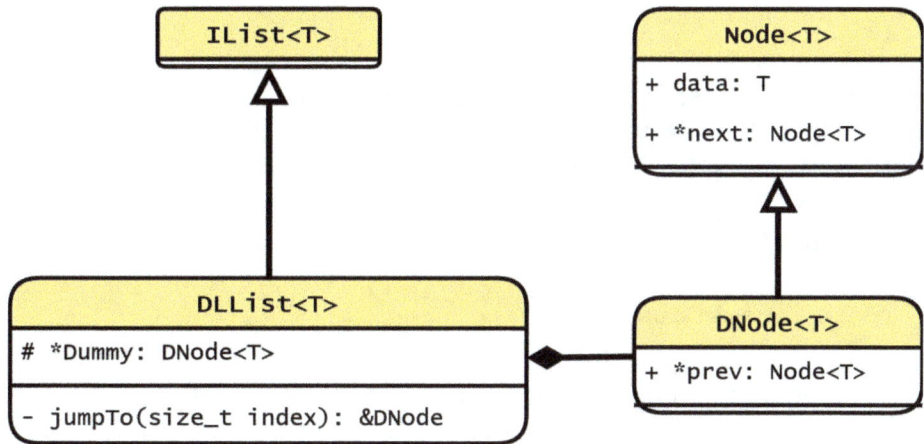

Figure 4.23: UML class diagram of `DLList` showing inheritance and relationships with `Node` and `DNode`

```
3      // (1) Create a new node
4      DNode<T>* newNode = new DNode<T>(item);
5
6      // (2) Link the new node with the
7      //     current last node and dummy node
8      newNode->prev = dummy->prev;
9      newNode->next = dummy;
10     dummy->prev->next = newNode;
11     dummy->prev = newNode;
12
13     // (3) Increment the size of the list
14     ++size;
15 }
```

pushBack Function: Add Element to End of List

PopBack

The `popBack` function removes an element from the end of the doubly-linked list. The time complexity of `popBack` is $O(1)$.

```
1 template <typename T>
2 T DLList<T>::popBack() {
3     assert(dummy->prev != dummy && size > 0);
4
5     // (1) Save a reference to the last node
6     DNode<T>* temp = dummy->prev;
7     T backData = temp->data;
8
```

```
 9        // (2) Update the dummy's previous node
10        dummy->prev = temp->prev;
11        temp->prev->next = dummy;
12
13        // (3) Delete the last node
14        delete temp;
15        --size;
16
17        return backData;
18    }
```
popBack Function: Remove Element from End of List

PushFront

The `pushFront` function adds an element to the beginning of the doubly-linked list. The time complexity of `pushFront` is $O(1)$.

```
 1 template <typename T>
 2 void DLList<T>::pushFront(const T item) {
 3     // (1) Create a new node
 4     DNode<T>* newNode = new DNode<T>(item);
 5
 6     // (2) Link the new node with
 7     //     the dummy node and the first node
 8     newNode->next = dummy->next;
 9     newNode->prev = dummy;
10     dummy->next->prev = newNode;
11     dummy->next = newNode;
12
13     // (3) Increment the size of the list
14     ++size;
15 }
```
pushFront Function: Add Element to Front of List

PopFront

The `popFront` function removes an element from the beginning of the doubly-linked list. The time complexity of `popFront` is $O(1)$.

```
 1 template <typename T>
 2 T DLList<T>::popFront() {
 3     assert(dummy->next != dummy && size > 0);
 4
 5     // (1) Save a reference to the first node
```

4.3 A Doubly-Linked List (DLList)

```
6        DNode<T>* temp = dummy->next;
7        T frontData = temp->data;
8
9        // (2) Update the dummy's next node
10       dummy->next = temp->next;
11       temp->next->prev = dummy;
12
13       // (3) Delete the first node
14       delete temp;
15       --size;
16
17       return frontData;
18 }
```

popFront Function: Remove Element from Front of List

4.3.4 Insert and Remove

In doubly-linked lists, both insertAt and removeAt operations can be optimized to $O(n/2)$ by leveraging the ability to traverse the list from either the head or the tail, whichever is closer to the target index. This effectively reduces the number of steps needed to reach the desired node by half on average, improving the overall performance of these operations.

Implementing this optimization involves checking the target index against the midpoint of the list. If the index is closer to the head, traverse from the head; if it is closer to the tail, traverse from the tail. This approach effectively balances the traversal time and enhances the efficiency of the doubly-linked list operations.

Jumping to Element at Index

For instance, with n elements, jumping to an element at index i involves
- Traversing from the dummy's next (Head) if i is less than or equal to $n/2$
- Traversing from the dummy's previous (Tail) if i is greater than $n/2$

The use of a dummy node in doubly-linked lists further simplifies these operations. The dummy node acts as a placeholder, ensuring that the list is never truly empty and that there are no special cases for inserting or removing the first or last elements. This uniform structure allows for consistent traversal and manipulation of nodes, enhancing both code simplicity and efficiency (see Figure 4.24).

JumpTo

The jumpTo function navigates to a specified index in the doubly-linked list. This function helps in optimizing the insertAt and removeAt operations by providing a starting point closer to the target index. The time complexity of jumpTo is $O(n/2)$ in the worst case.

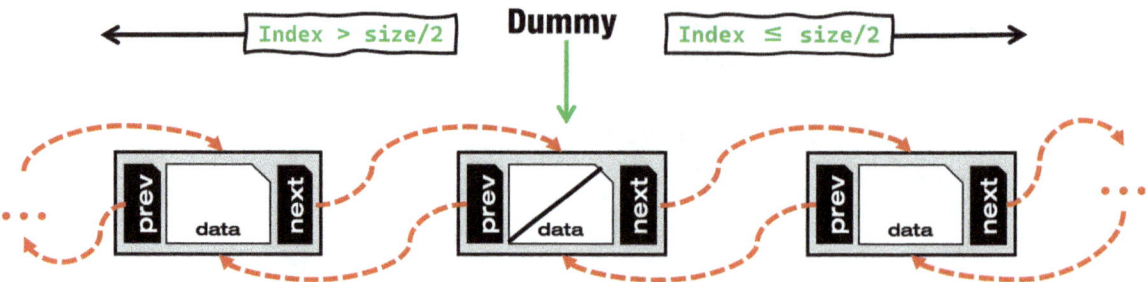

Figure 4.24: Jumping process in a DLList, showing how to move left or right through nodes based on the location of the target node

```cpp
template <typename T>
DNode<T>* DLList<T>::jumpTo(size_t index) const {
    assert(index >= 0 && index < size);

    DNode<T>* current;

    // (1) Determine the direction to traverse
    if (index < size / 2) {
        // (2) Traverse from the head
        //     if the index is in the first half
        current = dummy->next;
        for (size_t i = 0; i < index; ++i) {
            current = current->next;
        }
    } else {
        // (3) Traverse from the tail
        //     if the index is in the second half
        current = dummy;
        for (size_t i = size; i > index; --i) {
            current = current->prev;
        }
    }
    return current;
}
```

jumpTo Function: Navigate to Specified Index

Insert

The insertAt function adds an element at a specified location in the doubly-linked list. It verifies that the index is valid and updates the node connections to accommodate the new element (see Figure 4.25). This function operates in $O(n/2)$ time complexity in the worst case.

4.3 A Doubly-Linked List (DLList)

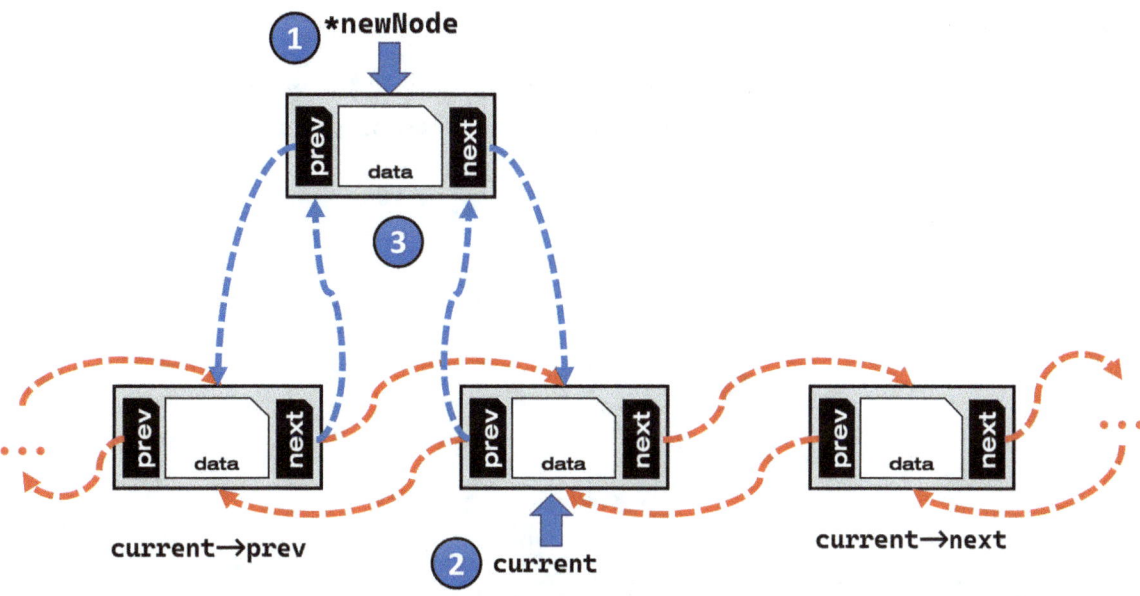

Figure 4.25: InsertAt operation with existing nodes in DLList, showing the steps to link the new node within the sequence by updating pointers

```
1  template <typename T>
2  void DLList<T>::insertAt(size_t index, const T item) {
3      assert(index >= 0 && index < size);
4
5      // (1) Create a new node
6      DNode<T>* newNode = new DNode<T>(item);
7
8      // (2) Jump to index location
9      DNode<T>* current = jumpTo(index);
10
11     // (3) Insert the new node
12     newNode->next = current;
13     newNode->prev = current->prev;
14     current->prev->next = newNode;
15     current->prev = newNode;
16
17     // (4) Increment the size of the list
18     ++size;
19 }
```

insertAt Function: Add Element at Specific Index

Remove

The `removeAt` function deletes an element from the doubly-linked list based on the specified index. It checks if the index is valid and updates the node connections to remove the selected item (see Figure 4.26). The time complexity of `removeAt` is $O(n/2)$ in the worst case.

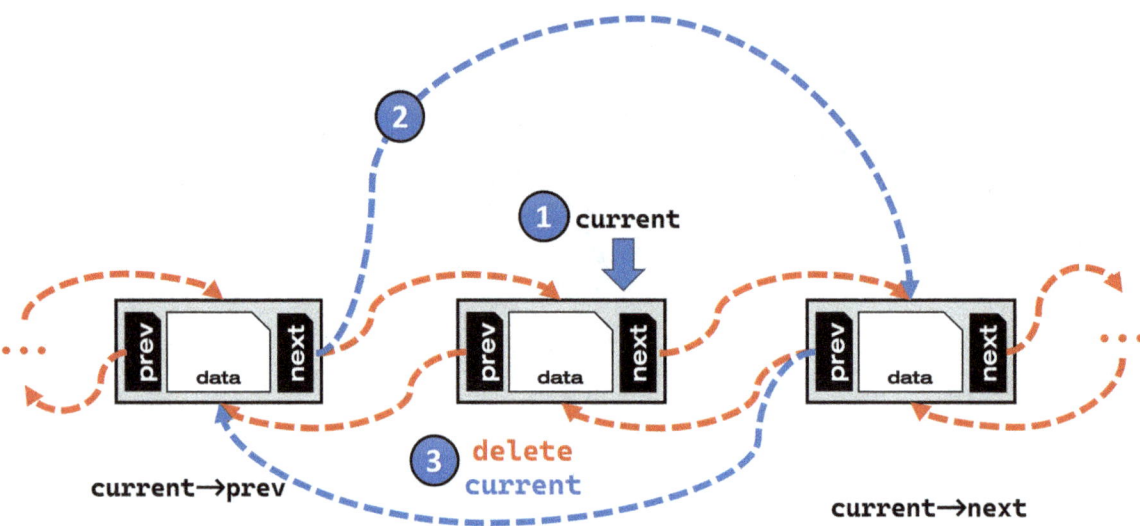

Figure 4.26: `RemoveAt` operation with existing nodes in DLList, showing the steps to update the links to exclude the current node and delete it

```
1  template <typename T>
2  void DLList<T>::removeAt(size_t index) {
3      assert(index >= 0 && index < size);
4
5      // (1) Jump to index location
6      DNode<T>* current = jumpTo(index);
7
8      // (2) Update the links
9      current->prev->next = current->next;
10     current->next->prev = current->prev;
11
12     // (3) Delete the current node
13     delete current;
14     --size;
15 }
```

removeAt Function: Remove Element at Specific Index

4.3.5 Accessing Elements

You can also access and modify elements in the doubly-linked list using the `operator[]`. The time complexity is $O(n/2)$ in the worst case, as it can be optimized by starting the traversal from the nearest end (head or tail).

```cpp
template <typename T>
T& DLList<T>::get(size_t index) {
    assert(index >= 0 && index < size);
    // (1) Jump to the specified index location
    DNode<T>* curr = jumpTo(index);
    // (2) Return the data at the index
    return curr->data;
}

template <typename T>
T& DLList<T>::operator[](size_t index) {
    return get(index);
}

template <typename T>
void DLList<T>::set(size_t index, const T item) {
    assert(index >= 0 && index < size);
    DNode<T>* curr = jumpTo(index);
    curr->data = item;
}
```
Access Elements using `get` and `operator[]` Functions

4.3.6 Traversing

To interact with the elements within a doubly-linked list, you need to traverse it from the dummy to the desired node. This process allows you to examine and print the contents of the list.

Printing the Doubly-Linked List

A fundamental operation is to print the elements in the doubly-linked list, providing a visual representation of its contents. The time complexity of the `print` function is $O(n)$.

```cpp
template <typename T>
void DLList<T>::print() const {
    DNode<T>* current = dummy->next;
    while (current != dummy) {
        std::cout << current->data << " ";
        current = current->next;
```

```
7    }
8    std::cout << std::endl;
9 }
```

print Function: Display Contents of the List

Destructor

The destructor ensures that all allocated memory for the doubly-linked list is properly released when the list goes out of scope or is explicitly destroyed, preventing memory leaks and promoting efficient resource management. The time complexity of the destructor is $O(n)$.

```
 1 template <typename T>
 2 void DLList<T>::clear() {
 3     DNode<T>* current = dummy->next;
 4     while (current != dummy) {
 5         DNode<T>* temp = current;
 6         current = current->next;
 7         delete temp;
 8     }
 9     dummy->next = dummy;
10     dummy->prev = dummy;
11     size = 0;
12 }
13
14 template <typename T>
15 DLList<T>::~DLList() {
16     clear();
17     delete dummy;
18 }
```

Destructor: Proper Memory Management

4.4 Performance Analysis

4.4.1 Linked Lists vs. Arrays

In the context of linked lists, there are pros and cons compared to arrays for managing lists of items.

Advantage: Flexibility

Linked lists are flexible. If you have a reference to a specific item in the list, you can easily delete that item or insert a new item next to it, no matter where it is located in the list. This operation takes a constant amount of time.

Disadvantage: Slower Access

On the downside, linked lists aren't as efficient when it comes to quickly accessing a specific item by its position (like using `get(i)` or `set(i,x)` in an array). With a linked list, you have to start at the beginning and walk through the list one item at a time until you reach the desired position, which takes more time.

4.4.2 Linked List Performance Comparison

The performance of linked lists varies based on whether they are singly-linked, singly-linked with a tail, or doubly-linked. Table 4.1 compares the time complexity of various operations for these types of linked lists and arrays.

Table 4.1: Time Complexity Comparison for Different Data Structures: Array, Singly-Linked List, Singly-Linked List with Tail, and Doubly-Linked List

Operation	Array	SLList	SLList with Tail	DLList
`pushFront(item)`	$O(n)$	$O(1)$	$O(1)$	$O(1)$
`topFront()`	$O(1)$	$O(1)$	$O(1)$	$O(1)$
`popFront()`	$O(n)$	$O(1)$	$O(1)$	$O(1)$
`pushBack(item)`	$O(1)$	$O(n)$	$O(1)$	$O(1)$
`topBack()`	$O(1)$	$O(n)$	$O(1)$	$O(1)$
`popBack()`	$O(1)$	$O(n)$	$O(n)$	$O(1)$
`indexOf(item)`	$O(n)$	$O(n)$	$O(n)$	$O(n)$
`set(index, item)`	$O(1)$	$O(n)$	$O(n)$	$O(n/2)$
`get(index)`	$O(1)$	$O(n)$	$O(n)$	$O(n/2)$
`insertAt(index, item)`	$O(n)$	$O(n)$	$O(n)$	$O(n/2)$
`removeAt(index)`	$O(n)$	$O(n)$	$O(n)$	$O(n/2)$

Performance Insights

The presence of a tail pointer in singly-linked lists simplifies and optimizes certain operations, particularly those related to adding elements at the end of the list, such as `pushBack`. In singly-linked lists without a tail, operations involving the end of the list, such as `pushBack`, `topBack`, and `popBack`, have a time complexity of $O(n)$ because they require traversing the entire list to reach the last node.

Operations like `topBack()` can be particularly inefficient in a singly-linked list without a tail because, to access the last element, the entire list must be traversed, resulting in an $O(n)$ time complexity. However, when a tail pointer is introduced, this operation becomes $O(1)$ because the tail pointer provides direct access to the last node.

Similarly, the operations `set`, `get`, `indexOf`, and `removeAt` also have $O(n)$ complexity in singly-linked lists, regardless of whether a tail is present, due to the potential need to traverse the entire list to locate or manipulate elements.

With the introduction of a tail pointer, the time complexity of appending an element at the end of the list (`pushBack`) improves significantly to $O(1)$. Additionally, `topBack` operations also become $O(1)$ due to direct access to the last element. Operations such as `popBack`, `set`, `get`, `insertAt`, and `removeAt` remain $O(n)$ as they still require traversing the list.

In contrast, the performance of doubly-linked lists (DLLists) is enhanced due to the additional backward reference (`prev`) in each node, allowing for more efficient operations in certain scenarios. For example, operations like `popBack` can be performed in $O(1)$ time because the `prev` pointer provides direct access to the preceding node. This reduces the need to traverse the entire list to find the second-to-last node, unlike in singly-linked lists.

Additionally, the `insertAt` and `removeAt` operations in doubly-linked lists benefit from the ability to traverse from either the head or the tail, depending on which is closer to the target index. This optimization allows these operations to achieve a time complexity of $O(n/2)$ in the worst case, effectively halving the average traversal distance compared to singly-linked lists.

By optimizing these operations to $O(n/2)$, doubly-linked lists offer a balanced and efficient solution for dynamic data structures that require flexible insertion and deletion capabilities, while maintaining manageable access times.

4.4.3 Best Practices and Common Use Cases

When working with linked lists, whether they are singly-linked, doubly-linked, or circular, adhering to best practices is crucial for efficient and error-free usage. Consider the following recommendations:

1. **Initialize Pointers:** Always initialize pointers correctly. Ensure that pointers to the next and previous nodes, as appropriate, are set to the correct initial values. For instance, in singly-linked lists, set the `next` pointer of the last node to `nullptr` to indicate the end of the list. In doubly-linked lists, initialize both the `next` and `prev` pointers properly.
2. **Memory Management:** Exercise caution and diligence in memory management. When deleting nodes or the entire list, release memory to prevent memory leaks.
3. **Consider Time Complexity:** Be mindful of the time complexity of your operations. Recognize that accessing elements by index in a singly-linked list is not efficient, as it requires traversing the list. If you require frequent random access, consider alternative data structures like dynamic arrays or doubly-linked lists, which offer faster indexing capabilities.
4. **Error Handling:** Implement robust error handling. Account for edge cases, such as attempting to delete a node that does not exist or accessing elements beyond the bounds of the list. Proper error handling ensures that your code behaves predictably and is more robust.

Additionally, understanding common use cases for each type of linked list can help you choose the appropriate data structure for your specific application. Consider the following use cases:

- **Singly-Linked List:** Ideal for applications where insertion and deletion operations are frequent and occur mostly at the beginning or the end of the list. Examples

include implementing stacks, queues, or managing a sequence of elements in a one-way traversal.
- **Doubly-Linked List:** Useful when there is a need for bidirectional traversal of the list. This makes it suitable for applications like navigation systems (e.g., browser history, undo-redo functionality in text editors) and implementing dequeues (double-ended queues).
- **Circular Linked List:** Best suited for applications that require a cyclic iteration over elements. Examples include implementing round-robin scheduling in operating systems, managing a playlist of songs, or designing a circular buffer.

4.5 Summary

In this chapter, we thoroughly explored various types of linked lists and their implementations. We examined the anatomy and operations of singly-linked lists, singly-linked lists with a tail, and doubly-linked lists. The introduction of a tail pointer in singly-linked lists significantly improved the efficiency of operations such as `pushBack` and `popBack`, making these operations more practical for real-world applications.

Doubly-linked lists (DLLists) provided enhanced flexibility with bidirectional traversal capabilities, allowing operations to be performed more efficiently by traversing the list from either end. This bidirectional nature is particularly advantageous for operations like `popBack`, `insertAt`, and `removeAt`, where accessing nodes closer to the tail can reduce the time complexity.

The complete class diagram for the data structures covered in this chapter, shown in Figure 4.27, illustrates the relationships and inheritance among the different linked list classes discussed in this chapter.

This comprehensive diagram provides a clear overview of the hierarchical structure and interaction between different linked list implementations, showcasing their design and functionality.

Our analysis of linked list performance reveals that while arrays offer faster access times due to their contiguous memory allocation, linked lists provide superior flexibility for insertion and deletion operations. Singly-linked lists with a tail pointer significantly enhance the efficiency of appending elements at the end of the list, making them more suitable for applications requiring frequent additions.

Doubly-linked lists, with their bidirectional traversal capabilities, offer further performance enhancements. The ability to traverse from either the head or the tail, depending on which is closer to the target index, optimizes operations such as `insertAt` and `removeAt`. This optimization allows these operations to achieve a time complexity of $O(n/2)$ in the worst case, effectively halving the average traversal distance compared to singly-linked lists.

By leveraging these bidirectional traversal strategies, doubly-linked lists offer a balanced and efficient solution for dynamic data structures that require flexible insertion and deletion capabilities, while maintaining manageable access times. This balance makes doubly-linked lists a robust choice for various applications, highlighting the importance of choosing the appropriate data structure based on specific operational requirements.

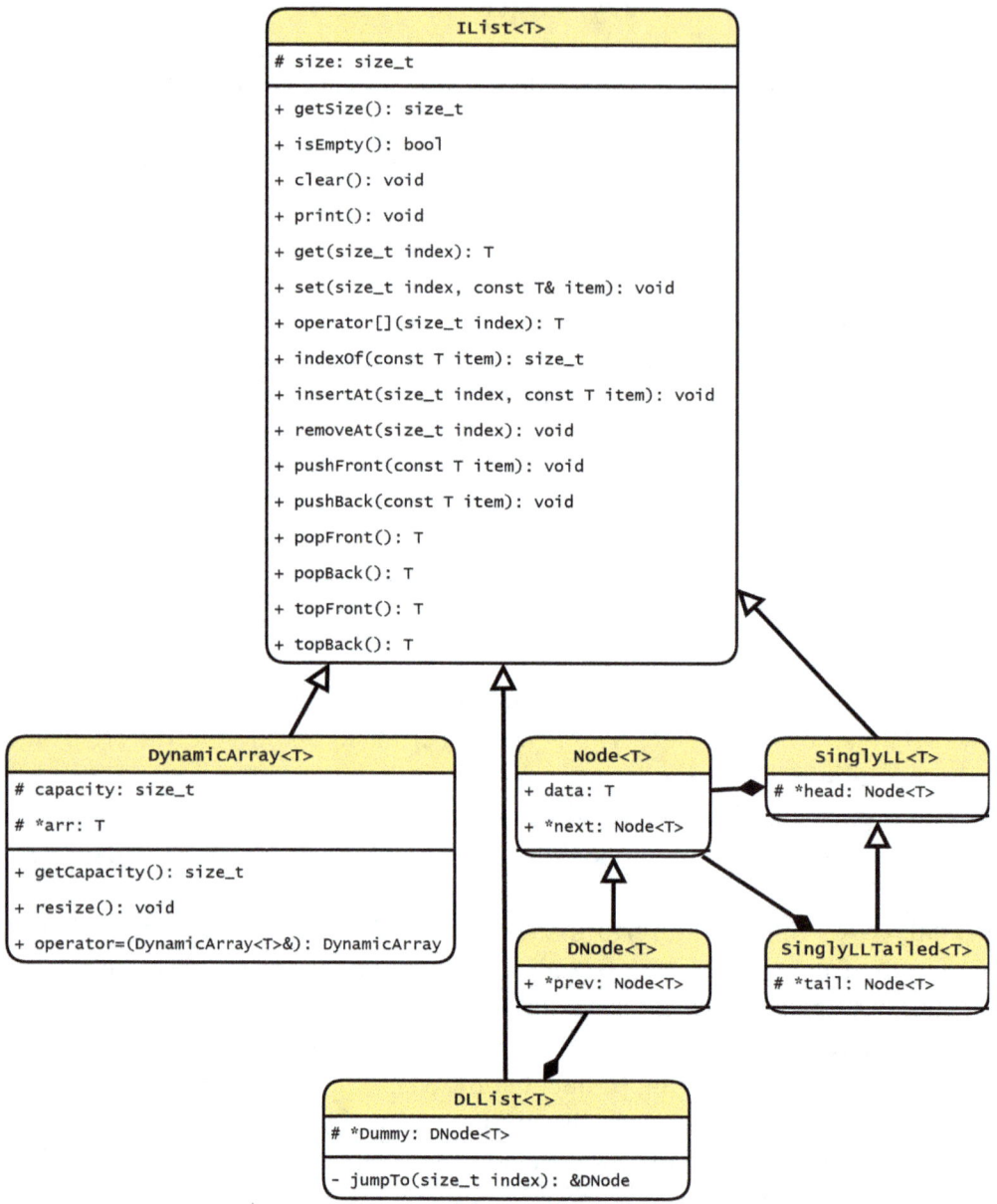

Figure 4.27: Full class diagram illustrating the relationships and inheritance among `Node`, `DNode`, `SinglyLL`, `SinglyLLTailed`, and `DLList`

Problems

Discussion

1. Explain how pointers enable the creation of linked data structures like linked lists. Provide examples to highlight the importance of pointers in building dynamic data structures.
2. Discuss the concept of nested pointers within data structures. Describe how nested pointers are created and accessed, and provide examples of their real-world applications in programming.
3. Explain why dynamic memory allocation is crucial in linked data structures that use the heap for storage. Discuss how dynamic allocation affects the flexibility and efficiency of linked lists and compare heap and stack memory allocation in linked data structures.
4. Describe the significance of the tail pointer in singly-linked lists. Explain how the tail pointer enhances the efficiency of certain operations like appending elements.

Multiple Choice Questions

1. What is the primary role of pointers in programming and data structures?
    (a) Enabling constant-time access
    (b) Establishing relationships between data elements
    (c) Allocating fixed-size memory blocks
    (d) Enhancing code readability
2. When creating a pointer to an object, how is the object's member accessed?
    (a) Using the . operator
    (b) By using the arrow operator (->) or the traditional dereference operator
    (c) Through a separate accessor function
    (d) By directly modifying the memory address
3. What does the arrow operator (->) represent when working with pointers to objects?
    (a) Direct assignment operator
    (b) Indirection operator
    (c) Pointer-to-member operator
    (d) Member access operator for pointers
4. In the structure Node containing int* pz, how do you allocate memory for pz?
    (a) `pz = new int;`
    (b) `Node.pz = new int;`
    (c) `(*Node).pz = new int;`
    (d) `ptr->pz = new int;`

5. Why is it good practice to initialize the `next` pointer to `nullptr` in a linked list node?
   (a) It avoids using uninitialized memory.
   (b) It prevents accidental pointer arithmetic.
   (c) It ensures a default state for the object.
   (d) It speeds up the linked list traversal.
6. In a linked list, what does the `next` member of a node typically point to?
   (a) The previous node in the list
   (b) The first node in the list
   (c) The last node in the list
   (d) The next node in the list
7. Why are linked lists created using pointers and stored in the heap?
   (a) To ensure constant-time access
   (b) To enable automatic memory deallocation
   (c) To allow dynamic growth and flexibility during program execution
   (d) To simplify memory management
8. What is a potential consequence of not properly deallocating memory in a linked list?
   (a) Improved program performance
   (b) Memory leaks and resource wastage
   (c) Increased code readability
   (d) Automatic memory cleanup by the system
9. In the context of linked lists, what is the significance of a doubly-linked list compared to a singly-linked list?
   (a) Doubly-linked lists have a faster traversal time.
   (b) Singly-linked lists are more memory-efficient.
   (c) Doubly-linked lists allow traversal in both directions.
   (d) Singly-linked lists provide better random access performance.
10. How does the presence of a `dummy` node simplify operations in a doubly-linked list (DLList)?
    (a) It reduces the overall memory usage of the DLList.
    (b) It eliminates the need for a tail pointer in the DLL.
    (c) It serves as a placeholder, ensuring a uniform structure and simplifying edge cases.
    (d) It enhances bidirectional traversal capabilities.
11. What is the primary advantage of having a `dummy` node in a doubly-linked list (DLList) when compared to a DLList without a `dummy` node?
    (a) It reduces the overall time complexity of DLList operations.
    (b) It simplifies edge cases and eliminates the need for `head` and `tail` pointers.
    (c) It improves the memory efficiency of the DLList.
    (d) It enhances bidirectional traversal capabilities.

4.5 Summary

12. What is the primary purpose of the `prev` pointer in a doubly-linked list (DLList)?
    (a) It points to the next node in the list.
    (b) It indicates the node with the maximum value.
    (c) It allows bidirectional traversal by pointing to the previous node in the list.
    (d) It is not a standard pointer used in DLList.
13. In a doubly-linked list with a `dummy` node, how can you efficiently add an element to the end of the list?
    (a) Use the `pushFront` method for constant-time insertion.
    (b) Iterate through the list to find the last node and append the new element to it.
    (c) Utilize the `tail` pointer for direct access to the last node.
    (d) Directly link the new element to the `dummy` node, updating the `dummy` node as the last node.
14. What is the time complexity of the `pushBack` operation in a doubly-linked list with a `dummy` node?
    (a) $O(1)$
    (b) $O(n)$
    (c) $O(\log n)$
    (d) $O(n \log n)$
15. In a doubly-linked list with a `dummy` node, how would you efficiently remove the last element?
    (a) Iterate through the list to find the second-to-last node and update its `next` pointer.
    (b) Utilize the `tail` pointer for direct access to the last node.
    (c) Directly link the `dummy` node to the second-to-last node, updating the `dummy` node as the new last node.
    (d) Traverse to the last node using the `prev` pointers and update the `prev` pointers accordingly.
16. In a doubly-linked list with a `dummy` node, what is the role of the `dummy` node in the `popBack` operation?
    (a) It is not involved in the `popBack` operation.
    (b) It serves as the placeholder for the removed element.
    (c) It is linked directly to the last node, facilitating constant-time removal.
    (d) It ensures a consistent structure by updating as the new last node after removal.

Challenge Questions

1. Write a C++ function to perform an in-place reversal of a singly-linked list. The function should take the head of the list as an argument and return the new head of the reversed list. After implementation, analyze the time and space complexity of the reversal operation.
2. Implement a C++ function that removes the first occurrence of a given value in a singly-linked list. If the value is not present in the list, the function should have no side effect. After implementation, analyze the time and space complexity of this deletion operation.

3. Write a C++ function that accepts two sorted singly-linked lists as input and merges them into a single sorted list. Analyze the time and space complexity of the merging process.
4. Write a function that finds the kth node from the end of a singly-linked list.
5. Implement a function to split a singly-linked list into two equal-sized lists. If the original list has an odd number of nodes, the extra node can be part of either of the two resulting lists.

Programming Problems

1. **DLList Palindrome Check**
   Write a c++ DLList method, isPalindrome(), that returns true if the list is a palindrome, i.e., the element at position i is equal to the element at position $n-i-1$ for all $i \in \{0,\ldots,n-1\}$. Your code should run in $O(n)$ time.

2. **DLList Rotation**
   Implement a c++ method, rotate(r), that "rotates" a DLList so that list item i becomes list item $(i+r) \mod n$. This method should run in $O(1+\min\{r, n-r\})$ time and should not modify any nodes in the list.

3. **DLList Truncation**
   Write a c++ method, truncate(i), that truncates a DLList at position i. After executing this method, the size of the list will be i, and it should contain only the elements at the indices $0,\ldots,i-1$. The return value is another DLList that contains the elements in the indices $i,\ldots,n-1$. This method should run in $O(\min\{i, n-i\})$ time.

5. Stack and Queue

Objectives

In this chapter, I will guide you through the essential concepts and operations of stack, queue, and deque data structures. We will explore their implementations, performance characteristics, and practical applications. Here are the key objectives we will cover:

1. **Stack:** We will explore the concept of a stack data structure and its utility in managing data. You will understand the basic push and pop operations in both array and singly-linked list implementations, and we will discuss the advantages and disadvantages of each approach.
2. **Queue:** We will understand the role of a queue in managing data access patterns. You will explore its array and singly-linked list implementations, covering enqueue and dequeue operations and highlighting their specific applications.
3. **Deque:** You will learn how to build a deque (double-ended queue) using arrays and understand the importance of efficient insertions and removals from both ends.
4. **Fast Implementations:** We will discuss techniques and optimizations for achieving fast implementations of stack, queue, and deque data structures. You will consider strategies such as amortized analysis, resizing, and other improvements to enhance performance in each context.

> 5. **Performance Analysis:** We will analyze the performance characteristics of stack, queue, and deque implementations in both array and linked list structures, taking into account the fast implementation techniques.

5.1 Stack

5.1.1 Introduction to Stack

A **stack** is a fundamental data structure that you will find very useful in managing data. It follows the Last In, First Out (**LIFO**) principle, meaning you add elements to the top and remove them from the top, just like a stack of plates. The primary operations you need to know are `push` (to add an element) and `pop` (to remove the top element). Figure 5.1 visually demonstrates these operations.

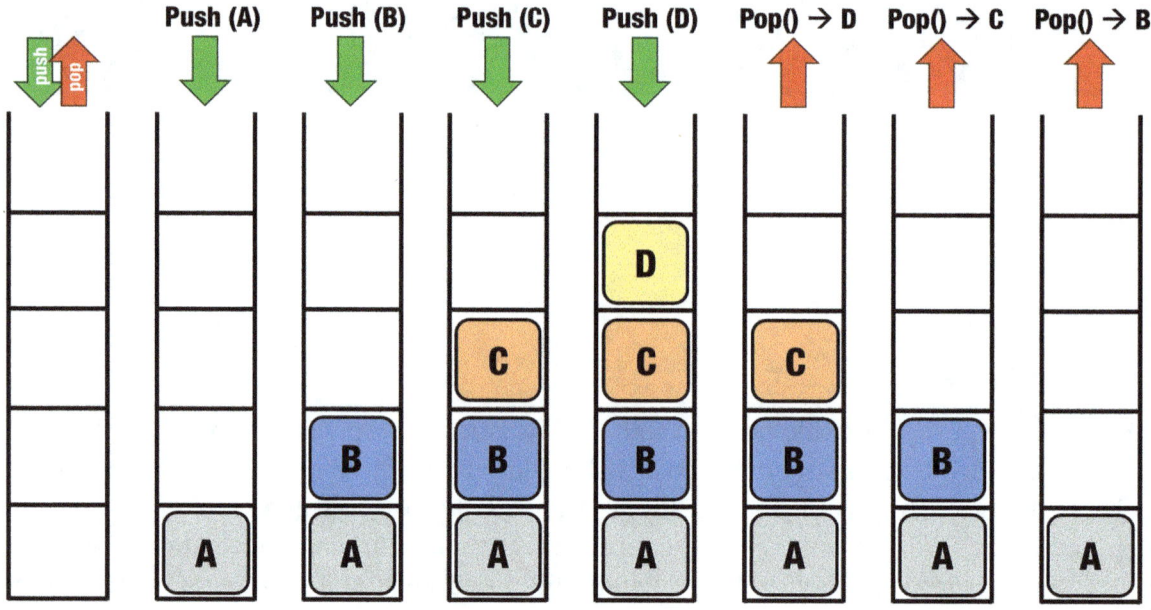

Figure 5.1: Illustration of stack operations: pushing and popping elements, demonstrating the Last In, First Out (LIFO) principle

5.1.2 Array-Based Stack

An **array-based stack** is a simple and efficient way to implement stack operations using an array. The top of the stack is indicated by a marker (called `top`), starting from −1. Figures 5.2 and 5.3 illustrate the process of pushing and popping elements onto and off the stack, respectively.

5.1 Stack

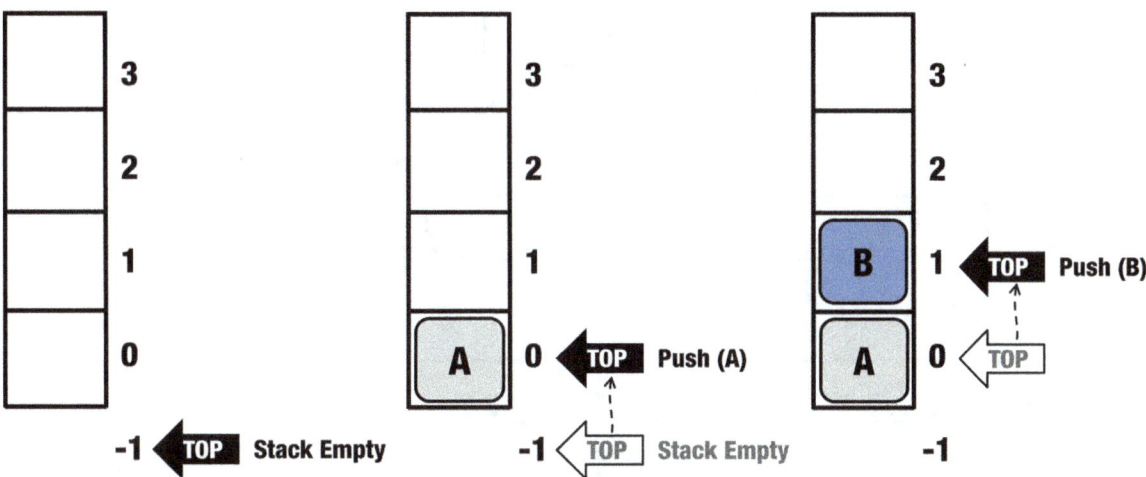

Figure 5.2: Array-based stack: push operation. The process starts with an empty array, and elements are added sequentially, updating the top marker

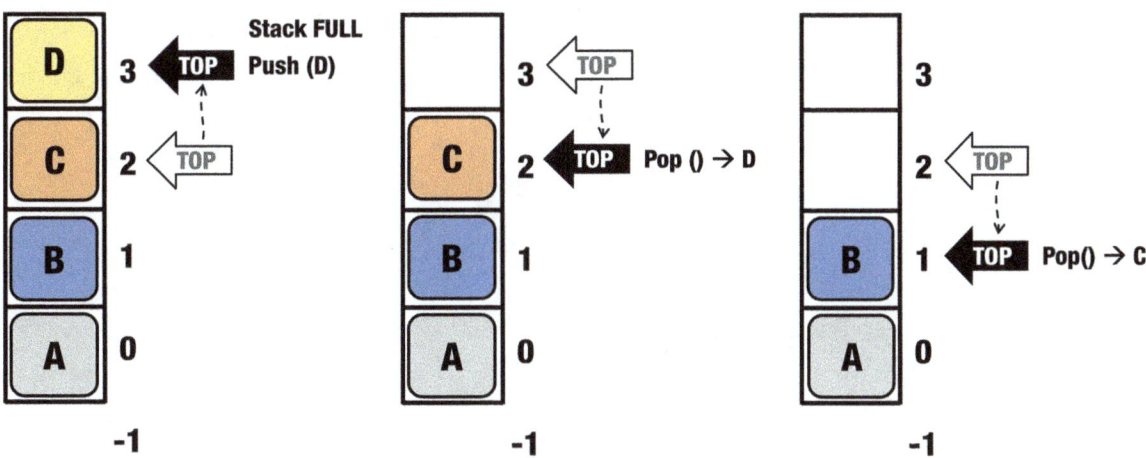

Figure 5.3: Array-based stack: pop operation. Elements are removed sequentially from the top of the stack

Implementation Interface

The `StackArray` class, inheriting from the `DynamicArray` class, implements the required functionalities. The class diagram in Figure 5.4 showcases the relationships and functions.

```cpp
template <typename T>
class StackArray : public DynamicArray<T> {
public:
    StackArray() : DynamicArray<T>() {}
    virtual ~StackArray(){}

```

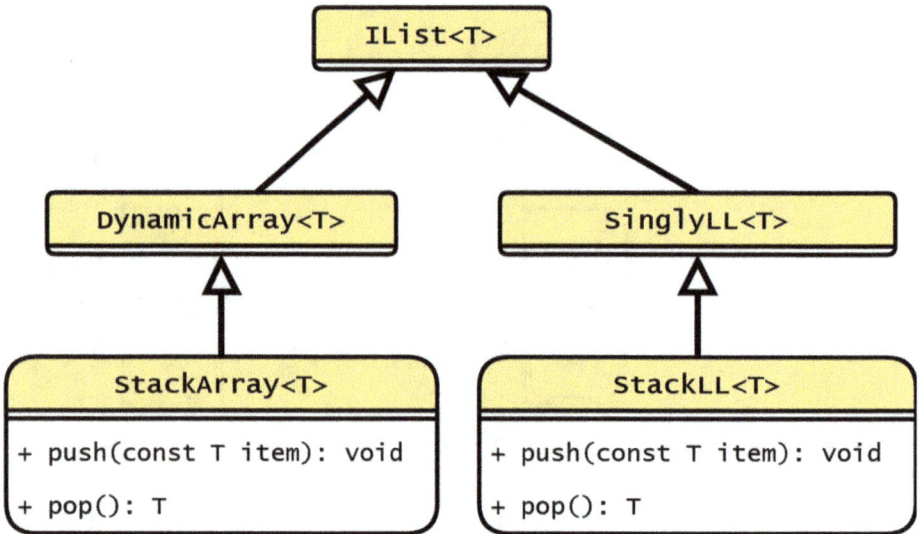

Figure 5.4: `StackArray` and `StackLL` UML class diagram. `StackArray` inherits from `DynamicArray<T>`, and `StackLL` inherits from `SinglyLL<T>`

```
7        // Stack-specific functions
8        virtual void push(const T item) {
9            this->pushBack(item);
10       }
11       virtual T pop() {
12           return this->popBack();
13       }
14   };
```

StackArray Class Interface

Note:
In the `DynamicArray` base class, `pushBack` appends an element to the end of the array, and `popBack` removes the last element. In the context of the `StackArray`, these operations are synonymous with pushing and popping from the top of the stack.

While the `top` is not explicitly managed as a separate variable in the implementation, the end of the array effectively represents the top of the stack.

5.1.3 Linked List Stack

The linked list stack efficiently leverages a singly-linked list (`SinglyLL`), where elements are inserted and removed from the front. The operations, `pushFront` and `popFront`, offer constant time complexity ($O(1)$), making it an efficient alternative to the array-based implementation.

Implementation Interface

The `StackLL` class inherits from a singly-linked list and implements the stack operations. Figure 5.4 shows the class diagram for `StackLL`.

```cpp
template <typename T>
class StackLL : public SinglyLL<T> {
public:
    StackLL() : SinglyLL<T>() {}
    virtual ~StackLL(){}

    // Stack-specific functions
    virtual void push(const T item) {
        this->pushFront(item);
    }
    virtual T pop() {
        return this->popFront();
    }
};
```

`StackLL` Class Interface

> **Note:**
> In the `StackLL` class, the `top` is not explicitly defined because the `SinglyLL` base class inherently manages the stack's top via its linked list structure. The `pushFront` and `popFront` methods add and remove elements at the front of the linked list, which effectively represents the top of the stack.
>
> In the `SinglyLL`, the order of items in the stack will be reversed compared to the `StackArray`. This is because `pushFront` in `SinglyLL` adds new elements to the front, while `pushBack` in `StackArray` adds them to the end.

5.2 Queue (Single-Ended Queue)

5.2.1 Introduction to Queue

A **queue** is a fundamental data structure that adheres to the First In, First Out (**FIFO**) principle. Elements are queued in the rear and dequeued from the front, creating a structure similar to a queue of people waiting in line. The primary operations on a queue are `enqueue` (to add an element) and `dequeue` (to remove the front element). Figure 5.5 visually demonstrates these operations.

5.2.2 Array-Based Queue

An **array-based queue** efficiently implements queue operations using an array. The front and rear of the queue are indicated by markers (`front` and `rear`), and elements are

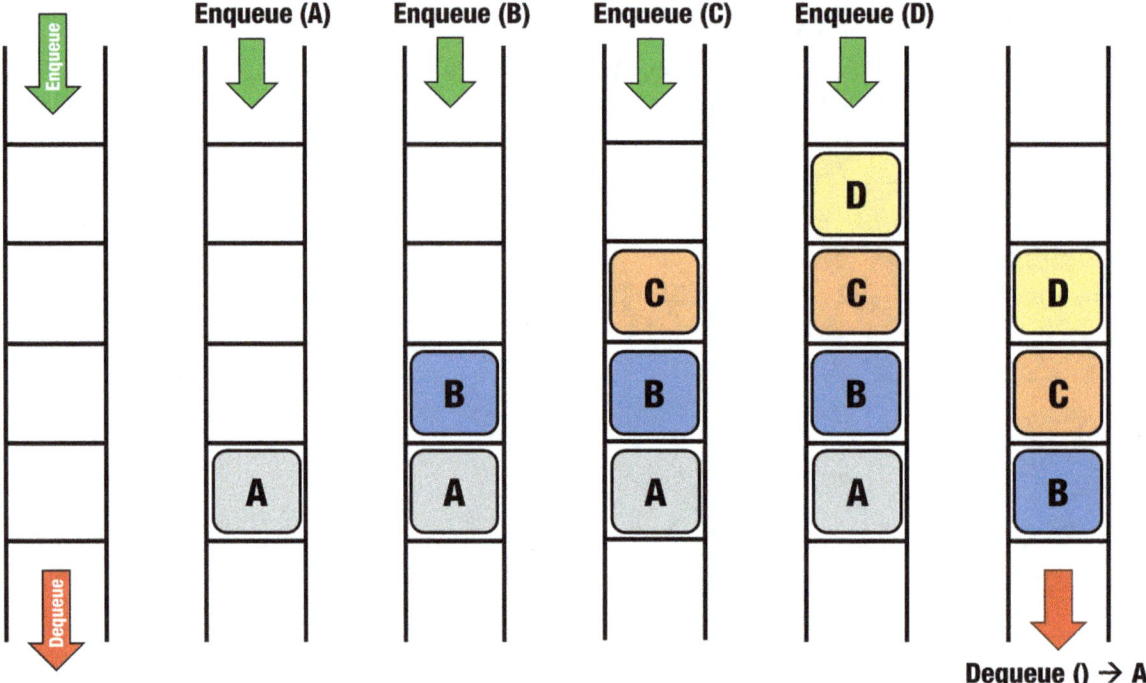

Figure 5.5: Illustration of queue operations: enqueuing and dequeuing elements, demonstrating the First In, First Out (FIFO) principle

enqueued at the rear and dequeued from the front. Figures 5.6 and 5.7 illustrate the process of handling an array as a circular list to represent a queue.

Circular Representation
- **Front and Rear Indices**
  - The front index (front) represents the position from where elements are dequeued.
  - The rear index (rear) represents the position at which elements are enqueued.
- **Circular Increment**
  - When enqueuing (enqueue), the rear index is incremented, and if it reaches the end of the array, it wraps around to the beginning.
  - When dequeuing (dequeue), the front index is incremented similarly.
  - This circular behavior ensures efficient space utilization.

Empty and Full Cases
- **Empty Queue**
  - In an empty queue, the front and rear indices are initially set to a specific value (e.g., 0) to indicate that the queue is empty.
  - When dequeuing, if front equals rear, the queue is empty.
- **Full Queue**
  - In a full queue, the rear index is about to catch up with the front index.

5.2 Queue (Single-Ended Queue)

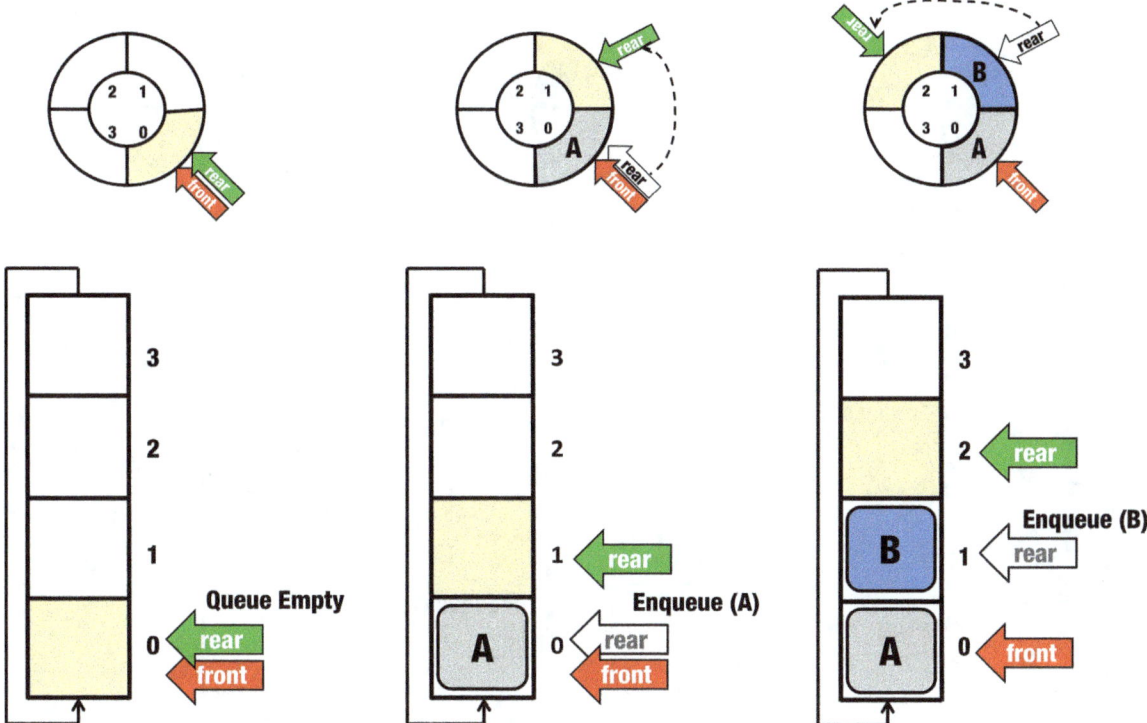

Figure 5.6: Array-based queue: enqueue and dequeue operations (I). The array is initially empty with front and rear markers at the start. Elements are enqueued at the rear

- To differentiate between a full and empty queue, one approach is to leave one slot unoccupied. This means that the maximum number of elements that can be stored is one less than the actual array size.
- When enqueuing, if `rear` is one less than `front`, the queue is full.

The figures (Figures 5.6 and 5.7) illustrate these operations:

- **Enqueue operation** is shown, demonstrating how `rear` is incremented in a circular fashion. The green arrow highlights the position where the next element will be *enqueued*.
- **Dequeue operation** is shown, demonstrating how `front` is incremented in a circular fashion. The red arrow indicates the position from which the elements will be *dequeued*.

These circular operations help manage the indices efficiently, ensuring a continuous representation of the queue within the array.

Implementation Interface

The `QueueArray` class, inheriting from the `DynamicArray` class, implements the required functionalities to manage a queue using an array-based approach. The class diagram in Figure 5.8 showcases the relationships and key functions of the `QueueArray` and `QueueLL` classes.

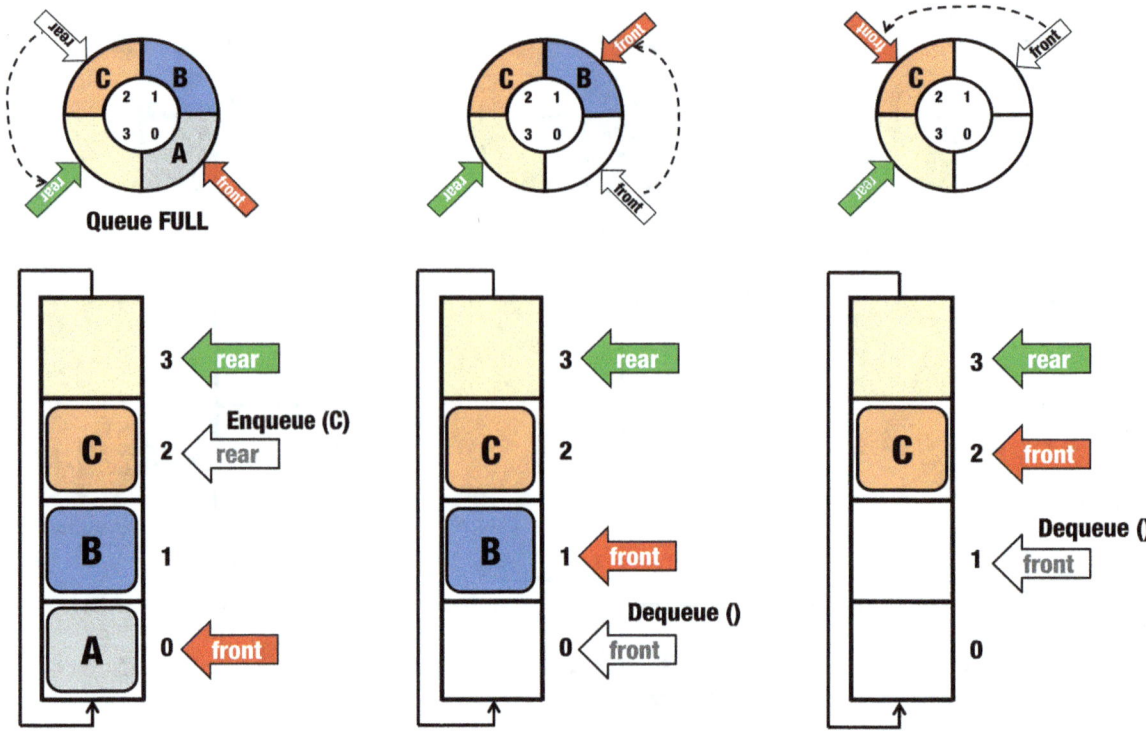

Figure 5.7: Array-based queue: enqueue and dequeue operations (II). When the queue is full, elements are dequeued from the front, and the front marker is updated accordingly

```
1  template <typename T>
2  class QueueArray : public DynamicArray<T> {
3  public:
4      QueueArray() : DynamicArray<T>(), front(0) {}
5      virtual ~QueueArray(){}
6
7      // DynamicArray functions
8      virtual void resize();
9      virtual void insertAt(size_t index, const T item);
10     virtual void removeAt(size_t index);
11     // Queue-specific functions
12     virtual void enqueue(const T item);
13     virtual T dequeue();
14     // ... Other relevant functions
15 protected:
16     size_t front;
17
18     // Inherited members to use directly
19     using DynamicArray<T>::size;
```

5.2 Queue (Single-Ended Queue)

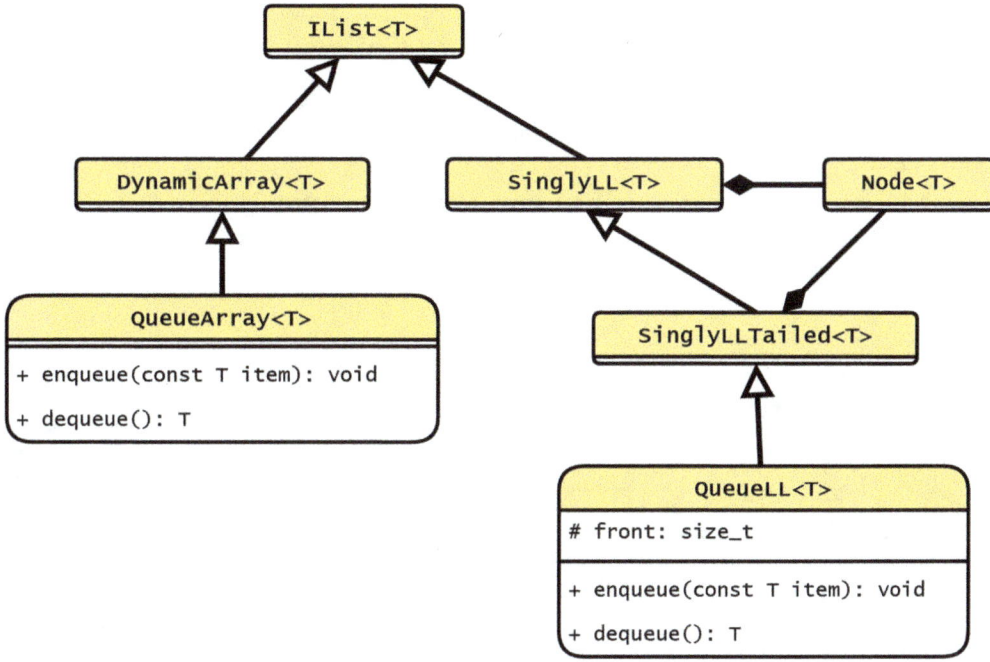

Figure 5.8: QueueArray and QueueLL UML class diagram. QueueArray inherits from DynamicArray<T>, and QueueLL inherits from SinglyLL<T>

```
20      using DynamicArray<T>::capacity;
21      using DynamicArray<T>::arr;
22   };
```

QueueArray Class Interface

Resize Operation

The resizing of the queue is illustrated in Figure 5.9. When capacity needs to be increased, the following steps are performed:
- Create a new array with the new capacity.
- Copy elements from the existing array to the new array in a circular fashion, starting from the front index.
- Delete the existing array.
- Update the array pointer to point to the new array.
- Update the capacity to the new capacity.
- Reset front to 0, and set rear to the current size.

> **Note:**
> Instead of explicitly maintaining a separate `rear` index, you can dynamically calculate the `rear` index using the size of the queue. The `rear` index is calculated as
>
> $$\mathtt{rear\ =\ (front\ +\ size)\ \%\ capacity}$$
>
> (Figure 5.10).

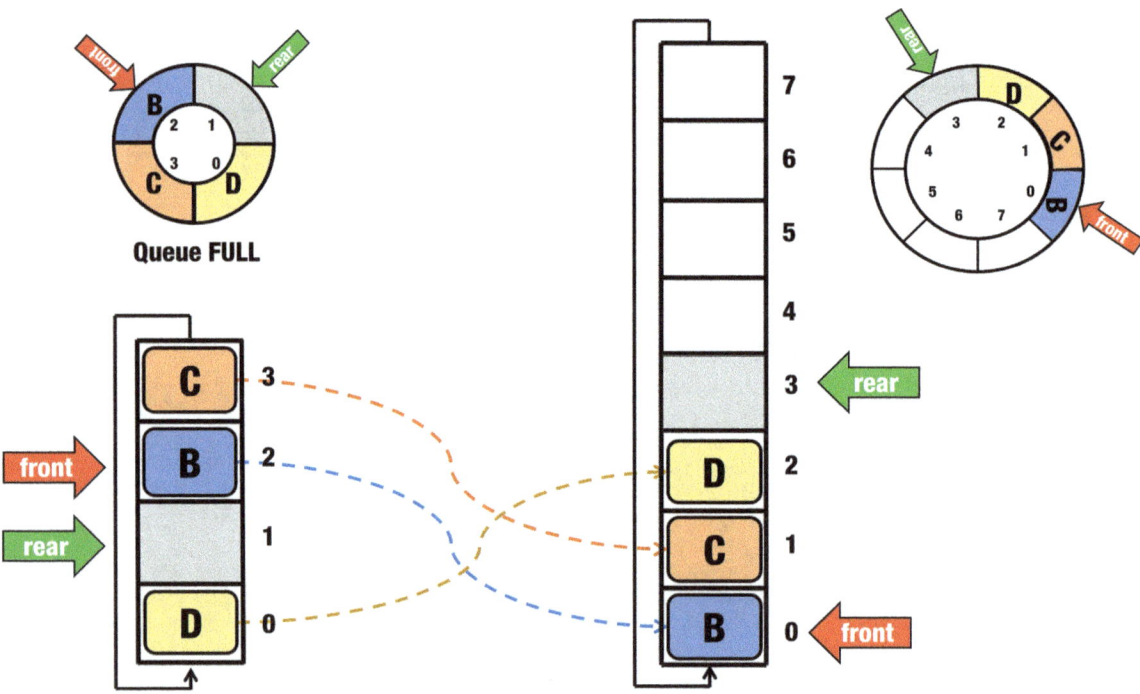

Figure 5.9: Resize queue operation. Demonstrating the process of resizing an array-based queue from a smaller capacity to a larger capacity, maintaining the order of elements

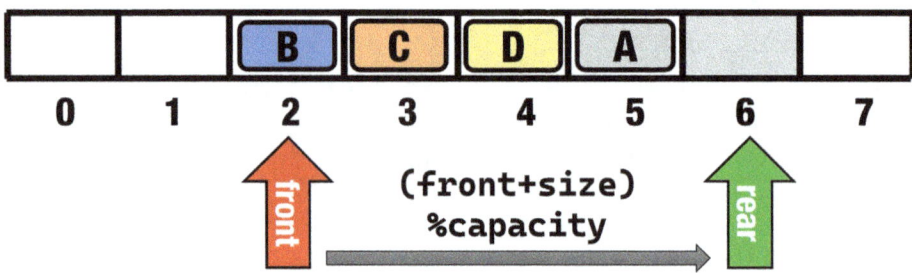

Figure 5.10: Queue's rear calculation. Showing how the rear index can be dynamically calculated using the front index and the current size of the queue

5.2 Queue (Single-Ended Queue)

```cpp
template <typename T>
void QueueArray<T>::resize() {
    size_t new_capacity =
        std::max(2*static_cast<int>(size), 2);
    T* brr = new T[new_capacity];
    for (size_t i=0; i< size; i++)
        brr[i] = arr[(front+i)% capacity];

    delete [] arr;
    arr = brr;
    capacity = new_capacity;
    front = 0; // rear = size;
}
```

resize Function: Adjust Capacity of Queue

Enqueue and Dequeue Operations

The enqueue operation adds an element to the rear of the queue. The enqueue function first checks if the size plus one is greater than the capacity, triggering a resize operation if necessary. The rear index is then updated to the next circular position, and the element is added to the updated rear index.

```cpp
template <typename T>
void QueueArray<T>::enqueue(const T item) {
    if (size+1 > capacity)
        resize();
    // calc rear position
    size_t rear=(front+size)%capacity;
    arr[rear] = item;
    // rear = (rear + 1) % capacity; // calculated
    ++size;
}
```

enqueue Function: Add Element to Queue

The dequeue operation removes and returns the front element of the queue. It first retrieves the element at the front index, updates the front index to the next circular position, and reduces the size of the queue. If the size becomes significantly smaller than the capacity, it triggers a resize operation to conserve space. The removed element is then returned.

```cpp
template <typename T>
T QueueArray<T>::dequeue() {
```

```
3      // Ensure the queue is not empty
4      assert(size > 0);
5      T item = arr[front];
6      front = (front + 1) % capacity;
7      --size;
8      if (3 * size < capacity)
9          resize();
10     return item;
11 }
```

dequeue Function: Remove Element from Queue

Insertion and Removal

The `insertAt` operation efficiently inserts an element at a specified position in the queue. The improved implementation takes advantage of the circular nature of the queue, reducing the number of operations needed to shift elements (Figure 5.11).

One of the *fast implementation* methods we utilize here is amortized analysis, which helps in understanding the average performance of the insertion operations. When the queue needs resizing, the entire queue is copied to a new larger array, ensuring that subsequent insertions are handled efficiently.

```
1  template <typename T>
2  void QueueArray<T>::insertAt(size_t i, const T item) {
3      assert(i <= size);
4      if (size+1 > capacity)
5          resize();
6      if (i < size/2) {
7        // Update front
8        front = (front == 0) ? capacity - 1 : front - 1;
9        // shift arr[0],..,arr[i-1] left one position
10       for (size_t k = 0; k < i; k++) {
11         arr[(front + k) % capacity]
12             = arr[(front + k + 1) % capacity];
13       }
14     } else {
15       // shift arr[i],..,arr[n-1] right one position
16       for (size_t k = size; k > i; k--) {
17         arr[(front + k) % capacity]
18             = arr[(front + k - 1) % capacity];
19       }
20     }
21     arr[(front+i)% capacity] = item;
22     ++size;
```

5.2 Queue (Single-Ended Queue)

23 }

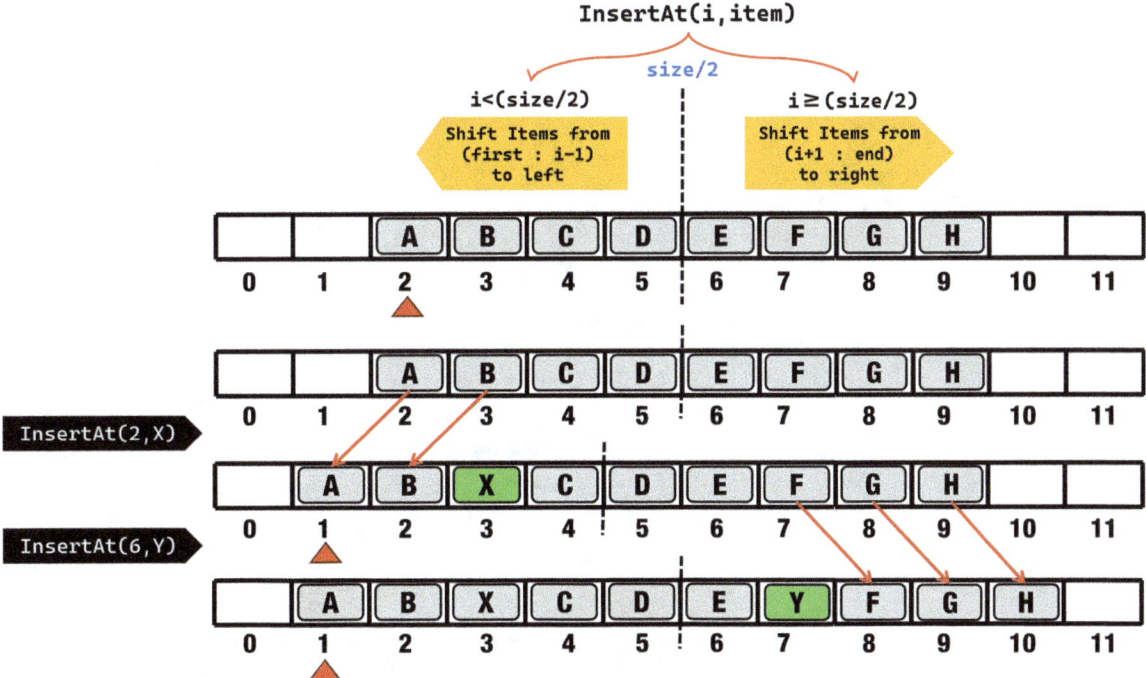

Figure 5.11: insertAt explanation. Demonstrating the process of inserting an element at a specific position in the queue, shifting elements as needed

This operation provides the flexibility to add elements at a specified position (insertAt) in the circular array-based queue with improved efficiency.

The removeAt operation removes an element at a specified position in the queue. The function efficiently shifts elements according to the removal position (i) (Figure 5.12).

Using a *fast implementation* method, such as the efficient use of circular indexing, ensures that the number of shifts required to remove an element is minimized. This is particularly beneficial in maintaining the overall performance of the queue.

```cpp
template <typename T>
void QueueArray<T>::removeAt(size_t i) {
    assert(i < size);
    if (i < size/2) {
        // shift arr[0],..,arr[i-1] right one position
        for (size_t k = i; k > 0; k--){
            arr[(front + k) % capacity]
                = arr[(front + k - 1) % capacity];
        }
```

```
10          // Update front index after shifting
11          front = (front + 1) % capacity;
12      } else {
13          // shift arr[i+1],..,arr[n-1] left one position
14          for (size_t k = i; k < size - 1; k++){
15              arr[(front + k) % capacity]
16                  = arr[(front + k + 1) % capacity];
17          }
18      }
19      --size;
20      if (3 * size < capacity)
21          resize();
22  }
```

removeAt Function: Remove Element at Specific Index

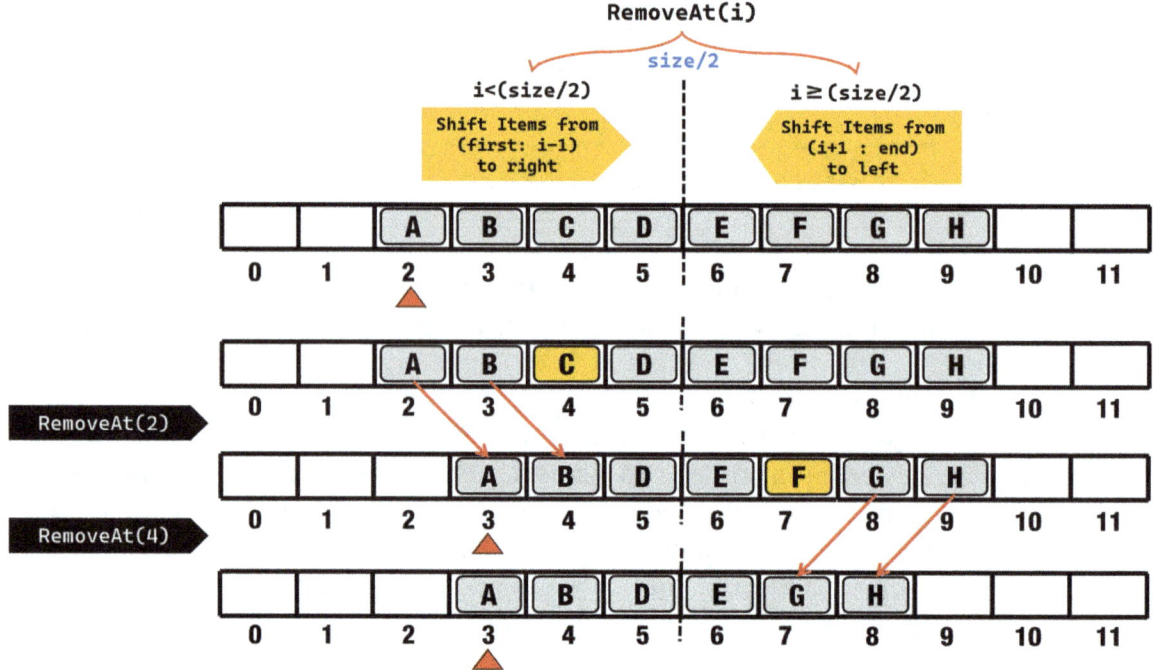

Figure 5.12: `removeAt` explanation. Demonstrating the process of removing an element at a specific position in the queue, shifting elements as needed

These removal operations provide the flexibility to remove elements at a specified position in the queue based on circular arrays. Using fast implementation methods, such as efficient circular indexing and resizing strategies, these operations maintain high performance even under varying load conditions.

5.2 Queue (Single-Ended Queue)

> **Note:**
> The `insertAt` and `removeAt` methods are available in the `QueueArray` class because they come from the `DynamicArray` class, which `QueueArray` inherits. However, queues are designed to work in a First In, First Out (FIFO) manner, meaning elements should be added at the back and removed from the front. Using `insertAt` and `removeAt` in a queue can mix up this order and cause the queue to behave incorrectly. Therefore, it is important to handle these methods carefully to make sure the queue works as expected.

5.2.3 Linked List Queue

The `QueueLL` is implemented using a singly-linked list (`SinglyLLTailed`) with a tail pointer. Elements are added at the rear (tail) and removed from the front, making it an efficient data structure for queue operations. The `enqueue` operation, which inserts elements at the rear, is optimized with constant time complexity due to the presence of the tail pointer.

Implementation Interface

The `QueueLL` class inherits from the `SinglyLLTailed` class and implements the required functionalities. The class diagram in Figure 5.8 showcases the relationships and functions.

The following are the implementations for the queue operations using the parent class methods:

```cpp
template <typename T>
class QueueLL : public SinglyLLTailed<T> {
public:
    QueueLL() : SinglyLLTailed<T>() {}
    virtual ~QueueLL(){}

    // Queue-specific functions
    virtual void enqueue(const T item) {
        this->pushBack(item);
    }
    virtual T dequeue() {
        return this->popFront();
    }
};
```

QueueLL Class Interface

This implementation takes advantage of the parent class methods `pushBack` and `popFront` to provide efficient enqueue and dequeue operations. The `enqueue` function adds an element to the rear of the queue, while the `dequeue` function removes and returns the front element of the queue.

5.3 Deque (Double-Ended Queue)

5.3.1 Introduction to Deque

A **double-ended queue (deque)** is a versatile data structure that facilitates insertion and deletion from both ends. Unlike a regular queue, a deque supports operations at both the front and rear, providing enhanced flexibility in managing data. Figure 5.13 visually illustrates these operations.

- **Enqueue Front Operation:** Adds an element to the front of the deque
- **Dequeue Front Operation:** Removes and returns the element from the front of the deque
- **Enqueue Rear Operation:** Adds an element to the rear of the deque
- **Dequeue Rear Operation:** Removes and returns the element from the rear of the deque

The deque utilizes two markers, `front` and `rear`, to signify its two ends. These markers enable efficient manipulation of the deque's elements from both sides. The `front` marker indicates the position from which elements are dequeued or enqueued at the front. Conversely, the `rear` marker signifies the position where elements are enqueued or dequeued from the rear.

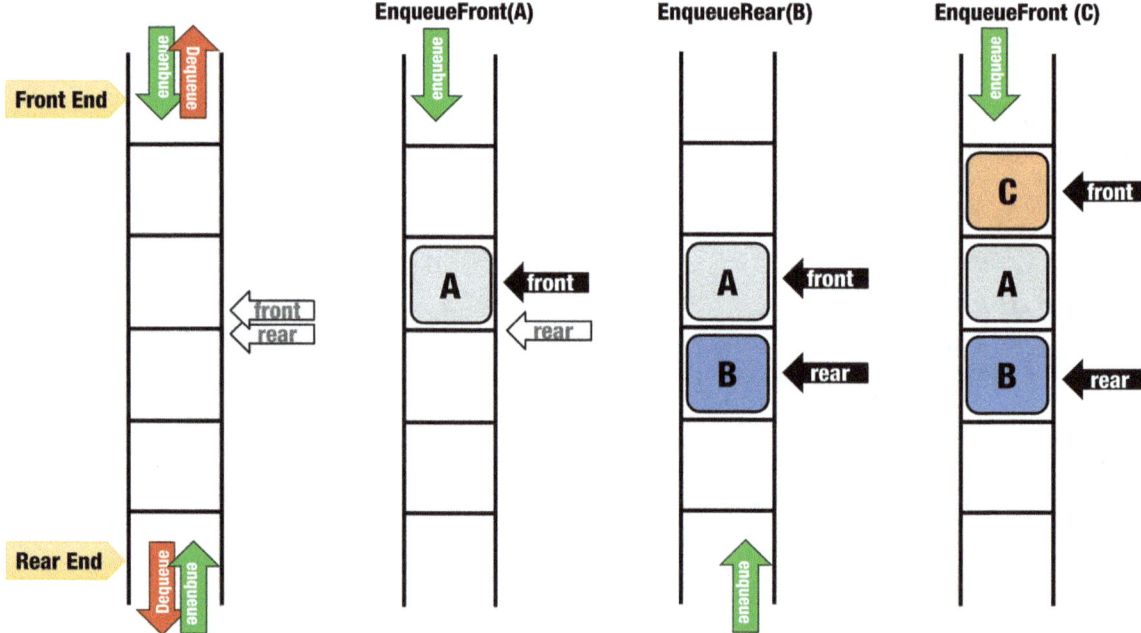

Figure 5.13: Visualizing operations on a deque. The figure demonstrates the operations of `enqueueFront(A)`, `enqueueRear(B)`, and `enqueueFront(C)`. Elements are added to both the front and rear of the deque, showcasing the versatility and flexibility of the deque data structure

5.3 Deque (Double-Ended Queue)

The circular representation of a deque efficiently handles scenarios where markers reach the end of the underlying array, ensuring a continuous and space-efficient structure. This design choice enhances the deque's performance and adaptability in various applications.

5.3.2 Array-Based Deque

An **array-based deque** efficiently implements deque operations using an array. Both the front and rear of the deque are indicated by markers (`front` and `rear`), allowing elements to be added or removed from either end.

Circular Representation

- **Front and Rear Indices**
    - The `front` index represents the position from where elements are dequeued or enqueued at the front.
    - The `rear` index represents the position where elements are enqueued or dequeued from the rear.
- **Circular Increment**
    - When enqueuing at the rear (`enqueueRear`), the `rear` index is incremented, and if it reaches the end of the array, it wraps around to the beginning.
    - When dequeuing from the front (`dequeueFront`), the `front` index is incremented similarly.
    - When enqueuing at the front (`enqueueFront`), the `front` index is decremented, and if it goes below zero, it wraps around to the end of the array.
    - When dequeuing from the rear (`dequeueRear`), the `rear` index is decremented similarly.

Empty and Full Cases

- **Empty Deque**
    - In an empty deque, the `front` and `rear` indices are initially set to a specific value (e.g., 0) to indicate that the deque is empty.
    - When dequeuing, if `front` equals `rear`, the deque is empty.
- **Full Deque**
    - In a full deque, the `rear` index is about to catch up with the `front` index.
    - To differentiate between a full and empty deque, one approach is to leave one slot unoccupied. This means that the maximum number of elements that can be stored is one less than the actual array size.
    - When enqueuing, if `rear` is one less than `front`, the deque is full.

Implementation Interface

The `DequeArray` class, inheriting from the `DynamicArray` class, implements the required functionalities. The class diagram in Figure 5.14 shows the relationships and functions.

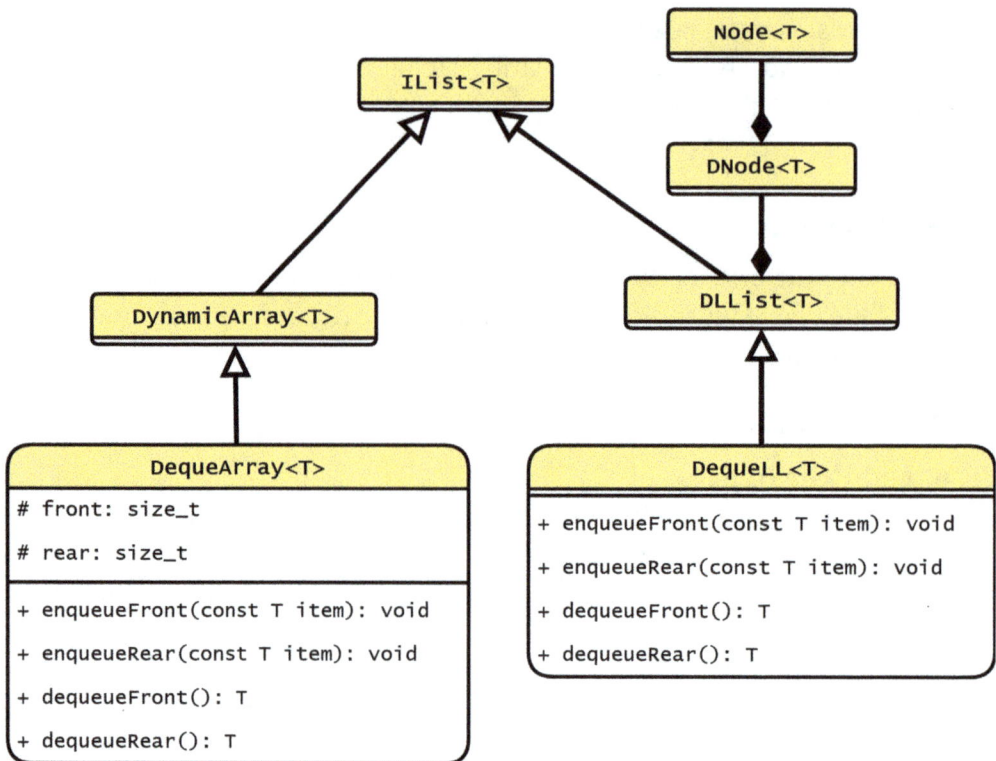

Figure 5.14: `DequeArray` and `DequeLL` UML class diagram

```cpp
template <typename T>
class DequeArray : public DynamicArray<T> {
public:
    DequeArray() : DynamicArray<T>(),
            front(0), rear(0) {}
    virtual ~DequeArray(){}

    // Deque-specific functions
    virtual void enqueueFront(const T item);
    virtual T dequeueFront();
    virtual void enqueueRear(const T item);
    virtual T dequeueRear();
    // ... Other relevant functions
    virtual void print() const;
    virtual void resize();
protected:
    size_t front;
    size_t rear;

    // Inherited members to use directly
```

5.3 Deque (Double-Ended Queue)

```
21        using DynamicArray<T>::size;
22        using DynamicArray<T>::capacity;
23        using DynamicArray<T>::arr;
24 };
```

DequeArray Class Interface

Enqueue and Dequeue Operations

Enqueue Front

The `enqueueFront` operation adds an element to the front of the deque. It first checks if the size plus one is greater than the capacity, triggering a resize operation if necessary. The front index is then decremented to the previous circular position, and the element is added to the updated front index.

```
1 template <typename T>
2 void DequeArray<T>::enqueueFront(const T item) {
3     if (size+1 > capacity)
4         resize();
5     // decrement front position circularly
6     front = (front == 0) ? capacity-1 : front - 1;
7     arr[front] = item;
8     ++size;
9 }
```

`enqueueFront` Function: Add Element to Front of Deque

Dequeue Front

The `dequeueFront` operation removes and returns the front element of the deque. It first retrieves the element at the front index (`front`), updates the front index to the next circular position, and reduces the size of the deque. If the size becomes significantly smaller than the capacity, it triggers a resize operation to conserve space. The removed element is then returned.

```
1 template <typename T>
2 T DequeArray<T>::dequeueFront() {
3     T item = arr[front];
4     front = (front + 1) % capacity;
5     --size;
6     if (3 * size < capacity)
7         resize();
8     return item;
9 }
```

`dequeueFront` Function: Remove Element from Front of Deque

Enqueue Rear

The `enqueueRear` operation adds an element to the rear of the deque. It first checks if the size plus one is greater than the capacity, triggering a resize operation if necessary. The rear index is then updated to the next circular position, and the element is added to the updated rear index.

```cpp
template <typename T>
void DequeArray<T>::enqueueRear(const T item) {
    if (size+1 > capacity)
        resize();
    // calc rear position
    size_t rear = (front + size) % capacity;
    arr[rear] = item;
    ++size;
}
```

enqueueRear Function: Add Element to Rear of Deque

Dequeue Rear

The `dequeueRear` operation removes and returns the rear element of the deque. It first retrieves the element at the rear index (`rear`), updates the rear index to the previous circular position, and reduces the size of the deque. If the size becomes significantly smaller than the capacity, it triggers a resize operation to conserve space. The removed element is then returned.

```cpp
template <typename T>
T DequeArray<T>::dequeueRear() {
    size_t rear = (front + size - 1) % capacity;
    T item = arr[rear];
    --size;
    if (3 * size < capacity)
        resize();
    return item;
}
```

dequeueRear Function: Remove Element from Rear of Deque

> **Note:**
> By utilizing the `insertAt` and `removeAt` methods from the parent `DynamicArray` class, the `enqueueFront`, `dequeueFront`, `enqueueRear`, and `dequeueRear` operations can be implemented efficiently. This approach utilizes the inherited functionalities to maintain efficient.

5.3 Deque (Double-Ended Queue)

```
1  template <typename T>
2  void DequeArray<T>::enqueueFront(const T item) {
3      this->insertAt(0, item);
4  }
5
6  template <typename T>
7  T DequeArray<T>::dequeueFront() {
8      T item = arr[front];
9      this->removeAt(0);
10     return item;
11 }
12
13 template <typename T>
14 void DequeArray<T>::enqueueRear(const T item) {
15     this->insertAt(size, item);
16 }
17
18 template <typename T>
19 T DequeArray<T>::dequeueRear() {
20     T item = arr[rear];
21     this->removeAt(size - 1);
22     return item;
23 }
```

Alternative Implementation Using Parent Methods

5.3.3 Linked List Deque

The `Linked List Deque` is implemented using a doubly-linked list (`DLList`). This implementation allows for efficient insertion and deletion at both ends of the deque. The `enqueueFront` and `enqueueRear` operations insert elements at the front and rear, respectively, while the `dequeueFront` and `dequeueRear` operations remove elements from the front and rear.

The `DequeLL` class inherits from the `DLList` class, providing an intuitive and efficient implementation for deque operations.

Implementation Interface

The following are the implementations for the deque operations using the parent class methods:

```
1  template <typename T>
2  class DequeLL : public DLList<T> {
3  public:
4      DequeLL() : DLList<T>() {}
```

```cpp
 5      virtual ~DequeLL(){}
 6
 7      // Deque-specific functions
 8      virtual void enqueueFront(const T item) {
 9          this->pushFront(item);
10      }
11      virtual T dequeueFront() {
12          return this->popFront();
13      }
14      virtual void enqueueRear(const T item) {
15          this->pushBack(item);
16      }
17      virtual T dequeueRear() {
18          return this->popBack();
19      }
20 };
```

DequeLL Class Interface

Operation Descriptions
- enqueueFront: Inserts an element at the front of the deque using the inherited pushFront method, which operates in $O(1)$ time
- dequeueFront: Removes and returns the front element using the inherited popFront method, also in $O(1)$ time
- enqueueRear: Adds an element to the rear of the deque via the pushBack method, ensuring efficient appending in constant time
- dequeueRear: Removes and returns the rear element using the popBack method, allowing for constant-time removal at the deque's end

Note:
In the DequeLL class, there is no need to define explicit front and rear pointers. This is because DequeLL inherits from DLList, which already manages the front and rear of the list internally. The doubly-linked nature of DLList ensures that all deque operations are performed efficiently, utilizing the existing pointers for optimal access and manipulation.

Advantages of Using DLList for Deque
- **Efficiency:** Both front and rear operations (enqueue and dequeue) are performed in constant time ($O(1)$), making the doubly-linked list an ideal choice for a deque implementation.
- **Bidirectional Access:** The use of a doubly-linked list enables efficient traversal from both ends, enhancing the flexibility of the deque for various use cases.
- **No Special Cases:** The presence of prev and next pointers in each node eliminates the need for special cases when adding or removing elements at either end of the deque, simplifying code maintenance and reducing error-prone scenarios.

5.4 Performance Analysis

5.4.1 Stack Performance Analysis
The stack operations have the following time complexities:
- **Push Operation:** $O(1)$ – Constant time complexity for adding an element to the top of the stack
- **Pop Operation:** $O(1)$ – Constant time complexity for removing the top element from the stack

5.4.2 Queue Performance Analysis
The queue operations have the following time complexities:
- **Enqueue and Dequeue Operations:** $O(1)$ – Constant time complexity for adding an element to the rear and removing the front element of the queue
- **InsertAt and RemoveAt Operations:** $O(\min(i, n-i))$ – Efficiently inserts or removes an element at a specified position in the queue, where n is the current size of the queue and i is the insertion or removal position

5.4.3 Deque Performance Analysis
The deque operations have the following time complexities:
- **Enqueue and Dequeue Operations:** $O(1)$ – Constant time complexity for adding or removing an element from the front or rear of the deque
- **InsertAt and RemoveAt Operations:** $O(\min(i, n-i))$ – Efficiently inserts or removes an element at a specified position in the deque, where n is the current size of the deque and i is the insertion or removal position

5.4.4 Choosing the Right Data Structure
The choice between array-based and linked list–based implementations of stacks, queues, and deques depends on the specific requirements of the application, such as expected size, the need for dynamic resizing, and the importance of random access.
- **Array-Based Structures**
    - **Advantages:** Efficient random access due to array indexing
    - **Disadvantages:** Requires resizing when the array reaches capacity
    - **Use Case:** Suitable for scenarios with a known or bounded maximum capacity
- **Linked List Structures**
    - **Advantages:** Dynamic structure with no need for resizing
    - **Disadvantages:** Overhead of maintaining and traversing linked nodes
    - **Use Case:** Suitable for scenarios with unpredictable or fluctuating sizes

5.5 Summary

In this chapter, we have explored the essential data structures of stacks, queues, and deques, delving into their array-based and linked list–based implementations, performance characteristics, and practical applications. The choice between these implementations depends on specific use cases and requirements, such as the need for dynamic resizing, memory efficiency, and access patterns.

In scenarios where there is no need to resize the underlying structure, the implementation of linked lists is particularly advantageous. The linked list can dynamically allocate memory for each element without requiring pre-allocation. Additionally, in situations where the size of the stack is unpredictable or varies significantly, the linked list implementation shines, as it adapts dynamically to the changing number of elements without incurring the cost of resizing an array. The decision between array-based and linked list–based implementations depends on the specific requirements of the application.

Queues can be implemented using two main data structures: a linked list with a tail pointer or an array. In both implementations, key operations (`enqueue` and `dequeue`) exhibit a constant time complexity of $O(1)$, ensuring efficient performance to add and remove elements from the queue. The choice between linked list and array-based queues depends on the specific requirements of the application, such as the expected queue size, the need for dynamic resizing, and the importance of random access.

Deques can be implemented using two main approaches: an array or a doubly-linked list. Each implementation provides constant time complexity for fundamental deque operations while offering unique advantages and trade-offs. The choice between these implementations depends on the specific requirements of the application, such as the expected deque size, the need for dynamic resizing, and the importance of random access or the simplicity of implementation.

The full class diagram for the data structures covered in this chapter is shown in Figure 5.15.

This comprehensive diagram showcases the hierarchical structure and interaction between different stack, queue, and deque implementations, providing a clear overview of their design and functionality.

Problems

Discussion

1. Explain LIFO and FIFO data structures. Compare how stacks and queues are used in real-world situations.
2. Explore how stacks are implemented using arrays and linked lists. Discuss their efficiency and when to use one over the other.
3. Investigate dynamic resizing in array-based stacks and queues. Describe its importance and how it affects overall efficiency.

5.5 Summary

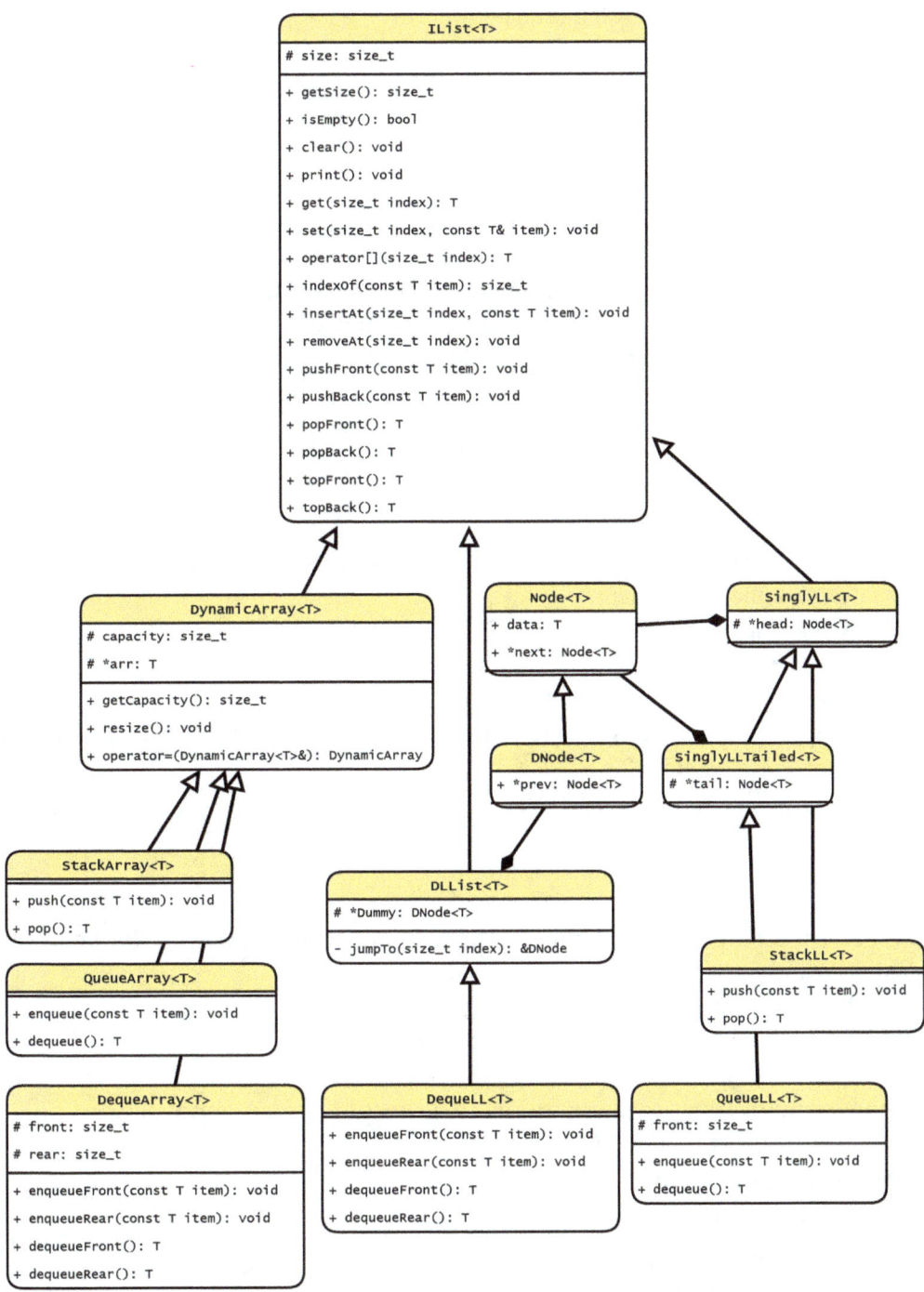

Figure 5.15: Full class diagram illustrating the relationships and inheritance among `StackArray`, `StackLL`, `QueueArray`, `QueueLL`, `DequeArray`, and `DequeLL`

4. Understand circular representation in array-based queues. Explain how circular indexing works and its advantages in memory efficiency.
5. Compare linked list–based queues with array-based queues. Discuss their strengths and weaknesses, considering factors like resizing and memory usage.

Multiple Choice Questions

1. What does the Last In, First Out (LIFO) principle mean in the context of a stack?
   (a) Elements are added to the top and removed from the bottom.
   (b) Elements are added to the bottom and removed from the top.
   (c) Elements are added to the top and removed from the top.
   (d) Elements are added to the bottom and removed from the bottom.
2. Which of the following operations is used to add an element to the top of a stack?
   (a) `enqueue`
   (b) `pop`
   (c) `push`
   (d) `dequeue`
3. What is the primary purpose of the `push` operation in a stack?
   (a) Remove the top element
   (b) Add an element to the top
   (c) Remove the bottom element
   (d) Add an element to the bottom
4. Which of the following is true regarding the time complexity of the push operation in an array-based stack?
   (a) $O(n)$
   (b) $O(\log n)$
   (c) $O(1)$
   (d) $O(n^2)$
5. What is the purpose of resizing the underlying array in an array-based stack?
   (a) To increase the time complexity of operations
   (b) To decrease the overall capacity of the stack
   (c) To efficiently manage the storage of elements
   (d) To prevent the stack from becoming empty
6. What principle does a queue follow in terms of element removal?
   (a) Last In, First Out (LIFO)
   (b) First In, First Out (FIFO)
   (c) Random Access
   (d) Stack Order
7. How are elements added to a queue?
   (a) At any random position
   (b) At the top
   (c) At the rear
   (d) At the front

5.5 Summary

8. What is a deque?
   (a) A data structure that follows the LIFO principle
   (b) A data structure that follows the FIFO principle
   (c) A versatile data structure allowing insertion and deletion from both ends
   (d) A data structure with efficient random access
9. Which implementation ensures efficient space utilization in a deque?
   (a) Linear representation
   (b) Circular representation
   (c) Stack implementation
   (d) Queue implementation
10. What is the purpose of the `front` marker in a deque?
    (a) Indicates the end of the deque
    (b) Represents the position for enqueuing at the front
    (c) Points to the middle of the deque
    (d) Specifies the position for dequeuing from the front
11. What operation adds an element to the front of the deque?
    (a) Enqueue Front
    (b) Dequeue Front
    (c) Enqueue Rear
    (d) Dequeue Rear
12. Which operation removes and returns the element from the front of the deque?
    (a) Enqueue Front
    (b) Dequeue Front
    (c) Enqueue Rear
    (d) Dequeue Rear
13. Which type of deque operation adds an element to the rear?
    (a) Enqueue Front
    (b) Dequeue Front
    (c) Enqueue Rear
    (d) Dequeue Rear
14. Which of the following operations removes and returns the element from the rear of the deque?
    (a) Enqueue Front
    (b) Dequeue Front
    (c) Enqueue Rear
    (d) Dequeue Rear
15. In a deque, what happens when markers reach the end of the underlying array?
    (a) Deque becomes empty.
    (b) Deque performs a resizing operation.
    (c) Circular representation ensures continuous structure.
    (d) Elements are shifted to a new array.
16. The deque supports operations at both ends, making it suitable for:
    (a) Implementing a stack
    (b) Implementing a queue

(c) Both implementing a stack and a queue
(d) Random access operations
17. What type of data structure is a deque?
    (a) Linear data structure
    (b) Tree data structure
    (c) Graph data structure
    (d) Hash data structure

Challenge Questions

1. Develop a data structure that efficiently supports the operations of both a stack and a queue. Analyze the time complexity of each operation and justify the design choices.
2. Design an algorithm to simulate the behavior of a double-ended queue (deque) using two stacks. Discuss the efficiency of your implementation in terms of time and space complexity.
3. Implement a stack using two queues. Explore different strategies for the push and pop operations and analyze the time complexity of each operation. Compare this approach with a traditional array-based stack.

Programming Problems

1. **Dyck Words**
   A Dyck word is a sequence of $+1$s and -1s with the property that the sum of any prefix of the sequence is never negative. For example, $+1, -1, +1, -1$ is a Dyck word, but $+1, -1, -1, +1$ is not a Dyck word since the prefix $+1 - 1 - 1 < 0$. Consider the relationship between Dyck words and stack operations.
   Provide a C++ code solution demonstrating how Stack push(x) and pop() operations can be related to Dyck words.

2. **Matched Strings**
   A matched string is a sequence of $\{, \}, (,), [,$ and $]$ characters that are properly matched. For example, ()[] is a matched string, but {()]} is not, since the second { is matched with a]. Utilize a Stack to determine if a given string of length n is a matched string.
   Provide a C++ code solution with a time complexity of $O(n)$.

3. **Reversing Stack Order**
   Suppose you have a Stack, s, that supports only the push(x) and pop() operations. Using only a FIFO Queue, reverse the order of all elements in a given Stack s, which supports only push(x) and pop() operations.
   Provide a C++ code solution for the reversal.

5.5 Summary

4. **Efficient addAll Operation**
   The `List` method `insertAll(i, c)` inserts all elements of the `Collection` c into the list at position i. (The `insertAt(i, x)` method is a special case where c=$\{x\}$.) Explain why it is not efficient to implement `insertAll(i, c)` by repeated calls to `insertAt(i, x)`. Design and implement a more efficient implementation.

5. **RandomQueue Design and Implementation**
   Design and implement a `RandomQueue`. This is an implementation of the `Queue` interface in which the `remove()` operation removes an element that is chosen uniformly at random among all the elements currently in the queue. (Think of a `RandomQueue` as a bag in which we can add elements or reach in and blindly remove some random element.) The `add(x)` and `remove()` operations in a `RandomQueue` should run in constant time per operation.

6. **Treque Design and Implementation**
   Design and implement a `Treque` (triple-ended queue). This is a `List` implementation in which `get(i)` and `set(i, x)` run in constant time, and `insertAt(i, x)` and `removeAt(i)` run in time $O(1 + \min\{i, n - i, |n/2 - i|\})$. In other words, modifications are fast if they are near either end or near the middle of the list.

7. **Array Rotation**
   Implement a method `rotate(a, r)` that "rotates" the array a so that `a[i]` moves to `a[(i+r) mod a.length]`, for all i in {0, ..., a.length}.

8. **List Rotation**
   Implement a method `rotate(r)` that "rotates" a `List` so that list item i becomes list item (i+r) mod n. When run on an `QueueArray`, `rotate(r)` should run in $O(1 + \min\{r, n - r\})$ time.

9. **Optimizing QueueArray Operations**
   Modify the `QueueArray` implementation so that the shifting done by `insertAt(i, x)`, `removeAt(i)`, and `resize()` is done using the faster `std::copy` method.

6. Hash Tables

Objectives

In this chapter, we will explore hash tables, an incredibly efficient data structure for storing and retrieving data. By the end of this chapter, you will have a thorough understanding of hash tables and their practical applications. Here's what you can look forward to:

1. **Introduction to Hashing:** We'll start with the basics of hashing and its importance in computer science.
2. **Comparison of Data Structures:** You'll learn to compare traditional data structures like arrays and linked lists in terms of storage efficiency and access speed, highlighting their strengths and weaknesses.
3. **Hash Functions:** We will delve into the properties of hash functions, understand what makes a good hash function, and see how they are used in hash tables.
4. **Collision Resolution:** Handling collisions is critical in hash tables. You'll explore different techniques such as chaining and open addressing and understand how they work.

> 5. **Implementation of Hash Tables:** We'll guide you through the implementation of hash tables using both chaining and open addressing techniques, with step-by-step code examples.
> 6. **Performance Analysis:** You'll learn to analyze the performance of hash tables, considering factors like time complexity, space complexity, and load factor.

6.1 Hashing Introduction

Hashing is a fundamental technique in computer science, providing an efficient way to map data to a fixed-size array for rapid data access. This process plays a crucial role in achieving a delicate balance between **storage efficiency** and **quick data access**. When confronted with the challenge of efficiently storing a large dataset or database while requiring speedy access, traditional data structures like arrays or linked lists may not be optimal choices. In this section, we will compare linked lists and arrays to highlight their efficiency trade-offs.

6.1.1 Array vs. Linked List

Arrays excel in providing constant-time direct access ($O(1)$), but their static allocation limits adaptability. Conversely, **linked lists** dynamically adjust to accommodate elements but can compromise search speed ($O(n)$) due to their sequential traversal nature. Table 6.1 offers a detailed comparison, highlighting these characteristics.

Table 6.1: Comparison Between Arrays and Linked Lists

Aspect	Array	Linked List
Access Time	Constant Time	Variable Time
Space Efficiency	Fixed Size	Dynamic Size
Adaptability	Limited	Flexible
Insertion/Deletion	May require resizing	No resizing needed
Memory Overhead	Minimal	Slightly higher (due to pointers)

The choice between arrays and linked lists depends on specific application needs, considering factors such as access patterns, adaptability, and memory efficiency.

6.1.2 Introducing Hash Tables

Hash tables emerge as a powerful solution to surpass the constraints of both arrays and linked lists. These tables adeptly store a small number, *n*, of integers from a broad range $U = \{0, \ldots, 2^w - 1\}$, with *w* representing the bit width. At the heart of hash tables is **hashing**, which employs hash functions to map data efficiently to designated locations within the table.

6.1.3 Applications of Hashing

Hashing finds diverse applications across various domains, providing efficient solutions to problems such as

- **Data Retrieval:** Hash tables are widely employed for quick and efficient data retrieval. They allow rapid access to stored information by mapping keys to specific locations, making them crucial for databases and data management systems.
- **Caching Mechanisms:** Hashing is used in caching mechanisms to store data that are frequently accessed. By associating data with unique hash codes, systems can quickly retrieve cached information, reducing latency and improving overall performance.
- **Symbol Tables:** Hash tables are fundamental in implementing symbol tables, mapping keys to values. This is particularly useful in compilers, interpreters, and other language processing applications.
- **File Systems:** Hashing is instrumental in managing file locations on disk, facilitating swift and organized access to stored data.

6.1.4 Usage Example: Management and Analysis of Access Logs

Imagine you are managing access logs for a web service and need to efficiently analyze these logs to quickly retrieve information about access counts from specific IP addresses within a defined timeframe. This can be quite challenging, especially when you need to answer queries promptly. Let's dive into how we can tackle this.

Consider the task of analyzing access logs and promptly answering queries such as the following.

IP Access Log Queries

To effectively manage and analyze these logs, you might need to answer several critical questions:

1. **Identifying Access from Specific IPs in the Last Hour:** How can we quickly determine if any user accessed the service from a particular IP address during the last hour?
2. **Counting Access Occurrences:** How can we efficiently calculate the number of times the service was accessed from a specific IP within a given time period?
3. **Unique IPs Accessed in the Last Hour:** How can we determine the count of distinct IP addresses that accessed the service during the last hour?

Given that one hour of logs can contain millions of lines, processing each query in real time would be impractical. To address this challenge, we need a way to keep track of how many times each IP appears in the last hour of the access log. Let's call this data structure C, which will store the mapping from IPs to their respective counters.

Addressing Challenges: IP Conversion

One effective approach is to convert IP addresses into a more manageable format, such as 32-bit integers. This conversion allows us to create an integer array for direct addressing, significantly improving the efficiency of tasks like access list updates and hourly access analysis.

Direct Addressing

Consider the fact that there are 2^{32} different IPv4 addresses. By converting each IP to a 32-bit integer, we can create an integer array A of size 2^{32}. This array can be used for direct addressing.

Analysis
- **Add:** The operation takes $O(1)$ time.
- **Update:** Each log line update takes $O(1)$ time.
- **Access:** Accessing an element also takes $O(1)$ time.
- **Memory Usage:** The space complexity is $O(N)$, where N is the size of the array.

List-Based Mapping

Direct addressing, however, requires an excessive amount of memory. An alternative is to store only active IPs in a list, retaining only the last occurrence of each IP and preserving the order of occurrence.

Analysis
If n is the number of active IPs:
- **Append:** The operation takes $\Theta(1)$ time.
- **Update:** Updating the list per log line takes $\Theta(n)$ time.
- **Access:** Accessing an element also takes $\Theta(n)$ time.
- **Memory Usage:** The space complexity is $\Theta(n)$.

Drawbacks of Array and Linked List-Based Approaches

When dealing with access log data, using arrays for direct addressing and linked lists for storing access counts comes with specific challenges:

First, consider the array-based approach. While employing an array to store access counts for each IP allows for constant time complexity in access, it requires a substantial amount of memory to encompass the entire IP address range. This becomes impractical when dealing with a large number of potential IP addresses, especially in scenarios such as IPv6, where the address space is significantly larger.

Next, think about the linked list–based approach. Utilizing linked lists to store access counts involves time-consuming processes of finding and erasing entries, with a time complexity of $\Theta(n)$, where n is the number of active IPs. This inefficiency becomes more pronounced with a substantial number of access log entries.

Hashing: A Compact Solution

Even with IP conversions, the sheer size of IP address spaces poses a memory challenge. This is where hashing comes into play as an elegant solution. Hashing allows for a more compact representation of IP-related data, minimizing memory usage while maintaining fast access times. By employing hash functions, you can efficiently map IP addresses to hash codes and store corresponding access counts. This approach strikes a balance between memory efficiency and query response time.

Using hashing, we can optimize both time and space complexities, enabling efficient management and analysis of large-scale access logs in real-time scenarios. This makes hashing an invaluable tool for handling extensive datasets with the need for quick access and minimal memory overhead.

6.2 Hash Functions

Hash functions play a fundamental role in the efficacy of **hash tables**. A hash function, denoted as $h : S \to \{0, 1, \ldots, m-1\}$ for any set of objects S and an integer $m > 0$ (where m is referred to as the cardinality of the hash function h), should possess the following desirable properties:

- **Fast Computation:** The hash function should be computationally efficient, facilitating the swift mapping of objects to hash values.
- **Uniqueness:** Different objects should map to distinct hash values, thereby preventing unnecessary collisions.
- **Limited Memory Usage:** The memory consumption of the hash function should ideally fall within the bounds of $O(m)$ space complexity.

6.2.1 Use of Hash Functions

In practice, hash functions are essential for efficient data storage and retrieval. They are used to convert data into hash codes, which serve as indices in a hash table. This process ensures quick access to data, making hash functions a cornerstone of effective data management.

One common application of hash functions is in databases, where they index data for rapid retrieval. For example, a database might use a hash function to convert a string (such as a username) into a numerical index, allowing for fast lookups. Hash functions are also crucial in caching, mapping data to cache slots for quick retrieval, thereby reducing latency and improving performance. Additionally, they are fundamental in implementing associative arrays, which store key-value pairs and use hash functions to compute indices into an array of buckets or slots.

In summary, hash functions are indispensable tools in computer science, enabling efficient data storage and retrieval across various applications. Their ability to quickly map data to specific locations in a hash table makes them vital for high-performance computing.

6.2.2 Multiplicative Hash Function

The multiplicative hash function is a widely used method for generating hash values for integers, taking advantage of modular arithmetic and integer division for efficient computation. The hash table utilized in this method has a size of 2^d, where d is an integer known as the dimension. The hash function is designed to hash an integer $x \in \{0, \ldots, 2^w - 1\}$ using the formula:

$$\text{hash}(x) = \frac{(z \cdot x) \mod 2^w}{2^{w-d}} \tag{6.1}$$

where

z is a randomly chosen odd integer in $[1, 2^w - 1]$.

w is the word size in bits (e.g., 32 or 64 bits), representing the size of the input domain.

d is the number of bits representing the size of the hash table, where the table size is 2^d.

The integer values in the range $[0, 2^w - 1]$ are mapped to corresponding hash values in the hash table, where hash(x) resides in the range $[0, 2^d - 1]$.

Note:
The multiplicative hash function takes advantage of the default integer operations being modulo 2^w, where w represents the number of bits in an integer. Additionally, the division by 2^{w-d} is effectively performed by right-shifting the bits by w − d, which discards the least significant bits, leaving the most significant bits as the hash value.

```
1 int hash(int x, int w, int d, int z) {
2     return ((long long)(z * x)) >> (w - d);
3 }
```

Multiplicative Hash Function Implementation

This code efficiently computes the hash value by performing the multiplication and right shift operations, where w and d represent the word size and the hash table dimension, respectively.

■ **Example 6.1** Consider an input value x = 15, with a word size w = 32, table size parameter d = 8, and a randomly chosen odd integer z = 4102541685.
Substitute the values into the formula:

$$\begin{aligned}\text{hash}(15) &= (x \cdot z) \mod 2^{32} \gg (32 - 8) \\ &= (x \cdot z) \mod 2^{32} \gg 24 \\ &= 83\end{aligned}$$

6.2 Hash Functions

Breaking it down into binary operations:

Binary representation of z	:	1111 0100 1000 0111 1101 0001 0111 0101
Binary representation of x	:	0000 1111
Multiplication x · z	:	1110 0101 0011 1111 0101 0100 0101 1101 1011
Modulo 2^{32}	:	0101 0011 1111 0101 0100 0101 1101 1011
Right shift 24	:	0101 0011

Therefore, the hash value for the input x = 15 using the multiplicative hash function is 83. ∎

■ **Example 6.2** Let us assume we have an input value x = 27 and the randomly chosen odd integer z = 3221225473.

Substitute the values into the formula:

$$\text{hash}(27) = (x \cdot z) \mod 2^{32} \gg (32 - 8)$$
$$= (x \cdot z) \mod 2^{32} \gg 24$$
$$= 64$$

Breaking it down into binary operations:

Binary representation of z	:	1100 0000 0000 0000 0000 0000 0000 0001
Binary representation of x	:	0001 1011
Multiplication x · z	:	1 0100 0100 0000 0000 0000 0000 0000 0001 1011
Modulo 2^{32}	:	0100 0000 0000 0000 0000 0000 0001 1011
Right shift 24	:	0100 0000

Therefore, the hash value for the input x = 27 using the multiplicative hash function with w = 32 and d = 8 is 64. ∎

6.2.3 Generating Hash Codes for Various Data Types

Hash functions are not limited to hashing integers; they can be extended to generate hash codes for strings, numbers, and other data types. Ensuring that different data types can be efficiently hashed is essential for the versatility and robustness of hash tables.

Hashing Strings

Hashing a string involves treating the string as a sequence of characters and then combining their ASCII values in a way that produces a unique hash code. A common method is to use polynomial rolling hash functions (see Equation 6.2).

$$\text{hash}(s) = \left(\sum_{i=0}^{|s|-1} s[i] \cdot p^i \right) \mod m \tag{6.2}$$

where

$s[i]$ is the ASCII value of the i-th character in the string s.

p is a small prime number, typically 31 or 37.

m is a large prime number to avoid overflow.

Here's how you can implement this in code:

```cpp
unsigned int hashString(const std::string &s) {
    int p = 31;          // Prime number base
    int m = 691;         // Large prime modulus
    unsigned int hash_value = 0;
    unsigned int p_pow = 1;
    for (char c : s) {
        hash_value =
            (hash_value + (c - 'a' + 1) * p_pow) % m;
        p_pow = (p_pow * p) % m;
    }
    return hash_value;
}
```

Polynomial Rolling Hash for Strings

This code computes a polynomial hash for the input string s, using p as the base and m to avoid overflow, ensuring unique hash values for different strings.

■ **Example 6.3** Let us assume that we have a string "hash" and use $p = 31$ and $m = 691$.
Substitute the values into the formula:

$$\begin{aligned}
\text{hash}(\text{"hash"}) &= (h \cdot 31^0 + a \cdot 31^1 + s \cdot 31^2 + h \cdot 31^3) \mod 691 \\
&= (8 \cdot 1 + 1 \cdot 31 + 19 \cdot 31^2 + 8 \cdot 31^3) \mod 691 \\
&= (8 + 31 + 18259 + 238328) \mod 691 \\
&= 256
\end{aligned}$$

Breaking it down into steps:

Character "h" (ASCII 104): $104 - 96 = 8$, contributes $8 \cdot 31^0 = 8$.
Character "a" (ASCII 97): $97 - 96 = 1$, contributes $1 \cdot 31^1 = 31$.
Character "s" (ASCII 115): $115 - 96 = 19$, contributes $19 \cdot 31^2 = 18259$.
Character "h" (ASCII 104): $104 - 96 = 8$, contributes $8 \cdot 31^3 = 238328$.

6.2 Hash Functions

Summing up:

$$8 + 31 + 18259 + 238328 = 256626.$$

Finally, taking modulo 691:

$$256626 \mod 691 = 256.$$

Therefore, the hash value for the string "hash" is 256. ∎

Hashing Floating-Point Numbers

Hashing floating-point numbers involves considering the bitwise representation of the floating-point value. Since floating-point numbers can have different representations due to precision issues, care must be taken to ensure that the hash function accounts for these.

The hash function for floating-point numbers can be expressed as

$$\text{hash}(f) = \sum_{i=0}^{n-1} (\text{hash}[i-1] \cdot p + \text{byte}(i)) \tag{6.3}$$

where

byte(i) is the i-th byte of the floating-point representation.

n is the number of bytes in the floating-point representation.

p is a small prime number (commonly 31 or 37).

hash$[-1] = 0$.

This approach sequentially processes each byte of the floating-point number, combining them with a prime multiplier to produce a unique hash code. Additionally, we can use the multiplicative method to ensure that the hash value fits within the table size.

```
1 unsigned int hashFloat(float f) {
2     unsigned int hash_value = 0;
3     unsigned char *p = reinterpret_cast<unsigned char*>(&f);
4     for (size_t i = 0; i < sizeof(f); ++i) {
5         hash_value = hash_value * 31 + p[i];
6     }
7     return hash_value;
8 }
```

Hashing Floating Point Numbers

This code processes each byte of the floating-point number's binary representation, multiplying the accumulated hash value by 31 (a small prime) and adding the current byte value, ensuring that the floating-point representation is uniquely hashed.

■ **Example 6.4** Let us assume we have a floating-point number 3.14. Substitute the value into the function:

Binary representation of 3.14 : 01000000 01001000 11110101 11000011

Byte values: $\{195, 245, 72, 64\}$

Hash value computation:
$$0 \cdot 31 + 195 = 195,$$
$$195 \cdot 31 + 245 = 6290,$$
$$6290 \cdot 31 + 72 = 195062,$$
$$195062 \cdot 31 + 64 = 6046986.$$

Therefore, the hash value for the floating-point number 3.14 is 6046986. ■

Hashing Compound Data Types

For compound data types, such as structures or classes, we can hash each member and combine their hash values. This can be achieved by using a combination of different hashing techniques to ensure that the resulting hash value is unique.

A common method to combine hash values is by using a prime multiplier, ensuring that the order and values of the fields uniquely determine the resulting hash code.

```
1 struct Point {
2     int x, y;
3 };
4
5 int zz = 31;   // A small prime number for combination
6
7 unsigned int hashPoint(const Point &p) {
8     // Compute hash for x-coordinate
9     unsigned int hash_x = hash(p.x);
10    // Compute hash for y-coordinate
11    unsigned int hash_y = hash(p.y);
12    // Combine using prime multiplier
13    return hash_x * zz + hash_y;
14 }
```

Hashing Compound Data Types

In this implementation, each member of the compound data type (e.g., coordinates of a point) is hashed individually, and their hash values are combined using a prime multiplier.

6.2 Hash Functions

> ■ **Example 6.5** Let us assume we have a point `(3, 4)`.
> Substitute the values into the function:
>
> $$\text{Assume hash}(3) = 83,$$
> $$\text{and hash}(4) = 110.$$
> $$\text{Then, hashPoint}((3, 4)) = 83 \cdot 31 + 110 = 2563 + 110 = 2673.$$
>
> Therefore, the hash value for the point `(3, 4)` is 2673. ■

By leveraging these techniques, we can generate efficient and reliable hash codes for various data types, ensuring that our hash tables are versatile and robust enough to handle different kinds of data effectively.

6.2.4 Collisions

Collisions occur when two distinct objects yield the same hash value, i.e., when $h(o_1) = h(o_2)$ and $o_1 \neq o_2$. Collisions are an inherent issue in hash tables because the finite number of hash values (m) often cannot uniquely represent every possible input from a much larger set (S). The effective handling of collisions is crucial for maintaining the integrity of a hash table.

Criteria for Good Hash Functions

A good hash function is indispensable to achieve efficient data retrieval and minimize collisions. It should exhibit the following characteristics:
- **Random Values:** The hash function should generate hash values with a broad distribution, minimizing clustering and promoting a uniform spread across the hash table.
- **Deterministic and Fast Computation:** The function must be deterministic, producing the same hash value for the same input every time it is used.
- **Uniform Distribution:** A good hash function ensures that hash values are uniformly distributed across the range.
- **Minimal Collisions:** The goal is to minimize collisions as much as possible. By reducing the frequency of collisions, the hash table can maintain efficient operations, preserving the constant time complexity ($O(1)$) that makes hash tables attractive for data storage and retrieval.

> **Note:**
> Collisions are unavoidable, especially when the input domain is much larger than the hash value range. However, a well-designed hash function reduces the number of collisions and spreads them evenly, ensuring that no single area of the hash table becomes a bottleneck.

In the next section, we will delve deeper into handling collisions through various techniques, such as chaining and open addressing. These strategies optimize hash table performance by efficiently resolving collisions, enhancing both the speed and reliability of data retrieval in real-world applications.

6.3 Hash Table Techniques

In this section, we will explore two primary techniques for implementing hash tables, each designed to address the challenge of collisions – instances where two different data items map to the same location.

6.3.1 Chaining

Chaining utilizes linked lists to efficiently store colliding elements. In this approach, linked lists are created at each hash table index to store colliding elements, allowing multiple items to coexist at the same index. This technique provides an effective way to handle collisions.

Figure 6.1 illustrates the concept of chaining in hashing. Each bucket in the hash table contains a linked list. When multiple items hash to the same index, they are added to the corresponding linked list. The hash key value and the length of the chain (denoted as c) are depicted to demonstrate how chaining accommodates collisions.

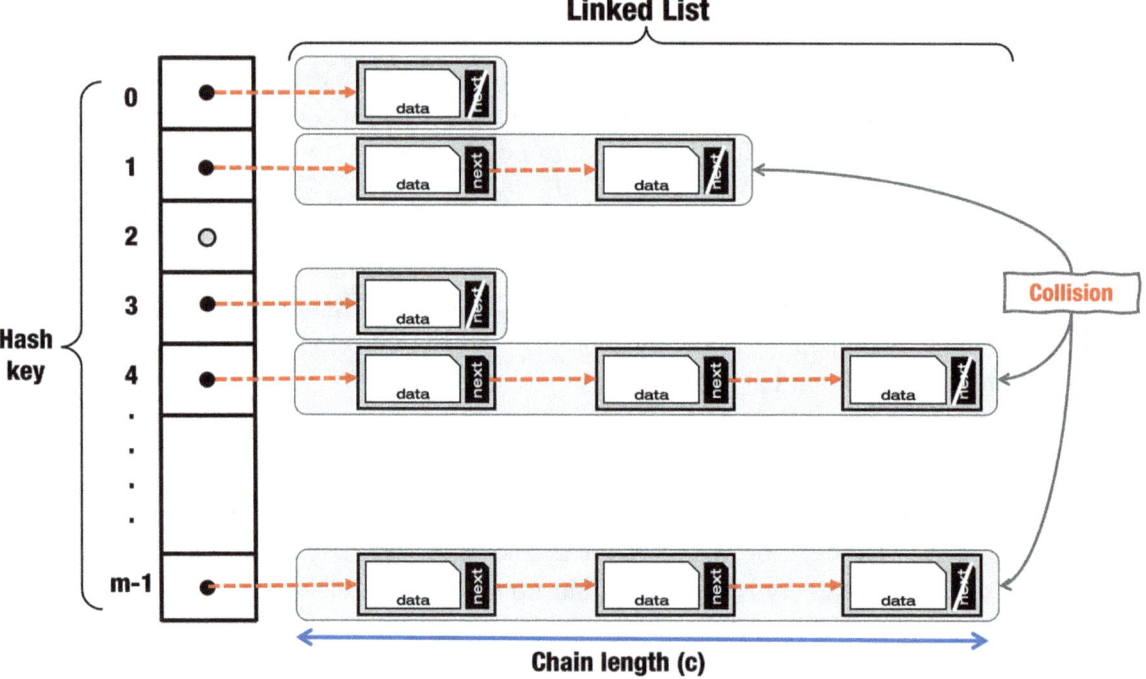

Figure 6.1: Chaining: hashing with linked list and collision handling

6.3 Hash Table Techniques

■ **Example 6.6** Consider the following problem: inserting elements (73, 15, 65, 41, 30, 69, 50) into a hash table using the hash function $h(x) = x \mod 7$. Figure 6.2 illustrates the chaining technique in action. Each item is hashed to the corresponding index, and when a collision occurs, it is added to the linked list at that index. The figure shows the resulting linked lists and their contents, demonstrating how chaining effectively handles collisions. ■

6.3.2 Open Addressing

Open addressing, also known as **probing**, seeks alternative locations within the table for placement when a collision occurs. This method involves linearly searching for the next available slot or employing more sophisticated probing strategies.

Linear probing is a straightforward example of open addressing. When a collision occurs, linear probing searches for the next available slot in a linear sequence. This technique can lead to clustering, where a group of consecutive slots is filled, increasing the chances of future collisions.

Figure 6.3 illustrates the concept of linear probing in hashing. When a collision occurs, probing searches for alternative locations to place the item within the hash table. The hash key values and the probing sequence are depicted to demonstrate how linear probing handles collisions.

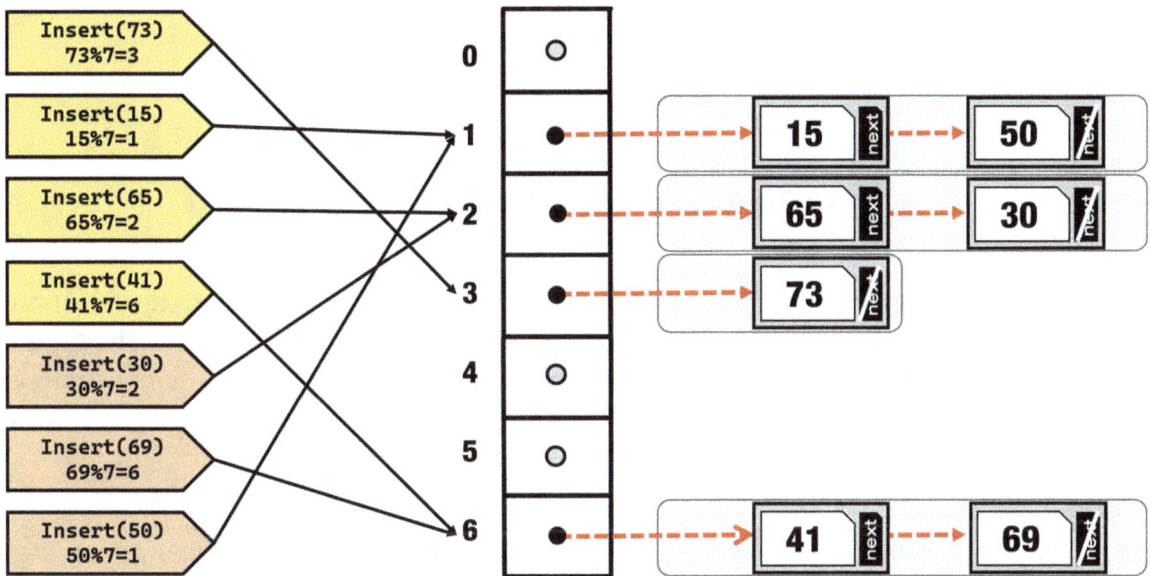

Figure 6.2: Chaining example: inserting 73, 15, 65, 41, 30, 69, 50 using hash function $h(x) = x \mod 7$

■ **Example 6.7** Consider the following problem: inserting elements (73, 15, 65, 41, 30, 69, 50) into a hash table using the hash function $h(x) = x \mod 7$. Figure 6.4 illustrates

Chapter 6. Hash Tables

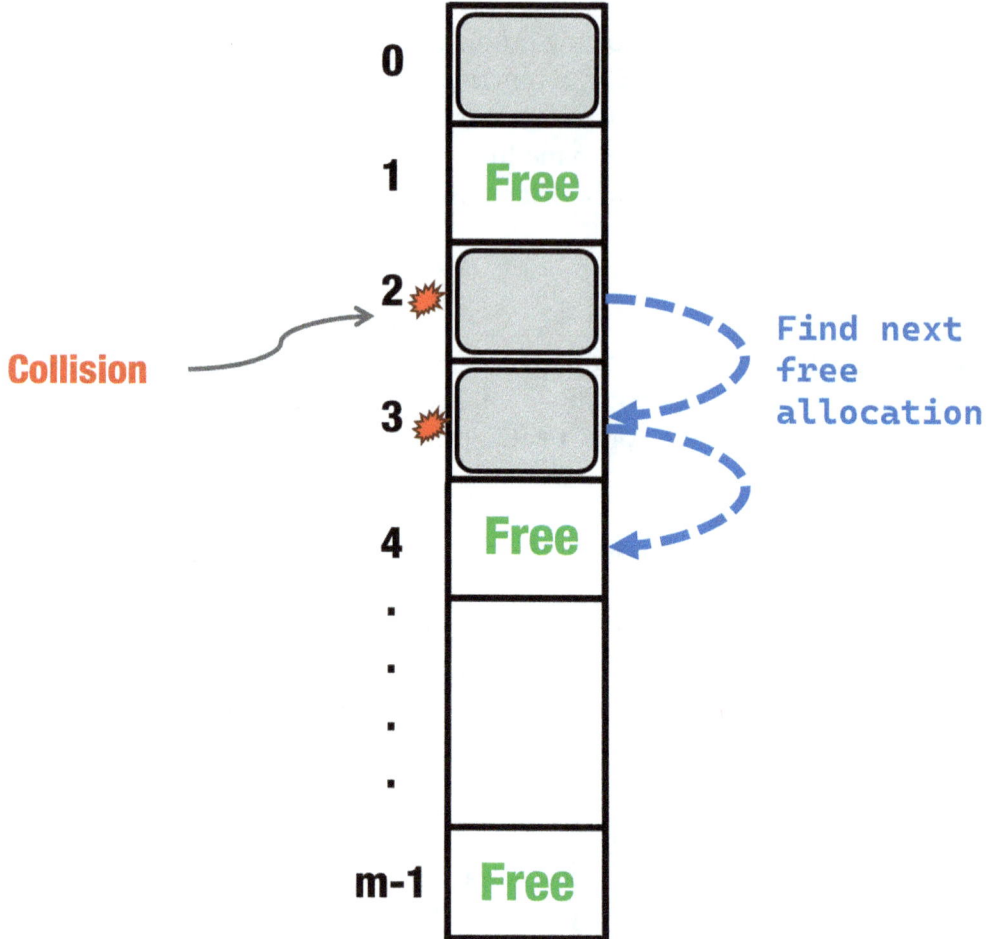

Figure 6.3: Probing: hashing with linear collision resolution

the probing technique in action. Probes occur when attempting to insert 30 at a location (2) already occupied, and the technique searches for the next available slot. The figure showcases the probing sequence and the corresponding hash key values, demonstrating how the technique efficiently resolves collisions. ■

Probing Variants

Open addressing involves several variants of probing techniques to handle collisions, including linear probing, quadratic probing, and double hashing.

Linear Probing

In linear probing, the probe sequence searches the table in a linear manner. When a collision occurs, the next index is checked in a sequential order.

$$\text{hash}(k,i) = (h(k)+i) \mod m \tag{6.4}$$

6.3 Hash Table Techniques

Figure 6.4: Probing example: inserting 73, 15, 65, 41, 30, 69, 50 using hash function $h(x) = x \mod 7$

where
- $h(k)$ is the initial hash value.
- i is the probe number.
- m is the size of the table.

■ **Example 6.8** Consider a hash table of size $m = 10$ and a hash function $h(k) = k \mod m$. For an element $k = 7$:

$$\text{hash}(7, 0) = (7 + 0) \mod 10 = 7$$
$$\text{hash}(7, 1) = (7 + 1) \mod 10 = 8$$
$$\text{hash}(7, 2) = (7 + 2) \mod 10 = 9$$

If index 7 is occupied, the algorithm will try 8, then 9, and so on until an empty slot is found. ■

Quadratic Probing

In quadratic probing, the probe sequence follows a quadratic function, which helps avoid primary clustering (consecutive filled slots).

$$\text{hash}(k,i) = (h(k) + c_1 \cdot i + c_2 \cdot i^2) \mod m \tag{6.5}$$

where c_1 and c_2 are constants chosen to avoid primary clustering.

■ **Example 6.9** For $k = 7$, $c_1 = 1$, $c_2 = 3$:

$$\text{hash}(7,0) = (7 + 1 \cdot 0 + 3 \cdot 0^2) \mod 10 = 7$$
$$\text{hash}(7,1) = (7 + 1 \cdot 1 + 3 \cdot 1^2) \mod 10 = 1$$
$$\text{hash}(7,2) = (7 + 1 \cdot 2 + 3 \cdot 2^2) \mod 10 = 7$$

If index 7 is occupied, the algorithm will try 1, then 7 again, and so on until an empty slot is found. ■

Double Hashing

Double hashing uses a secondary hash function to calculate the step size for the probe sequence, reducing the chances of clustering and providing a more uniform distribution of probes.

$$\text{hash}(k,i) = (h_1(k) + i \cdot h_2(k)) \mod m \tag{6.6}$$

where h_1 and h_2 are two different hash functions.

■ **Example 6.10** Let $h_1(k) = k \mod 10$ and $h_2(k) = 1 + (k \mod 5)$:

$$\text{hash}(7,0) = (7 + 0 \cdot (1 + 7 \mod 5)) \mod 10 = 7$$
$$\text{hash}(7,1) = (7 + 1 \cdot (1 + 7 \mod 5)) \mod 10 = 0$$
$$\text{hash}(7,2) = (7 + 2 \cdot (1 + 7 \mod 5)) \mod 10 = 3$$

If index 7 is occupied, the algorithm will try 0, then 3, and so on until an empty slot is found. ■

6.3.3 Performance Analysis

Understanding the performance of hash tables involves assessing their time and space complexity. Let us consider the analysis for both chaining and probing approaches.

6.3 Hash Table Techniques

Before diving into the specifics, let's define the key parameters involved in the analysis:
- n: The number of different keys currently in the hash table
- m: The cardinality of the hash function, which is also the size of the hash table
- c: The length of the longest chain in the hash table
- α: The load factor, which indicates the average number of elements per bucket

Chaining Analysis
Chaining is a technique to implement a hash table by using linked lists to handle collisions.

Space Complexity
The space complexity of chaining is $O(n+m)$:
- $O(n)$ to store n pairs (key, value)
- $O(m)$ to store the array A of size m

Time Complexity
The time complexity of chaining is $O(c+1)$, where c is the length of the longest chain. This time complexity arises because, in the worst case, you may need to traverse the longest chain to find, insert, or delete an element.

To optimize both m and c, consider
- Improving the hash function to generate more unique hash codes
- Redistributing elements between buckets
- Using techniques such as dynamic resizing

Advantages
- Simple and straightforward to implement.
- Handles collisions dynamically by growing the linked lists, allowing for a flexible table size.
- Deletion is straightforward as it involves removing an element from a linked list.

Disadvantages
- May result in unevenly distributed chains, especially if the hash function does not distribute values uniformly.
- Linked lists introduce additional memory overhead due to pointer storage.
- Performance degrades as the load factor increases, especially if chains grow significantly longer.

Probing Analysis
The time complexity of probing depends on the specific probing strategy employed. In the worst case, with linear probing, the time complexity can degrade to $\Theta(m)$ when the table is nearly full. Let's examine the advantages and disadvantages of the different probing variants.

Linear Probing
Advantages
- Simple to implement.
- Requires only one hash function.

Disadvantages
- Prone to primary clustering.
- Performance degrades as the load factor increases.

Quadratic Probing
Advantages
- Reduces primary clustering compared to linear probing.
- Effective for moderate load factors.

Disadvantages
- Secondary clustering can still occur.
- Requires careful selection of constants to ensure all slots are visited.
- May not find an empty slot if the table is more than half full.

Double Hashing
Advantages
- Minimizes clustering by using two independent hash functions.
- Provides a uniform distribution of probes.

Disadvantages
- More complex to implement due to the need for two hash functions.
- Requires careful selection of hash functions to avoid common multiples.
- Requires two good hash functions.

Load Factor

The load factor (α) is a critical parameter that influences the performance of hash tables. It is defined as

$$\alpha = \frac{n}{m} \tag{6.7}$$

> **Note:**
> A high load factor indicates a high table occupancy, potentially leading to more collisions. Maintaining a balanced load factor is crucial for efficient hash table performance. Generally, keeping α below 0.7 helps balance performance and memory usage.

Comparison

While chaining has a relatively constant time complexity, probing's time complexity can degrade as the table occupancy increases. Chaining often outperforms probing in terms of average-case performance, but the choice between them depends on factors such as expected data distribution and the specific use case (see Table 6.2).

6.4 Hash Table Implementation

Table 6.2: Comparison Between Chaining and Probing Techniques

Aspect	Chaining	Probing
Time Complexity	Consistent	May degrade with higher occupancy
Space Complexity	Higher (linked lists)	Lower
Load Factor Tolerance	More tolerant	May suffer from increased collisions
Dynamic Resizing	Suitable	May require rehashing

Understanding these techniques and their performance implications is crucial for effectively using hash tables in various applications. In the next chapter, we will delve into advanced hash table techniques, further exploring their implementation details, performance characteristics, and practical applications.

6.4 Hash Table Implementation

Implementing a hash table involves translating the abstract concepts discussed earlier into concrete code. This section will guide you through implementing a hash table using two common techniques: chaining and open addressing.

6.4.1 Chaining

In the chaining implementation, we use an array of linked lists. Specifically, we utilize an array of dynamic arrays, where each dynamic array holds a linked list of elements. This approach helps in managing collisions by storing multiple elements in the same index through linked lists.

The `ChainedHashTable` class, inheriting from the `ISet` interface, implements the required functionalities using the composition of `SinglyLL` and `DynamicArray`. The class diagram in Figure 6.5 showcases the relationships and functions.

```cpp
template <typename T>
class ChainedHashTable : public ISet<T> {

public:
    ChainedHashTable(size_t initialCapacity = 1024)
        : table(initialCapacity, SinglyLL<T>()),
          D((int)(std::log2(initialCapacity))) {}

    // ..... Other Abstract Interface methods
private:
    DynamicArray<SinglyLL<T>> table;

    // Multiplicative hash parameters
    static const int W = 32;
```

Chapter 6. Hash Tables

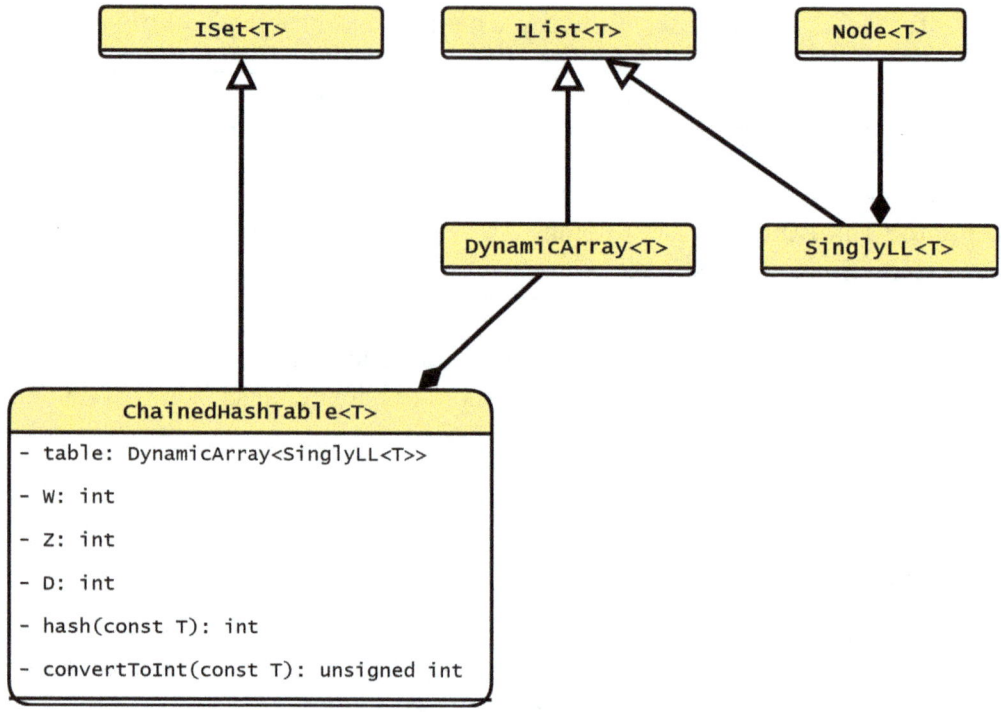

Figure 6.5: UML class diagram of `ChainedHashTable`. The `ChainedHashTable` class inherits from `ISet` and is composed of `SinglyLL` and `DynamicArray`

```cpp
15      int D;
16
17      // A randomly chosen odd number in [1:2^W-1]
18      static const long long Z = 2654435769;
19
20      // Hash function using multiplicative hashing
21      unsigned int hash(const T item) const {
22          unsigned int x = convertToInt(item);
23          return ((Z * x) >> (W - D)) % table.getCapacity();
24      }
25
26      // Conversion based on the problem
27      unsigned int convertToInt(const T x) const;
28  };
```

ChainedHashTable Class Interface

6.4 Hash Table Implementation

The `ChainedHashTable` class incorporates a `DynamicArray` named `table` to store linked lists. The hash function, using multiplicative hashing, is implemented with parameters such as `W` (word size), `D` (table size), and `Z` (a randomly chosen odd number).

Lookup Operation

The `contains` function searches for an element in the hash table. It looks for the element in the linked list at the computed index. The average-case **time complexity** is $O(1)$, but it can degrade to $O(c)$ in the worst case.

```cpp
template <typename T>
bool ChainedHashTable<T>::contains(const T item) const {
    size_t index = hash(item);
    // Ensure the index is within the bounds
    assert(index < table.getCapacity());

    // Using indexOf to check if item exists
    const SinglyLL<T>& bucket = table[index];
    return bucket.indexOf(item) != -1;
}
```

`contains` Function: Check Element Existence

Add Operation

The `add` function is responsible for adding an element to the hash table. It checks if the element is already present using the `contains` function and adds it to the linked list at the computed index. The average-case **time complexity** is $O(1)$ due to uniform distribution, but it can degrade to $O(c)$ in the worst case, where c is the length of the longest chain.

```cpp
template <typename T>
bool ChainedHashTable<T>::add(const T x) {
    size_t index = hash(x);
    // Ensure the index is within the bounds
    assert(index < table.getCapacity());

    // Using indexOf to check if x exists
    if (table[index].indexOf(x) == -1) {
        table[index].pushFront(x);
        ++size;
        return true;
    }
    return false;
}
```

`add` Function: Insert Element

Remove Operation

The `remove` function removes an element from the hash table. It searches for the element in the linked list at the computed index and removes it if found. The average-case **time complexity** is $O(1)$, but it can degrade to $O(c)$ in the worst case.

```
1  template <typename T>
2  bool ChainedHashTable<T>::remove(const T x) {
3      size_t index = hash(x);
4      // Ensure the index is within the bounds
5      assert(index < table.getCapacity());
6      int pos = table[index].indexOf(x);
7
8      // Using indexOf to check if x exists
9      if (pos != -1) {
10         --size;
11         // Remove specific element in SinglyLL
12         table[index].removeAt(pos);
13         return true;
14     }
15     return false;
16 }
```

remove Function: Delete Element

6.4.2 Linear Probing

In the probing implementation, we use an array of elements represented by `Dynamic Array`. In a `LinearHashTable`, there are three types of entries that can be stored:
- DATA: Actual values in the `ISet` that we are representing
- FREE values: At array locations where no data has ever been stored
- DELETED values: At array locations where data was once stored but has since been deleted

We introduce an additional array named `status` to keep track of the status of each slot in the table. The `status` array uses 0 to represent FREE slots, 1 for OCCUPIED slots, and 2 for slots that have been marked as DELETED. This enables us to distinguish between null values and deleted values.

```
1  template <typename T>
2  class LinearHashTable : public ISet<T> {
3  public:
4      // Constructor
5      LinearHashTable(size_t capacity)
6          : table(new DynamicArray<T>(capacity)),
7            status(new DynamicArray<SlotStatus>(capacity,FREE)) {}
8
```

6.4 Hash Table Implementation

```cpp
 9      virtual ~LinearHashTable() {
10          delete table;
11          delete status;
12      }
13      // ..... Other Abstract Interface methods
14  private:
15      // 0 for free, 1 for occupied, 2 for deleted
16      enum SlotStatus { FREE, OCCUPIED, DELETED };
17
18      DynamicArray<T> *table;
19      DynamicArray<SlotStatus> *status;
20
21      // Hash function using Modulo
22      int hash(const T item) const {
23          unsigned int x = convertToInt(item);
24          return x % table->getCapacity();
25      }
26
27      // Conversion based on the problem
28      unsigned int convertToInt(const T item) const;
29
30      void resize();
31
32  protected:
33      // Inherited members to use directly
34      using ISet<T>::size;
35  };
```

LinearHashTable Class Interface

To efficiently handle the operations, we maintain the invariant that the table's capacity is greater than or equal to twice the number of non-null values (capacity - size).

The class diagram in Figure 6.6 shows the relationships and functions of LinearHash Table, which inherits from ISet and is composed of DynamicArray.

Let's delve into the operations of linear probing in hash tables with a series of illustrative examples and corresponding figures to provide clarity.

First, consider the initial state of the table where all slots are marked as FREE. When we add the element 73, the hash function computes its index as hash(73) = 73 % 7 = 3. As shown in Figure 6.7, index 3 becomes OCCUPIED and the count of non-FREE slots, size, is incremented to 1.

Next, we demonstrate the process of adding another element, 30. The hash function determines the initial index as 2, which is already OCCUPIED. Linear probing directs us to the next index, 3, which is also OCCUPIED. Continuing the search, we find index 4 is FREE. Hence, 30 is inserted at index 4, changing its state to OCCUPIED, and size is updated to 5, as illustrated in Figure 6.8.

Chapter 6. Hash Tables

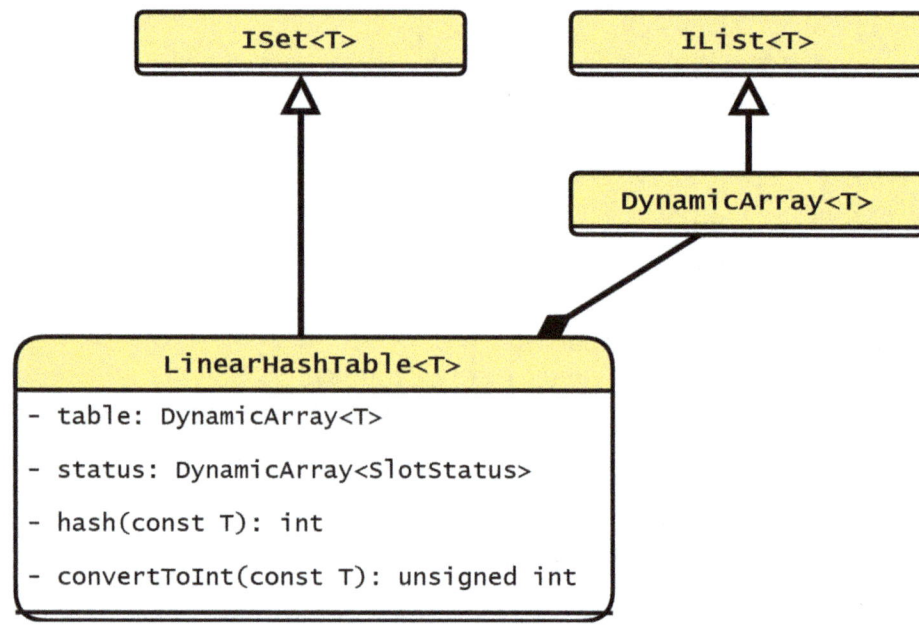

Figure 6.6: `LinearHashTable` UML class diagram. `LinearHashTable` inherits from `ISet` and is composed of `DynamicArray<T>`

When an element needs to be removed, such as 73, the hash function locates it at index 3, which is in the OCCUPIED state. After removal, index 3's state is changed to DELETED, as depicted in Figure 6.9.

Lastly, Figure 6.10 showcases the addition of the element 50. The hash function calculates the index as `hash(50) = 50 % 7 = 1`. Both indexes 1 and 2 are OCCUPIED. The probing continues until it reaches index 3, which is DELETED. Therefore, 50 is inserted at index 3, and its state is updated to OCCUPIED.

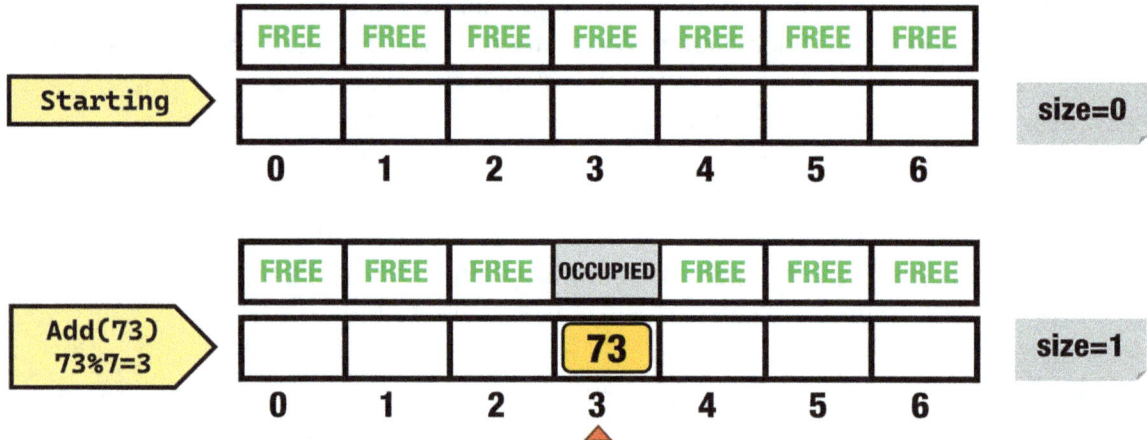

Figure 6.7: Initial state of the table with all slots marked as FREE and the state changed after adding 73

6.4 Hash Table Implementation

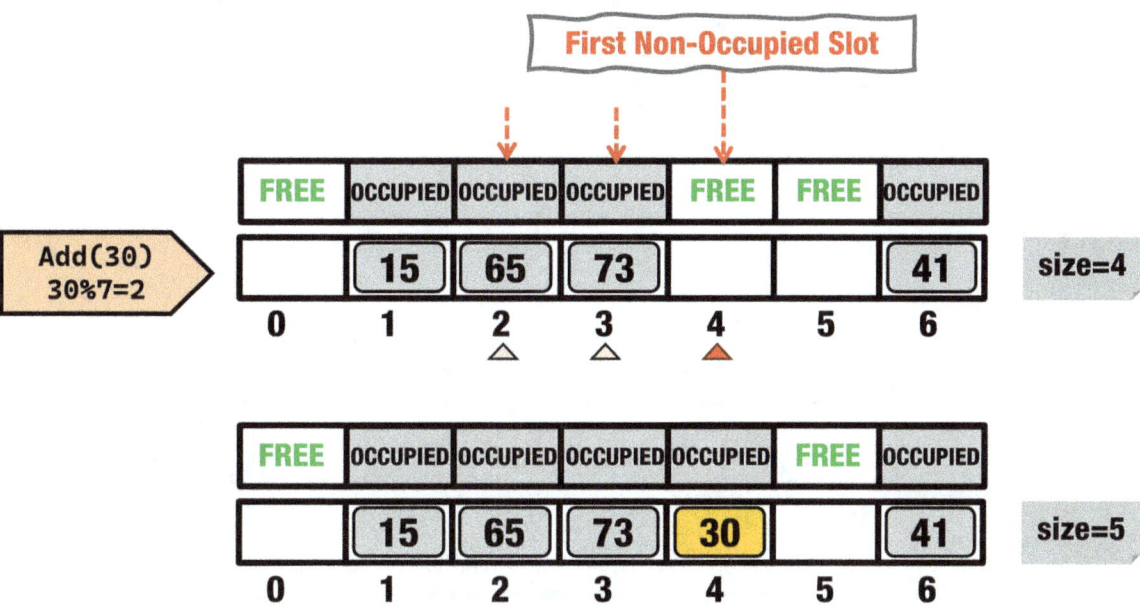

Figure 6.8: Adding the element 30. Initial index 2 is OCCUPIED, continuing to index 3 (OCCUPIED), and finally inserting 30 at index 4 (FREE), changing its state to OCCUPIED and setting size = 5

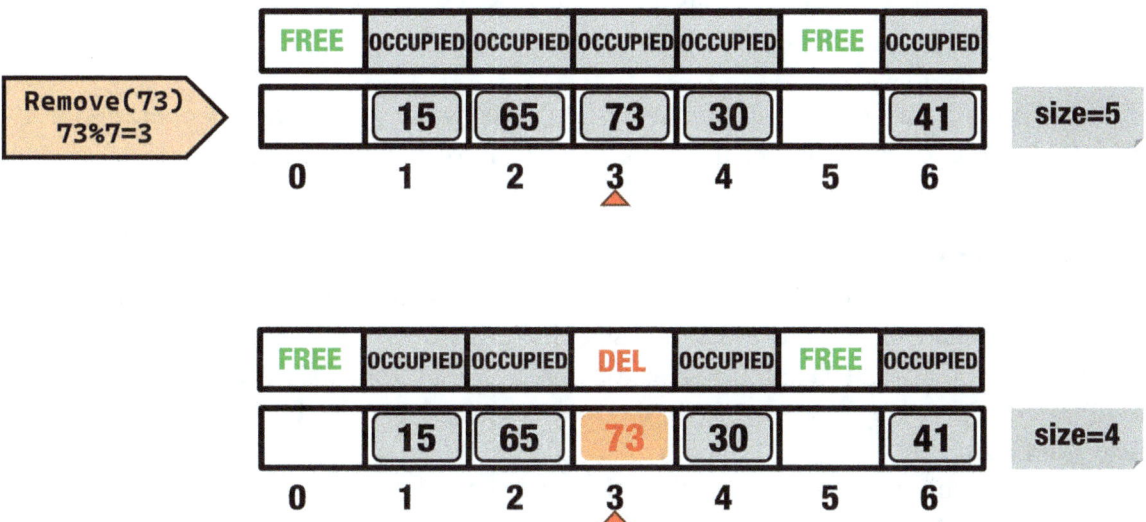

Figure 6.9: Removing the element 73. Located at index 3 with state OCCUPIED. After removal, index 3's state becomes DELETED

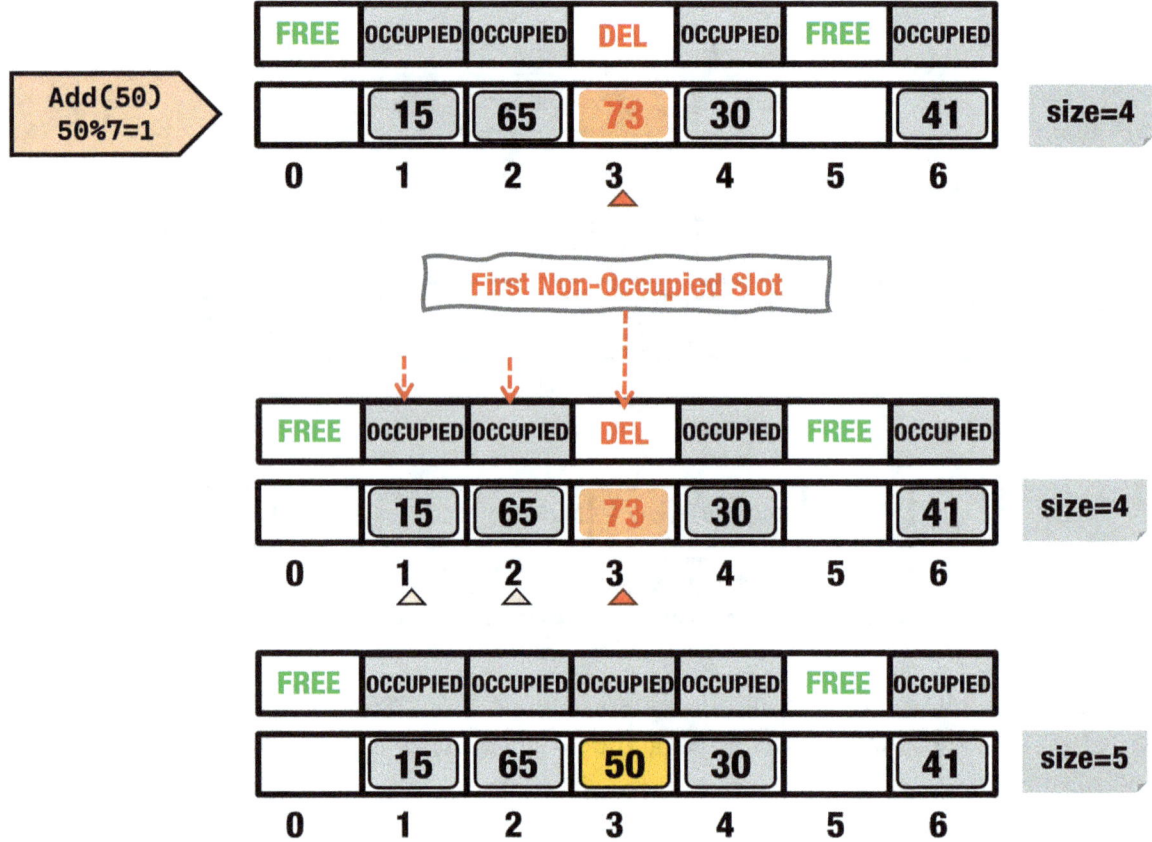

Figure 6.10: Adding the element 50. The hash value is calculated as `hash(50) = 50 % 7 = 1`, but indexes 1 and 2 are `OCCUPIED`. The first non-`OCCUPIED` index found is 3, which has a state of `DELETED`. Therefore, 50 is inserted at index 3, and its state is changed to `OCCUPIED`

Tracking the state of each slot in the hash table is essential for efficient operation of the hash table. It allows for proper handling of insertions, deletions, and searches, ensuring that the table remains effective even as elements are added and removed.

Lookup Operation

The `contains` operation in a `LinearHashTable` is straightforward. We start at array entry `t[i]`, where `i = hash(x)`, and search entries `t[i]`, `t[(i+1) mod capacity]`, `t[(i+2) mod capacity]`, and so on, until we find an index `i'` such that either `t[i'] = x` or `t[i'] = null`. In the former case, we return `t[i']`, and in the latter case, we return `null`.

When searching for an element, the following scenarios may occur:
- **Case 1:** The desired element is found at the initial index `i`, and its status is not `DELETED`. In this case, the element is returned directly.
- **Case 2:** We encounter `DELETED` slots or `OCCUPIED` slots that do not match the desired element. We continue the search by incrementing the index until a `FREE` slot is found, indicating that the element is not present.

6.4 Hash Table Implementation

The worst-case **time complexity** for `contains` is $O(\text{size})$, as it depends on the number of slots traversed during the search.

```
1  template <typename T>
2  bool LinearHashTable<T>::contains(const T x) const {
3      size_t i = hash(x);
4      // Loop until an unoccupied slot is found
5      while ((*status)[i] != SlotStatus::FREE) {
6          // Case 1: Found and status is not DELETED
7          if ((*status)[i] != SlotStatus::DELETED
8                          && (*table)[i] == x)
9              return true;
10
11         // Case 2: DELETED or OCCUPIED, continue the search
12         i = (i + 1) % table->getCapacity();
13     }
14     // Element not found
15     return false;
16 }
```
contains Function: Check Element Existence

Add Operation

The `add` operation in a `LinearHashTable` aims to insert an element into the hash table. It checks if the element is already present using `contains(x)`. The operation then searches for the next available slot and stores x at that location, incrementing `size` if necessary.

When adding an element using `add`, the following scenarios may occur:
- **Case 1:** The desired element is already present in the table. The `find` operation identifies a match, and the function returns `false`, indicating that the addition was unsuccessful.
- **Case 2:** The table exceeds 80% occupancy. In this situation, the table is resized to accommodate more elements efficiently.
- **Case 3:** The next available slot for insertion is found by probing through the table. The element is added to the table, and the counter `size` is updated accordingly.

The average-case **time complexity** is $O(1)$, but in the worst case, it can degrade to $O(n)$, where n is the table capacity.

```
1  template <typename T>
2  bool LinearHashTable<T>::add(const T x) {
3      // Case 1: Check if the element is already present
4      if (contains(x))
5          return false;
```

```cpp
 6
 7      // Case 2: Resize the table if it exceeds 80% occupancy
 8      if (size >= 0.8 * table->getCapacity())
 9          resize();
10
11      // Case 3: Find the next available slot for insertion
12      size_t i = hash(x);
13      // Loop until an unoccupied slot is found
14      while ((*status)[i] == SlotStatus::OCCUPIED) {
15          i = (i + 1) % table->getCapacity();
16      }
17
18      // Update counters and insert the element
19      ++size;
20      (*table)[i] = x;
21      (*status)[i] = SlotStatus::OCCUPIED;
22      // Successfully added the element
23      return true;
24 }
```

add Function: Insert Element

Remove Operation

The `remove` operation removes an element from the hash table. It searches for the element and sets the corresponding entry to `DELETED`. The average-case **time complexity** is $O(1)$, but in the worst case, it can degrade to $O(n)$.

```cpp
 1 template <typename T>
 2 bool LinearHashTable<T>::remove(const T x) {
 3     size_t i = hash(x);
 4     // Loop until an unoccupied slot is found
 5     while ((*status)[i] != SlotStatus::FREE) {
 6         T y = (*table)[i];
 7         if ((*status)[i] != SlotStatus::DELETED && x == y) {
 8             (*status)[i] = SlotStatus::DELETED;
 9             --size;
10             // Min 12.5% occupancy
11             if (8 * size < table->getCapacity())
12                 resize();
13             return true;
14         }
15         i = (i + 1) % table->getCapacity();
16     }
17     // Element not found
```

```
18        return false;
19 }
```

remove Function: Delete Element

Resize Operation

The `resize` operation is responsible for resizing the hash table when needed. The new capacity (`newCapacity`) is determined based on the current number of elements (`size`), ensuring sufficient space to maintain efficient performance. A new array `tnew` is created with the updated size, and all occupied elements from the existing array `table` are rehashed and inserted into `tnew`.

```cpp
1  template <typename T>
2  void LinearHashTable<T>::resize() {
3      size_t newCapacity = 1;
4      while (newCapacity < 3 * size) newCapacity <<= 1;
5  
6      DynamicArray<T>* newTable
7          = new DynamicArray<T>(newCapacity);
8      DynamicArray<SlotStatus>* newStatus
9          = new DynamicArray<SlotStatus>(newCapacity, FREE);
10 
11     // Insert everything into newTable
12     for (size_t k = 0; k < table->getCapacity(); ++k) {
13         if ((*status)[k] == SlotStatus::OCCUPIED) {
14             size_t i = hash((*table)[k]);
15             while ((*newStatus)[i] == SlotStatus::OCCUPIED) {
16                 i = (i + 1) % newTable->getCapacity();
17             }
18             (*newTable)[i] = (*table)[k];
19             (*newStatus)[i] = SlotStatus::OCCUPIED;
20         }
21     }
22 
23     // Update arrays
24     delete table;
25     delete status;
26 
27     table = newTable;
28     status = newStatus;
29 }
```

resize Function: Resizes and Rehashes Elements in `LinearHashTable`

The `resize` operation ensures that the new size accommodates at least three times the number of elements (3 * size). This approach helps in maintaining a balanced load factor, minimizing collisions, and ensuring efficient performance. The resizing process involves
- Calculating the **new capacity** by left-shifting («) until it is at least three times the current size
- Creating new arrays for `table` and `status`, both initialized with the new capacity
- Rehashing and reinserting all elements from the old table to the new one, ensuring that each element is placed correctly in the resized array
- Deleting the old arrays and updating the class pointers to reference the new, resized arrays

The **time complexity** for `resize` is $O(n)$, where n is the number of elements in the hash table, as each element must be rehashed and inserted into the new table.

6.4.3 Hash Table Performance Comparison

The performance of hash tables varies based on the collision resolution strategy used, such as chaining or probing. Table 6.3 compares the worst-case time complexity of various operations for chaining and probing techniques, highlighting the potential performance differences between these approaches.

Table 6.3: Worst-Case Time Complexity Comparison for Hash Table Operations Using Chaining and Probing

Operation	Chaining	Probing
add(item)	$O(c)$	$O(n)$
contains(item)	$O(c)$	$O(n)$
remove(item)	$O(c)$	$O(n)$

- **Chaining:** The time complexity for operations such as `add`, `contains`, and `remove` is $O(c)$, where c is the length of the longest chain in the hash table. This is because each operation may need to traverse the linked list (chain) to find, add, or remove the desired item.
- **Probing:** In probing, the worst-case time complexity for the operations can degrade to $O(n)$, where n is the number of elements in the table. This degradation occurs due to the linear search required to find an open slot or the desired element, especially when the table is nearly full.

While chaining provides relatively consistent performance by managing collisions through linked lists, probing can suffer from performance degradation as the table occupancy increases, making it more suitable for scenarios with low to moderate load factors.

6.5 Summary

In this chapter, we have explored hash tables, a fundamental data structure in computer science that allows for efficient data storage and retrieval. We began by comparing traditional data structures, such as arrays and linked lists, highlighting their respective advantages and limitations. This comparison set the stage for understanding why hash tables are a superior choice in many scenarios.

We then introduced the concept of hashing, discussing the properties of good hash functions, including fast computation, uniqueness, and minimal memory usage. Understanding these properties is crucial for implementing effective hash tables.

Next, we examined different methods for handling collisions, such as chaining and open addressing. Detailed explanations, examples, and illustrations were provided to clarify these techniques. We also delved into the implementation of hash tables using both chaining and open addressing. The code examples and diagrams offered a practical guide to these implementations.

Performance analysis of hash tables was another key focus, emphasizing the importance of the load factor and the impact of different collision resolution strategies on time and space complexity. This analysis helps to select the most appropriate technique based on specific requirements.

Finally, we explored the applications of hashing in various domains, demonstrating its versatility and efficiency in tasks such as data retrieval, caching, and managing symbol tables and file systems.

Overall, this chapter has equipped you with a solid understanding of hash tables, their implementation, and their applications. You are now well prepared to leverage hash tables in your own projects, ensuring efficient data management and retrieval.

The class diagram in Figure 6.11 provides an overview of the hash table implementations discussed in this chapter, highlighting the relationships and interactions between the various components.

Problems

Discussion

1. What are the trade-offs inherent in traditional data structures such as arrays and linked lists in terms of storage efficiency and access speed?
2. How do hash tables efficiently store a small number of integers from an extensive range, and what role do hash functions play in this process?
3. What are the essential characteristics of good hash functions, and why is collision resolution crucial to maintaining the integrity of a hash table?
4. Explain the concept of a multiplicative hash function and describe its implementation involving modular arithmetic and integer division.
5. Compare and contrast the collision resolution techniques of chaining and linear probing in hash tables.

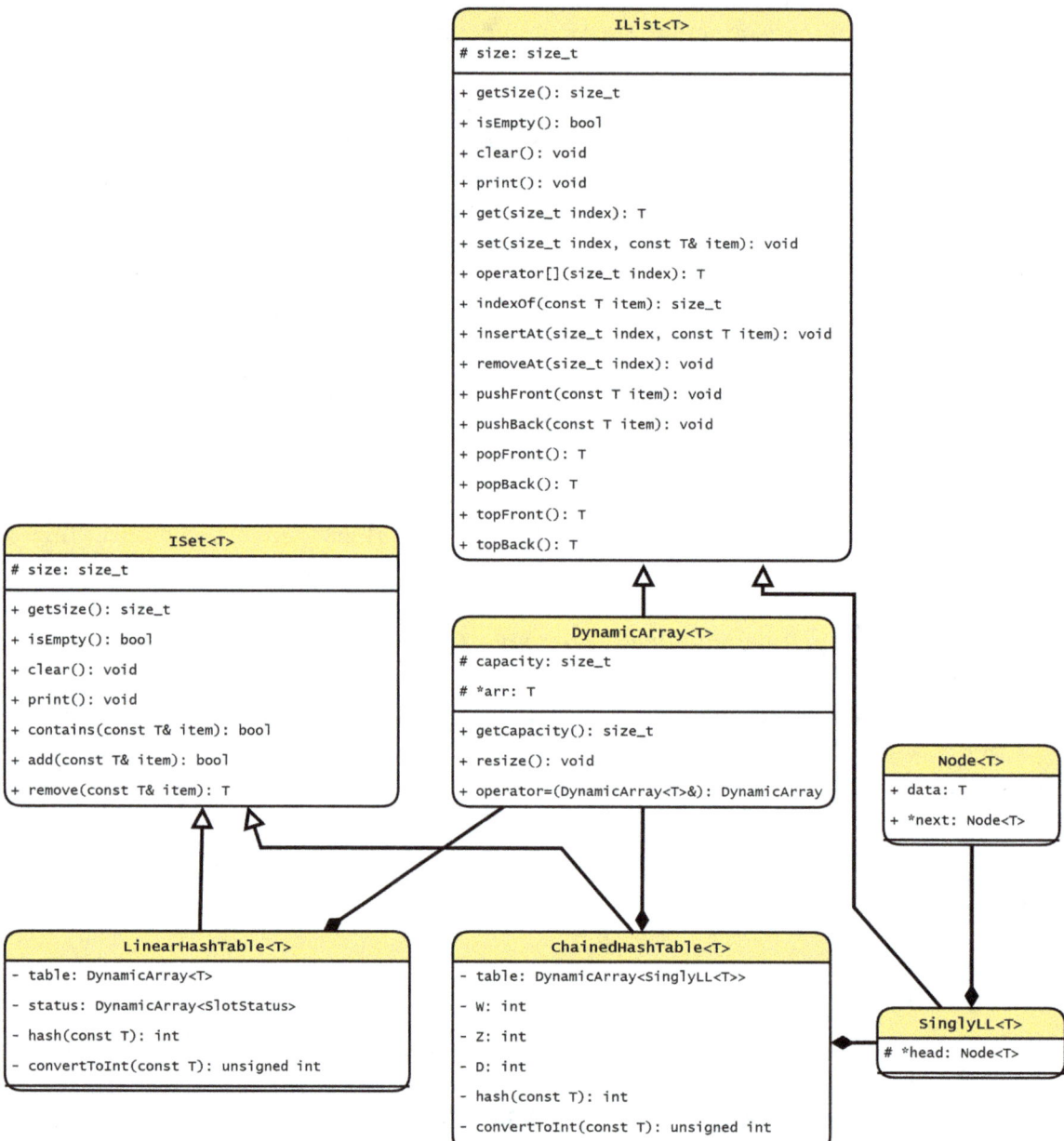

Figure 6.11: Class diagram for hash table implementations. This diagram includes `ChainedHashTable`, `LinearHashTable`, and their relationships with other classes

6.5 Summary

6. What factors should be considered when evaluating the strengths and weaknesses of chaining and linear probing, including time complexity, space complexity, load factor tolerance, and dynamic resizing?
7. How does hashing find applications in various domains, including data retrieval, caching mechanisms, symbol tables, and file systems?
8. Describe the key components of a hash function, including fast computation, uniqueness, and limited memory usage. Why are these properties important for efficient hash functions?
9. Walk through the steps of the multiplicative hash function for a given input value and the randomly chosen odd integer, demonstrating the calculation of the hash value.
10. Discuss the potential impact of a poorly designed hash function on the performance of a hash table. Provide examples of hash functions that might lead to suboptimal results and explain why.
11. Why is it important to track the status of slots in a hash table? Discuss how marking slots as DELETED can impact performance and future insertions.
12. Describe the process and challenges of resizing a hash table. What considerations should be taken into account to maintain efficiency?
13. How do probing techniques like quadratic probing and double hashing differ from linear probing in terms of handling collisions?

Multiple Choice Questions

1. In the context of hashing, what is the role of hash functions?
    (a) Determine the load factor
    (b) Map data to specific locations in a fixed-size array
    (c) Perform arithmetic operations
    (d) Sort the data
2. Which technique involves using linked lists to handle collisions in hash tables?
    (a) Probing
    (b) Chaining
    (c) Clustering
    (d) Hash folding
3. What is the advantage of a multiplicative hash function in generating hash values?
    (a) Limited distribution
    (b) Slow computation
    (c) Modular arithmetic
    (d) Fixed hash table size
4. When comparing arrays and linked lists in terms of space efficiency, which statement is correct?
    (a) Arrays have dynamic size, while linked lists have a fixed size.
    (b) Arrays have constant access time, while linked lists have variable time.

(c) Arrays have limited adaptability, while linked lists are flexible.//
(d) Arrays have minimal memory overhead, while linked lists have higher overhead.

5. What is a key characteristic of a good hash function?
   (a) Slow computation
   (b) Limited memory usage
   (c) Frequent collisions
   (d) Deterministic

6. In a hash table with open addressing, what happens when all slots are occupied, and an insertion is attempted?
   (a) Dynamic resizing occurs automatically.
   (b) The hash table rejects the insertion.
   (c) Collision resolution strategy is applied.
   (d) The insertion is delayed until a slot is available.

7. How does dynamic resizing contribute to the efficiency of a hash table?
   (a) Reduces the need for a good hash function
   (b) Eliminates collisions entirely
   (c) Adjusts the table size to maintain a suitable load factor
   (d) Increases the space complexity

8. Consider a hash table with a load factor close to 1. What impact does this high load factor have on the table's performance?
   (a) Improved adaptability
   (b) Reduced number of collisions
   (c) Increased likelihood of collisions
   (d) Faster access times

9. Which of the following is a disadvantage of using chaining for collision resolution in hash tables?
   (a) Increased memory usage due to linked lists
   (b) Difficulty in handling deletions
   (c) Inability to store different data types
   (d) Complexity of the hash function

10. In linear probing, what is the primary cause of performance degradation as the hash table fills up?
    (a) Hash function complexity
    (b) Clustering
    (c) Dynamic resizing
    (d) Load factor

11. Which of the following best describes quadratic probing?
    (a) Probing linearly to resolve collisions
    (b) Using two hash functions for probing
    (c) Probing using a quadratic function to resolve collisions
    (d) Probing randomly to resolve collisions

12. What is a common characteristic of double hashing?
    (a) Using a single hash function twice
    (b) Using two independent hash functions

(c) Applying a quadratic function to the hash values
   (d) Probing with a constant interval
13. Why is it essential to reset the status array during the resize operation in a hash table?
    (a) To free up memory
    (b) To reinitialize hash values
    (c) To ensure accurate tracking of slot statuses
    (d) To improve hash function efficiency

Challenge Questions

1. Investigate the concept of cuckoo hashing. Explain how it works, its advantages, and scenarios where it outperforms other collision resolution strategies. Discuss any potential challenges or limitations associated with cuckoo hashing.
2. Consider the implementation of a distributed hash table (DHT) in a peer-to-peer network. Discuss the key challenges involved in designing and maintaining a DHT, including issues related to scalability, fault tolerance, and load balancing.
3. Delve into the world of cryptographic hash functions. Explain the properties that make a hash function suitable for cryptographic applications. Discuss common cryptographic hash functions, their use cases, and any vulnerabilities or attacks associated with them.

Programming Problems

1. **Basic Multiplicative Hash Function Calculation**
   Given an input value x and a predefined odd integer z, calculate the hash value using the multiplicative hash function. Assume $w = 32$ and $d = 10$.
   - Input value $x = 12345$
   - Odd integer $z = 2654435769$

   Calculate the hash value and provide a step-by-step breakdown of the computation, including the binary representation of each step.

2. **Implementing and Analyzing Hash Function Distribution**
   Implement a multiplicative hash function in C++ and analyze the distribution of hash values. Use the following parameters for the hash function:
   - Odd integer $z = 2654435769$ (simplified for ease of calculation)
   - Parameters $w = 32$, $d = 8$
   - A series of input values: $x = 1, 2, 3, \ldots, 100$

   (a) Implement the multiplicative hash function in C++.
   (b) Compute the hash values for each input value from $x = 1$ to $x = 100$.
   (c) Analyze and discuss the distribution of the hash values.

3. **Hash Table Operations**
   Implement a hash table using chaining and linear probing in C++. Perform the following operations and analyze their performance:
   (a) Insert elements: 5, 28, 19, 15, 20, 33, 12, 17, 10
   (b) Find elements: 19, 20, 99
   (c) Remove elements: 28, 15, 33
   Compare the time complexity of each operation in both implementations and discuss any differences observed.

4. **Load Factor and Performance**
   Design an experiment to analyze the impact of the load factor on the performance of a hash table with linear probing. Vary the load factor from 0.1 to 0.9 and measure the average time taken for insertion, search, and deletion operations. Plot the results and provide an analysis.

5. **Evaluating Hash Functions**
   Given two hash functions:
   - $h_1(k) = k \mod 11$
   - $h_2(k) = 1 + (k \mod 10)$

   Evaluate the performance of double hashing using these hash functions. Implement the hash table and perform a series of insertions, searches, and deletions. Compare the results with those of linear and quadratic probing.

6. **Optimal Hash Code Assignment**
   A certain university assigns sequential integers as student numbers, starting from zero and now in the millions. For a class of 100 first-year students, we need to determine whether it is more sensible to use the first two digits or the last two digits of their student numbers to generate hash codes. Provide a C++ solution and justify your choice based on efficiency and potential issues.

7. **Designing a Hash Table for Usernames**
   A social media platform needs to design a hash table to store user profiles, each identified by a unique username. The usernames are alphanumeric and can be up to 15 characters long. Design a hash function that minimizes collisions and justifies your choice. Implement the hash function in C++ and simulate the insertion of the following usernames: "alice123," "bob_smith," "charlie789," "david456," and "eve_jones." Analyze the distribution of these usernames in the hash table.

7. Trees

Objectives

In this chapter, we will explore binary search trees (BSTs) and AVL trees, essential data structures for efficient data storage, retrieval, and manipulation. By the end of this chapter, you will have a thorough understanding of these tree structures and their practical applications. Here's what you can look forward to:

1. **Fundamentals of Binary Search Trees:** We will start with the basics of BSTs, their structure, and their importance in computer science. You will understand how BSTs maintain an ordered structure that facilitates efficient search operations.
2. **Basic Operations in BSTs:** You will learn how to perform insertion, deletion, and searching operations in BSTs. We will delve into the mechanics of these operations, ensuring you understand how they maintain the BST properties.
3. **Properties and Variants of Binary Trees:** We will explore different types of binary trees, including full, complete, and perfect binary trees. You will learn their unique properties and how these properties impact their applications.
4. **Introduction to AVL Trees:** AVL trees are introduced as a solution to the unbalancing problem in BSTs. You will understand their self-balancing property and how it ensures logarithmic operation times.

5. **Rotations in AVL Trees:** Handling imbalances in AVL trees involves rotations. We will discuss different rotation techniques, such as left rotation, right rotation, left-right rotation, and right-left rotation, and see how they maintain the AVL property.
6. **Implementation of AVL Trees:** We will guide you through the implementation of AVL trees, covering class definitions and methods for insertion, deletion, and balancing the tree. Step-by-step code examples will help you solidify your understanding.
7. **Performance Analysis:** Finally, you will learn to analyze the performance of AVL trees, considering factors like time complexity and space complexity. We will compare the efficiency of operations in AVL trees to those in unbalanced BSTs.

7.1 Binary Trees

A tree is a nonlinear data structure that consists of nodes connected by edges. It is defined as a collection of nodes, where each node can have zero or more child nodes, and there is exactly one root node with no parent. In this section, we will delve into a specific type of tree known as a binary tree.

7.1.1 Introduction to Binary Trees

Binary trees are a type of data structure where each node has at most two children, referred to as the left child and the right child. This structure allows for efficient data storage, retrieval, and manipulation. Binary trees are used in various applications, such as expression parsing, decision-making processes, and data sorting.

Figure 7.1 illustrates a typical binary tree structure, showing the parent and the left and right children of a node u in a binary tree.

7.1.2 Properties of Binary Trees

Before we explore different types of binary trees, let's first understand some fundamental properties they possess.

Binary trees possess several key properties that make them useful:
- **Maximum Nodes:** A binary tree of height h has at most $2^{h+1} - 1$ nodes.
- **Minimum Height:** A binary tree with n nodes has a minimum height of $\lceil \log_2(n+1) \rceil - 1$.
- **Leaf Nodes:** A binary tree with n nodes has at least $\lceil \frac{n}{2} \rceil$ leaf nodes.

7.1.3 Types of Binary Trees

Binary trees come in several varieties, each with its unique properties and applications:
- **Full Binary Trees:** Every node has either zero or two children.

7.1 Binary Trees

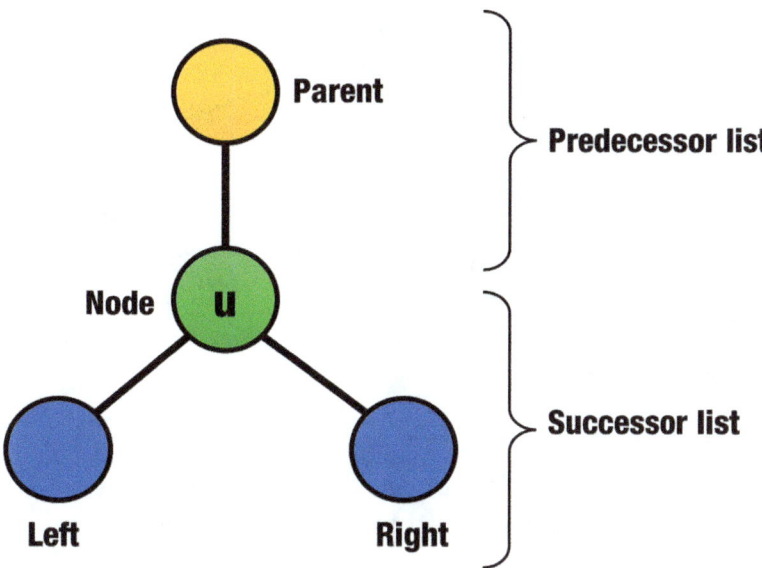

Figure 7.1: The parent, left child, and right child of the node u in a `BinaryTree`

- **Complete Binary Trees:** All levels are fully filled except possibly for the last level, which is filled from left to right.
- **Perfect Binary Trees:** All internal nodes have exactly two children, and all leaf nodes are at the same level.

Figures 7.2, 7.3, and 7.4 illustrate these types of binary trees.

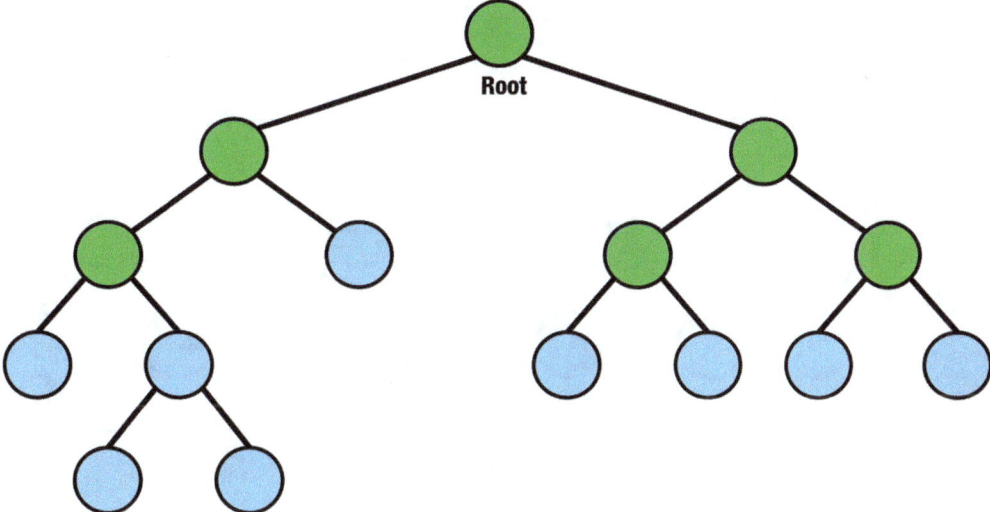

Figure 7.2: An example of a full binary tree where every node has either zero or two children

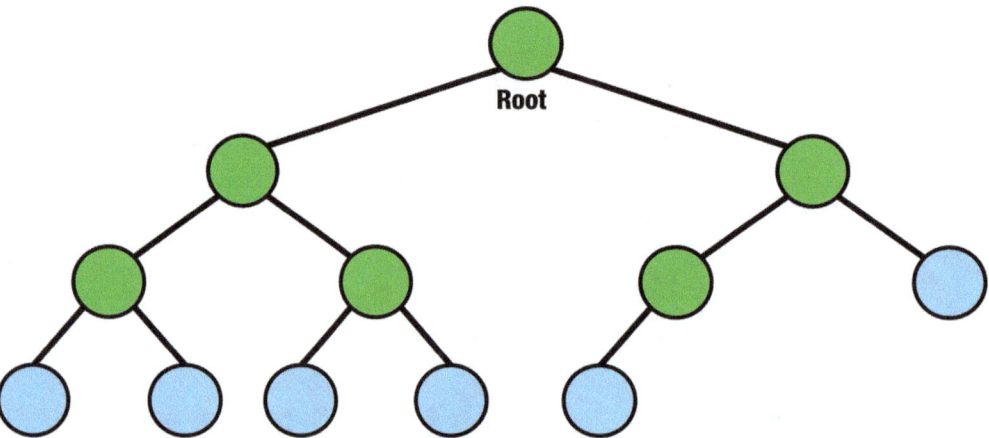

Figure 7.3: An example of a complete binary tree where all levels are fully filled except possibly for the last level, which is filled from left to right

7.1.4 Representation of Binary Trees

Binary trees can be represented in various ways in memory, primarily using arrays or linked lists.

Using Arrays

In an array representation, a binary tree is stored in a sequential manner. For a node at index i:

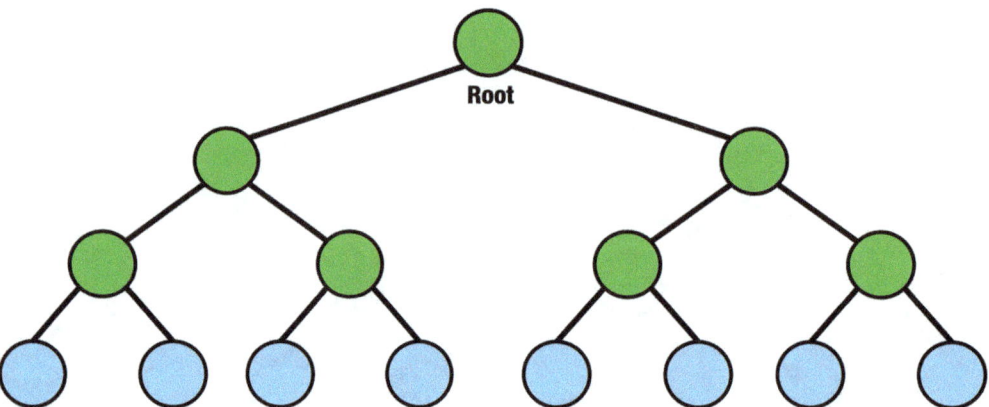

Figure 7.4: An example of a perfect binary tree where all internal nodes have exactly two children, and all leaf nodes are at the same level

- The left child is at index $2i + 1$.
- The right child is at index $2i + 2$.
- The parent is at index $\lfloor \frac{i-1}{2} \rfloor$.

This representation is particularly efficient for complete binary trees. Figure 7.5 shows the array representation of a binary tree.

7.1 Binary Trees

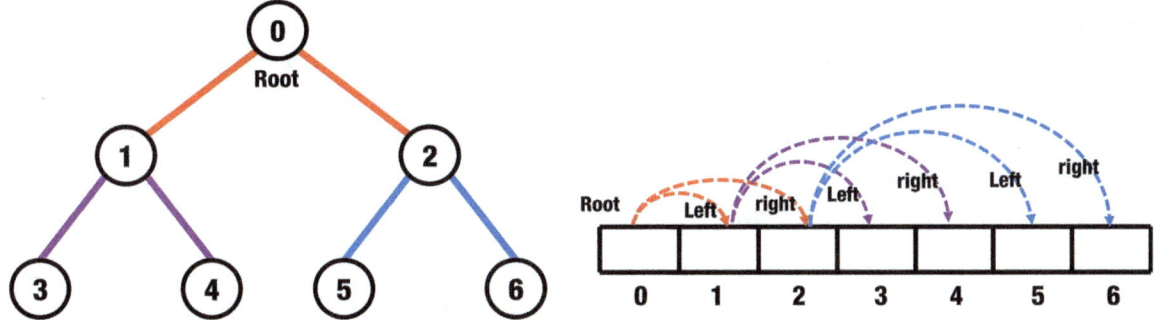

Figure 7.5: Array representation of a binary tree. The left child of the node at index i is at index $2i+1$, and the right child is at index $2i+2$. The parent is at index $\lfloor \frac{i-1}{2} \rfloor$

To implement a binary tree using a dynamic array class, consider the following code:

```
1  template<typename T>
2  class BinaryTreeArray : public DynamicArray<T> {
3  public:
4      BinaryTreeArray(size_t initialCapacity = 8)
5          : DynamicArray<T>(initialCapacity) {}
6
7      T getLeftChild(size_t index) {
8          size_t leftIndex = 2 * index + 1;
9          return (leftIndex < this->capacity) ?
10                 this->get(leftIndex) : T();
11     }
12
13     T getRightChild(size_t index) {
14         size_t rightIndex = 2 * index + 2;
15         return (rightIndex < this->capacity) ?
16                this->get(rightIndex) : T();
17     }
18
19     T getParent(size_t index) {
20         return (index == 0) ?
21                T() : this->get((index - 1) / 2);
22     }
23 };
```

BinaryTreeArray Class Interface

Using Linked Lists

In a linked list representation, each node is an object containing **four** fields: the data, a pointer to the left child, a pointer to the right child, and a pointer to the parent. This representation is flexible and supports dynamic binary trees where the structure can change frequently.

Figure 7.6 shows the structure of a node in a linked list representation.

Figure 7.6: A node in a linked list representation of a binary tree, containing data, pointers to the left and right children, and a pointer to the parent

Each node in a binary tree can be represented by a `struct`, which includes pointers to the left child, right child, and the parent:

```cpp
template<typename T>
struct BTreeNode {
    T key;
    BTreeNode *parent, *left, *right;
    int height;

    BTreeNode(T data) : key(data), parent(nullptr),
            left(nullptr), right(nullptr),
            height(0) {}
};
```

`BTreeNode` Struct Definition

Figure 7.7 illustrates a node in a binary tree with its left and right pointers pointing to new nodes, while the parent pointer is set to `nullptr`, indicating that it is the root node.

7.1 Binary Trees

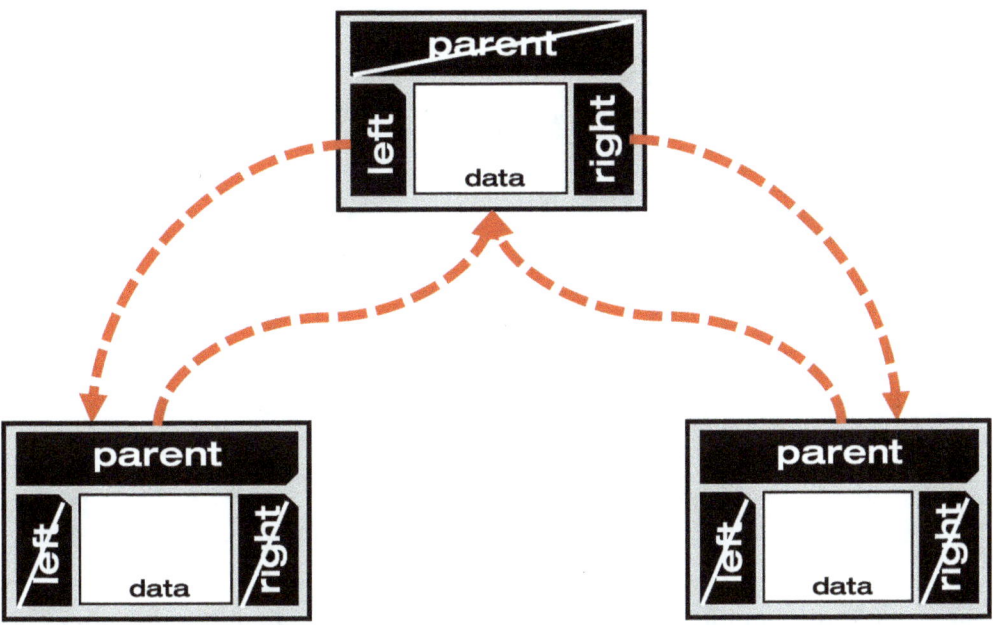

Figure 7.7: A binary tree node with left and right pointers pointing to new nodes. The parent pointer is set to `nullptr`, indicating it is the root node

The binary tree itself can be represented by a pointer to its root node, denoted as `root`.

```
1 template <typename T=int>
2 class BinaryTree : public ITree<BTreeNode<T>, T> {
3 public:
4     BinaryTree() : root(nullptr) {}
5
6     virtual ~BinaryTree();
7
8     // ... Other relevant functions
9
10 protected:
11     BTreeNode<T> *root;
12 };
```
`BinaryTree` Class Interface

7.1.5 Computing Size, Height, and Depth

In binary trees, certain properties, such as the size, height, and depth of the nodes, are important metrics. These can be computed using recursive algorithms.

Depth of a Node

The **depth** of a node is the number of edges from the node to the tree root node. The implementation of the depth computation is shown below:

```cpp
template <typename T>
size_t BinaryTree<T>::depth(BTreeNode<T> *u) const {
    size_t d = 0;
    while (u != nullptr) {
        u = u->parent;
        d++;
    }
    return d;
}
```

depth Function: Node Depth Calculation

For an array representation, the depth of a node at index i can be computed using the formula $\lfloor \log_2(i+1) \rfloor$.

```cpp
#include <cmath>

int depth(int i) {
    return std::floor(std::log2(i + 1));
}
```

depth Function: Array Representation

Size of the Tree

The **size** of a tree is the total number of nodes present in the tree. The following recursive implementation computes the size of the tree:

```cpp
template <typename T>
size_t BinaryTree<T>::getSize(BTreeNode<T> *u) const {
    if (u == nullptr) return 0;
    return 1 + getSize(u->left) + getSize(u->right);
}

template <typename T>
size_t BinaryTree<T>::getSize() const {
    return getSize(root);
}
```

getSize Function: Tree Size Calculation

For an array representation, the size of the tree is simply the length of the array.

7.1 Binary Trees

Height of a Node

The **height** of a node is the number of edges on the longest path from the node to a leaf. The following code implements the height computation:

```cpp
template <typename T>
size_t BinaryTree<T>::height(BTreeNode<T> *u) const {
    if (u == nullptr) return -1;
    return 1 + std::max(height(u->left), height(u->right));
}

template <typename T>
size_t BinaryTree<T>::height() const {
    return height(root);
}
```

`height` Function: Node Height Calculation

For an array representation, the height of the tree can be computed using the formula $\lfloor \log_2(n) \rfloor$, where n is the number of nodes. The following code for this calculation is

```cpp
#include <cmath>

int height() {
    return std::floor(std::log2(this->capacity));
}
```

`height` Function: Array Representation

7.1.6 Destroying a Binary Tree

Properly destroying a binary tree is crucial to avoid memory leaks, especially in dynamic tree structures where nodes are allocated on the heap. Destruction involves recursively deleting all nodes, starting from the leaves and progressing up to the root.

The following destructor method ensures that the binary tree is safely and completely deleted:

```cpp
template <typename T>
BinaryTree<T>::~BinaryTree() {
    clear();
}

template <typename T>
void BinaryTree<T>::clear() {
    deleteSubTree(root);
```

```
 9        root = nullptr;
10 }
11
12 template <typename T>
13 void BinaryTree<T>::deleteSubTree(BTreeNode<T> *node) {
14     if (node != nullptr) {
15         deleteSubTree(node->left);
16         deleteSubTree(node->right);
17         delete node;
18     }
19 }
```

Destructor and Deletion of a Binary Tree

The `deleteSubTree` function recursively deletes the left and right subtrees of a node before deleting the node itself, ensuring that all allocated memory is released properly.

7.1.7 Binary Tree Traversal Methods

Traversing a binary tree involves visiting all its nodes in a specific order to perform various operations such as search, sort, or modify the tree. Traversal strategies are broadly classified into two categories: Depth-First Search (DFS) and Breadth-First Search (BFS).

Depth-First Traversal

Depth-First Traversal explores as deep as possible down each branch before backtracking. This category includes the following methods, as illustrated in Figure 7.8:

- **In-Order Traversal (Left-Root-Right):** Processes the left subtree, the current node, and then the right subtree. It is especially useful for binary search trees to retrieve data in sorted order.
- **Pre-order Traversal (Root-Left-Right):** Visits the current node before its subtrees. This method is advantageous for cloning a tree or evaluating prefix expressions.
- **Post-Order Traversal (Left-Right-Root):** Accesses the current node after its subtrees. It is typically employed for deleting a tree or evaluating postfix expressions.

Recursion is an intuitive and efficient way to implement tree traversals due to the recursive nature of trees themselves.

Breadth-First Traversal

Breadth-First Traversal, or Level-Order Traversal, visits nodes across each level before proceeding to the next. This approach is executed using a queue and is ideal when all nodes at one level must be processed before moving to the next, as shown in Figure 7.9.

- **Level-Order Traversal:** Begins at the root, moving level by level and from left to right across the tree. It is often used in scenarios that require processing at each level, such as in Breadth-First Search algorithms.

7.1.8 Implementation of Traversal Techniques

There are four primary methods of traversal that suit different needs, detailed below.

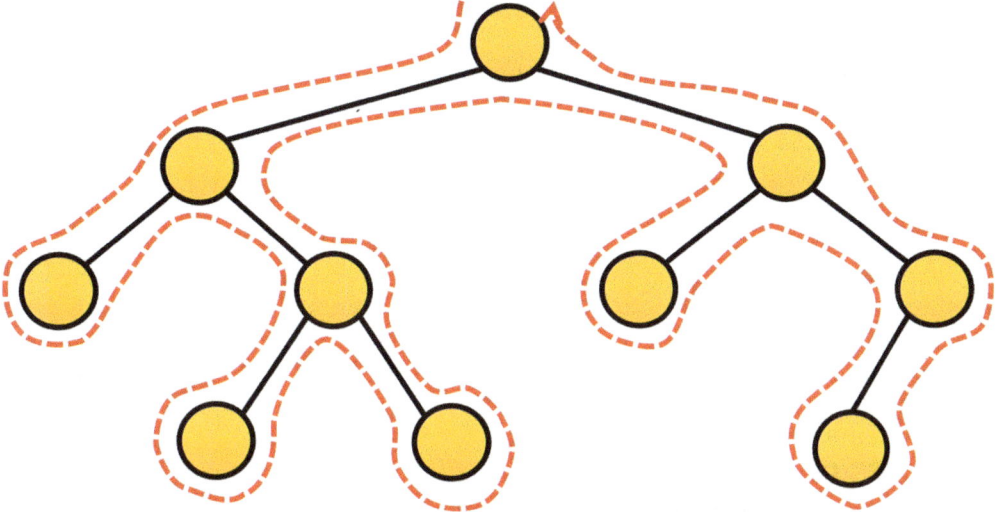

Figure 7.8: Illustration of Depth-First Traversal methods on a binary tree

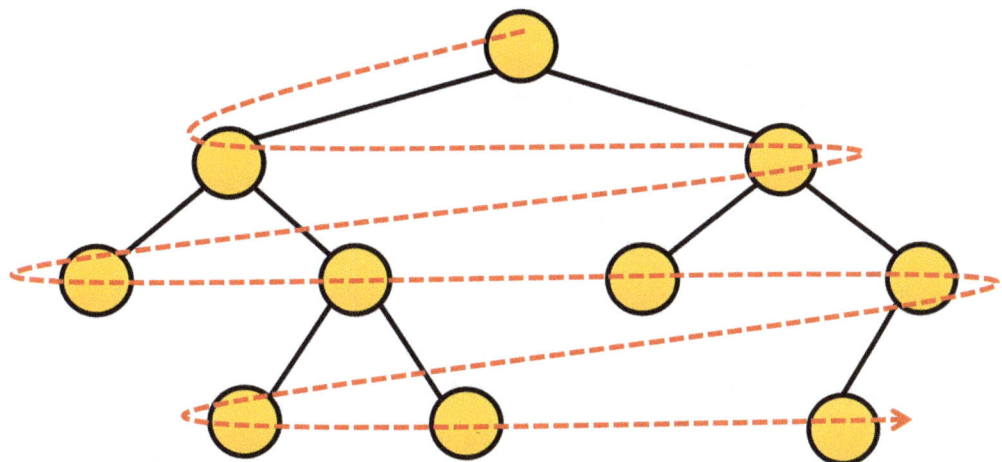

Figure 7.9: Illustration of Breadth-First (Level-Order) Traversal on a binary tree

Pre-order Traversal

In Pre-order Traversal, each node is processed before its child nodes. It is particularly useful for copying the tree or constructing prefix expressions. The order of visitation is as follows: root, left subtree, right subtree.

```cpp
template <typename T>
void BinaryTree<T>::
    preOrderTraversal(BTreeNode<T>*node) const{

    if (node == nullptr) return;
    // Process the root
    std::cout << node->key << " ";
    // Traverse left subtree
    preOrderTraversal(node->left);
    // Traverse right subtree
    preOrderTraversal(node->right);
}
```

`preOrderTraversal` Function: Performs Pre-order Traversal of a `BinaryTree`

In-Order Traversal

In In-Order Traversal, nodes are visited in a manner that results in visiting them in an ascending order, which is especially beneficial in binary search trees to retrieve data in sorted order. The order is as follows: left subtree, root, right subtree.

```cpp
template <typename T>
void BinaryTree<T>::
    inOrderTraversal(BTreeNode<T>*node) const{

    if (node == nullptr) return;
    // Traverse left subtree
    inOrderTraversal(node->left);
    // Process the root
    std::cout << node->key << " ";
    // Traverse right subtree
    inOrderTraversal(node->right);
}
```

`inOrderTraversal` Function: Performs In-order Traversal of a `BinaryTree`

Post-Order Traversal

Post-Order Traversal processes a node after its child nodes have been processed, making it suitable for operations like tree deletions or evaluating postfix expressions. The sequence is as follows: left subtree, right subtree, root.

```cpp
template <typename T>
void BinaryTree<T>::
    postOrderTraversal(BTreeNode<T>*node) const{
```

7.1 Binary Trees

```
4
5       if (node == nullptr) return;
6       // Traverse left subtree
7       postOrderTraversal(node->left);
8       // Traverse right subtree
9       postOrderTraversal(node->right);
10      // Process the root
11      std::cout << node->key << " ";
12 }
```

`postOrderTraversal` Function: Performs Post-order Traversal of a `BinaryTree`

Level-Order Traversal

Level-Order Traversal visits each level of the tree from left to right and is typically implemented using a queue. This method is ideal for scenarios that require visiting nodes in a breadth-first manner.

```
1  template <typename T>
2  void BinaryTree<T>::
3      levelOrderTraversal(BTreeNode<T>*root) const{
4
5       if (root == nullptr) return;
6       QueueArray<BTreeNode<T>*> q;
7       q.enqueue(root);
8       while (!q.isEmpty()) {
9           BTreeNode<T>* node = q.dequeue();
10          // Process the current node
11          std::cout << node->key << " ";
12          if (node->left != nullptr)
13              // Enqueue left child
14              q.enqueue(node->left);
15          if (node->right != nullptr)
16              // Enqueue right child
17              q.enqueue(node->right);
18      }
19 }
```

`levelOrderTraversal` Function: Performs Level-order Traversal of a `BinaryTree`

7.1.9 Traversing Binary Trees – Examples

To illustrate the practical use and distinct order of visits of each traversal method, consider the binary tree shown in Figure 7.10.

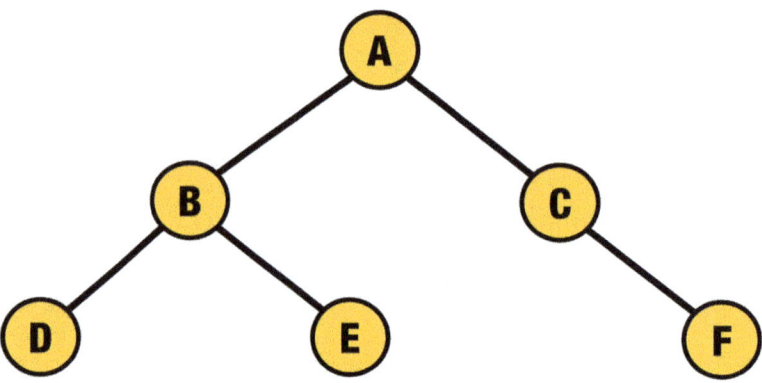

Figure 7.10: A binary tree example

Example of Pre-order Traversal

▪ **Example 7.1** For the given tree (Figure 7.10), in Pre-order Traversal, we first visit the node, then the left subtree, and finally the right subtree. The Pre-order Traversal would be

A, B, D, E, C, F

▪

Example of In-Order Traversal

▪ **Example 7.2** For the given tree (Figure 7.10), in In-Order Traversal, we first visit the left subtree, then the node, and finally the right subtree. The In-Order Traversal would be

D, B, E, A, C, F

▪

Example of Post-Order Traversal

▪ **Example 7.3** For the given tree (Figure 7.10), in Post-Order Traversal, we first visit the left and right subtrees and then the node itself. The Post-Order Traversal would be

D, E, B, F, C, A

▪

7.2 Binary Search Trees (BSTs)

Example of Level-Order Traversal

■ **Example 7.4** For the given tree (Figure 7.10), in Level-Order Traversal, we visit the nodes level by level from left to right. The Level-Order Traversal would be

A, B, C, D, E, F

■

7.1.10 Comparison of Tree Traversal Methods

Table 7.1 compares the DFS and BFS traversal methods based on the order in which nodes are visited and their typical applications.

Table 7.1: Comparison of Depth-First and Breadth-First Tree Traversal Methods

Traversal Type	Order of Visitation	Typical Applications
In-Order	Left subtree, **Node**, Right subtree	Retrieving data in sorted order in binary search trees
Pre-order	**Node**, Left subtree, Right subtree	Cloning trees, evaluating prefix expressions
Post-Order	Left subtree, Right subtree, **Node**	Deleting trees, evaluating postfix expressions
Level-Order	Across each level, from Left to Right	Processing nodes level by level, as in Breadth-First Search algorithms

Each traversal strategy is tailored to specific applications, making the understanding of their order of visitation and use cases essential for effectively working with binary trees.

This section has provided an overview of binary trees, their properties, and traversal methods. The next section will delve into binary search trees, their properties, and the primary operations that can be performed on them, including insertion, searching, and deletion.

7.2 Binary Search Trees (BSTs)

In this section, we will explore the properties of BSTs, their basic operations (insertion, searching, and deletion), and the underlying tree structure that enables efficient data manipulation.

7.2.1 Introduction to Binary Search Trees

A **binary search tree** is a binary tree that maintains a specific order among its elements to facilitate efficient search, insertion, and deletion operations. Each node in a BST follows the rule that its left child's value is less than its own value, and its right child's value is greater than or equal to its own. This property makes BSTs efficient for various operations, ensuring that the tree remains ordered and allows for fast data retrieval and modification.

7.2.2 Properties of Binary Search Trees

BSTs possess the following properties:
- **Ordering Property:** For any node u in a BST, all keys in the left subtree are less than or equal to the key of u, and all keys in the right subtree are greater than the key of u.
- **Unique Path:** There is a unique path from the root to any other node.
- **Efficient Search:** The ordering property allows for efficient searching, with average and worst-case time complexities of $O(\log n)$ and $O(n)$, respectively, depending on the tree's balance.

7.2.3 Basic Operations in BST

BSTs are capable of efficient data manipulation through fundamental operations:
- **Insertion:** Inserts new elements while maintaining the BST's ordered property. The insertion finds the correct position for the new node to keep the tree sorted.
- **Deletion:** Handles three scenarios: deleting a leaf node, a node with a single child, or a node with two children. Each case is managed to preserve the BST's ordered structure.
- **Searching:** Involves comparing the target value with the nodes, starting from the root and traversing the tree accordingly. This process repeats until the target is found or the search reaches a leaf node.

BST Insertion

Insertion in a BST follows an ordered approach to find the correct node position. The element is inserted as a leaf, with the traversal from the root directed left or right based on the new element's value, until the appropriate insertion point is found.

> ■ **Example 7.5** Consider starting with an empty BST. We sequentially insert nodes with the values 15, 10, 20, 8, 12, 17, 25 in that order. Each insertion is made by comparing the value to be inserted with the existing nodes, starting from the root, and finding the appropriate position so that the left child is always less than the parent node, and the right child is greater than or equal to the parent node.
>
> The resulting BST after these insertions is illustrated in Figure 7.11. ■

```cpp
template <typename T>
BTreeNode<T>* BinarySearchTree<T>::
    insertNode(BTreeNode<T>* node, T key) {

    if (node == nullptr)
```

7.2 Binary Search Trees (BSTs)

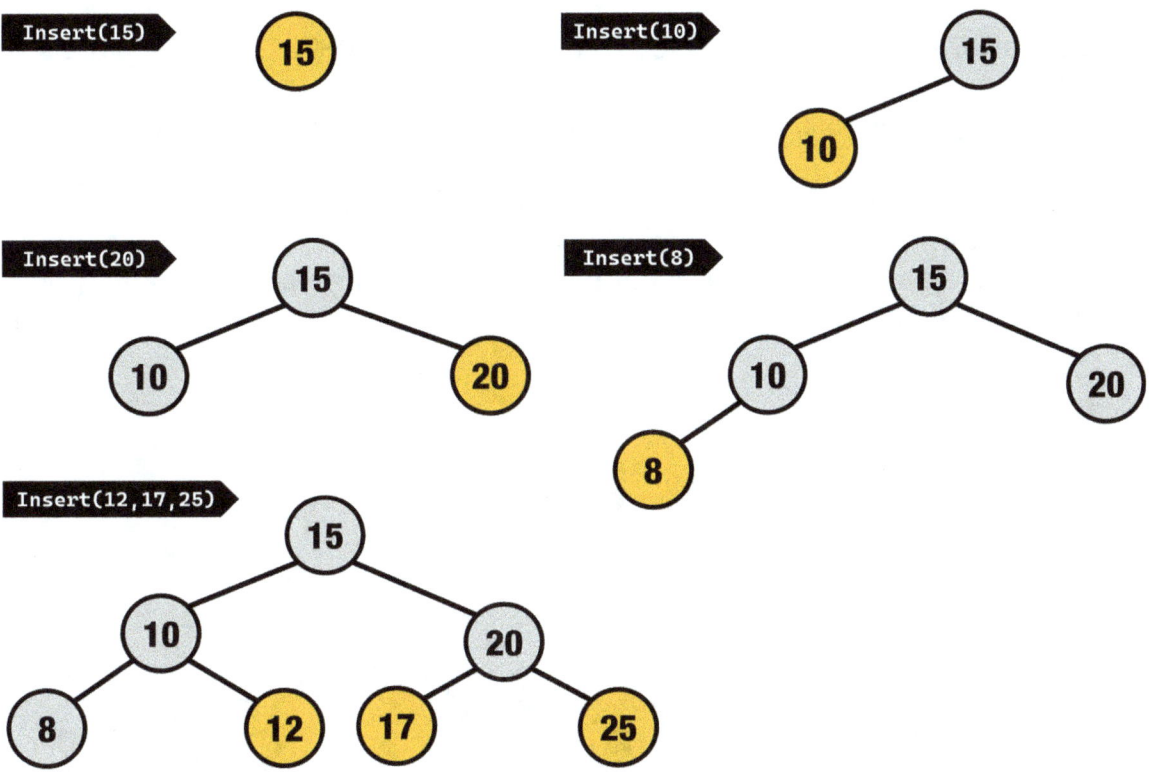

Figure 7.11: A binary search tree after inserting elements 15, 10, 20, 8, 12, 17, and 25

```
6            return new BTreeNode<T>(key);
7        if (key < node->key)
8            node->left = insertNode(node->left, key);
9        else if (key > node->key)
10           node->right = insertNode(node->right, key);
11       return node;
12   }
13
14   template <typename T>
15   bool BinarySearchTree<T>::insert(const T key) {
16       root = insertNode(root, key);
17       return true;
18   }
```

insert Functions: Insertion of a Node

BST Searching

Searching for a value in a BST follows a specific path from the root, based on binary search principles.

■ **Example 7.6** Assume we need to find the value 12 in a BST. The search process is as follows:
1. Starting at the root, compare 12 with 15. Since 12 is smaller, move to the left child.
2. Compare 12 with 10. As 12 is larger, proceed to the right child.
3. The search leads us to 12, successfully locating it in the tree.

This process is visually depicted in Figure 7.12, showing each step in the search path. ■

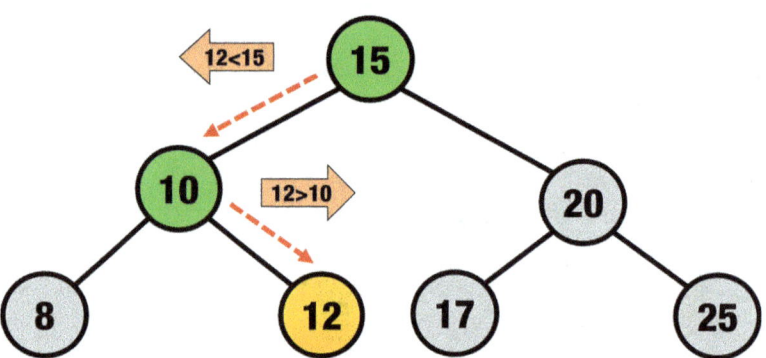

Figure 7.12: A step-by-step illustration of searching for the value 12 in a BST

```
1  template <typename T>
2  BTreeNode<T>* BinarySearchTree<T>::
3      searchNode(BTreeNode<T>* root, T key) const{
4
5      if (root == nullptr || root->key == key)
6          return root;
7      if (key < root->key)
8          return searchNode(root->left, key);
9      return searchNode(root->right, key);
10 }
11
12 template <typename T>
13 BTreeNode<T>* BinarySearchTree<T>::
14     find(const T key) const {
15
16     return searchNode(root, key);
17 }
```

searchNode and find Functions: Searching for a Node

7.2 Binary Search Trees (BSTs)

BST Deletion

Deletion in a BST depends on the structure of the node to be deleted, which can be a leaf node, a node with one child, or a node with two children. The deletion process in a BST involves three primary cases:

1. **Leaf Node:** Direct removal from the tree.
2. **One Child:** The node is replaced by its child.
3. **Two Children:** The node's value is replaced with its inorder successor or predecessor, and then the successor/predecessor is deleted, simplifying to one of the first two cases.

This method preserves the BST's properties during deletion. Figure 7.13 illustrates the three cases of deletion.

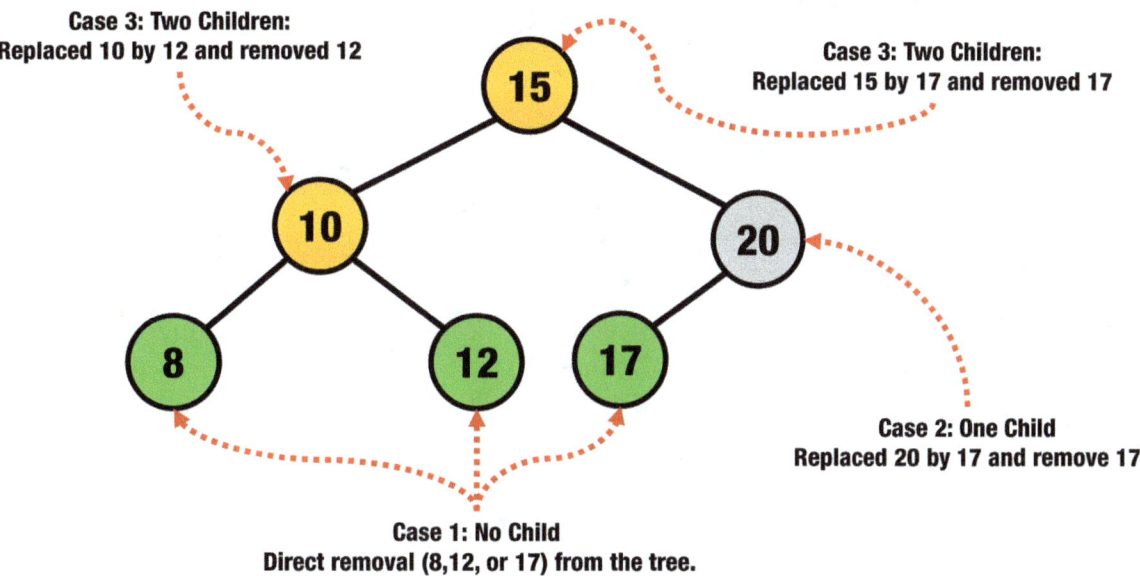

Figure 7.13: An illustration of the three cases of deletion in a BST: (case 1) deleting a leaf node, (case 2) deleting a node with one child, and (case 3) deleting a node with two children

■ **Example 7.7** In our example tree, to delete the node with the value 10, which has two children, we replace it with its inorder successor, which is 12. The process involves two steps: first, replacing the value 10 with 12 in its position and then removing the node originally containing the value 12. This process ensures the BST properties are preserved after deletion.

The detailed steps of this deletion process are illustrated in Figure 7.14. ■

```
1 template <typename T>
2 BTreeNode<T>* BinarySearchTree<T>::
3     deleteNode(BTreeNode<T>* root, T key) {
```

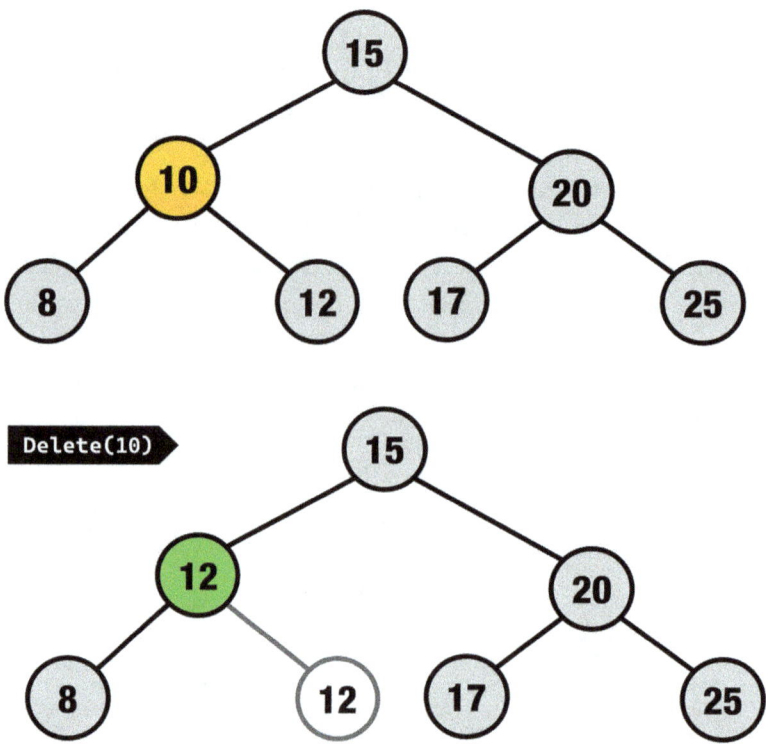

Figure 7.14: Step-by-step illustration of deleting the value 10 in a BST, highlighting the replacement with the inorder successor (value 12)

```
 4
 5      // Base case: If the root is nullptr, the tree is empty
 6      if (root == nullptr) return root;
 7
 8      // Recur down the tree to find the node to delete
 9      if (key < root->key) {
10          // The key to be deleted is in the left subtree
11          root->left = deleteNode(root->left, key);
12      } else if (key > root->key) {
13          // The key to be deleted is in the right subtree
14          root->right = deleteNode(root->right, key);
15      } else {
16          // Case 1: Node with only one child or no child
17          if (root->left == nullptr) {
18              // Node has no left child (or is a leaf node),
19              // replace it with the right child
20              BTreeNode<T>* temp = root->right;
21              delete root;
22              return temp;
23          } else if (root->right == nullptr) {
```

```
24              // Node has no right child,
25              // replace it with the left child
26              BTreeNode<T>* temp = root->left;
27              delete root;
28              return temp;
29          }
30
31          // Case 2: Node with two children
32          // Get the inorder predecessor
33          BTreeNode<T>* temp = this->findMax(root->left);
34
35          // Replace with the inorder predecessor's key
36          root->key = temp->key;
37
38          // Delete the inorder predecessor
39          root->left = deleteNode(root->left, temp->key);
40      }
41      return root;
42 }
43
44 template <typename T>
45 bool BinarySearchTree<T>::remove(const T key) {
46      size_t initialSize = this->getSize();
47      root = deleteNode(root, key);;
48      return this->getSize() < initialSize;
49 }
```

deleteNode and remove Functions: Deletion of a Node

Finding Min and Max Nodes

When working with BSTs, it is often necessary to find the minimum or maximum value within a subtree. These helper functions are particularly useful during the deletion process.

```
1  // Find the minimum value node
2  template <typename T>
3  BTreeNode<T>* BinarySearchTree<T>::
4      findMin(BTreeNode<T>* node) const {
5
6      BTreeNode<T>* current = node;
7      while (current && current->left != nullptr)
8          current = current->left;
9      return current;
10 }
11
```

```
12 // Find the maximum value node
13 template <typename T>
14 BTreeNode<T>* BinarySearchTree<T>::
15     findMax(BTreeNode<T>* node) const {
16
17     BTreeNode<T>* current = node;
18     while (current && current->right != nullptr)
19         current = current->right;
20     return current;
21 }
```
findMin and findMax Functions: Finding Minimum and Maximum Nodes

These functions are integral to maintaining the structure and properties of the BST during complex operations like deletion.

7.2.4 Performance Analysis

The performance of basic operations in a BST (insertion, searching, and deletion) depends on the height of the tree (h). The time complexity of insertion, searching, and deletion operations is $O(h)$. In the best case, where the tree is balanced, this complexity is $O(\log n)$, where n is the number of nodes in the tree. In the worst-case scenario, where the tree degenerates into a linked list, the complexity becomes $O(n)$.

7.2.5 Class Implementation of BST

A typical implementation of a BST in C++, along with functions for insertion, deletion, searching, and traversal:

```
1  template <typename T=int>
2  class BinarySearchTree : public BinaryTree<T> {
3  public:
4      BinarySearchTree() : BinaryTree<T>() {}
5      virtual ~BinarySearchTree() {}
6
7      // Implementation of the pure virtual functions
8      virtual bool insert(const T key);
9      virtual bool remove(const T key);
10     virtual BTreeNode<T>* find(const T key) const ;
11     virtual void traverse() const;
12
13 private:
14     // Helper functions to implement the required operations
15     BTreeNode<T>* insertNode(BTreeNode<T>* node, T key);
16     BTreeNode<T>* deleteNode(BTreeNode<T>* node, T key);
17     BTreeNode<T>* searchNode(BTreeNode<T>* node, T key) const;
```

```
18
19 protected:
20     // Inherited members to use directly
21     using BinaryTree<T>::root;
22
23     BTreeNode<T>* findMin(BTreeNode<T>* node) const;
24     BTreeNode<T>* findMax(BTreeNode<T>* node) const;
25 };
```
`BinarySearchTree` Class Interface

7.2.6 Summary

The efficiency of a BST, akin to a binary search in an array, relies on the tree's balance. A well-balanced BST minimizes depth, optimizing search operations. If the tree becomes unbalanced, performance can degrade to $O(n)$ in the worst case. Self-balancing trees address this issue by maintaining balance automatically.

This section has covered the fundamental aspects of binary search trees, including their properties, basic operations, and structural efficiency. The next section will explore self-balancing binary search trees, which ensure that the tree remains balanced for optimal performance.

7.3 Balanced Binary Trees

Binary search trees (BSTs) are highly efficient for search operations due to their ordered structure. However, their performance can degrade significantly when the tree becomes unbalanced. In an unbalanced BST, where the height difference between the left and right subtrees is significant, the tree's height can become linear with respect to the number of nodes. This leads to inefficiencies, as the time complexity for search, insertion, and deletion operations can degrade to $O(n)$ instead of $O(\log n)$.

To address this issue, balanced binary trees are employed. These trees use various balancing techniques to ensure that the tree maintains a low height, regardless of the order of insertions and deletions. By keeping the tree balanced, we can guarantee consistent efficient operations with time complexities close to $O(\log n)$.

Balancing techniques are crucial for maintaining the operational efficiency of BSTs. They ensure that the tree does not degenerate into a linear structure, thus preserving the advantages of the binary search algorithm.

7.3.1 Unbalanced Binary Search Trees

Unbalanced binary search trees can take various shapes, leading to inefficient operations. Below are common shapes of unbalanced BSTs.

Skewed Trees

A skewed tree is a degenerate form of a binary tree where each node has only one child. This can happen when elements are inserted in a strictly increasing or decreasing order.

In a right-skewed BST, all nodes have only a right child, forming a structure similar to a linked list, as shown in Figure 7.15. Conversely, a left-skewed BST, where each node has only a left child, forms when elements are inserted in decreasing order (Figure 7.16).

Sparse Trees

A sparse tree has nodes that are not uniformly distributed, leading to significant height differences between subtrees. This irregular shape can result from random insertions and deletions over time without rebalancing.

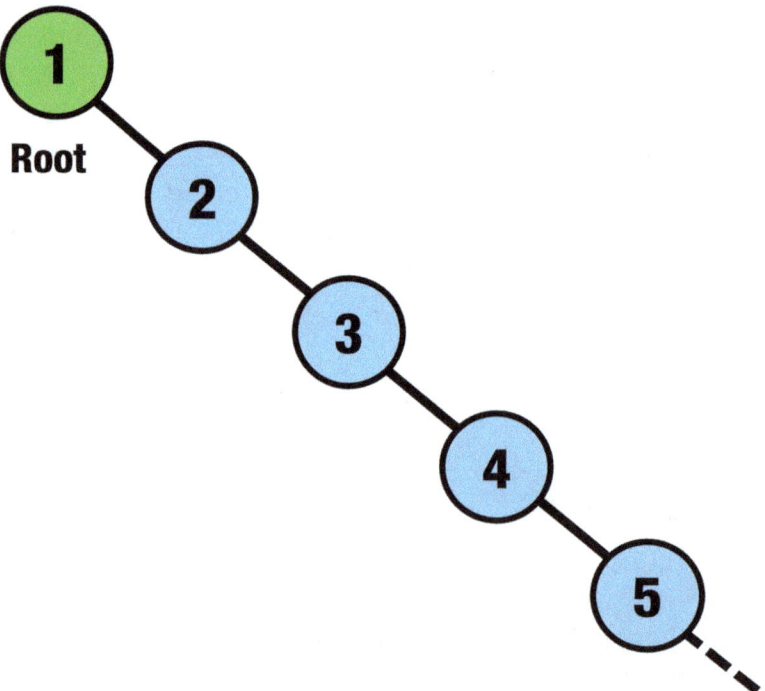

Figure 7.15: A right-skewed BST (inserting elements in increasing order)

Figures 7.15, 7.16, and 7.17 illustrate examples of unbalanced BSTs, highlighting how their structures can degrade operational efficiency. These unbalanced shapes emphasize the need for balancing techniques to maintain a low height and ensure efficient operations.

7.3.2 Self-Balancing Binary Search Trees

Self-balancing binary search trees are a category of BSTs designed to maintain a balanced structure, ensuring optimal time complexity for search, insertion, and deletion operations. By automatically balancing the tree after modifications, these trees prevent performance degradation that can occur with unbalanced BSTs.

7.3 Balanced Binary Trees

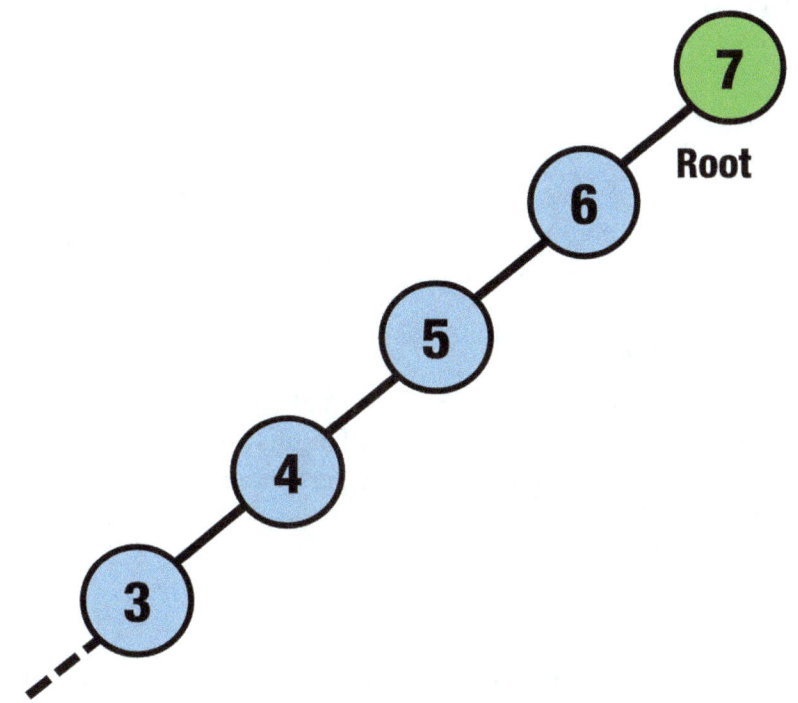

Figure 7.16: A left-skewed BST (inserting elements in decreasing order)

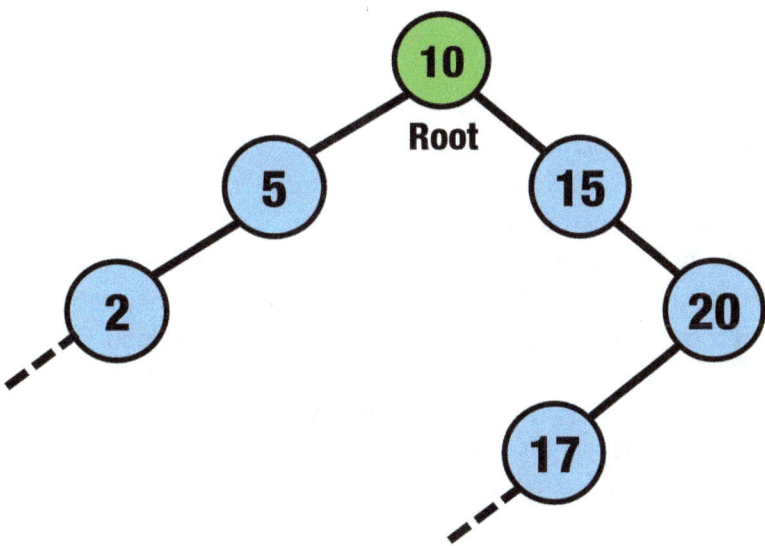

Figure 7.17: A sparse BST with irregular node distribution

In the next section, we will explore a type of balanced binary trees, such as AVL trees, which implement specific rules and rotations to maintain balance after every insertion and deletion.

7.4 AVL Trees

In this section, you will learn how to create an AVL tree class, understand the basic operations necessary for maintaining the AVL properties, and see how insertion and deletion operations are performed to keep the tree balanced.

7.4.1 Introduction to AVL Trees

AVL trees, named after their inventors **Adelson-Velsky** and **Landis**, are a type of self-balancing binary search tree. In AVL trees, the heights of the two child subtrees of any node differ by no more than one. *Rebalancing* is performed whenever this property is violated during insertions or deletions, ensuring that the tree remains balanced and operations remain efficient.

7.4.2 AVL Property

The AVL property is defined by the **balance factor** of a node, which is the difference in height between its right and left subtrees. The permissible balance factors for a node in an AVL tree are -1, 0, or 1, ensuring a balanced height across all nodes.

The defining characteristic of AVL trees is

> For any node N in an AVL tree, the absolute difference in heights between its left and right subtrees is at most one: $|N.Left.Height - N.Right.Height| \leq 1$.

This property guarantees the tree's balanced nature, allowing operations to run in logarithmic time.

Proof of AVL Balance Property

The AVL balance property ensures that the tree's height is logarithmic relative to its number of nodes. This can be demonstrated as follows:
- A node at height h in an AVL tree has a subtree of size at least $2^{h/2}$. Therefore, a tree of height h has a minimum number of nodes that grows exponentially with h.
- Inversely, if a tree contains n nodes, its height h is bounded by $h \leq 2\log_2(n)$, which is $O(\log(n))$.

This height-node relationship is fundamental to AVL trees' efficiency. Since the height of an AVL tree with n nodes is $O(\log(n))$, all basic operations, such as insertion, deletion, and searching, can be performed in $O(\log(n))$ time.

7.4.3 Balanced and Unbalanced AVL Trees

The following figures illustrate examples of balanced and unbalanced AVL trees, showing the height of the children at each node:
- Figure 7.18 represents a balanced AVL tree, where the height of the subtrees of each node differs by no more than one.
- Figure 7.19 illustrates a left-unbalanced AVL tree, where the height difference between the left and right subtrees of node 30 is more than one.
- Figure 7.20 shows a right-unbalanced AVL tree, where the height difference between the right and left subtrees of node 30 is more than one.

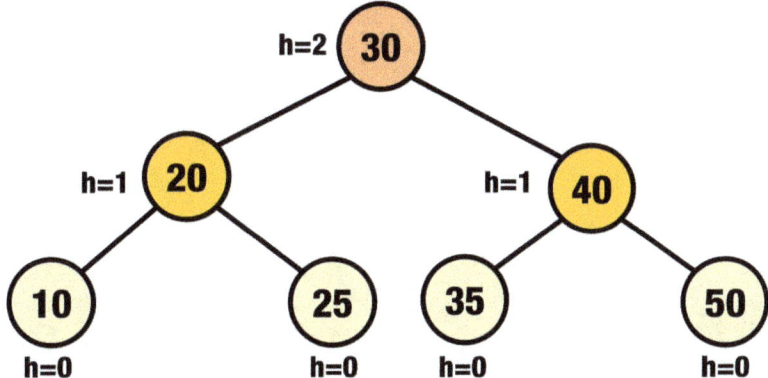

Figure 7.18: A balanced AVL tree. The height of the subtrees of each node differs by no more than one

7.4.4 Rotations in AVL Trees

To maintain balance, AVL trees perform rotations when the balance factor of a node becomes −2 or 2. There are **four** types of rotations used to rebalance the tree:
- **Left Rotation (LR):** Applied when the right subtree is taller than the left subtree
- **Right Rotation (RR):** Applied when the left subtree is taller than the right subtree
- **Left-Right Rotation (LRR):** A combination of left and right rotations used when the left subtree's right child is taller
- **Right-Left Rotation (RLR):** A combination of right and left rotations used when the right subtree's left child is taller

Left Rotation

A left rotation (LR) is applied when the right subtree is taller than the left subtree. This operation moves the root of the right subtree to the root position, and the original root becomes the left child of the new root (Figure 7.21). The steps for a left rotation are as follows:

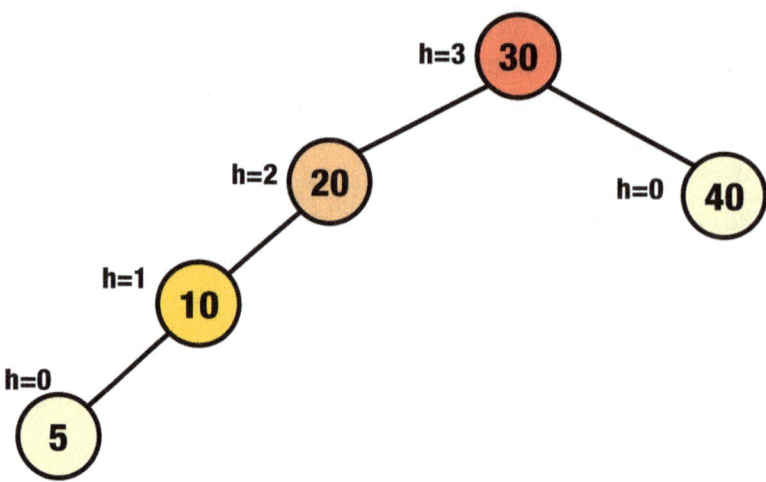

Figure 7.19: A left-unbalanced AVL tree. The height difference between the left and right subtrees of node 30 is more than one

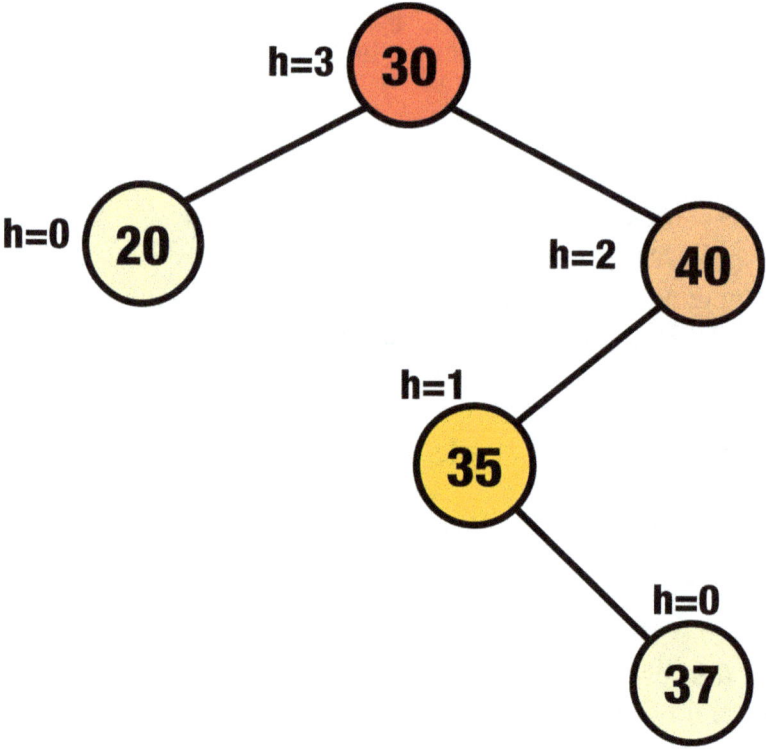

Figure 7.20: A right-unbalanced AVL tree. The height difference between the right and left subtrees of node 30 is more than one

7.4 AVL Trees

1. The right child of *x*, denoted as *y*, becomes the new root.
2. The left child of *y*, denoted as *z*, becomes the right child of *x*.
3. *x* becomes the left child of *y*.
4. Update the right child of *x* to be *z*.
5. Update the heights of *x* and *y*.

```
template<typename T>
BTreeNode<T>* AVLTree<T>::leftRotate(BTreeNode<T>* x) {
    // (1) The right child of x, pointer as y
    BTreeNode<T>* y = x->right;
    // (2) The left child of y, pointer as z
    BTreeNode<T>* z = y->left;
    // (3) x becomes the left child of y
    y->left = x;
    // (4) Update the right child of x to be z
    x->right = z;
    // (5) Update the heights of x and y
    updateHeight(x);
    updateHeight(y);
    // Return new root
    return y;
}
```

`leftRotate` Function: Performs Left Rotation in an `AVLTree`

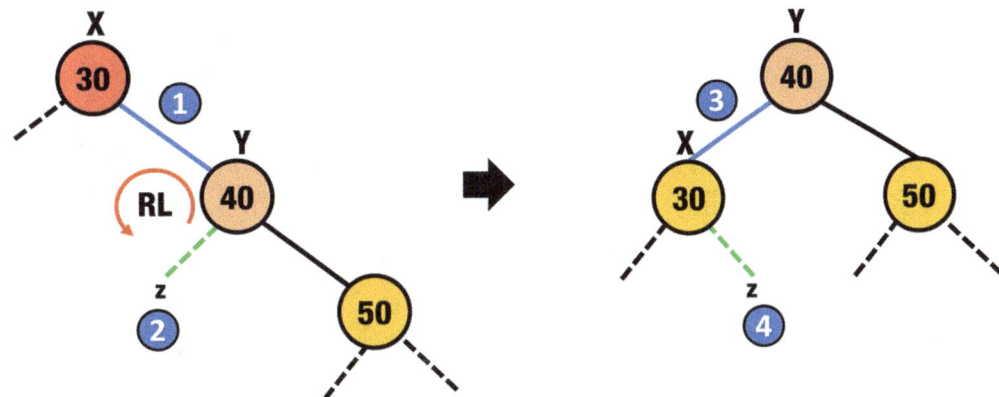

Figure 7.21: Left rotation: applied when the right subtree is taller than the left subtree

Right Rotation

A right rotation (RR) is applied when the left subtree is taller than the right subtree. This operation moves the root of the left subtree to the root position, and the original root becomes the right child of the new root (Figure 7.22). The steps for a right rotation are as follows:

1. The left child of *y*, denoted as *x*, becomes the new root.
2. The right child of *x*, denoted as *z*, becomes the left child of *y*.
3. *y* becomes the right child of *x*.
4. Update the left child of *y* to be *z*.
5. Update the heights of *y* and *x*.

```
template<typename T>
BTreeNode<T>* AVLTree<T>::rightRotate(BTreeNode<T>* y) {
    // (1) The left child of y, pointer as x
    BTreeNode<T>* x = y->left;
    // (2) The right child of x, pointer as z
    BTreeNode<T>* z = x->right;
    // (3) y becomes the right child of x
    x->right = y;
    // (4) Update the left child of y to be z
    y->left = z;
    // (5) Update the heights of y and x
    updateHeight(y);
    updateHeight(x);
    // Return new root
    return x;
}
```

`rightRotate` Function: Performs Right Rotation in an `AVLTree`

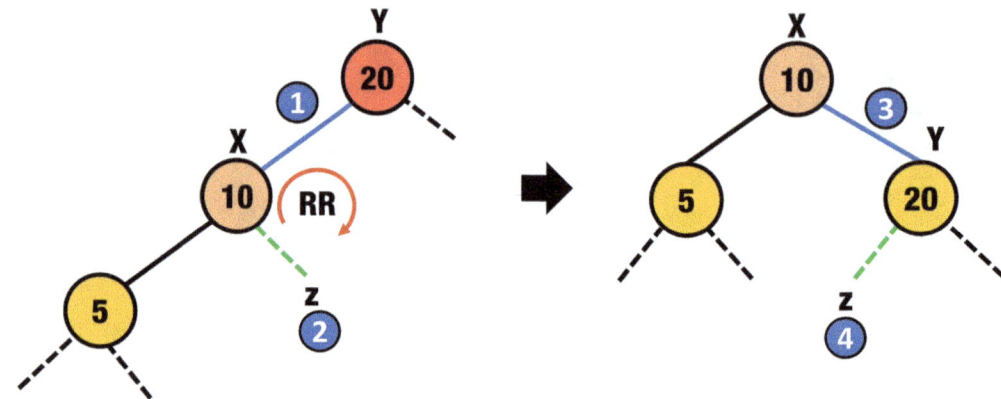

Figure 7.22: Right rotation: applied when the left subtree is taller than the right subtree

Left-Right Rotation

A left-right rotation (LRR) is a combination of left and right rotations used when the left subtree's right child is taller. This operation first performs a left rotation on the left child,

7.4 AVL Trees

then a right rotation on the root (Figure 7.23). The steps for a left-right rotation are as follows:
1. Perform a left rotation (LR) on the left child of the root.
2. Perform a right rotation (RR) on the root.

```
1 template<typename T>
2 BTreeNode<T>* AVLTree<T>::leftRightRotate(BTreeNode<T>* u) {
3     // (1) Perform a LR on the left child of the root
4     u->left = leftRotate(u->left);
5     // (2) Perform a RR on the root
6     return rightRotate(u);
7 }
```

`leftRightRotate` Function: Performs Left-Right Rotation in an `AVLTree`

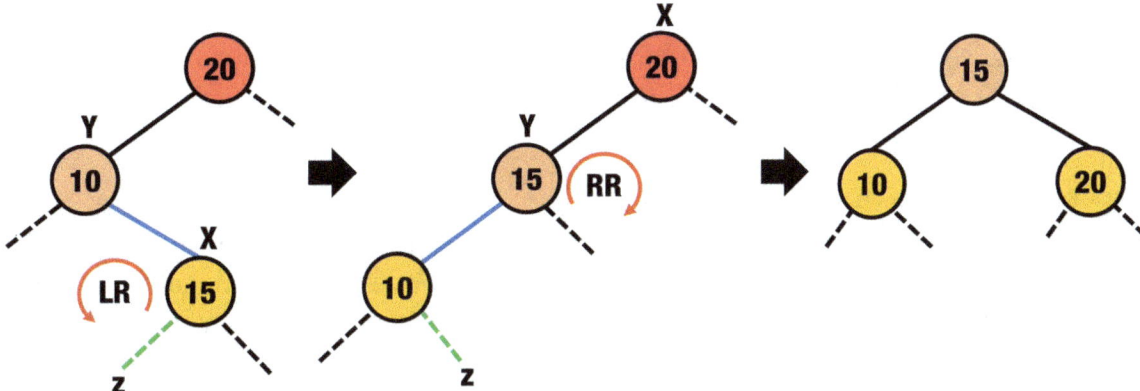

Figure 7.23: Left-right rotation: a combination of left and right rotations used when the left subtree's right child is taller

Right-Left Rotation

A right-left rotation (RLR) is a combination of right and left rotations used when the right subtree's left child is taller. This operation first performs a right rotation on the right child, then a left rotation on the root (Figure 7.24). The steps for a right-left rotation are as follows:
1. Perform a right rotation on the right child of the root.
2. Perform a left rotation on the root.

```
1 template<typename T>
2 BTreeNode<T>* AVLTree<T>::rightLeftRotate(BTreeNode<T>* u) {
3     // (1) Perform a RR on the right child of the root
4     u->right = rightRotate(u->right);
5     // (2) Perform a LR on the root
```

```
6        return leftRotate(u);
7    }
```

rightLeftRotate Function: Performs Right-Left Rotation in an AVLTree

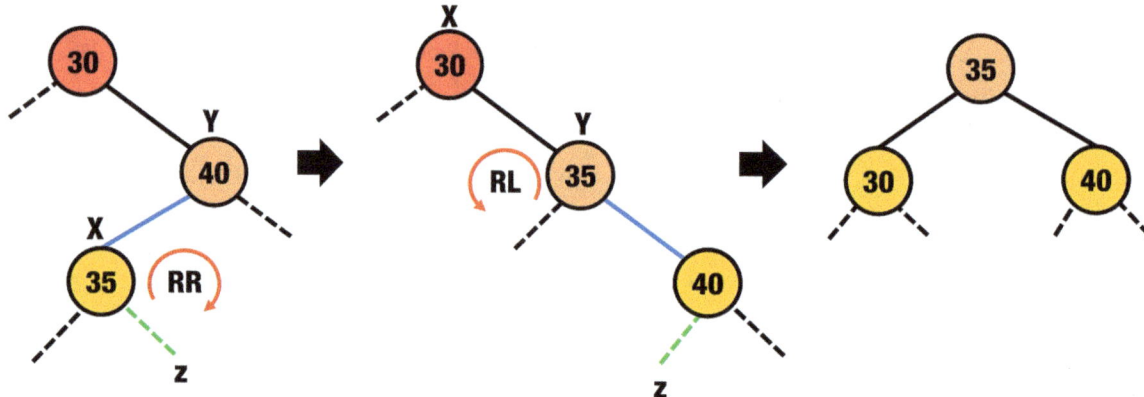

Figure 7.24: Right-left rotation: a combination of right and left rotations used when the right subtree's left child is taller

7.4.5 Implementation of AVL Tree

Let's begin by defining our AVLTree class. This class will inherit from the BinarySearchTree class, which already provides basic BST functionalities such as insertion, deletion, and searching. The AVL tree implementation enhances these operations by ensuring the tree remains balanced after every insertion or deletion.

AVL Tree Class Definition

```
1  template<typename T=int>
2  class AVLTree : public BinarySearchTree<T> {
3  public:
4      AVLTree() : BinarySearchTree<T>() {}
5      virtual ~AVLTree() { }
6
7      // Override interface methods from the base class
8      virtual bool remove(const T);
9      virtual bool insert(const T);
10     virtual void print() const
11     {
12         this->inOrderTraversal(this->root);
13     }
14
15 private:
16     // Rotation methods for balancing the tree
```

7.4 AVL Trees

```
17      BTreeNode<T>* rightRotate(BTreeNode<T>* u);
18      BTreeNode<T>* leftRotate(BTreeNode<T>* u);
19      BTreeNode<T>* leftRightRotate(BTreeNode<T>* u);
20      BTreeNode<T>* rightLeftRotate(BTreeNode<T>* u);
21      BTreeNode<T>* balanceTree(BTreeNode<T>* u);
22
23      // Insertion and deletion methods with balancing
24      BTreeNode<T>* insertAVL(BTreeNode<T>* u, T key);
25      BTreeNode<T>* deleteAVL(BTreeNode<T>* u, T key);
26
27  protected:
28      using BinarySearchTree<T>::root;
29
30      // Utility methods to manage node heights and balance
31      void updateHeight(BTreeNode<T>* node);
32      int getBalance(BTreeNode<T>* node) const;
33  };
```

`AVLTree` Class Interface

Basic Operations

The following basic operations are essential for maintaining the AVL tree properties: determining the balance factor of a node, updating the height of a node, and balancing the tree after insertions or deletions.

Determining Balance Factor

The balance factor of a node is the difference in heights between the left and right subtrees. It helps in determining whether the node is balanced.

```
1  template<typename T>
2  int AVLTree<T>::getBalance(BTreeNode<T>* u) const {
3      if (u == nullptr) return 0;
4      return this->height(u->left) - this->height(u->right);
5  }
```

`getBalance` Function: Calculates Balance Factor in an `AVLTree`

Updating Height

The height of a node is updated based on the heights of its left and right children. This is essential after insertion and deletion operations.

```
1  template<typename T>
2  void AVLTree<T>::updateHeight(BTreeNode<T>* u) {
3      if (u != nullptr) {
```

```
4            u->height = 1 + std::max(height(u->left),
5                                     height(u->right));
6        }
7 }
```

updateHeight Function: Updates the Height of a Node in an `AVLTree`

Balancing the AVL Tree

Balancing the AVL tree involves performing rotations to maintain the AVL property, which ensures that the tree remains balanced after insertions or deletions. The `balanceTree` function is responsible for this process.

Steps for Balancing

1. Get the balance factor of the node.
2. If the balance factor indicates the tree is unbalanced, perform the necessary rotation:
    - Right rotation if the left subtree is taller and unbalanced.
    - Left rotation if the right subtree is taller and unbalanced.
    - Left-right rotation if the left subtree's right child is taller.
    - Right-left rotation if the right subtree's left child is taller.

```
1  template<typename T>
2  BTreeNode<T>* AVLTree<T>::balanceTree(BTreeNode<T>* u) {
3      int balance = getBalance(u);
4
5      if (balance > 1) {
6          // Left subtree is taller
7          if (getBalance(u->left) >= 0) {
8              return rightRotate(u);
9          } else {
10             return leftRightRotate(u);
11         }
12     } else if (balance < -1) {
13         // Right subtree is taller
14         if (getBalance(u->right) <= 0) {
15             return leftRotate(u);
16         } else {
17             return rightLeftRotate(u);
18         }
19     }
20     return u;
21 }
```

`balanceTree` Function: Balances the Nodes in an `AVLTree`

7.4 AVL Trees

Insertion in AVL Trees

Insertion in an AVL tree follows the same steps as in a binary search tree (BST), with the additional step of updating the balance factors and performing rotations to maintain balance.

Steps for Insertion
1. Perform standard BST insertion.
2. Update the height of the ancestor node.
3. Get the balance factor of the ancestor node to check if it became unbalanced.
4. If unbalanced, perform the appropriate rotation.

```cpp
template<typename T>
BTreeNode<T>* AVLTree<T>::
    insertAVL(BTreeNode<T>* u, T key) {

    // Step 1: Perform standard BST insertion
    if (u == nullptr) {
        return new BTreeNode<T>(key);
    }

    if (key < u->key) {
        u->left = insertAVL(u->left, key);
    } else if (key > u->key) {
        u->right = insertAVL(u->right, key);
    } else {
        // Duplicate keys are not allowed
        return u;
    }

    // Step 2: Update the height of the current node
    updateHeight(u);

    // Step 3: Check and Balance the tree
    return balanceTree(u);
}

template<typename T>
bool AVLTree<T>::insert(const T key) {
    root = insertAVL(root, key);
    return true;
}
```

`insert` Functions: Insertion and Balancing in an `AVLTree`

Deletion in AVL Trees

Deletion in an AVL tree also follows the same path as in a BST, with balance factor updates and rotations to maintain the AVL property.

Steps for Deletion
1. Perform standard BST deletion.
2. Update the height of the ancestor node.
3. Get the balance factor of the ancestor node to check if it became unbalanced.
4. If unbalanced, perform the appropriate rotation.

```cpp
template<typename T>
BTreeNode<T>* AVLTree<T>::
    deleteAVL(BTreeNode<T>* root, T key) {

    if (root == nullptr) return root;

    // Step 1: Perform standard BST deletion
    if (key < root->key) {
        root->left = deleteAVL(root->left, key);
    } else if (key > root->key) {
        root->right = deleteAVL(root->right, key);
    } else {
        // Node with only one child or no child
        if (root->left == nullptr ||
                root->right == nullptr) {
            BTreeNode<T>* temp = root->left ?
                        root->left : root->right;
            if (temp == nullptr) {
                // No child case
                temp = root;
                root = nullptr;
            } else {
                // One child case
                *root = *temp;
            }
            delete temp;
        } else {
            // Node with two children
            // Get the inorder successor
            BTreeNode<T>* temp = this->findMin(root->right);
            root->key = temp->key;
            root->right = deleteAVL(root->right, temp->key);
        }
    }

```

```
36        if (root == nullptr) return root;
37
38        // Step 2: Update the height of the current node
39        updateHeight(root);
40
41        // Step 3: Check and balance the tree
42        return balanceTree(root);
43 }
44
45 template<typename T>
46 bool AVLTree<T>::remove(const T key) {
47     size_t initialSize = this->getSize();
48     root = deleteAVL(root, key);
49     return this->getSize() < initialSize;
50 }
```

remove Functions: Deletion and Balancing in an AVLTree

7.4.6 Performance Analysis

The performance of basic operations in an AVL tree (insertion, deletion, and searching) depends on the height of the tree (h). Since AVL trees are balanced, the height is $O(\log n)$, where n is the number of nodes in the tree. Therefore, the time complexity for insertion, searching, and deletion operations is $O(\log n)$.

7.5 Summary

In this chapter, we delved into the world of binary trees, specifically focusing on binary search trees (BSTs) and AVL trees. We started with an introduction to binary trees, discussing their structure, properties, and various types. Then, we moved on to the basic operations in BSTs, including insertion, deletion, and searching, emphasizing how these operations ensure that the BST remains ordered and efficient for data manipulation.

We then examined AVL trees, a type of self-balancing binary search tree. AVL trees automatically maintain their balance through rotations, ensuring that the height difference between the left and right subtrees of any node is no more than one. This balancing act guarantees that all basic operations – such as insertion, deletion, and searching – are performed in logarithmic time, enhancing the tree's overall efficiency.

A key part of this chapter was the comparison between balanced and unbalanced trees. We discussed how unbalanced BSTs can degrade to a linear structure, similar to linked lists, resulting in inefficient operations with time complexities of $O(n)$ for insertion, deletion, and searching. Conversely, AVL trees maintain their balance, ensuring that the tree's height remains logarithmic in relation to the number of nodes, which results in $O(\log n)$ time complexity for all basic operations, thereby significantly improving performance.

Lastly, we implemented the AVL tree class, demonstrating its inheritance structure. The AVL tree class inherits from the `BinarySearchTree` class, which in turn inherits from the `BinaryTree` class. The `BinaryTree` class itself inherits from the `ITree` interface and includes a root node of type `BTreeNode<T>`. This structure enables the AVL tree to efficiently manage tree operations while maintaining balance, providing a robust solution for dynamic data storage and retrieval.

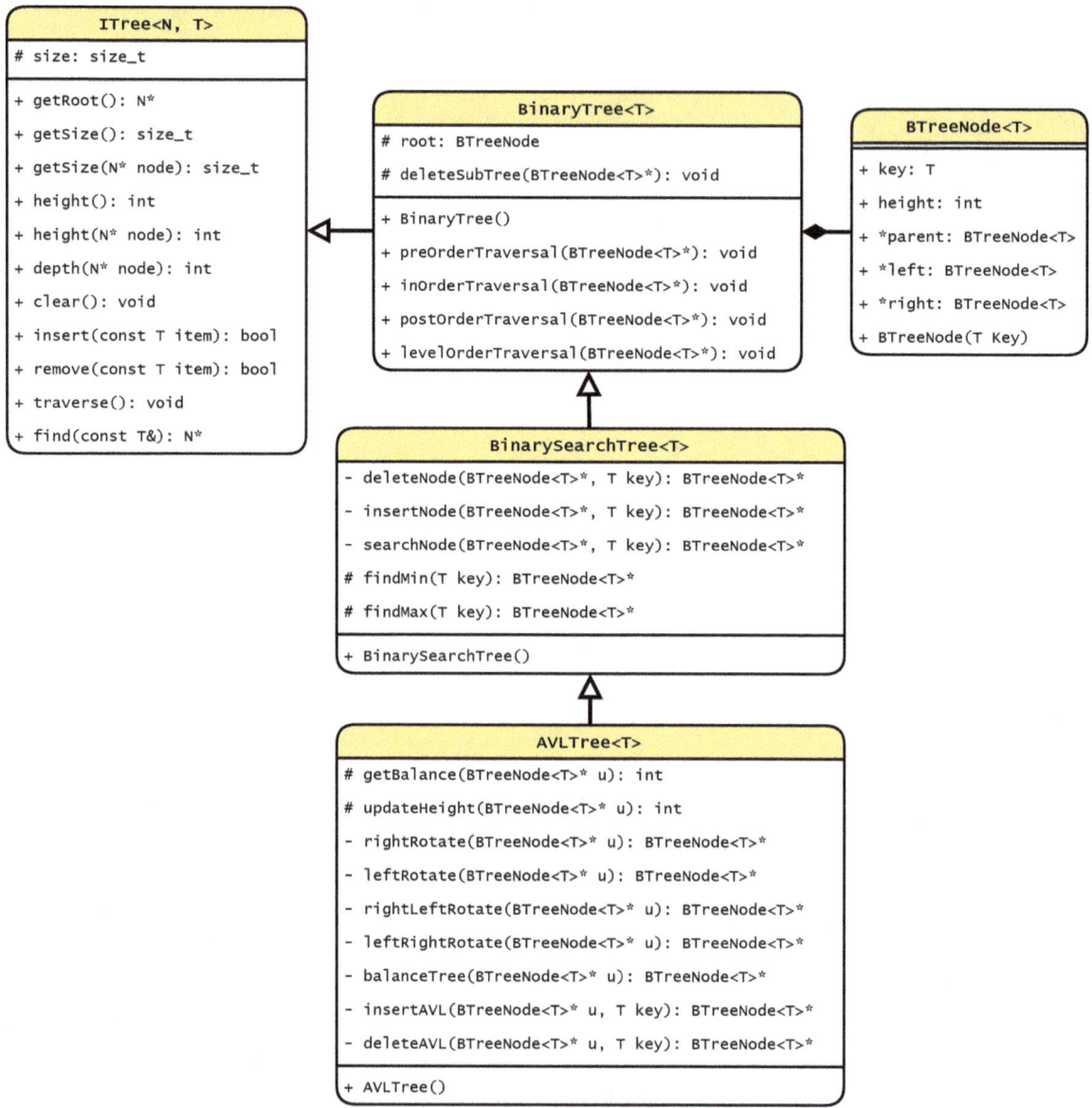

Figure 7.25: Class diagram for AVL tree implementations. This diagram illustrates the inheritance relationships between `AVLTree`, `BinarySearchTree`, `BinaryTree`, and `ITree` classes

The class diagram in Figure 7.25 provides an overview of the AVL tree implementation discussed in this chapter, highlighting the relationships and interactions between the various components. This diagram underscores the hierarchical structure that allows AVL trees to maintain balance and ensure efficient performance.

7.5 Summary

Problems

Discussion

1. What is a binary search tree (BST)? Describe the fundamental structure and properties of a BST.
2. How do In-Order, Pre-order, Post-Order, and Level-Order traversals differ in a binary search tree? Compare these traversal methods in terms of their order of visiting nodes and their typical applications in BSTs.
3. How does the insertion operation work in a BST? Explain the steps involved in inserting a new element into a BST.
4. What are the challenges associated with an unbalanced BST? Discuss how an unbalanced BST can affect the performance of search operations.
5. How do AVL trees ensure balance? Describe the mechanism AVL trees use to maintain balance after insertions and deletions.
6. What is the balance factor in an AVL tree, and what are its permissible values? Explain the concept of balance factor and its importance in AVL trees.
7. Describe the process of searching for a value in a BST.
8. What are the different scenarios for the deletion operation in a BST? Explain how deletion is handled in the cases of a leaf node, a node with one child, and a node with two children.
9. How does the balance property of AVL trees contribute to their efficiency?
10. In the context of BSTs, compare and contrast insertion, deletion, and searching in terms of their complexity. Discuss how these operations differ in terms of their execution and complexity.
11. Why are balancing techniques important in BSTs, particularly in AVL trees? Explain the role of balancing techniques in maintaining the efficiency of BST operations.
12. **Insertion and Deletion in BSTs:** Given the following sequence of numbers: 15, 10, 20, 8, 12, 17, 25, insert them into an initially empty BST. Then, delete the node with value 10 and provide the resulting tree.
13. **Balancing an AVL Tree:** Insert the following sequence of numbers into an initially empty AVL tree: 30, 20, 40, 10, 25, 35, 50, 5. Show the tree after each insertion and the necessary rotations to maintain balance.

Multiple Choice Questions

1. What property must be satisfied by all nodes in a binary search tree (BST)?
    (a) Each node must have exactly two children.
    (b) The left child's value is always greater than its parent's value.
    (c) The left child's value is less than its parent's, and the right child's value is greater.
    (d) Each node must have at least one child.

2. Which traversal method visits the left subtree, the node, and then the right subtree in that order?
   (a) Pre-order Traversal
   (b) Post-Order Traversal
   (c) In-Order Traversal
   (d) Level-Order Traversal
3. What is the height of a node in a binary tree?
   (a) The number of edges from the root to the node
   (b) The number of edges on the longest path from the node to a leaf
   (c) The total number of descendants of the node
   (d) The number of edges from the node to the deepest leaf
4. In AVL trees, what is the maximum allowable difference in heights of the left and right subtrees of any node?
   (a) 0
   (b) 1
   (c) 2
   (d) There is no specific limit.
5. Which type of traversal in a binary tree visits all the nodes at a given depth level before moving to the next level?
   (a) In-Order Traversal
   (b) Pre-order Traversal
   (c) Post-Order Traversal
   (d) Level-Order Traversal
6. What does the size of a binary tree represent?
   (a) The height of the tree
   (b) The depth of the deepest node
   (c) The number of nodes in the tree
   (d) The number of leaf nodes
7. When deleting a node with two children in a BST, what node is typically used to replace the deleted node?
   (a) The leftmost child of the left subtree
   (b) The rightmost child of the right subtree
   (c) The inorder successor or predecessor
   (d) Any leaf node
8. What is a primary advantage of keeping a binary tree balanced?
   (a) Increases the number of leaf nodes
   (b) Enhances the visual appeal of the tree
   (c) Ensures all operations are performed in linear time
   (d) Optimizes search, insertion, and deletion operations to logarithmic time
9. In a balanced binary tree, what is the relationship between the number of nodes (n) and the height (h) of the tree?
   (a) $h = n$
   (b) $h = \log_2(n)$
   (c) $h = n^2$
   (d) $h = 2^n$

7.5 Summary

10. Which of the following best describes the Pre-order Traversal in a binary tree?
    (a) Visits the node, then the left subtree, and finally the right subtree
    (b) Visits the left subtree, then the node, and finally the right subtree
    (c) Visits the left subtree, then the right subtree, and finally the node
    (d) Visits nodes level by level, from left to right
11. What is the balance factor of a node in an AVL tree?
    (a) The difference between the heights of its left and right subtrees
    (b) The number of nodes in its left and right subtrees
    (c) The depth of the node in the tree
    (d) The height of the node in the tree
12. What happens if the balance factor of a node in an AVL tree is outside the range [−1, 1]?
    (a) The tree remains unchanged.
    (b) The node is removed from the tree.
    (c) The tree is rebalanced using rotations.
    (d) The tree is converted into a linked list.
13. Which of the following is a self-balancing binary search tree?
    (a) Binary tree
    (b) Binary search tree
    (c) AVL tree
    (d) Linked list
14. What type of rotation is performed when the right subtree is taller than the left subtree and a new node is inserted into the right subtree of the right child?
    (a) Left rotation
    (b) Right rotation
    (c) Left-right rotation
    (d) Right-left rotation
15. What is the time complexity of insertion in an AVL tree?
    (a) $O(1)$
    (b) $O(n)$
    (c) $O(\log n)$
    (d) $O(n \log n)$
16. Which of the following operations is not directly affected by the balance factor of a node in an AVL tree?
    (a) Insertion
    (b) Deletion
    (c) Searching
    (d) Rotations

Programming Problems

1. **Find Kth Smallest Element:** Implement a function to find the kth smallest element in a BST, and analyze its complexity. Consider both recursive and iterative approaches.
2. **Range Sum Query:** Implement a function to calculate the sum of all nodes' values within a given range $[L, R]$ in a BST, and analyze its complexity. Discuss the efficiency of your approach.
3. **Validate BST:** Implement a function to check if a given binary tree is a valid BST, and analyze its complexity. Explain the approach used for validation.
4. **Find Closest Element:** Implement a function to find the value in a BST that is closest to a given target, and analyze its complexity. Discuss how your implementation handles ties.
5. **Inorder Predecessor and Successor:** Implement functions to find the inorder predecessor and successor of a given node in a BST. Provide the theoretical time complexity of each function.
6. **Merge Two BSTs:** Implement a function to merge two BSTs into a single balanced BST. Analyze the complexity of your merging algorithm.
7. **Count Nodes in Range:** Implement a function to count the number of nodes within a given range $[L, R]$ in a BST. Analyze the time complexity of your solution.
8. **Convert BST to Greater Sum Tree:** Implement a function to convert a BST into a Greater Sum Tree, where each node contains the sum of all nodes greater than itself. Analyze the complexity of your algorithm.
9. **Find Lowest Common Ancestor:** Implement a function to find the lowest common ancestor (LCA) of two nodes in a BST. Provide an analysis of the time complexity.
10. **Check AVL Property:** Implement a function to check if a given BST is also an AVL tree (i.e., it is balanced). Analyze the complexity of your function.
11. **Balance Factor Calculation:** Implement a function to calculate and print the balance factor of each node in an AVL tree. Discuss the time complexity of your implementation.
12. **Depth of Deepest Odd Level Leaf:** Implement a function to find the depth of the deepest odd level leaf node in a BST. Analyze the complexity of your solution.
13. **Convert Sorted Array to BST:** Implement a function to convert a sorted array into a height-balanced BST. Analyze the time complexity of the conversion process.
14. **Maximum Path Sum:** Implement a function to find the maximum path sum in a BST. The path can start and end at any node. Provide a complexity analysis of your solution.
15. **Find Nodes at K Distance:** Implement a function to find all nodes at distance K from a given target node in a BST. Analyze the time complexity of your algorithm.

8. Graphs

Objectives

In this chapter, we will explore the versatile and powerful world of graph data structures. Graphs are essential for modeling relationships and connections in various domains. By the end of this chapter, you will have a comprehensive understanding of graph structures and their practical applications. Here's what you can look forward to:

1. **Fundamentals of Graphs:** We will start with the basic concepts and terminology associated with graphs. You will understand the significance of vertices, edges, and the different types of graphs, such as directed, undirected, weighted, and unweighted.
2. **Graph Representations:** Learn about various ways to represent graphs, including adjacency matrices and adjacency lists. You will discover how to implement essential operations on graphs, such as adding and removing vertices and edges efficiently, and understand their impact on the graph structure.
3. **Graph Traversal Techniques:** We will delve into Depth-First Search (DFS) and Breadth-First Search (BFS), two fundamental algorithms for exploring graphs. You will learn how these algorithms work, their applications, and how to implement them.

4. **Advanced Graph Operations:** Explore more complex graph operations, including checking connectivity and performing path existence queries. These operations are crucial for many real-world applications and algorithms.
5. **Performance Analysis:** Finally, you will analyze the performance of different graph representations and operations. We will discuss the time and space complexity of various algorithms and provide guidelines for optimizing graph-related tasks.

8.1 Introduction to Graphs

In this section, we introduce graphs, a fundamental data structure used to model pairwise relations between objects. A graph G is defined as a set of vertices V and a set of edges E, where each edge connects two vertices.

8.1.1 What Is a Graph?

A graph G can be represented as $G = (V, E)$, where
- V is a finite set of vertices.
- E is a finite set of edges.

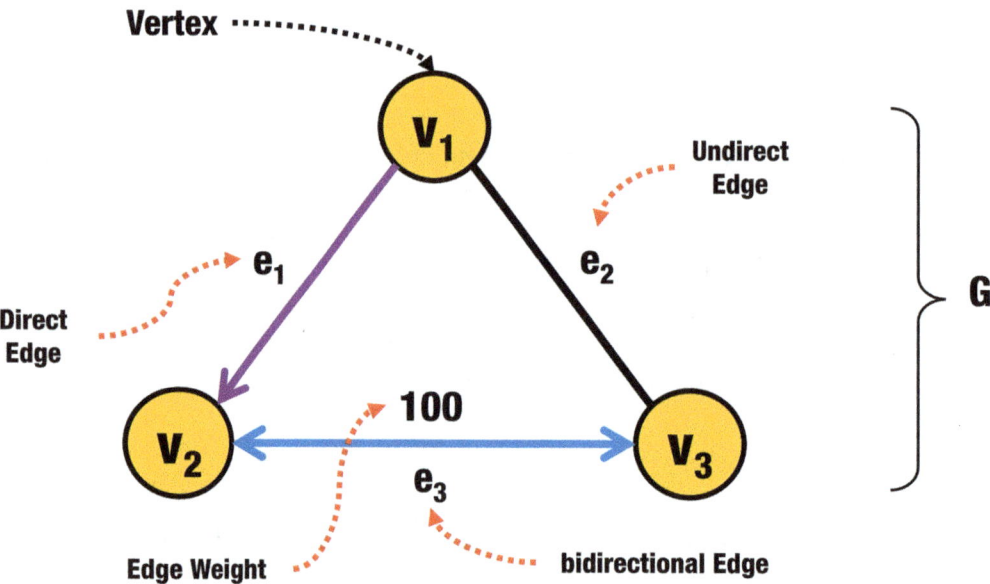

Figure 8.1: Graph with three vertices, v_1, v_2, v_3, and three types of edges: e_1 is directed, e_2 is undirected, and e_3 is bidirectional weighted

As shown in Figure 8.1, a graph consists of vertices and edges, which can have various properties such as direction and weight. These properties, including the distinctions between directed, undirected, and bidirectional edges, will be discussed in detail in the following subsection.

8.1 Introduction to Graphs

8.1.2 Graph Terminology

Graph terminology includes the following key terms and properties:

Terms
- **Vertices (Nodes):** The fundamental units represented as points or circles in a graph. A vertex can represent a physical object, concept, or abstract entity. In Figure 8.1, v_1, v_2, and v_3 are vertices.
- **Edges (Links):** The connections between vertices, represented as lines connecting pairs of vertices. Edges can be directed, undirected, or bidirectional. In Figure 8.1, e_1 is a directed edge from v_1 to v_2, e_2 is an undirected edge between v_1 and v_3, and e_3 is a bidirectional weighted edge between v_2 and v_3.
- **Weight:** A value assigned to an edge, representing the cost or distance between vertices. In Figure 8.1, the edge e_3 has an associated weight.
- **Degree:** The number of edges incident to a vertex. In Figure 8.1, the degree of v_1 is 2 (edges e_1 and e_2).
- **Path:** A sequence of edges that connect a sequence of vertices. For example, in Figure 8.1, $v_1 \to v_2 \to v_3$ forms a path.
- **Cycle:** A path that starts and ends at the same vertex with no other repetitions of vertices and edges. An example cycle in Figure 8.1 is $v_1 \to v_2 \to v_3 \to v_1$ if such edges exist.

Properties
- **Connectedness:** A graph is connected if there is a path between any pair of vertices (see Figure 8.2(1)).
- **Planarity:** A graph is planar if it can be drawn on a plane without any edges crossing (see Figure 8.2(2)).
- **Bipartiteness:** A graph is bipartite if its vertices can be divided into two disjoint sets such that no two vertices within the same set are adjacent (see Figure 8.2(3)).

8.1.3 Types of Graphs

Using graphs, you can model a variety of relationships. Graphs can be classified into several types based on their properties:
- **Directed Graphs:** These graphs model one-way relationships where edges have a direction, indicating the relationship flows from one vertex to another.
- **Undirected Graphs:** Represent two-way relationships where edges have no direction, signifying mutual connections.

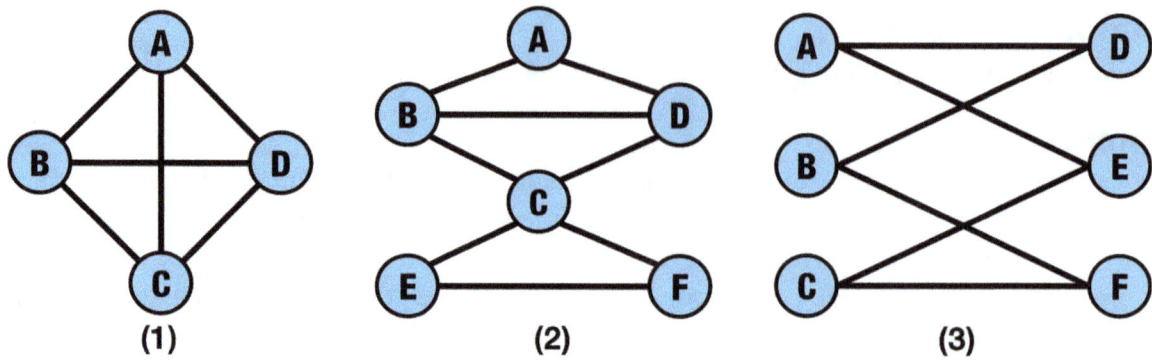

Figure 8.2: Graph properties: (1) Example of a connected graph. This graph shows four vertices A, B, C, and D with paths between each pair of vertices. (2) Example of a planar graph. This graph demonstrates six vertices A, B, C, D, E, and F with edges that do not cross each other. (3) Example of a bipartite graph. This graph displays six vertices divided into two sets: A, B, C on the left and D, E, F on the right. Edges only connect vertices from one set to the other

- **Weighted Graphs:** By assigning weights to edges, these graphs model the cost or distance between vertices.
- **Unweighted Graphs:** These simpler models represent uniform cost or distance between vertices, with all edges treated equally.
- **Simple Graphs:** Simple graphs avoid loops and multiple edges between the same pair of vertices, creating straightforward structures.
- **Multigraphs:** Multigraphs allow multiple edges between the same vertices, representing complex or redundant connections.

Graph Density

Graphs can also be classified based on their density, which is the ratio of the number of edges to the number of possible edges:

- **Sparse Graph:** A graph with relatively few edges compared to the number of possible edges, meaning most vertices are connected to only a few other vertices (see Figure 8.3(1)).
- **Dense Graph:** A graph with a number of edges close to the maximum possible, which is $V(V-1)/2$ for an undirected graph or $V(V-1)$ for a directed graph, implying most vertices are connected to many other vertices (see Figure 8.3(2)).
- **Complete Graph:** A special case of a dense graph where every pair of distinct vertices is connected by a unique edge, representing the maximum edge density $V(V-1)/2$ for an undirected graph (see Figure 8.3(3)).

8.1 Introduction to Graphs

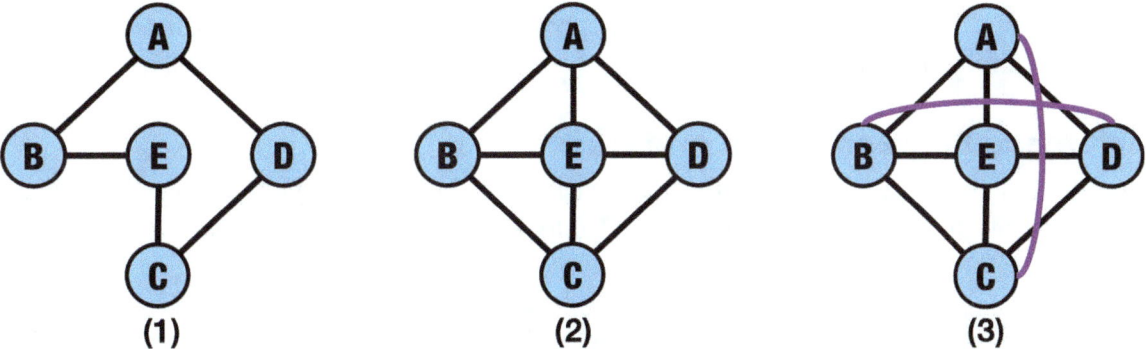

Figure 8.3: Graph density. (1) Sparse graph: Most vertices are connected to only a few other vertices. (2) Dense graph: Most vertices are connected to many other vertices. (3) Complete graph: Every pair of distinct vertices is connected by a unique edge

Understanding graph density helps in selecting the most appropriate data structure for representing a graph, optimizing performance for various graph operations.

8.1.4 Examples and Applications

Using graphs, you can solve various real-world problems:
- **Computer Networks:** Represent computers as nodes and network connections as edges to model network topologies.
- **Social Networks:** By representing individuals as nodes and their relationships as edges, you can analyze social structures.
- **Road Maps:** Model intersections as nodes and roads as edges to find the shortest paths or optimize routes.

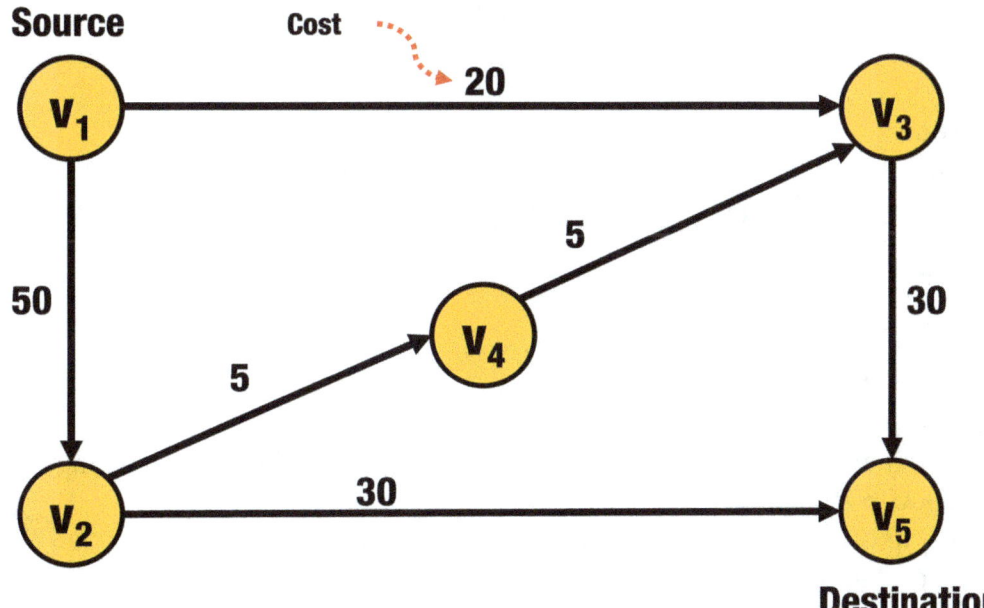

Figure 8.4: Example of a graph showing source, destination, and cost on every edge

As shown in Figure 8.4, graphs can represent various types of information such as source, destination, and cost.

8.1.5 Difference Between Graph and Tree

Graphs and trees are both important data structures but have key differences that make them suitable for different applications. Table 8.1 provides a comparison of their main differences.

In the next section, you will explore various ways to represent graphs, perform operations on them, and understand their applications in different domains.

8.2 Graph Representations

Graphs can be represented in several ways, each with its own advantages and disadvantages. The choice of representation affects the efficiency of graph operations such as traversal, insertion, and deletion. By understanding different representations, you can choose the most appropriate one for your specific use case.

In general, a graph can be stored as a 2D matrix. In the case of an unweighted graph, a 1 or 0 is used to represent the presence or absence of a connection between vertices. In the case of a weighted graph, a value w is used to represent the connection with weight.

Figure 8.5 shows a simple graph with its equivalent matrix representation.

Table 8.1: Key Differences Between Graph and Tree

Feature	Graph	Tree
Definition	A collection of vertices and edges	A hierarchical structure with nodes
Structure	Can have cycles	Acyclic (no cycles)
Connectedness	Not necessarily connected	Always connected
Edges	Can have multiple edges between nodes	Only one edge between nodes
Root Node	No root node	Has a root node
Relationship	General	Hierarchical
Examples	Computer networks, social networks	File system hierarchy, organizational chart

8.2.1 Basic Graph Operations

Below are the basic operations on graphs:
- **Addition of Nodes:** Adding a new vertex v to the graph involves updating the graph structure to include the new vertex.
- **Removal of Nodes:** Removing a vertex v involves deleting the vertex and all edges connected to it.

8.2 Graph Representations

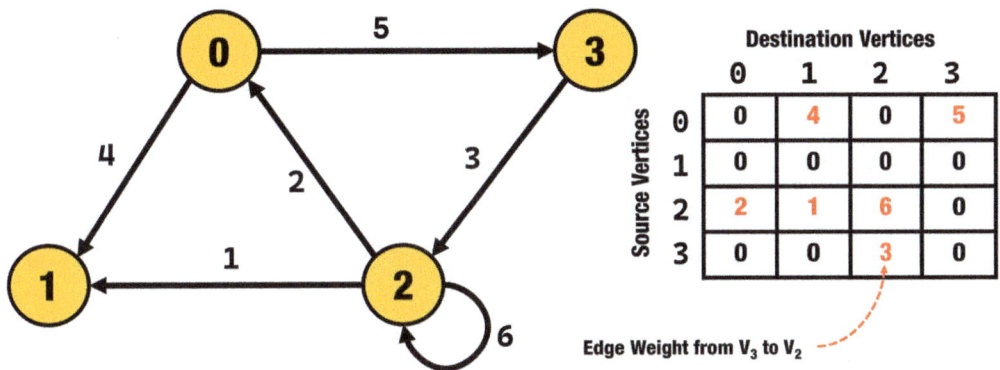

Figure 8.5: A simple graph with its equivalent matrix representation. The graph consists of vertices connected by edges with weights. The adjacency matrix on the right illustrates the connections between vertices, where non-zero values represent the weights of the edges

- **Addition of Edges:** Adding a new edge $e = (u,v)$ between two vertices involves updating the adjacency structure to reflect the new edge.
- **Removal of Edges:** Removing an existing edge $e = (u,v)$ involves updating the adjacency structure to remove the specified edge.
- **Searching:** Finding whether a particular vertex $v \in V$ or edge $e = (u,v) \in E$ exists in the graph.
- **Traversal:** Visiting all the vertices and edges in the graph, typically using Depth-First Search (DFS) or Breadth-First Search (BFS).
- **Pathfinding:** Determining a path $P = \{v_1, v_2, \ldots, v_k\}$ between two vertices v_1 and v_k.
- **Connectivity Checking:** Verifying if the graph is connected, i.e., if there is a path between any pair of vertices $u, v \in V$.

8.2.2 Abstract Interface for Graph Class

To ensure that different graph representations follow a consistent structure, we define an abstract interface called `IGraph`. This interface specifies the operations that any graph class should implement, providing a uniform way to interact with different graph representations.

In this interface, we use template parameters `L1` and `L2` to allow for flexible customization of the internal list structures. `L1` represents the outer list structure, and `L2` represents the inner list structure. By using these template parameters, different graph implementations can customize `L1` and `L2` as needed. For example, using `Array` with `L2` will represent an adjacency matrix, while using `Linked List` will represent an adjacency list.

The combination of `L1` and `L2` (i.e., `L1 × L2`) allows for flexible and efficient graph representations. The outer list `L1` represents all vertices (0 to $V - 1$), while the inner list `L2` represents the vertices connected to each vertex, as illustrated in Figure 8.6.

Figure 8.7 shows the UML class diagram that presents the structure of the `IGraph` interface.

```cpp
template <typename T,
    template <typename> class L1,
    template <typename> class L2>
class IGraph {
protected:
    L1<L2<T>*> graph;
    // Number of Vertices
    size_t V;
public:
    IGraph(size_t num_vertices) :
        V(num_vertices),
        graph(num_vertices) {}
    virtual ~IGraph() {}

    // Add/Remove a vertex
    virtual void addVertex() = 0;
    virtual void removeVertex(int i) = 0;

    // Add/Remove an edge between vertices i and j
    virtual void addEdge(int i, int j) = 0;
    virtual void removeEdge(int i, int j) = 0;

    // Check if there is an edge between two vertices
    virtual bool hasEdge(int i, int j) const = 0;

    // Get the number of edges in the graph
    virtual int edgeCount() const = 0;

    // Get a list of all integers j such i->j is an edge
    virtual L1<int> outEdges(int i) const = 0;

    // Get a list of all integers j such j->i is an edge
    virtual L1<int> inEdges(int i) const = 0;

    // Print the graph representation
    virtual void printGraph() const = 0;

    // Get the number of vertices in the graph
    int vertexCount() const;

    // Access the graph data structure
    const L1<L2<T>>& getGraph() const{
        return graph;
    }
```

8.2 Graph Representations

```
45
46      // Get the degree of a vertex
47      virtual int getDegree(int v) const;
48      virtual int getOutDegree(int v) const = 0;
49      virtual int getInDegree(int v) const = 0;
50 };
```
IGraph Abstract Interface Definition

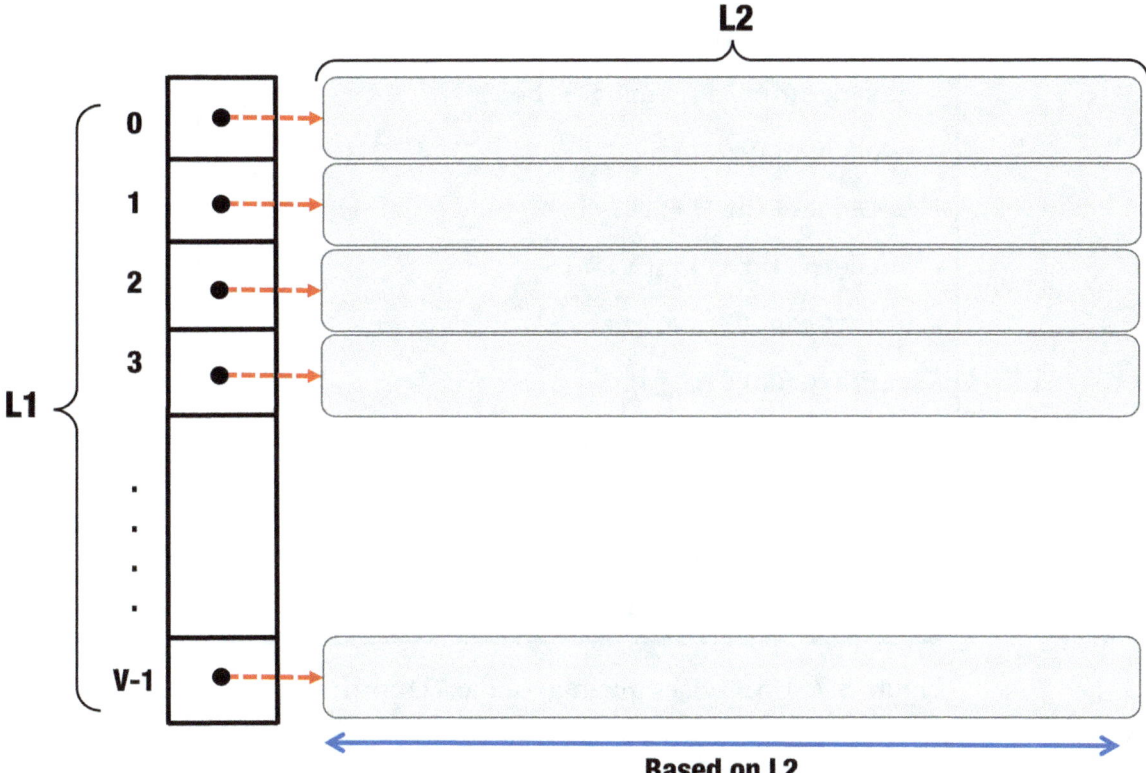

Figure 8.6: Illustration of L1 and L2 in a graph representation. The outer list (L1) represents all vertices, and the inner lists (L2) represent the vertices connected to each vertex. This structure allows for flexible customization of the internal list structures. For instance, L2 can be an Array or Linked List, facilitating the representation of graphs as adjacency matrices or adjacency lists, respectively

The IGraph interface defines the following virtual and pure functions:
- addVertex(): Adds a new vertex to the graph
- removeVertex(int i): Removes the vertex i and all its associated edges from the graph
- addEdge(int i, int j): Adds an edge between vertices i and j
- removeEdge(int i, int j): Removes the edge between vertices i and j
- hasEdge(int i, int j) const: Checks if there is an edge between vertices i and j

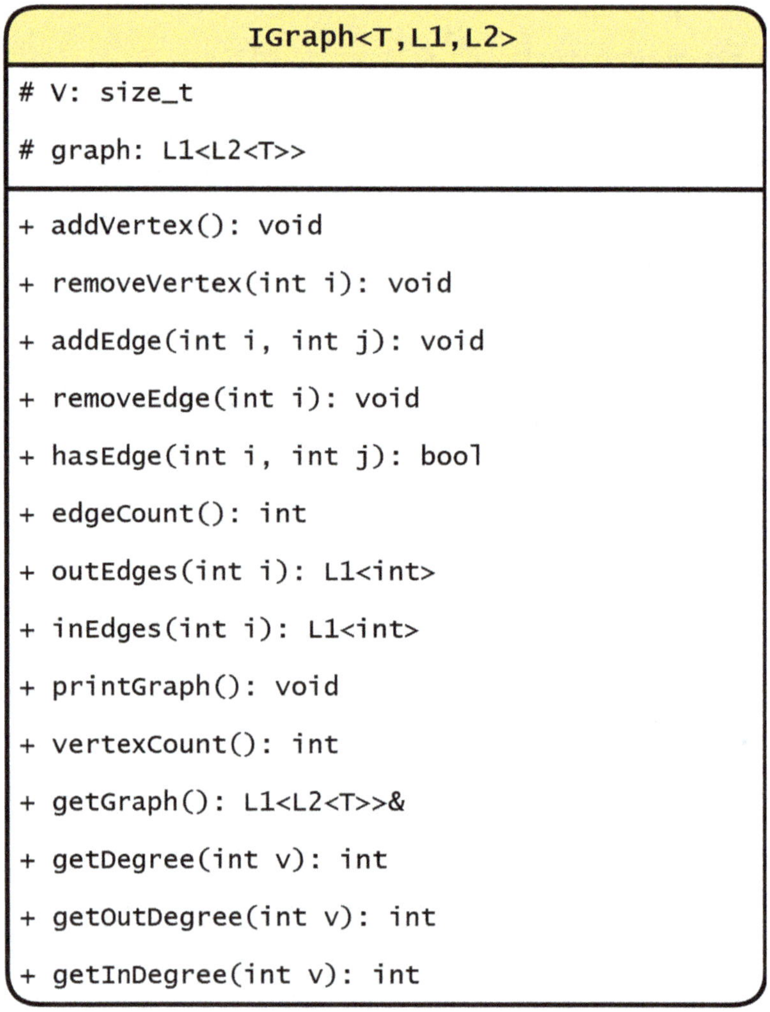

```
┌─────────────────────────────────────────┐
│           IGraph<T,L1,L2>               │
├─────────────────────────────────────────┤
│ # V: size_t                             │
│ # graph: L1<L2<T>>                      │
├─────────────────────────────────────────┤
│ + addVertex(): void                     │
│ + removeVertex(int i): void             │
│ + addEdge(int i, int j): void           │
│ + removeEdge(int i): void               │
│ + hasEdge(int i, int j): bool           │
│ + edgeCount(): int                      │
│ + outEdges(int i): L1<int>              │
│ + inEdges(int i): L1<int>               │
│ + printGraph(): void                    │
│ + vertexCount(): int                    │
│ + getGraph(): L1<L2<T>>&                │
│ + getDegree(int v): int                 │
│ + getOutDegree(int v): int              │
│ + getInDegree(int v): int               │
└─────────────────────────────────────────┘
```

Figure 8.7: UML class diagram of the `IGraph` interface

- `printGraph() const`: Prints the graph representation
- `vertexCount() const`: Returns the number of vertices in the graph
- `edgeCount() const`: Returns the number of edges in the graph
- `outEdges(int i) const`: Returns a list of vertices that are directly reachable from vertex `i`
- `inEdges(int i) const`: Returns a list of vertices from which vertex `i` is directly reachable
- `getGraph() const`: Returns a constant reference to the underlying graph data structure
- `getDegree(int v) const`: Returns the degree of the vertex `v`
- `getOutDegree(int v) const`: Returns the out-degree of the vertex `v` (for directed graphs)
- `getInDegree(int v) const`: Returns the in-degree of the vertex `v` (for directed graphs)

8.2 Graph Representations

By using the `IGraph` interface with the `L1` and `L2` template parameters, you can implement various graph representations while ensuring they all adhere to the same set of operations.

Vertex Count

The `vertexCount` function returns the number of vertices in the graph. This operation is $O(1)$ as it simply returns the value of V.

```
1 int vertexCount() const {
2     return V;
3 }
```

`vertexCount` Function: Counts the Number of Vertices in a Graph

Finding Degree of Vertices

The degree of a vertex is the number of edges connected to it. For directed graphs, this includes both in-degree and out-degree.

```
1 int getDegree(int v) const {
2     return getInDegree(v) + getOutDegree(v);
3 }
```

`getDegree` Function: Calculates the Degree of a Vertex in a Graph

Next, you will explore specific implementations of this interface using different graph representations.

8.2.3 Adjacency Matrix

The adjacency matrix is a 2D array of size $V \times V$, where V is the number of vertices in the graph. Each cell in the matrix $A[i][j]$ indicates whether there is an edge from vertex i to vertex j.

> **Definition:** An adjacency matrix for a graph G with vertices V and edges E is a $V \times V$ matrix A where $A[i][j] = 1$ if there is an edge from vertex i to vertex j, and $A[i][j] = 0$ otherwise. For weighted graphs, $A[i][j]$ can store the weight of the edge.
>
> **Symmetric for Undirected Graphs:** For undirected graphs, the adjacency matrix is symmetric, i.e., $A[i][j] = A[j][i]$.

The structure of an adjacency matrix using `Array` for both `L1` and `L2` is illustrated in Figure 8.8.

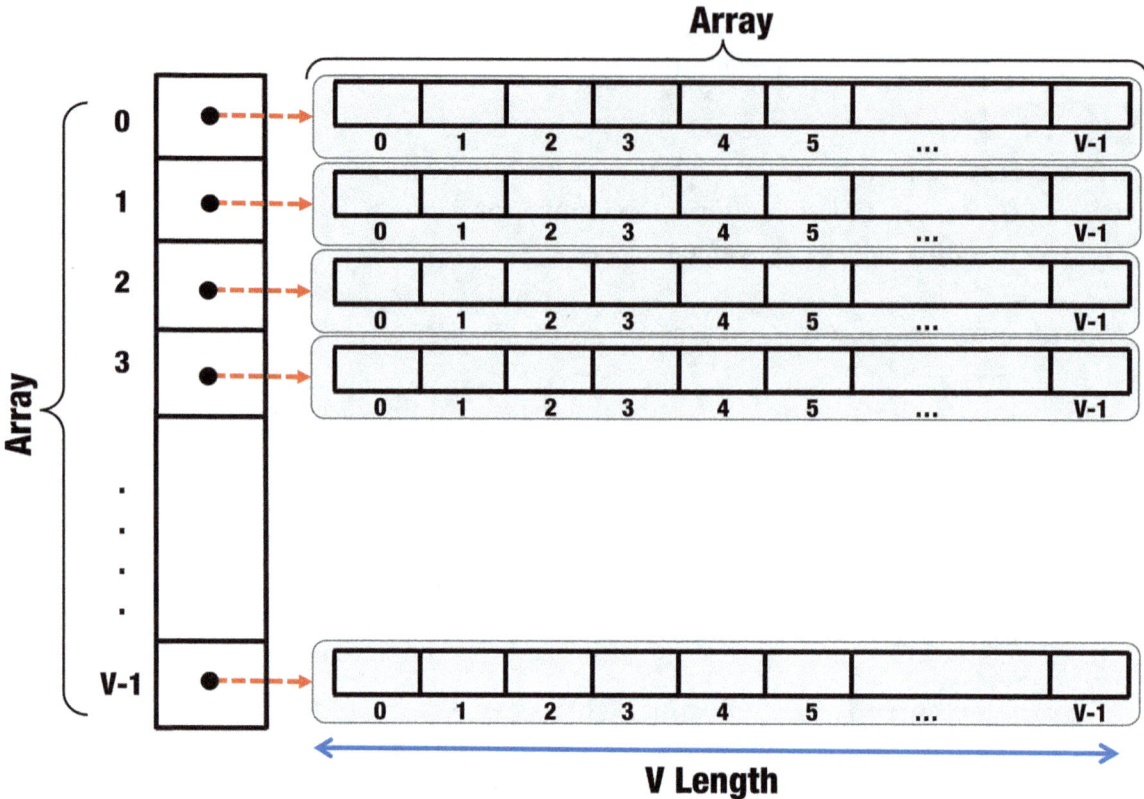

Figure 8.8: Illustration of an adjacency matrix where both `L1` and `L2` are represented using `Array`

Implementing `IGraph` with Adjacency Matrix

The following code demonstrates how to implement the `IGraph` interface using an adjacency matrix representation by customizing the `L1` and `L2` templates:

```
template <typename T>
class GraphAdjMatrix :
    public IGraph<T, DynamicArray, DynamicArray> {
public:
    GraphAdjMatrix(int nVertices) :
        IGraph<T, DynamicArray, DynamicArray>(nVertices) {
        // Initialize graph with the given number of vertices
        for (int i = 0; i < nVertices; ++i) {
            graph.pushBack(new DynamicArray<T>(nVertices,0));
        }
    }

    ~GraphAdjMatrix(){}

```

8.2 Graph Representations

```
15      // IGraph Interface Methods
16      void addVertex();
17      void removeVertex(int i);
18      void addEdge(int i, int j);
19      void addEdge(int i, int j, T w = 1);
20
21      void removeEdge(int i, int j);
22      bool hasEdge(int i, int j) const;
23      void print() const;
24      int edgeCount() const;
25      DynamicArray<int> outEdges(int i) const;
26      DynamicArray<int> inEdges(int i) const;
27      int getOutDegree(int v) const;
28      int getInDegree(int v) const;
29
30 protected:
31      // Inherited members to use directly
32      using IGraph<T, DynamicArray, DynamicArray>::V;
33      using IGraph<T, DynamicArray, DynamicArray>::graph;
34 };
```

GraphAdjMatrix Class Interface

In this implementation, we define a class `GraphAdjMatrix` where both L1 and L2 are arrays, making it an adjacency matrix to store graph edges.

The class diagram in Figure 8.9 shows the relationships and functions where `GraphAdjMatrix` inherits from `IGraph`, with composition of `DynamicArray`.

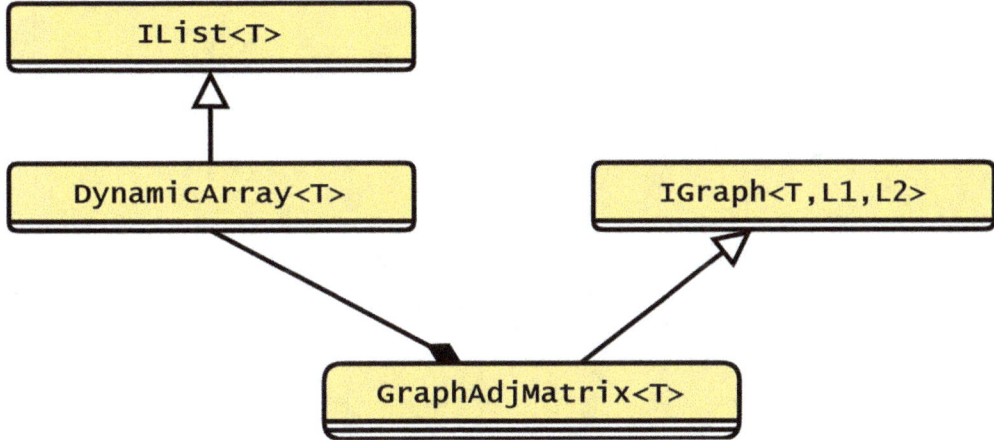

Figure 8.9: Class diagram of `GraphAdjMatrix` inheriting from `IGraph` with `DynamicArray<int>`

Addition of Vertices

The `addVertex` function adds a new vertex to the graph. This process involves two key steps: resizing all existing edge lists to include the new vertex and adding the new vertex to the vertex list itself, as shown in Figure 8.10. The time complexity for adding a vertex is $O(V)$ due to the need to resize each row in the adjacency matrix.

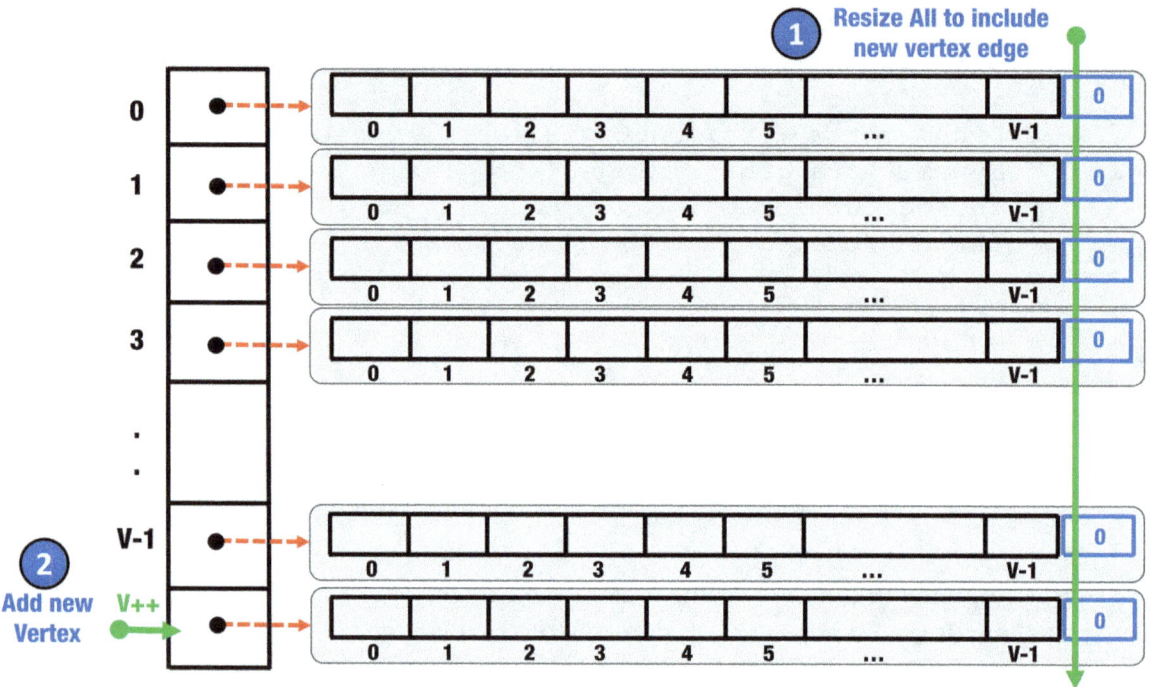

Figure 8.10: Adding a vertex. (1) Resizing the edge lists to accommodate the new vertex. (2) Adding the new vertex to the vertex list

```
1  template <typename T>
2  void GraphAdjMatrix<T>::addVertex() {
3      V++;
4      // (1) Resize all existing edge lists to accommodate
5      // the new vertex by adding 0 to represent no edge
6      for (size_t i = 0; i < graph.getSize(); ++i) {
7          graph[i]->pushBack(0);
8      }
9      // (2) Add the new vertex and initialize its row with 0s
10     DynamicArray<T>* newRow = new DynamicArray<T>(V,0);
11     graph.pushBack(newRow);
12 }
```

addVertex Function: Adds a New Vertex

8.2 Graph Representations

Removal of Vertices

The `removeVertex` function removes a vertex and all its associated edges from the graph. This process involves two main steps: removing the row corresponding to the vertex and removing the column corresponding to the vertex from all other edge lists, as shown in Figure 8.11. The time complexity for removing a vertex is $O(V)$ because each column in the adjacency matrix must be updated.

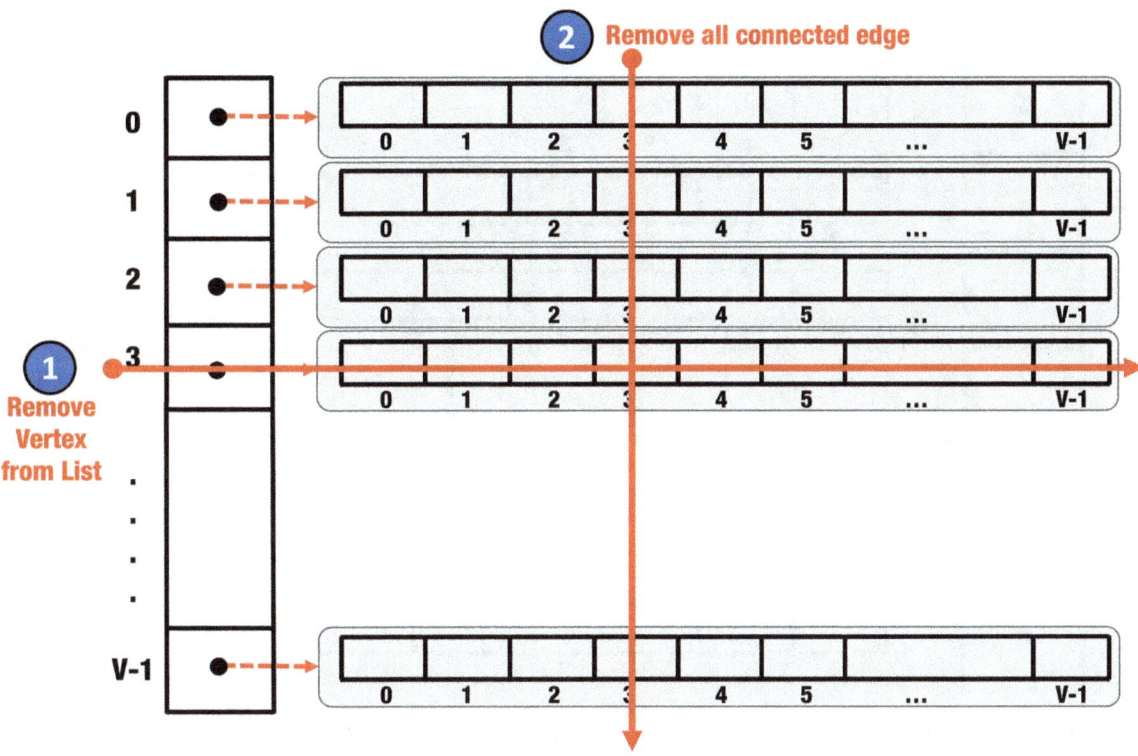

Figure 8.11: Removing a vertex. (1) Removing the row corresponding to the vertex. (2) Removing the column corresponding to the vertex

```
1  template <typename T>
2  void GraphAdjMatrix<T>::removeVertex(int i) {
3      if (i < 0 || (size_t)i >= V) return;
4      // (a) Remove the row of the vertex
5      graph.removeAt(i);
6
7      for (size_t j = 0; j < graph.getSize(); ++j) {
8          // (b) Remove the column of the vertex
9          graph[j]->removeAt(i);
10     }
11     V--;
12 }
```

removeVertex Function: Removes a Vertex

Addition and Removal of Edges

The `addEdge` function adds an edge from vertex *i* to vertex *j*, with an optional weight parameter *w*. For unweighted graphs, *w* defaults to 1. The `removeEdge` function removes the edge by setting the corresponding matrix entry to zero. Both operations run in $O(1)$ time. Figure 8.12 illustrates the process of changing the edge status.

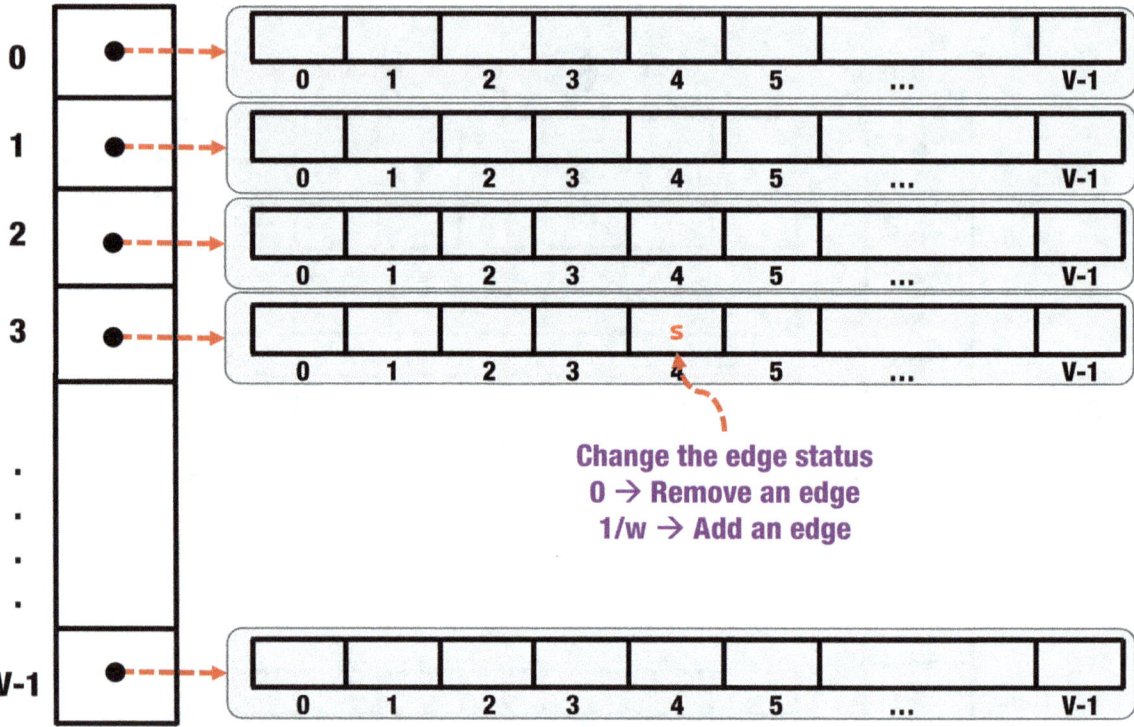

Figure 8.12: Changing the edge status: 0 represents no connection (removing an edge), and 1 or *w* represents a connection (adding an edge)

```
1  template <typename T>
2  void GraphAdjMatrix<T>::addEdge(int i, int j) {
3      (*graph[i])[j] = 1;
4  }
5
6  template <typename T>
7  void GraphAdjMatrix<T>::addEdge(int i, int j, T w) {
8      (*graph[i])[j] = w;
9  }
10
11 template <typename T>
12 void GraphAdjMatrix<T>::removeEdge(int i, int j) {
13     (*graph[i])[j] = 0;
14 }
```

`addEdge` and `removeEdge` Functions: Manipulating Edges

8.2 Graph Representations

Edge Existence Check

The `hasEdge` function checks if there is an edge from vertex *i* to vertex *j*. It returns true if the matrix entry is non-zero, indicating the presence of an edge. This operation runs in $O(1)$ time.

```
1 template <typename T>
2 bool GraphAdjMatrix<T>::hasEdge(int i, int j) const {
3     return graph[i][j] != 0;
4 }
```

`hasEdge` Function: Checks for the Existence of an Edge

Graph Printing

The `printGraph` function prints the adjacency matrix, providing a visual representation of the graph. Each row corresponds to a vertex, and each column within a row represents the edges from that vertex to other vertices. The time complexity of this function is $O(V^2)$.

```
1 template <typename T>
2 void GraphAdjMatrix<T>::print() const {
3     for (size_t i = 0; i < V; ++i) {
4         for (size_t j = 0; j < V; ++j) {
5             std::cout << (*graph[i])[j] << " ";
6         }
7         std::cout << std::endl;
8     }
9 }
```

`print` Function: Displays the Adjacency Matrix

Edge Count

The `edgeCount` function counts and returns the number of edges in the graph by iterating through the adjacency matrix and counting non-zero entries. The time complexity of this function is $O(V^2)$.

```
1 template <typename T>
2 int GraphAdjMatrix<T>::edgeCount() const {
3     int count = 0;
4     for (size_t i = 0; i < V; ++i) {
5         for (size_t j = 0; j < V; ++j) {
6             if ((*graph[i])[j] != 0) {
7                 count++;
8             }
9         }
```

```
10    }
11    return count;
12 }
```

edgeCount Function: Counts the Number of Edges

Outgoing and Incoming Edges

The `outEdges` function returns a list of vertices that are directly reachable from vertex i (i.e., outgoing edges). It iterates through the row corresponding to vertex i and collects all vertices j where the matrix entry $A[i][j]$ is non-zero. The `inEdges` function returns a list of vertices from which vertex i is directly reachable (i.e., incoming edges). It iterates through the column corresponding to vertex i and collects all vertices j where the matrix entry $A[j][i]$ is non-zero. The time complexity for both functions is $O(V)$.

```
 1 template <typename T>
 2 DynamicArray<int> GraphAdjMatrix<T>::outEdges(int i) const {
 3     DynamicArray<int> edges;
 4     for (size_t j = 0; j < V; ++j) {
 5         if ((*graph[i])[j] != 0) {
 6             edges.pushBack(j);
 7         }
 8     }
 9     return edges;
10 }
11
12 template <typename T>
13 DynamicArray<int> GraphAdjMatrix<T>::inEdges(int i) const {
14     DynamicArray<int> edges;
15     for (size_t j = 0; j < V; ++j) {
16         if ((*graph[j])[i] != 0) {
17             edges.pushBack(j);
18         }
19     }
20     return edges;
21 }
```

`outEdges` and `inEdges` Functions: Retrieves Outgoing and Incoming Edges

Finding Degrees of Vertices

The `getOutDegree` function returns the out-degree of a vertex v by counting the number of non-zero entries in the row corresponding to v. The `getInDegree` function returns the in-degree of a vertex v by counting the number of non-zero entries in the column corresponding to v. The time complexity for both functions is $O(V)$.

8.2 Graph Representations

```
 1 template <typename T>
 2 int GraphAdjMatrix<T>::getOutDegree(int v) const {
 3     int outDegree = 0;
 4     for (size_t j = 0; j < V; ++j) {
 5         if ((*graph[v])[j] != 0) {
 6             outDegree++;
 7         }
 8     }
 9     return outDegree;
10 }
11
12 template <typename T>
13 int GraphAdjMatrix<T>::getInDegree(int v) const {
14     int inDegree = 0;
15     for (size_t i = 0; i < V; ++i) {
16         if ((*graph[i])[v] != 0) {
17             inDegree++;
18         }
19     }
20     return inDegree;
21 }
```

`getOutDegree` and `getInDegree` Functions: Calculates the Out-Degree and In-Degree of a Vertex

Example

Figure 8.13 illustrates an example of an adjacency matrix representation for a simple graph. Each cell in the matrix contains the weight of the edge between two vertices, with 0 representing no connection.

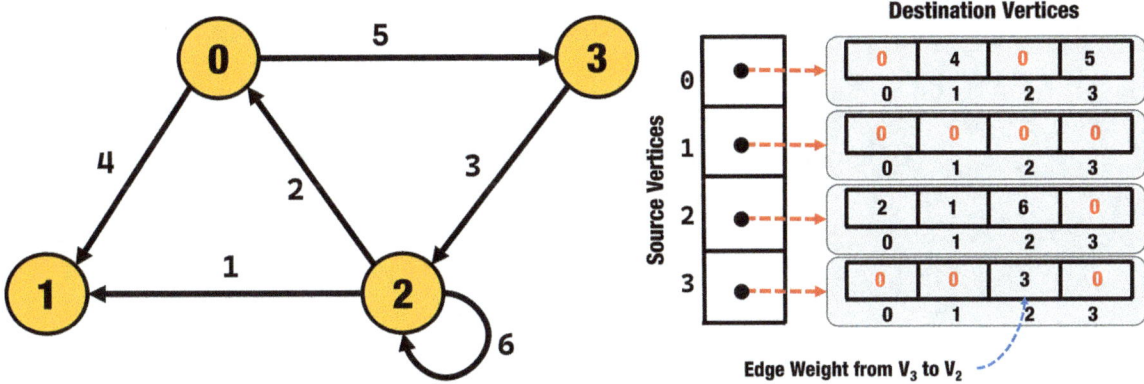

Figure 8.13: Example of an adjacency matrix. This figure shows a simple graph represented as an adjacency matrix, where each cell contains the weights of the edges

```cpp
int main() {
    GraphAdjMatrix<int> g(5);

    g.addEdge(0, 1, 4);
    g.addEdge(0, 3, 5);
    g.addEdge(2, 1, 1);
    g.addEdge(2, 0, 2);
    g.addEdge(2, 2, 6);
    g.addEdge(3, 2, 3);

    std::cout << "Graph adjacency matrix:" << std::endl;
    g.print();

    std::cout << "Number of vertices: "
              << g.vertexCount() << std::endl;
    std::cout << "Number of edges: "
              << g.edgeCount() << std::endl;

    std::cout << "Outgoing edges from vertex 0: ";
    DynamicArray<int> outEdges = g.outEdges(0);
    for (size_t i = 0; i < outEdges.getSize(); ++i) {
        std::cout << outEdges[i] << " ";
    }
    std::cout << std::endl;

    std::cout << "Incoming edges to vertex 3: ";
    DynamicArray<int> inEdges = g.inEdges(3);
    for (size_t i = 0; i < inEdges.getSize(); ++i) {
        std::cout << inEdges[i] << " ";
    }
    std::cout << std::endl;

    return 0;
}
```

Example usage of a graph using an adjacency matrix

8.2 Graph Representations

Output
The following output displays the adjacency matrix of the graph, the total number of vertices and edges, and lists the outgoing edges from vertex 0 and the incoming edges to vertex 3:

```
Graph adjacency matrix:
0 4 0 5 0
0 0 0 0 0
2 1 6 0 0
0 0 3 0 0
0 0 0 0 0
Number of vertices: 5
Number of edges: 6
Outgoing edges from vertex 0: 1 3
Incoming edges to vertex 3: 0
```

8.2.4 Adjacency List

The adjacency list is an array of lists. The size of the array is equal to the number of vertices. Each element of the array is a list containing all adjacent vertices of the corresponding vertex, along with the weight of the edges.

> **Definition:** An adjacency list for a graph G with vertices V and edges E consists of an array of V lists. Each list at index i contains pairs (j, w), where j is a vertex such that there is an edge from vertex i to vertex j, and w is the weight of the edge.

The structure of an adjacency list using `Array` for `L1` and `SinglyLL` for `L2` is illustrated in Figure 8.14.

Implementing with Adjacency List
The following code demonstrates how to implement the `IGraph` interface using an adjacency list representation by customizing the `L1` and `L2` templates:

```cpp
template <typename T>
struct Vertex{
    T weight;
    int index;

    // Default constructor
    Vertex() : weight(T()), index(-1) {}
    Vertex(T w, int idx) : weight(w), index(idx) {}

    operator int() const { return index; }
};
```
Vertex Struct Definition

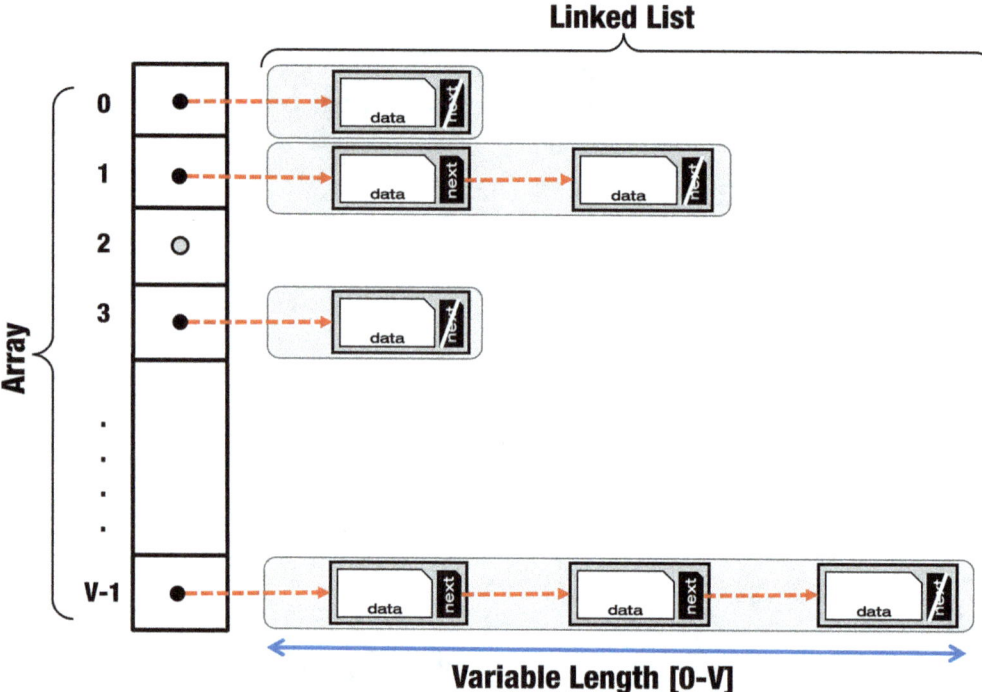

Figure 8.14: Illustration of an adjacency list where `L1` is represented using `Array` and `L2` is represented using `Linked List`. Each element of the array (`L1`) contains a type of linked list (`L2`) of vertices adjacent to the corresponding vertex, along with the weights of the edges

```cpp
template <typename T>
class GraphAdjList :
    public IGraph<Vertex<T>, DynamicArray, DLList> {

public:
    GraphAdjList(int nVertices)
        : IGraph<Vertex<T>, DynamicArray, DLList>(nVertices) {
        // Initialize graph with the given number of vertices
        for (int i = 0; i < nVertices; ++i) {
            graph.pushBack(new DLList<Vertex<T>>(););
        }
    }
    ~GraphAdjList() {
        for (size_t i = 0; i < graph.getSize(); ++i) {
            if (graph[i] != nullptr) {
                graph[i]->clear();   // Clear the list
                delete graph[i];     // Delete the list
                graph[i] = nullptr;
```

```
19          }
20        }
21     }
22
23     // IGraph Interface Methods
24     void addVertex();
25     void removeVertex(int i);
26     void addEdge(int i, int j);
27     void addEdge(int i, int j, T w);
28     void removeEdge(int i, int j);
29     bool hasEdge(int i, int j) const;
30     void print() const;
31     int edgeCount() const;
32     DynamicArray<int> outEdges(int i) const;
33     DynamicArray<int> inEdges(int i) const;
34     int getOutDegree(int v) const;
35     int getInDegree(int v) const;
36 };
```

GraphAdjList Class Interface

In this implementation, we define a class GraphAdjList that uses an adjacency list to store graph edges by customizing the L1 and L2 templates as DynamicArray and DLList, respectively. The IGraph interface methods are inherited and implemented in the parent class.

The class diagram in Figure 8.15 illustrates the relationships and functions where GraphAdjList inherits from IGraph, with composition of DynamicArray<int> and DLList<int>.

Addition of Vertices

The addVertex function adds a new vertex to the graph by adding a new list to the adjacency list, as shown in Figure 8.16. This operation is efficient, with a time complexity of $O(1)$.

```
1 template <typename T>
2 void GraphAdjList<T>::addVertex() {
3     // Add new vertex
4     graph.pushBack(new DLList<Vertex<T>>());
5     ++V;
6 }
```

addVertex Function: Adds a New Vertex

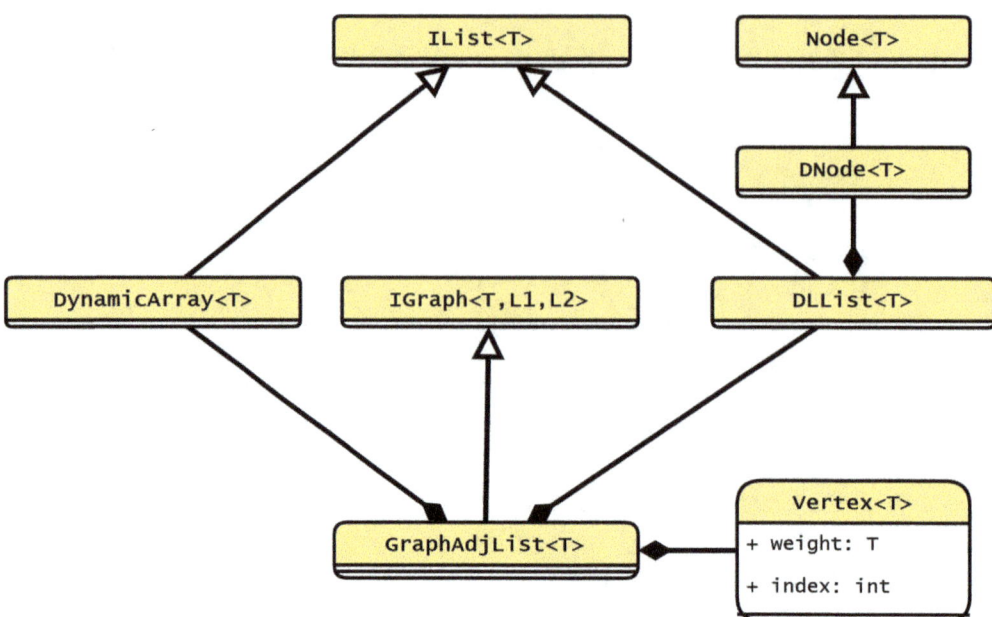

Figure 8.15: Class diagram of `GraphAdjList` inheriting from `IGraph` with `DynamicArray` and `DLList`

Removal of Vertices

The `removeVertex` function removes a vertex and all its associated edges from the graph. This involves two main steps: removing the list for the vertex and searching through all other lists to remove references to the removed vertex, as shown in Figure 8.17. The time complexity for removing a vertex is $O(V + E)$ due to the need to update all lists.

```cpp
template <typename T>
void GraphAdjList<T>::removeVertex(int i) {
    if (i < 0 || (size_t)i >= V) return;
    // (1) Remove the list for the vertex
    graph.removeAt(i);
    V--;
    // (2) Search through all vertices to
    //     remove the removed vertex
    for (size_t j = 0; j < V; ++j) {
        for (size_t k = 0; k < graph[j]->getSize(); ++k) {
            auto& glist = *graph[j];
            // Find the index of the vertex and remove it
            if (glist[k].index == i) {
                graph[j]->removeAt(k);
                --k; // Ensure we don't skip elements
            } else if (glist[k].index > i) {
                // Adjust indices after the removed one
```

8.2 Graph Representations

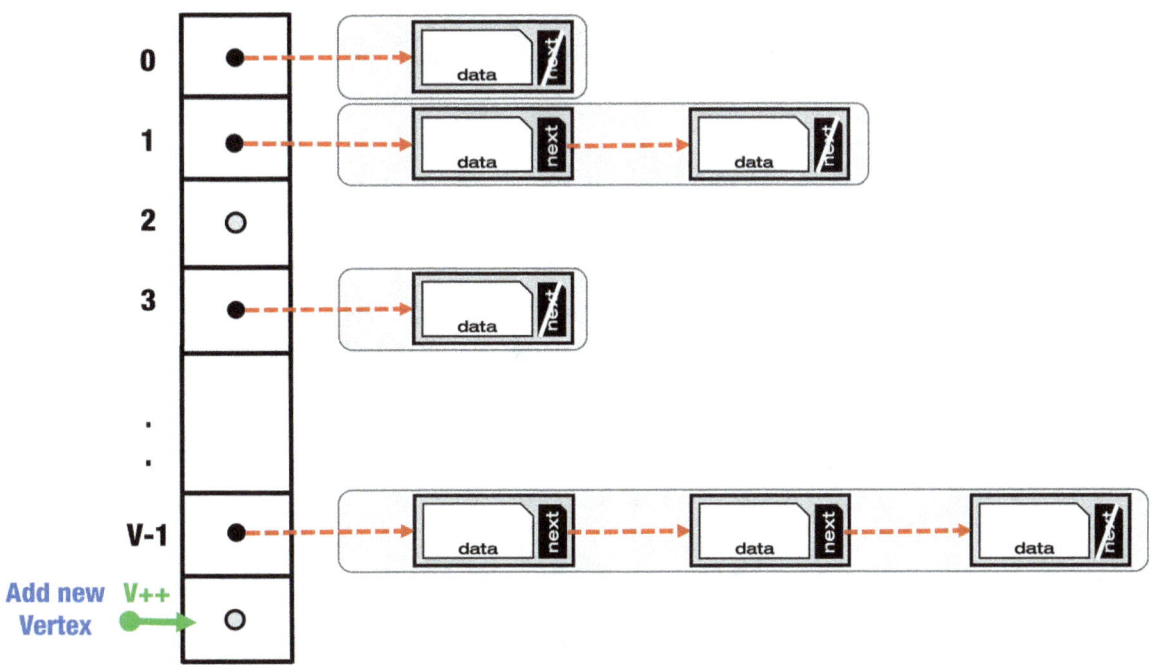

Figure 8.16: Adding a vertex: adding a new list for the new vertex in the adjacency list

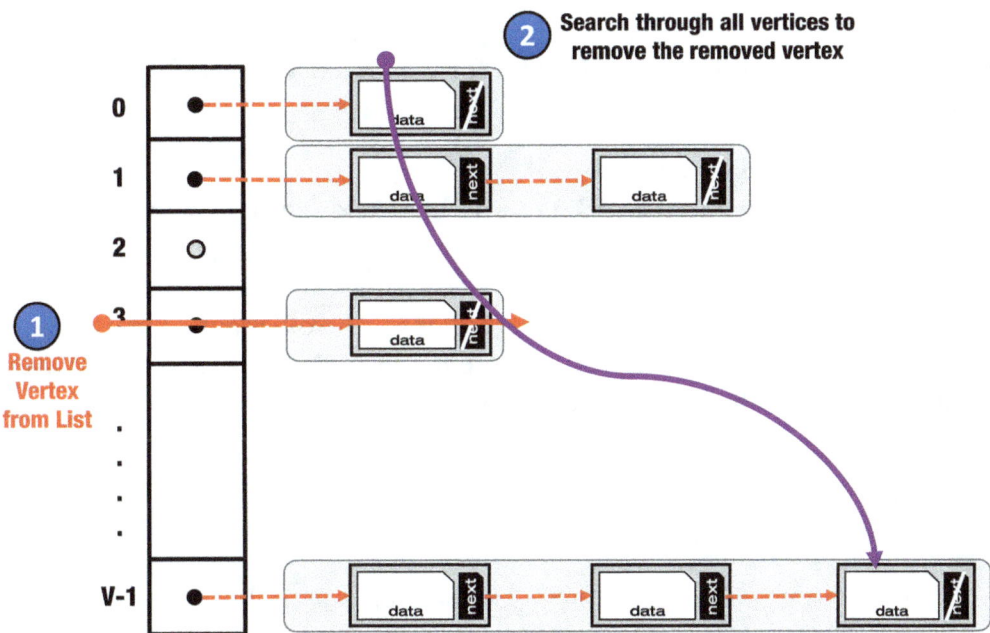

Figure 8.17: Removing a vertex. (1) Removing the list for the vertex. (2) Searching through all other lists to remove references to the removed vertex

```
18                    glist[k].index--;
19                }
20            }
21        }
22 }
```

removeVertex Function: Removes a Vertex

Edge Existence Check

The `hasEdge` function checks if there is an edge from vertex *i* to vertex *j*. It iterates through the list at index *i* and returns true if vertex *j* is found. This operation runs in $O(E)$ in the worst case.

```
1 template <typename T>
2 bool GraphAdjList<T>::hasEdge(int i, int j) const {
3     if (i < 0 || i >= V || j < 0 || j >= V) {
4         return false; // Invalid indices
5     }
6     for (size_t k = 0; k < graph[i].getSize(); ++k) {
7         if ((*graph[i])[k].index == j) {
8             return true;
9         }
10    }
11    return false;
12 }
```

hasEdge Function: Checks for the Existence of an Edge

Addition and Removal of Edges

The `addEdge` function in the `GraphAdjList` class adds an edge between two vertices *i* and *j*, with an optional weight parameter *w*. For an unweighted graph, *w* defaults to 1. The `removeEdge` function removes the edge between the specified vertices.

The time complexity for adding an edge is $O(1)$, as it involves appending a new element to the adjacency list. The time complexity for removing an edge is $O(E/V)$ on average, as it may require searching through the adjacency list of vertex *i* to find and remove the edge to vertex *j*.

```
1 // Add a unweighted edge from vertex i to vertex j
2 template <typename T>
3 void GraphAdjList<T>::addEdge(int i, int j) {
4     addEdge(i,j,1);
5 }
6
```

8.2 Graph Representations

```cpp
7  // Add a weighted edge from vertex i to vertex j
8  template <typename T>
9  void GraphAdjList<T>::addEdge(int i, int j, T w) {
10     if (i >= 0 && i < V && j >= 0 && j < V) {
11         graph[i]->pushBack(Vertex<T>(w, j));
12     }
13 }
14
15 // Remove the edge between vertices i and j
16 template <typename T>
17 void GraphAdjList<T>::removeEdge(int i, int j) {
18     if (i >= 0 && i < V) {
19         for (size_t k = 0; k < graph[i]->getSize(); ++k) {
20             if ((*graph[i])[k].index == j) {
21                 graph[i]->removeAt(k);
22                 return;
23             }
24         }
25     }
26 }
```

addEdge and removeEdge Functions: Manipulating Edges

Graph Printing

The `print` function prints the adjacency list, providing a visual representation of the graph. Each index corresponds to a vertex, and the list at each index represents the edges from that vertex to other vertices. The time complexity of this function is $O(V+E)$.

```cpp
1  template <typename T>
2  void GraphAdjList<T>::print() const {
3      for (size_t i = 0; i < V; ++i) {
4          std::cout << "Vertex " << i << ": ";
5          for (size_t j = 0; j < graph[i]->getSize(); ++j) {
6              std::cout << (*graph[i])[j].index << " ";
7          }
8          std::cout << std::endl;
9      }
10 }
```

print Function: Displays the Adjacency List

Edge Count

The `edgeCount` function counts and returns the number of edges in the graph by iterating through all the adjacency lists and counting their elements. The time complexity of this function is $O(V+E)$.

```
1  template <typename T>
2  int GraphAdjList<T>::edgeCount() const {
3      int count = 0;
4      for (size_t i = 0; i < V; ++i) {
5          count += graph[i]->getSize();
6      }
7      return count;
8  }
```

edgeCount Function: Counts the Number of Edges

Outgoing and Incoming Edges

The `outEdges` function returns a list of vertices that are directly reachable from vertex i (i.e., outgoing edges). It iterates through the list at index i and collects all vertices. The `inEdges` function returns a list of vertices from which vertex i is directly reachable (i.e., incoming edges). The time complexity for `outEdges` is $O(E)$ and for `inEdges` is $O(V + E)$.

```
1   template <typename T>
2   DynamicArray<int> GraphAdjList<T>::outEdges(int i) const {
3       DynamicArray<int> edges;
4       for (size_t j = 0; j < graph[i]->getSize(); ++j) {
5           edges.pushBack((*graph[i])[j].index);
6       }
7       return edges;
8   }
9   template <typename T>
10  DynamicArray<int> GraphAdjList<T>::inEdges(int i) const {
11      DynamicArray<int> edges;
12      for (size_t j = 0; j < V; ++j) {
13        for (size_t k = 0; k < graph[j]->getSize(); ++k) {
14            if ((*graph[j])[k].index == i) {
15                edges.pushBack(j);
16            }
17        }
18      }
19      return edges;
20  }
```

outEdges and inEdges Functions: Retrieves Outgoing and Incoming Edges

Finding Degrees of Vertices

The `getOutDegree` function simply returns the size of the adjacency list of vertex v. The `getInDegree` function iterates through all vertices and counts how many times the

8.2 Graph Representations

given vertex v appears in their adjacency lists. The time complexity for `getInDegree` is $O(V+E)$, and for `getOutDegree`, it is $O(1)$.

```
1 template <typename T>
2 int GraphAdjList<T>::getOutDegree(int v) const {
3     if (v >= 0 && v < V) {
4         return graph[v]->getSize();
5     }
6     return 0;
7 }
8 template <typename T>
9 int GraphAdjList<T>::getInDegree(int v) const {
10    int inDegree = 0;
11    for (size_t i = 0; i < V; ++i) {
12      for (size_t j = 0; j < graph[i]->getSize(); ++j){
13        if ((*graph[i])[j].index == v) {
14          inDegree++;
15        }
16      }
17    }
18    return inDegree;
19 }
```

`getOutDegree` and `getInDegree` Functions: Calculates the Out-Degree and In-Degree of a Vertex

Example

Here is an example of an adjacency list representation for a simple graph.

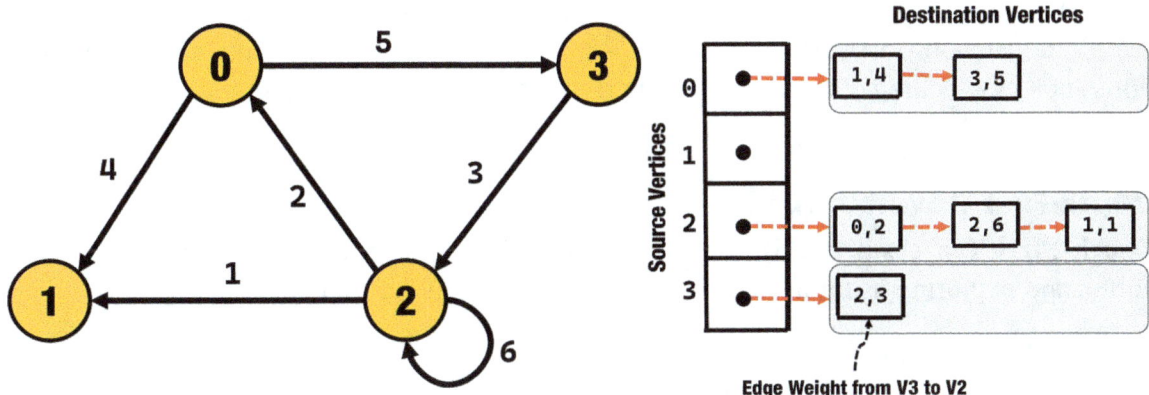

Figure 8.18: Example of an adjacency list. This figure shows a simple graph represented as an adjacency list, where each vertex points to a list of its adjacent vertices

Figure 8.18 illustrates an adjacency list for a graph with vertices connected by edges. Each vertex has a list of adjacent vertices, showcasing the connections in the graph.

8.2.5 Other Representations

Edge List

The **edge list** is a straightforward representation of a graph that consists of a list of all edges. Each edge is represented as a pair of vertices (i, j), and for weighted graphs, each pair can also include the edge's weight (i, j, w).

This representation is simple and efficient for graphs with a relatively small number of edges compared to vertices, making it particularly useful for sparse graphs.

Incidence Matrix

The **incidence matrix** is a 2D array of size $V \times E$, where V is the number of vertices and E is the number of edges. Each cell $A[i][j]$ indicates whether vertex i is incident to edge j. Specifically, $A[i][j] = 1$ if vertex i is an endpoint of edge j, and 0 otherwise.

This representation is particularly useful in applications that require direct manipulation of edges based on their relationship to vertices, such as network flows and bipartite graph algorithms.

8.2.6 Conclusion

In this section, we covered various representations of graphs, specifically using the adjacency matrix and adjacency list. Each representation has its advantages and trade-offs, depending on the type of operations and the characteristics of the graph being modeled.

In the next section, we will delve deeper into specific operations and modifications for these graph representations, focusing on graph traversals and advanced operations such as checking connectivity and performing path existence queries.

8.3 Graph Traversals and Advanced Operations

In this section, we will explore the fundamental operations used to navigate through the vertices and edges of a graph. Two primary traversal techniques are Depth-First Traversal (DFS) and Breadth-First Traversal (BFS). Additionally, we will delve into advanced operations such as checking connectivity and performing path existence queries. Let's start with the basics and build up to more complex functionalities.

8.3.1 Depth-First Traversal (DFS)

Depth-First Traversal (DFS) is a method of exploring a graph by starting at a source vertex and exploring as far as possible along each branch before backtracking.

Concept and Uses

DFS follows the Last In, First Out (LIFO) principle using a stack (either explicitly or via recursion). It is particularly useful in various scenarios, such as
- Pathfinding and maze-solving algorithms
- Topological sorting
- Detecting cycles in graphs
- Finding connected components in a graph

8.3 Graph Traversals and Advanced Operations

Implementing DFS in Graphs

Let's see how DFS can be implemented using an adjacency list. We'll use a utility function `DFSUtil` that performs the actual traversal. This function uses a stack to manage the vertices to be explored, ensuring a LIFO order of traversal. The `DFS` function initializes a visited array and calls `DFSUtil` for the specified start vertex. The `DFS()` function iterates through all vertices to handle disconnected components, calling `DFSUtil` for any unvisited vertex.

The **time complexity** of DFS is $O(V+E)$. Each vertex V is pushed and popped from the stack once, and each edge E is considered once.

```cpp
// Utility function for DFS traversal
template <typename T>
void GraphAdjList<T>::
    DFSUtil(int v, DynamicArray<bool>& visited) const {
    StackArray<int> stack;
    stack.push(v);

    while (!stack.isEmpty()) {
        int current = stack.pop();

        if (!visited[current]) {
            std::cout << current << " ";
            visited[current] = true;
        }

        const auto& adjList = *graph[current];
        for (size_t i = 0; i < adjList.getSize(); ++i) {
            int neighbor = adjList[i].index;
            if (!visited[neighbor]) {
                stack.push(neighbor);
            }
        }
    }
}

// Perform DFS starting from a given vertex
template <typename T>
void GraphAdjList<T>::DFS(int v) const {
    DynamicArray<bool> visited(V, false);
    DFSUtil(v, visited);
}

// Perform DFS for the entire graph to
// handle disconnected components
```

```
35  template <typename T>
36  void GraphAdjList<T>::DFS() const {
37      DynamicArray<bool> visited(V, false);
38      for (size_t v = 0; v < V; ++v) {
39          if (!visited[v]) {
40              DFSUtil(v, visited);
41          }
42      }
43  }
```

DFS Function: Depth-First Search Traversal

Figure 8.19 shows an example of Depth-First Search starting at node 0. Nodes are numbered with the order in which they are added to the stack, from 0 to 9. The edges used to add the next nodes to the stack are colored in red.

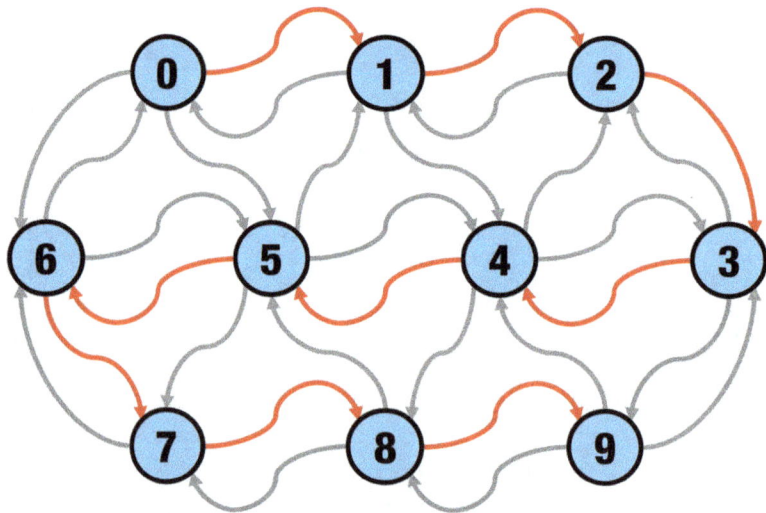

Figure 8.19: Example of Depth-First Search starting at node 0. Nodes are numbered with the order in which they are added to the stack, from 0 to 9. Edges used to add the next nodes to the stack are colored in red

8.3.2 Breadth-First Traversal (BFS)

Breadth-First Traversal (BFS) explores a graph level by level. Imagine that you are spreading out from a central point, covering all neighboring areas before moving further out. This technique is ideal for finding the shortest path in unweighted graphs.

8.3 Graph Traversals and Advanced Operations

Concept and Uses

BFS follows the First In, First Out (FIFO) principle using a queue. It is used in various applications, including
- Finding the shortest path in unweighted graphs
- Level-Order Traversal in trees
- Checking bipartiteness of a graph

Implementing BFS in Graphs

Now, let's implement BFS using an adjacency list. This function uses a queue to manage the vertices to be explored, ensuring a FIFO order of traversal. The function initializes a visited array and starts from the specified vertex s. It processes each vertex by marking it visited and enqueuing its unvisited neighbors.

The **time complexity** of BFS is $O(V+E)$. Each vertex is enqueued and dequeued once, and each edge is considered once.

```cpp
template <typename T>
void GraphAdjList<T>::BFS(int s) const {
    DynamicArray<bool> visited(V, false);
    QueueArray<int> queue;
    visited[s] = true;
    queue.enqueue(s);

    while (!queue.isEmpty()) {
        int current = queue.dequeue();

        std::cout << current << " ";

        const auto& adjList = *graph[current];
        for (size_t i = 0; i < adjList.getSize(); ++i) {
            int neighbor = adjList[i].index;
            if (!visited[neighbor]) {
                visited[neighbor] = true;
                queue.enqueue(neighbor);
            }
        }
    }
}
```

BFS Function: Breadth-First Search Traversal

Figure 8.20 shows an example of Breadth-First Search starting at node 0. The nodes are numbered with the order in which they are added to the queue, from 0 to 9. The edges used to add the next nodes to the queue are colored in red.

8.3.3 Advanced Graph Operations

Beyond basic traversals, graphs often require more sophisticated operations. Let's enhance the functionality of graph data structures by checking for connectivity and performing path existence queries.

Checking for Connectivity

Checking for connectivity involves determining if there is a path between any two vertices in the graph. This can be achieved using graph traversal algorithms like DFS or BFS.

In this implementation, `isConnected` checks if all vertices are reachable from the starting vertex (0). It uses DFS to mark all reachable vertices and then verifies if all vertices are visited.

The **time complexity** for checking connectivity is $O(V+E)$, as it uses DFS which traverses all vertices and edges.

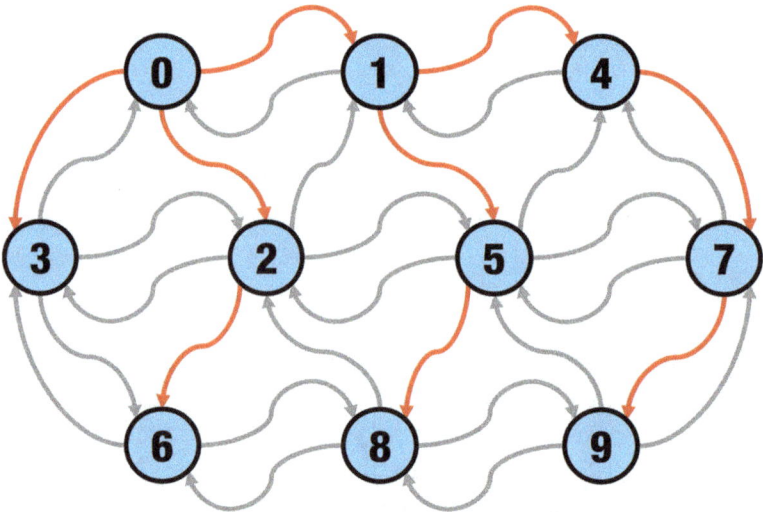

Figure 8.20: Example of Breadth-First Search starting at node 0. Nodes are numbered with the order in which they are added to the queue, from 0 to 9. Edges used to add the next nodes to the queue are colored in red

```
1 template <typename T>
2 bool GraphAdjList<T>::isConnected() const {
3     DynamicArray<bool> visited(V, false);
4     // Start DFS from vertex 0
5     DFSUtil(0, visited);
6
7     for (size_t i = 0; i < V; ++i) {
8         if (!visited[i]) {
```

8.3 Graph Traversals and Advanced Operations

```
9                // If any vertex isn't visited
10               // the graph isn't connected
11               return false;
12           }
13       }
14       return true;
15  }
```

isConnected Function: Checks Connectivity of the GraphAdjList

Path Existence Queries

Path existence queries determine whether there is a path between two vertices. This is useful in many real-world applications, like finding if there is a route between two locations on a map.

In this implementation, pathExists uses DFS to determine if there is a path from src to dest. The recursive function marks the source vertex as visited and explores its neighbors. If it reaches the destination, it returns true.

The **time complexity** for path existence queries is $O(V + E)$, as it uses DFS which traverses all vertices and edges.

```
1  template <typename T>
2  bool GraphAdjList<T>::DFS(int src, int dest,
3             DynamicArray<bool>& visited) const {
4
5      visited[v] = true;
6      if (v == dest) return true;
7
8      for (size_t i = 0; i < graph[v]->getSize(); ++i) {
9          int neighbor = (*graph[v])[i].index;
10         if (!visited[neighbor] &&
11             DFS(neighbor, dest, visited)) {
12             return true;
13         }
14     }
15     return false;
16 }
17
18 template <typename T>
19 bool GraphAdjList<T>::pathExists(int src, int dest) const {
20     DynamicArray<bool> visited(V, false);
21     return DFS(src, dest, visited);
22 }
```

DFS and pathExists Functions: Path Existence Check using DFS

8.3.4 Graph Traversal Class Updates

To summarize, here is the updated class definition for `GraphAdjList`, which includes methods for both DFS and BFS, as well as advanced operations like checking connectivity and path existence queries:

```cpp
template <typename T>
class GraphAdjList :
    public IGraph<T, DynamicArray, DLList> {

public:
    void BFS(int) const;
    void DFS(int) const;
    void DFS() const;
    bool isConnected() const;
    bool pathExists(int, int) const;

    // Other Methods ...
private:
    void DFSUtil(int, DynamicArray<bool>& ) const;
    bool DFS(int, int, DynamicArray<bool>&) const;

    // Other Methods ...
};
```

Update `GraphAdjList` Class Interface with Traversal

Design Considerations

When designing DFS and BFS for a graph, consider the following points:

- Ensure the graph's vertices and edges are accurately represented.
- Handle disconnected graphs by initiating traversal from all unvisited vertices.
- Avoid stack overflow in deep or infinite graphs by using an iterative approach for DFS if necessary.
- Optimize space usage by keeping track of visited vertices to avoid reprocessing in BFS.

In this section, we covered both fundamental and advanced graph operations. We explored the concepts, implementations, and design considerations for Depth-First Traversal (DFS), Breadth-First Traversal (BFS), checking connectivity, and path existence queries. With these tools, you can effectively navigate and manipulate graph data structures in your applications.

8.4 Performance Considerations

This section discusses the performance considerations for graph operations, storage requirements, and the trade-offs involved in choosing different graph representations, specifically adjacency matrix vs. adjacency list.

8.4.1 Time Complexity of Graph Operations

The time complexity of graph operations varies depending on the representation of the graph. Table 8.2 summarizes the time complexities for insertion, deletion, and search operations in different graph representations.

Table 8.2: Comparison of Time Complexity for Different Graph Operations

Operation	Adjacency Matrix	Adjacency List
Insertion of Vertex	$O(V^2)$	$O(1)$
Removal of Vertex	$O(V^2)$	$O(V+E)$
Insertion of Edge	$O(1)$	$O(1)$
Removal of Edge	$O(1)$	$O(E/V)$ on average, $O(E)$ worst case
Check Edge Existence	$O(1)$	$O(E/V)$ on average, $O(E)$ worst case
Iterate Over All Edges	$O(V^2)$	$O(V+E)$

Summary of Key Operations

- **Adjacency Matrix:** Efficient for dense graphs where the number of edges is close to V^2. Operations such as insertion, deletion, and edge existence checks are very fast. However, inserting or removing a vertex requires resizing the entire matrix, which is time-consuming.
- **Adjacency List:** Efficient for sparse graphs where the number of edges is much less than V^2. Allows for fast insertion of vertices and edges. However, removing a vertex or an edge can be slower compared to the adjacency matrix due to the need to update multiple lists.

8.4.2 Space Complexity

The space complexity of a graph depends on its representation and the density of the graph (i.e., the number of edges relative to the number of vertices). Table 8.3 compares the space complexity for adjacency matrix and adjacency list representations.

Table 8.3: Comparison of Space Complexity for Different Graph Representations

Representation	Space Complexity	Suitability
Adjacency Matrix	$O(V^2)$	Dense Graphs ($E \approx V^2$)
Adjacency List	$O(V+E)$	Sparse Graphs ($E \ll V^2$)

8.4.3 Choosing the Right Representation

Choosing the appropriate graph representation depends on the graph's density and the specific requirements of the operations to be performed. For dense graphs with a high number of edges, the adjacency matrix is beneficial due to its constant-time edge operations. For sparse graphs, the adjacency list is preferred due to its lower space complexity and efficient edge iteration capabilities.

When to Use Which Representation

Use Adjacency Matrix If
- The graph is dense (i.e., the number of edges is close to V^2).
- Quick edge existence checks are crucial.
- The graph structure does not change frequently, and space is not a constraint.

Use Adjacency List If
- The graph is sparse (i.e., the number of edges is much less than V^2).
- Efficient memory usage is necessary.
- The graph structure changes frequently, requiring dynamic edge insertions and deletions.

Understanding the trade-offs between different graph representations allows for informed decisions based on the specific requirements of the application. Each representation has its advantages and disadvantages, making it suitable for different scenarios.

This section provided an overview of performance considerations for graph data structures, including time complexity, space complexity, and trade-offs when choosing different graph representations.

8.5 Summary

In this chapter, we explored the versatile and powerful data structure known as graphs. We began with an introduction to the basic concepts and terminology of graphs, covering vertices, edges, and various graph properties such as connectedness, planarity, and bipartiteness.

We then delved into different ways to represent graphs, focusing on adjacency matrices and adjacency lists. These representations were thoroughly discussed, including their implementation and the trade-offs involved in terms of time and space complexity.

Graph traversal techniques, specifically Depth-First Search (DFS) and Breadth-First Search (BFS), were covered in detail. We provided implementations and discussed their uses, concepts, and complexities.

Advanced graph operations were also examined, such as checking connectivity and determining the path existence between vertices. These operations are crucial for real-world applications such as network analysis and pathfinding.

Finally, we discussed performance considerations, comparing the efficiency of various graph operations and representations. This comprehensive understanding equips you with the knowledge to choose the appropriate graph representation and perform efficient graph operations based on the specific requirements of your application.

8.5 Summary

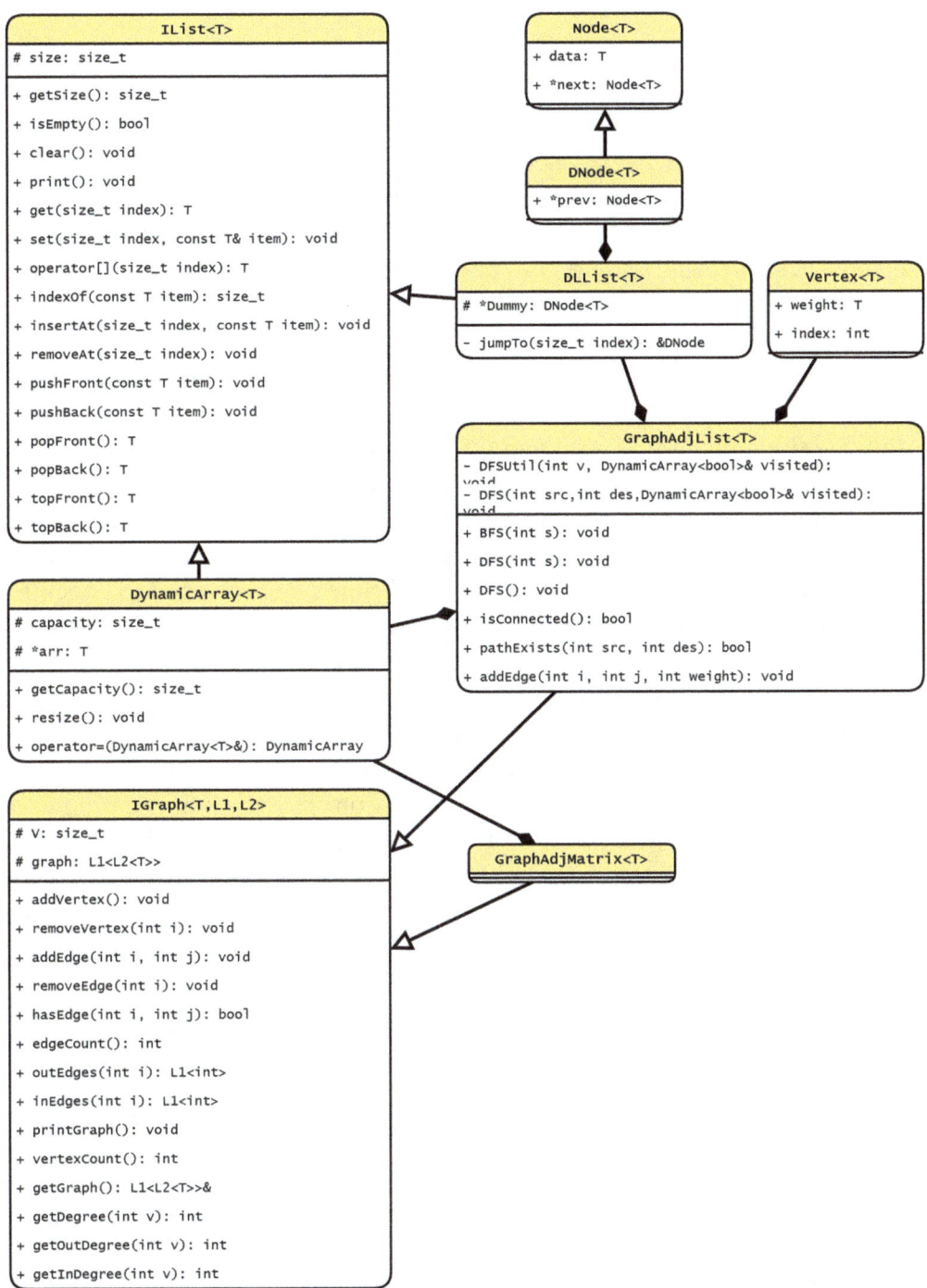

Figure 8.21: Class diagram for graph implementations. This diagram includes `GraphAdjMatrix`, `GraphAdjList`, and their relationships with other classes

The class diagram in Figure 8.21 provides an overview of the graph implementations discussed in this chapter, showcasing the relationships and interactions between the various components.

Problems

Discussion

1. Explain the differences between directed and undirected graphs. Provide examples of real-world scenarios where each type would be applicable.
2. Compare and contrast adjacency matrices and adjacency lists. What are the main advantages and disadvantages of each representation?
3. Describe the Depth-First Search (DFS) algorithm. What are its main uses and in what scenarios is it most effective?
4. Explain the Breadth-First Search (BFS) algorithm. How does it differ from DFS, and what are its primary applications?
5. In what situations would it be more beneficial to use an adjacency matrix over an adjacency list? Explain your reasoning with examples.
6. What are the key considerations when designing a graph data structure for a dynamic environment where edges and vertices are frequently added or removed?
7. How can graph traversal algorithms like DFS and BFS be used to check for connectivity in a graph? Provide a step-by-step explanation.
8. Discuss the time and space complexities of graph operations (insertion, deletion, and search) for both adjacency matrices and adjacency lists.
9. Describe a real-world application where path existence queries are crucial. How would you implement this in a graph data structure?
10. How do the concepts of graph density and connectivity influence the choice of algorithms and data structures for graph traversal and modification?

Multiple Choice Questions

1. Which of the following graph representations is more space-efficient for a sparse graph?
   (a) Adjacency matrix
   (b) Incidence matrix
   (c) Adjacency list
   (d) Edge list
2. What is the time complexity of checking if an edge exists between two vertices in an adjacency matrix?
   (a) $O(1)$
   (b) $O(V)$
   (c) $O(E)$
   (d) $O(\log V)$
3. In which graph representation are all neighbors of a vertex stored in a list associated with that vertex?
   (a) Adjacency matrix
   (b) Incidence matrix

(c) Adjacency list
(d) Edge list
4. Which of the following algorithms can be used to detect cycles in a graph?
    (a) Depth-First Search (DFS)
    (b) Breadth-First Search (BFS)
    (c) Dijkstra's Algorithm
    (d) Prim's Algorithm
5. What is the space complexity of an adjacency matrix for a graph with V vertices?
    (a) $O(V)$
    (b) $O(E)$
    (c) $O(V+E)$
    (d) $O(V^2)$
6. In a Breadth-First Search (BFS), what data structure is typically used to manage the vertices to be explored?
    (a) Stack
    (b) Queue
    (c) Priority queue
    (d) Linked list
7. Which graph traversal algorithm is best suited for finding the shortest path in an unweighted graph?
    (a) Depth-First Search (DFS)
    (b) Breadth-First Search (BFS)
8. What is the primary advantage of using an adjacency list over an adjacency matrix?
    (a) Faster edge existence checks
    (b) Lower space complexity for sparse graphs
    (c) Easier to implement
    (d) Better suited for dense graphs
9. How can you determine if a graph is connected?
    (a) By performing a Depth-First Search (DFS) or Breadth-First Search (BFS) and checking if all vertices are visited
    (b) By counting the number of edges
    (c) By checking the degree of each vertex
10. Which of the following is a key characteristic of a dense graph?
    (a) The number of edges is close to the square of the number of vertices.
    (b) The number of edges is much less than the number of vertices.
    (c) There are no cycles.
    (d) All vertices have the same degree.
11. What is the time complexity of iterating over all edges in an adjacency list?
    (a) $O(V)$
    (b) $O(E)$
    (c) $O(V^2)$
    (d) $O(V+E)$
12. Which of the following is not a typical use of Depth-First Search (DFS)?
    (a) Pathfinding in mazes
    (b) Topological sorting

- (c) Finding connected components
- (d) Finding shortest paths in weighted graphs
13. What is the primary disadvantage of using an adjacency matrix for representing sparse graphs?
    - (a) Difficult to implement
    - (b) High space complexity
    - (c) Slow edge existence checks
    - (d) Inefficient iteration over edges
14. Which of the following graph traversal algorithms is guaranteed to visit all vertices exactly once in a connected graph?
    - (a) Depth-First Search (DFS)
    - (b) Breadth-First Search (BFS)
    - (c) Both DFS and BFS
    - (d) Neither DFS nor BFS
15. In an undirected graph, how many edges are present if the adjacency matrix is fully populated (i.e., dense graph)?
    - (a) V
    - (b) V^2
    - (c) $V(V-1)/2$
    - (d) $V(V-1)$

Programming Problems

1. **Graph Connectivity:** Write a function that determines if a graph is connected using Depth-First Search (DFS). Discuss the time complexity of your solution.
2. **Shortest Path in Unweighted Graph:** Implement a function to find the shortest path between two vertices in an unweighted graph using BFS. Analyze the time complexity of your solution.
3. **Detect Cycle in Directed Graph:** Write a function to detect a cycle in a directed graph using Depth-First Search (DFS). Provide a complexity analysis of your approach.
4. **Connected Components:** Implement a function to find all connected components in an undirected graph using DFS. Explain the logic and analyze its time complexity.
5. **Topological Sort:** Write a function to perform a topological sort on a directed acyclic graph (DAG). Discuss the applications of topological sorting and analyze its time complexity.
6. **Graph Coloring:** Implement a function to determine if a graph can be colored using two colors such that no two adjacent vertices share the same color (i.e., bipartite graph). Analyze the complexity of your solution.

9. Specialized Data Structures and Techniques

Objective

In this chapter, we will explore specialized data structures that offer unique solutions to specific computational problems. These structures are designed to enhance performance in terms of speed and memory usage in scenarios where fundamental data structures may not be sufficient. By the end of this chapter, you will have a comprehensive understanding of these advanced data structures and their practical applications. Here's what you can look forward to:

1. **Exploring Heaps:** We will begin with heaps, both Max-Heaps and Min-Heaps, discussing their properties, applications, and operations like insertion, deletion, and heapification.
2. **Priority Queues:** Learn about priority queues, which are often implemented using heaps, and understand how they manage tasks efficiently by always keeping the highest (or lowest) priority element accessible. You will explore their structure, operations, and performance in various use cases.

3. **Building and Using Maps:** Learn about map data structures, focusing on key-value pairs, hash functions, and collision handling using chained hash tables. You will understand how to implement and utilize maps efficiently.
4. **Space-Efficient Linked Lists:** Discover how space-efficient linked lists minimize pointer overhead by storing multiple elements in each node. We will cover their structure, operations, and performance benefits.
5. **Understanding Skip Lists:** Dive into skip lists, a probabilistic data structure that allows fast search, insertion, and deletion operations. You will learn about their layered structure, rules, and implementation.
6. **Performance Analysis and Applications:** Finally, we will analyze the performance of these specialized data structures and explore their applications in various real-world scenarios. This will include a comparison with other data structures and a discussion on their advantages.

9.1 Introduction

In the world of computer science, data structures play a crucial role in organizing and managing data efficiently. While basic structures like arrays, linked lists, and trees form the foundation, specialized data structures offer unique solutions to complex problems. In this chapter, we will explore a variety of advanced data structures designed to enhance performance regarding speed and memory usage in specific scenario. By diving into heaps, maps, space-efficient linked lists, and skip lists, you will learn how to optimize algorithms and tackle computational challenges more effectively. Let's explore the functionality of these specialized data structures, their implementation specifics, and their real-world uses. By the conclusion of this chapter, you will have the expertise to select and apply the appropriate data structure for any problem, guaranteeing that your solutions are both effective and refined.

9.2 Heaps

9.2.1 Introduction to Heaps

Heaps are specialized tree-based data structures that satisfy the heap property, making them ideal for implementing priority queues.

Heaps are commonly used in scenarios where quick access to the *largest* or *smallest* element is required, such as in scheduling algorithms, graph algorithms (like Dijkstra's shortest path), and efficient priority queues. Therefore, there are two types of heaps: **Max-Heap** and **Min-Heap**.

9.2 Heaps

In a Max-Heap, for any given node u, the value of u is greater than or equal to the values of its children (successors), ensuring that the largest element is at the root. Mathematically:

$$\forall \text{node } u, \text{value}(u) \geq \text{value}(\text{successor}(u))$$

Conversely, in a Min-Heap, the value of u is less than or equal to the values of its children (successors), ensuring that the smallest element is at the root. Mathematically:

$$\forall \text{node } u, \text{value}(u) \leq \text{value}(\text{successor}(u))$$

As shown in Figure 9.1, the structure of a heap can either be a Max-Heap (1) or a Min-Heap (2) depending on whether the root is the maximum or minimum element in the heap.

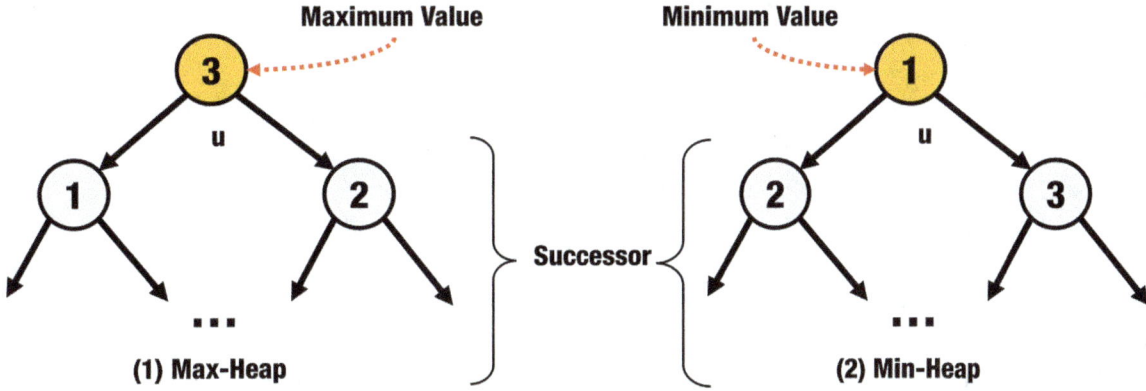

Figure 9.1: An illustration of (1) a Max-Heap where the value of node u is greater than or equal to the values of its successors and (2) a Min-Heap where the value of node u is less than or equal to the values of its successors. This ensures the root of the heap is the largest element in a Max-Heap and the smallest element in a Min-Heap

Properties of Heaps

Heaps have several essential properties:
- **Complete Binary Tree:** A heap is a complete binary tree, meaning all levels are fully filled except possibly for the last level, which is filled from left to right (see "Types of Binary Trees" in Chapter 7).
- **Heap Property:** The specific heap property (max or min) must be satisfied by every parent-child (successor) relationship.

Max-Heap

A Max-Heap ensures that the largest element is always at the root. Each parent node has a value greater than or equal to its children's values.

Chapter 9. Specialized Data Structures and Techniques

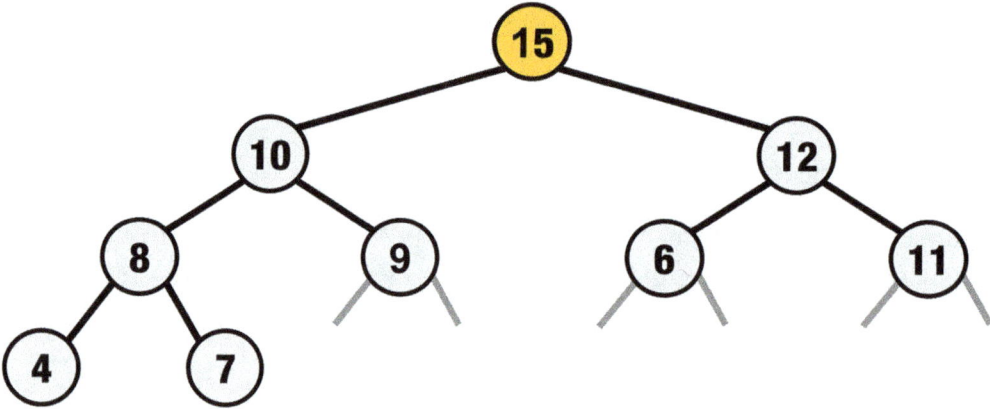

Figure 9.2: An example of a Max-Heap

■ **Example 9.1 Max-Heap Property**
In the example shown in Figure 9.2:
- The root node (15) is the largest element.
- The value of the root node (15) is greater than its children (10 and 12).
- The value of node 10 is greater than its children (8 and 9).
- The value of node 12 is greater than its child (11).
- The value of node 8 is greater than its children (4 and 7).

■

Min-Heap

A Min-Heap ensures that the smallest element is always at the root. Each parent node has a value less than or equal to its children's values.

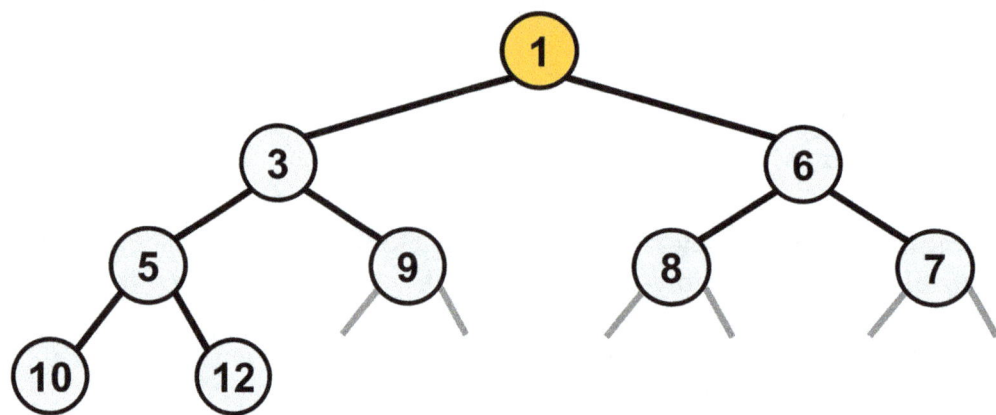

Figure 9.3: An example of a Min-Heap

9.2 Heaps

> **Example 9.2 Min-Heap Property**
> In the example shown in Figure 9.3:
> - The root node (1) is the smallest element.
> - The value of the root node (1) is less than its children (3 and 6).
> - The value of node 3 is less than its children (5 and 9).
> - The value of node 6 is less than its children (8 and 7).
> - The value of node 5 is less than its children (10 and 12).

9.2.2 Binary Heaps

Binary heaps are the most common form of heaps, implemented using arrays for efficient access and manipulation.

As shown in Figure 9.4, binary heaps can be efficiently represented using arrays. The array representation allows easy access to the parent and child nodes. For a node at index i:
- The parent node is at index $\lfloor (i-1)/2 \rfloor$.
- The left child is at index $2i+1$.
- The right child is at index $2i+2$.

The following code defines a `BinaryHeap` class with basic functions to access parent and child nodes, as well as other essential heap operations:

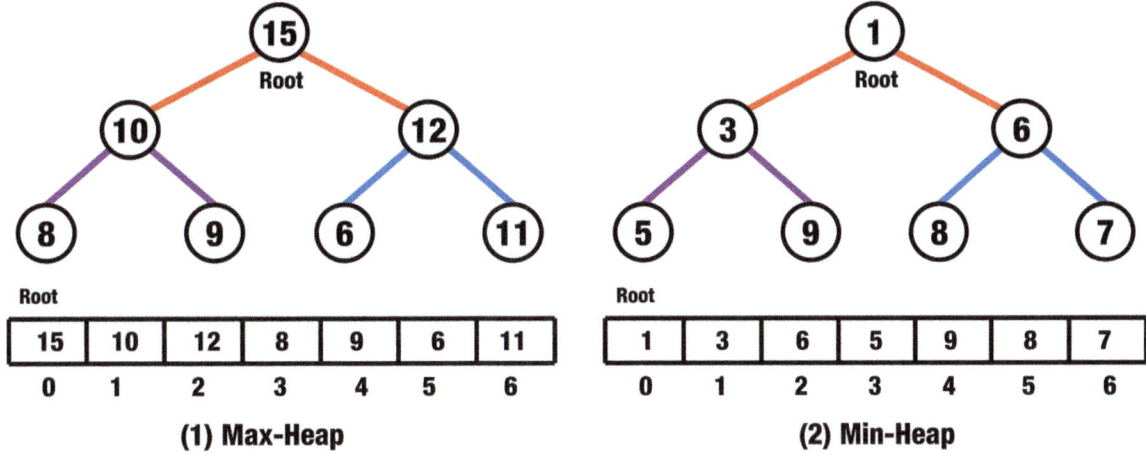

Figure 9.4: A representation of binary heaps using trees and corresponding arrays. (1) The Max-Heap tree on the right has the root node 15 and is represented by the array. (2) The Min-Heap tree on the left has the root node 1 and is represented by the array

```
1 template <typename T>
2 class BinaryHeap {
3 public:
4     // Inserts a new element into the heap
5     virtual void add(const T value);
```

```cpp
 6
 7      // Removes an element by value
 8      virtual void remove(const T value);
 9
10      // Deletes the root element
11      virtual void deleteRoot();
12
13      // Builds a heap from an arbitrary array of elements
14      virtual void buildHeap();
15
16      // Sorts the elements
17      virtual void heapSort();
18
19      // Heapifies the array
20      virtual void heapify(DynamicArray<T>& arr);
21
22      // Utility function to print the heap
23      virtual void print() const;
24
25      // Returns the element at the root
26      virtual T peek() const;
27
28      virtual size_t getSize() const {
29          return heap.getSize();
30      }
31 protected:
32      DynamicArray<T> heap;
33
34      // Maintains the heap by "bubbling down" at index i to n
35      void heapifyDown(int i, int n);
36
37      // Maintains the heap by "bubbling up" at index i
38      void heapifyUp(int i);
39 private:
40      // Returns the index of the parent/children node
41      int parent(int i) const { return (i - 1) / 2; }
42      int left(int i) const { return 2 * i + 1; }
43      int right(int i) const { return 2 * i + 2; }
44 };
```

BinaryHeap Class Interface

9.2 Heaps

The class diagram (refer to Figure 9.5) provides an overview of the structure and relationships within the `BinaryHeap` class.

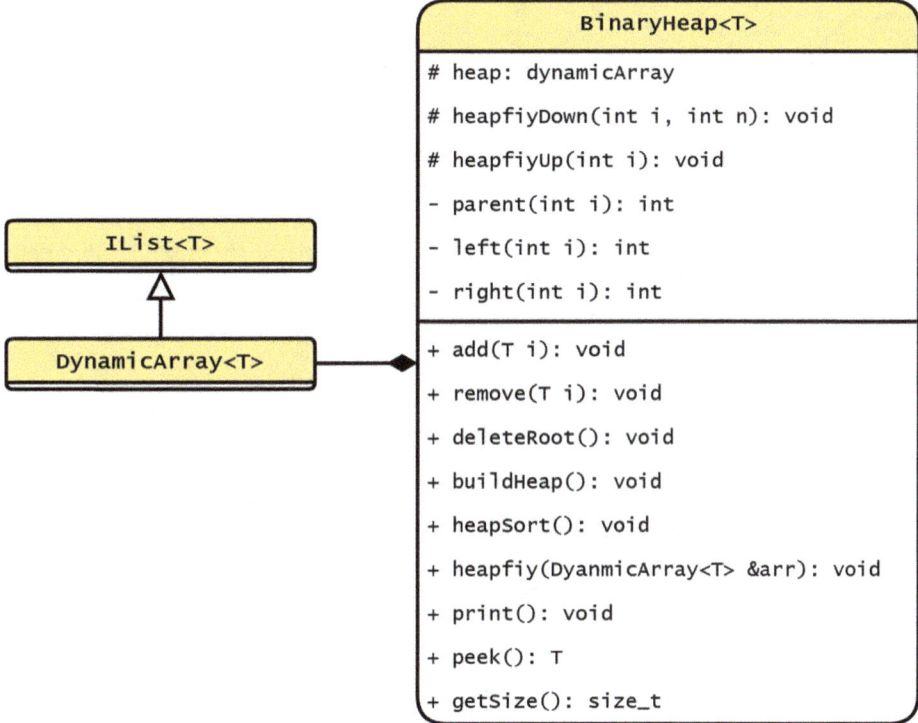

Figure 9.5: Class diagram of `BinaryHeap`

Heap Operations

Heaps support several fundamental operations, including insertion, deletion, and heapification. The following are typical implementations for binary heaps.

Insertion

Insertion in a heap involves adding a new element at the end of the heap (tree or array) to maintain the complete tree property and then "bubbling up" the element to its correct position to restore the heap property. This process is also known as "heapify-up."

> ■ **Example 9.3** Inserting a Value into a Min-Heap
> As shown in Figure 9.6, inserting the element 2 into the Min-Heap starts by adding the new element at the end of the array. It then bubbles up to maintain the heap property. Initially, 2 is swapped with 9, then with 3, ensuring the heap property is maintained. The root node (1) remains the smallest element. ■

256　Chapter 9. Specialized Data Structures and Techniques

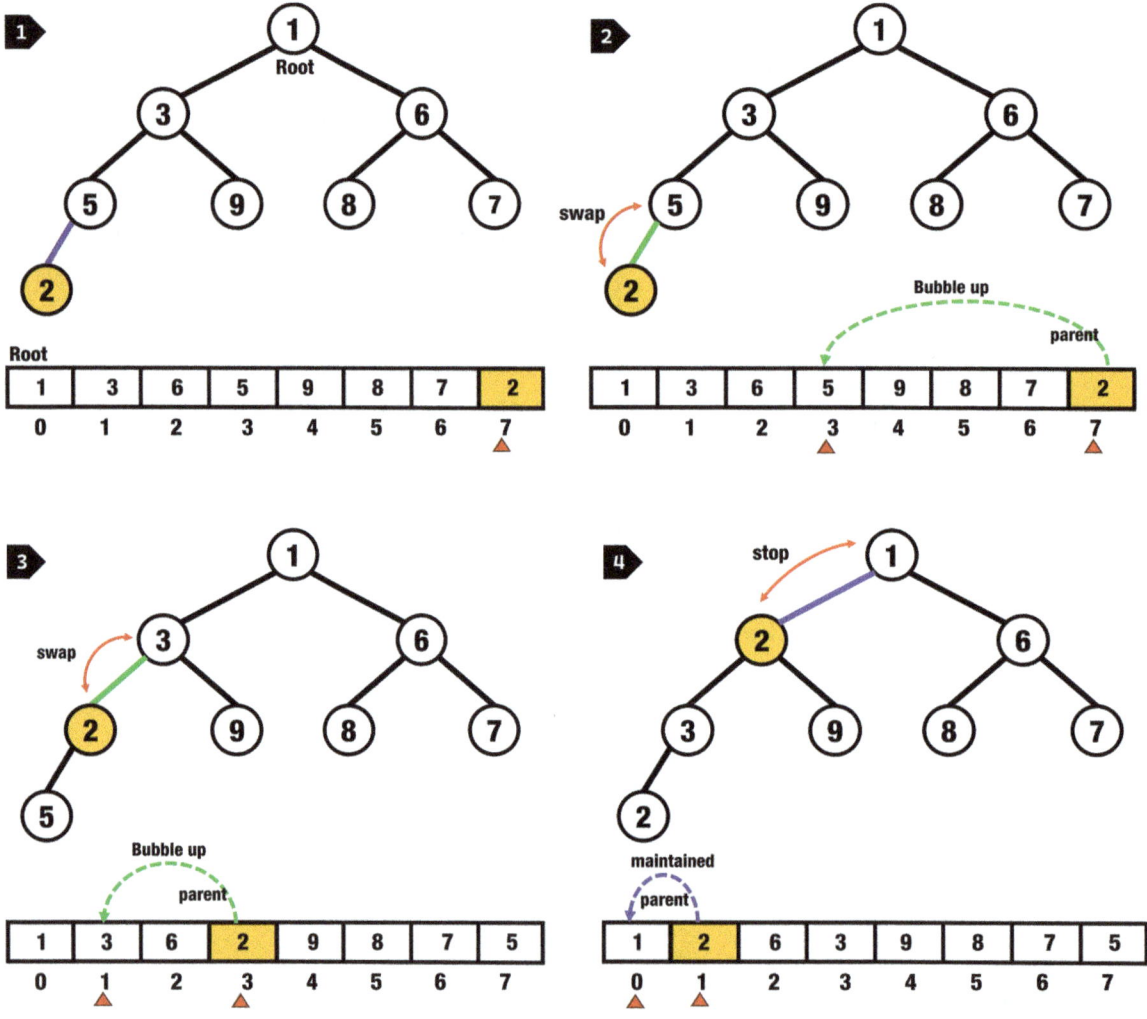

Figure 9.6: Insertion of the element 2 into a Min-Heap. The new element 2 is added at the end of the array and then bubbled up to its correct position. Initially, 2 is swapped with 9, then with 3, ensuring the heap property is maintained. The root node (1) remains the smallest element

```cpp
template <typename T>
void BinaryHeap<T>::heapifyUp(int i) {
    while (i != 0 && heap[parent(i)] > heap[i]) {
        std::swap(heap[i], heap[parent(i)]);
        i = parent(i);
    }
}

template <typename T>
void BinaryHeap<T>::add(const T value) {
```

9.2 Heaps

```
11        heap.pushBack(value);
12        heapifyUp(heap.getSize() - 1);
13 }
```

`heapifyUp` and `add` Functions: Adding and Maintaining Order in a `BinaryHeap`

The `add` function inserts a new element at the end of the heap array and then calls `heapifyUp` to ensure the heap property is maintained by swapping the new element with its parent until it is in the correct position.

Deletion (Remove Min/Max)

Deletion typically involves removing the root element, which is either the maximum or minimum element in the heap, depending on whether it is a **Max-Heap** or **Min-Heap**. The last element in the heap is then moved to the root position, and the heap property is restored by "bubbling down" this element. This process is known as "heapify-down."

■ **Example 9.4** Deletion in a Min-Heap

As illustrated in Figure 9.7, the root element (1) is removed from the Min-Heap. The last element (7) is moved to the root position, and then the heap property is restored by "bubbling down" the new root. Initially, 7 is swapped with 3, then with 5, ensuring the heap property is maintained. ■

```
1 template <typename T>
2 void BinaryHeap<T>::deleteRoot() {
3     if (heap.getSize() == 0)
4         return;
5     heap[0] = heap.popBack();
6     heapifyDown(0, heap.getSize());
7 }
8
9 template <typename T>
10 void BinaryHeap::heapifyDown(int i, int n) {
11    int lChild   = left(i);
12    int rChild   = right(i);
13    int smallest = i;
14
15    if (lChild < n  &&  heap[lChild] < heap[smallest])
16        smallest = lChild;
17
18    if (rChild < n && heap[rChild] < heap[smallest])
19        smallest = rChild;
20
21    if (smallest != i) {
```

258 Chapter 9. Specialized Data Structures and Techniques

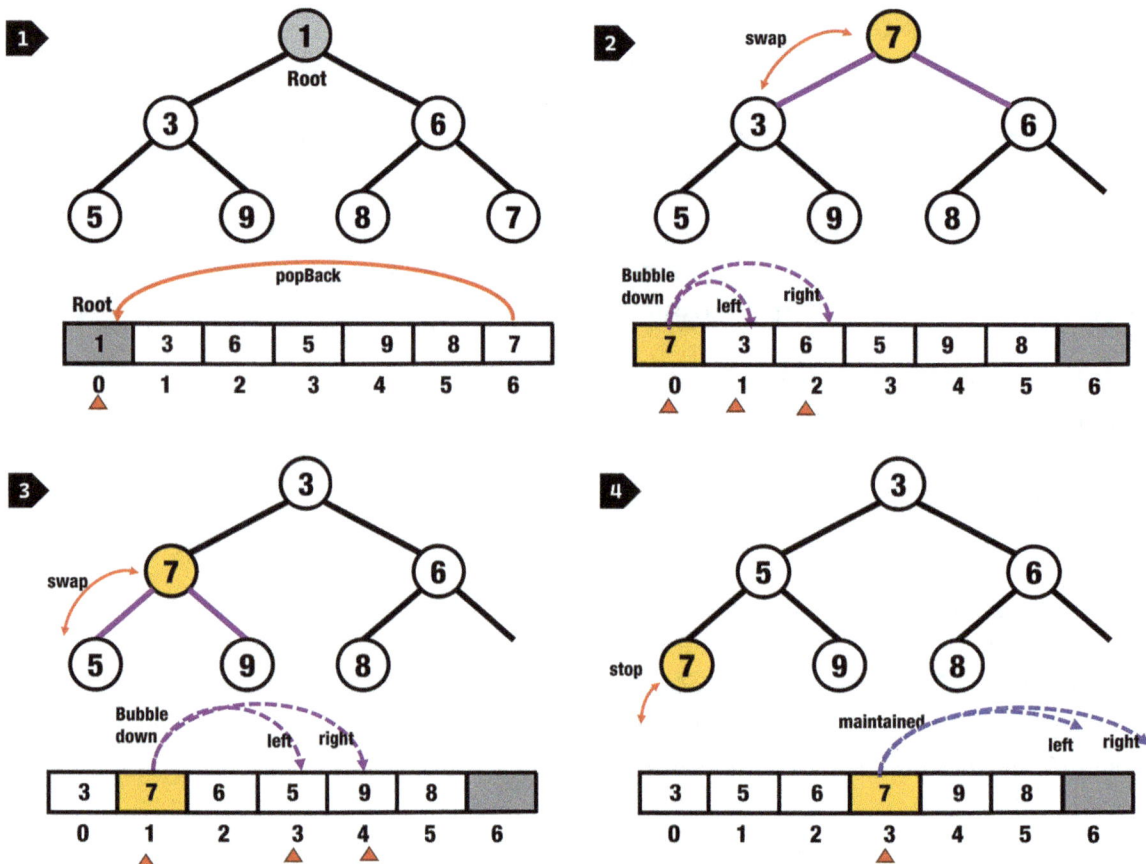

Figure 9.7: Removal of the minimum element (1) from a Min-Heap. The root element (1) is swapped with the last element (7), and then the heap property is restored by "bubbling down" the new root. The new root (7) is swapped with 3 and then with 5 to maintain the Min-Heap property

```
22          swap(heap[i], heap[smallest]);
23          heapifyDown(smallest, n);
24      }
25 }
```

`deleteRoot` and `heapifyDown` Functions: Removing the Root and Reordering in a `BinaryHeap`

The `deleteRoot` function removes the root element by swapping it with the last element in the heap, then calling `heapifyDown` to restore the heap property.

9.2 Heaps

Remove an Element

This operation removes a specific value from the heap and maintains the heap property.

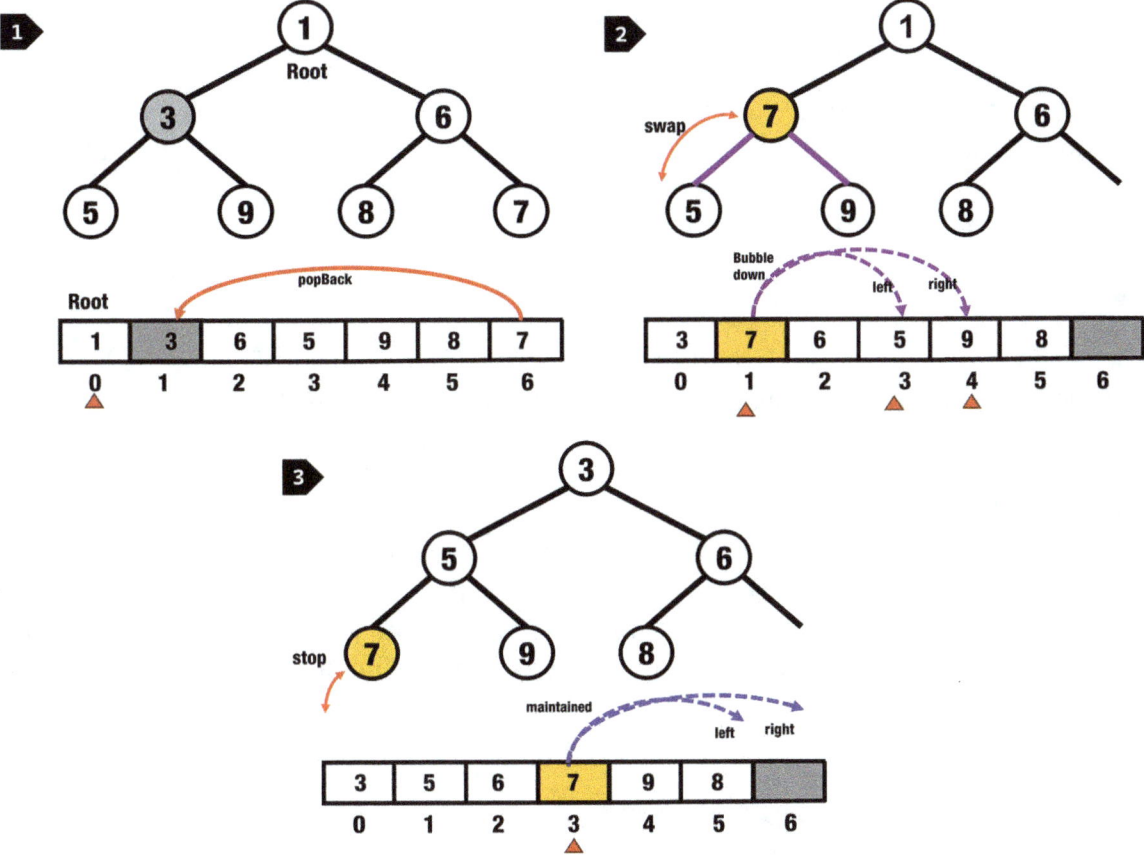

Figure 9.8: Removal of the element 3 from a Min-Heap. The element 3 is located and replaced with the last element (7). The heap property is restored by "bubbling down" the new value (7), which is swapped with 5 to maintain the Min-Heap property

> ■ **Example 9.5** **Removing an Element in a Min-Heap**
> As illustrated in Figure 9.8, the element 3 is removed from the Min-Heap. After locating the element 3, it is replaced with the last element (7). To maintain the Min-Heap property, the new value (7) is bubbled down by swapping it with 5. ■

Here is the code that performs the remove operation:

```
1 template <typename T>
2 void BinaryHeap<T>::remove(const T value) {
3     int index = heap.indexOf(value);
4     if (index == -1) return;
5
```

```
6        heap[index] = heap.popBack();
7        heapifyDown(index, heap.getSize());
8 }
```
remove Function: Removes a Specified Value

In the `remove` function, the element to be removed is first located using the `indexOf` function. If the element is found, it is replaced with the last element in the heap array. The `heapifyDown` function is then called to restore the heap property by bubbling down the replaced element to its correct position.

Heapify

The heapify operation is used to build a heap from an arbitrary array of elements. It ensures that the heap property is satisfied for all elements in the array. The heapify process can be performed efficiently in $O(n)$ time using a bottom-up approach.

■ **Example 9.6 Heapify**
As illustrated in Figure 9.9, the heapify operation transforms an arbitrary array into a Min-Heap. Initially, the element 3 at index 2 is swapped with 1, its smaller child. Next, the element 8 at index 1 is swapped with 2, maintaining the Min-Heap property. Finally, the root element 7 is bubbled down, resulting in a valid Min-Heap. ■

```
1  template <typename T>
2  void BinaryHeap<T>::buildHeap() {
3      int n = heap.getSize();
4      for (int i = (n / 2) - 1; i >= 0; i--) {
5          heapifyDown(i, n);
6      }
7  }
8
9  template <typename T>
10 void BinaryHeap<T>::heapify(DynamicArray<T>& arr) {
11     heap = arr;
12     buildHeap();
13 }
```
buildHeap and heapify Functions: Constructing and Reordering a BinaryHeap

The `buildHeap` function starts from the last non-leaf node and applies the `heapifyDown` function to each node in a bottom-up manner. This ensures that all subtrees are valid heaps, resulting in an overall heapified array.

Note: When building the heap from an array, avoid unnecessary copying of the array. Use the original array and build the heap in place.

9.2 Heaps

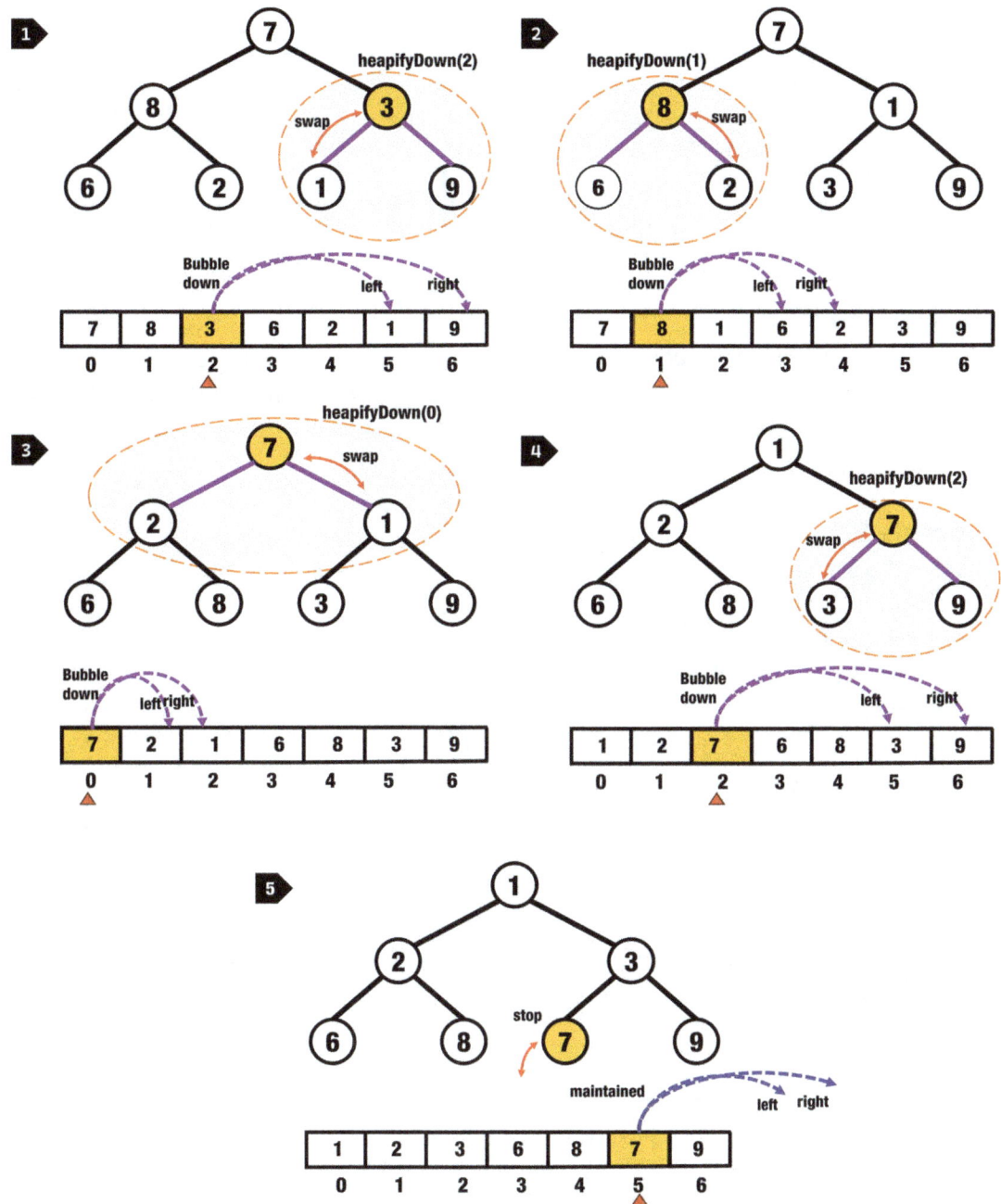

Figure 9.9: Illustration of the heapify operation. Starting with the array representation of a tree, the heapify operation adjusts the elements to maintain the heap property. The process involves "bubbling down" elements to their correct positions

Peek
The `peek` function retrieves the root element of the heap without removing it. This function is particularly useful in priority queues (discussed in the next section) where you want to inspect the highest priority element without modifying the heap.

```cpp
1 template <typename T>
2 T BinaryHeap<T>::peek() const {
3     assert(heap.getSize() > 0 && "Heap is empty");
4     return heap[0];
5 }
```

peek Function: Returns the Top Element Without Removing It

Heap Sort Algorithm

Heap sort is a comparison-based sorting algorithm that leverages the heap data structure to sort elements. The algorithm involves building a heap from the input data and then repeatedly extracting the maximum (for a Max-Heap) or minimum (for a Min-Heap) element from the heap and placing it at the end of the sorted array.

■ **Example 9.7** Heap Sort with a Min-Heap

Consider the array $[4, 10, 3, 5, 1]$. The heap sort process is as follows:
- Build a Min-Heap: $[1, 4, 3, 10, 5]$
- Swap the root with the last element and reduce the heap size: $[5, 4, 3, 10, 1]$
- Heapify the root: $[3, 4, 5, 10, 1]$
- Repeat the process:
    - Swap: $[3, 4, 5, 10, 1] \to [10, 4, 5, 3, 1]$
    - Heapify: $[4, 10, 5, 3, 1]$
    - Swap: $[4, 10, 5, 3, 1] \to [5, 10, 4, 3, 1]$
    - Heapify: $[4, 10, 5, 3, 1]$
    - Swap: $[4, 10, 5, 3, 1] \to [10, 5, 4, 3, 1]$
    - Heapify: $[5, 10, 4, 3, 1]$

The sorted array in descending order is $[10, 5, 4, 3, 1]$. Reversing this gives the sorted array in ascending order: $[1, 3, 4, 5, 10]$. ■

```cpp
1 template <typename T>
2 void BinaryHeap<T>::heapSort() {
3     buildHeap(); // First build the heap
4     for (int i = heap.getSize() - 1; i >= 0; i--) {
5         std::swap(heap[0], heap[i]);
6         heapifyDown(0, i);
7     }
8 }
```

heapSort Function: Performs Heap Sort

9.2 Heaps

In the `heapSort` function, the smallest element (root of the heap) is swapped with the last element in the heap and removed from the heap. The `heapifyDown` function is called to restore the heap property, and this process is repeated until all elements are sorted.

Performance Analysis

Heap sort is an efficient sorting algorithm with a time complexity of $O(n \log n)$. This efficiency comes from the heap operations, which ensure that both insertion and removal operations run in $O(\log n)$ time. The algorithm performs well with large datasets and is not sensitive to the initial ordering of the data.

- **Time Complexity:** The heap construction phase takes $O(n)$ time, and each of the n removal operations takes $O(\log n)$ time, leading to an overall time complexity of $O(n \log n)$.
- **Space Complexity:** Heap sort has a space complexity of $O(1)$ because it is an in-place sorting algorithm that requires no additional storage beyond the input array.

9.2.3 Optimizing Binary Heap Operations

Optimizing the performance of binary heap operations can lead to significant improvements in efficiency, particularly for large data or frequent operations.

Optimized HeapifyDown

In the `heapifyDown` function, our aim is to minimize the number of swaps by determining the smallest (or largest, in the case of a Max-Heap) among the current node and its children before performing any swaps. This approach ensures that only the necessary swaps are made, reducing the overall number of swaps.

Implementing `heapifyDown` iteratively avoids the overhead associated with recursive function calls and eliminates the risk of stack overflow in deep-recursion scenarios. The iterative approach uses a loop that continues until the heap property is restored, making it generally more efficient than a recursive implementation.

```
void BinaryHeap<T>::heapifyDown(int i, int n) {
    while (true) {
        int lChild = left(i);
        int rChild = right(i);
        int smallest = i;

        if (lChild < n && heap[lChild] < heap[smallest])
            smallest = lChild;

        if (rChild < n && heap[rChild] < heap[smallest])
            smallest = rChild;

        if (smallest == i) break;
```

```
15        std::swap(heap[i], heap[smallest]);
16        i = smallest;
17    }
18 }
```

Optimized Iterative `heapifyDown` Function

The function starts by checking the children on the left and right of the current node to determine the smallest element. If either child is smaller than the current node, a swap is performed, and the process continues iteratively. The loop ends when the current node is smaller than both of its children, ensuring that the heap property is maintained.

Batch Insertions

If multiple elements need to be inserted, consider inserting them all at once and then performing a single `buildHeap` operation. This reduces the number of heapify operations needed and optimizes the overall insertion time.

9.2.4 Customizing Binary Heaps with `HeapType`

In the previous section, we discussed the standard implementation of binary heaps, which could be either a Min-Heap or a Max-Heap. To make our `BinaryHeap` class more customizable, we introduce an enumeration `HeapType` that allows the heap to be configured as either a Min-Heap or a Max-Heap at the time of creation.

HeapType Enumeration

The `HeapType` enumeration is defined as follows:

```
1 enum class HeapType { MIN_HEAP, MAX_HEAP };
```

`HeapType` Enumeration: Defines Types of Heaps

This enumeration enables the user to specify the desired heap type when instantiating a `BinaryHeap` object. Depending on the `HeapType` provided, the heap will either maintain the smallest element at the root (Min-Heap) or the largest element at the root (Max-Heap).

Customizing the `BinaryHeap` Class

The `BinaryHeap` class has been modified to include a `HeapType` member, which is initialized through the constructor. The class now supports both Min-Heaps and Max-Heaps using the same underlying implementation, with the behavior controlled by the `HeapType`.

```
1 template <typename T>
2 class BinaryHeap {
3 public:
```

9.2 Heaps

```
 4      // Constructor to initialize the desired type
 5      BinaryHeap(HeapType type = HeapType::MIN_HEAP);
 6
 7      // Other functions (add, remove, deleteRoot, etc.)
 8
 9  protected:
10      // Heap type: MIN_HEAP or MAX_HEAP
11      HeapType type;
12
13  private:
14      // Helper function for comparison
15      bool compare(int i, int j) const;
16  };
17
18  template <typename T>
19  BinaryHeap<T>::BinaryHeap(HeapType type)
20      : type(type) {}
```
Customized `BinaryHeap` Class Interface

Helper Functions for Comparison

A key change in this implementation is the introduction of a comparison helper function, `compare`, which determines the correct order of elements based on the heap type.

```
 1  template <typename T>
 2  bool BinaryHeap<T>::compare(int i, int j) const {
 3      if (type == HeapType::MIN_HEAP) {
 4          // Min-heap: Parent should be less than children
 5          return heap[i] > heap[j];
 6      } else {
 7          // Max-heap: Parent should be greater than children
 8          return heap[i] < heap[j];
 9      }
10  }
```
`compare` Function: Compares Elements in the `BinaryHeap` Based on `HeapType`

Updating Heapify Functions

The `heapifyUp` and `heapifyDown` functions have been updated to use the `compare` function, ensuring that elements are correctly ordered according to the specified heap type.

```
 1  template <typename T>
 2  void BinaryHeap<T>::heapifyUp(int i) {
 3      while (i != 0 && compare(parent(i), i)) {
```

```cpp
4            std::swap(heap[i], heap[parent(i)]);
5            i = parent(i);
6        }
7    }
8    template <typename T>
9    void BinaryHeap<T>::heapifyDown(int i, int n) {
10       while (true) {
11           int lChild = left(i);
12           int rChild = right(i);
13           int target = i;
14
15           if (lChild < n && compare(target, lChild))
16               target = lChild;
17
18           if (rChild < n && compare(target, rChild))
19               target = rChild;
20
21           if (target == i) break;
22
23           std::swap(heap[i], heap[target]);
24           i = target;
25       }
26   }
```

Updated `heapifyUp` and `heapifyDown` Functions Using `compare` in `BinaryHeap`

These changes ensure that the `BinaryHeap` class is flexible and can be used to implement Min-Heaps and Max-Heaps efficiently, depending on the needs of the application.

Benefits of Customization

This customization allows for a single, unified implementation of the `BinaryHeap` class that can cater to different use cases. Whether the application requires a priority queue that prioritizes the smallest or the largest element, this flexible implementation provides a robust solution. The use of the `HeapType` enumeration enhances code readability and maintainability, as the heap's behavior is clearly defined and controlled through the constructor.

Overall, this update makes the `BinaryHeap` class a more powerful and adaptable data structure, suitable for a wide range of applications that rely on heap-based algorithms.

9.3 Priority Queues

9.3.1 Introduction to Priority Queues

A **priority queue** is a data structure that manages elements based on their priority rather than their insertion order. This makes priority queues particularly useful in scenarios such as task scheduling, where tasks with higher priority need immediate attention.

Priority queues are commonly implemented using a **heap**, a dynamic structure that efficiently maintains the highest (or lowest) priority element at the root. This arrangement allows for quick access and modification of elements based on their priority.

9.3.2 Implementing a Priority Queue with a Heap

As shown in Figure 9.10, the priority queue is built using a Max-Heap, where each element is represented as a `PQNode` that contains data and its associated priority. The heap structure ensures that the node with the highest priority is always at the root, facilitating efficient operations on the highest priority elements.

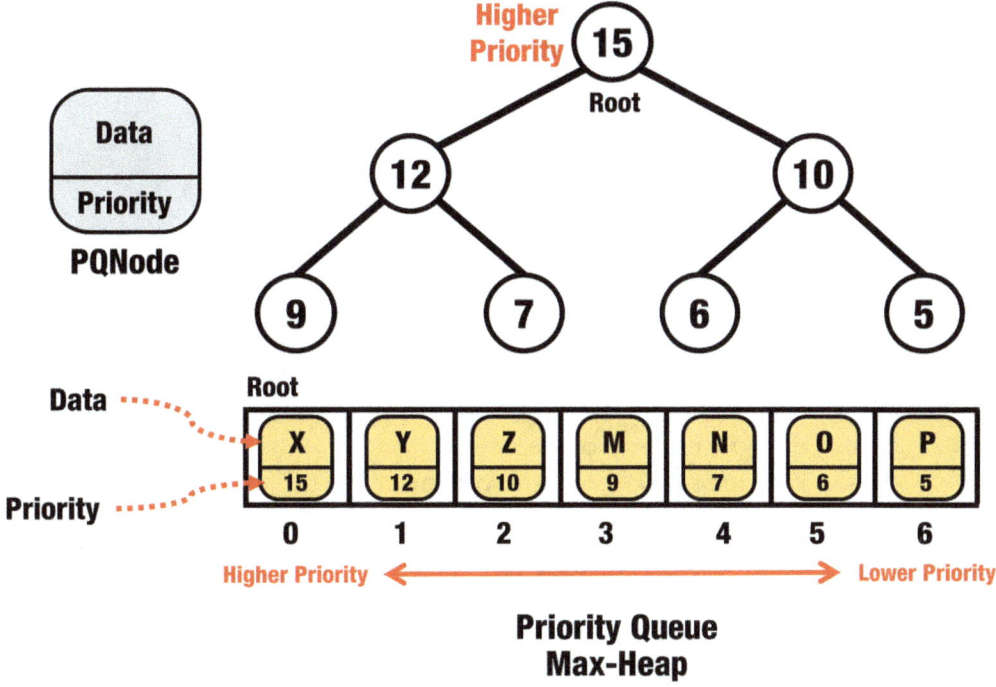

Figure 9.10: An illustration of a Max-Heap with an array representation where each element is a `PQNode` containing data and priority. The heap orders nodes by priority, keeping the highest priority node at the root

Node Structure Definition

The `PQNode` class represents each element in the priority queue, storing both data and its priority. This structure supports comparison operations, ensuring that the heap can correctly organize nodes by priority.

```cpp
template <typename T>
class PQNode {
public:
    T data;
    int priority;

    // Constructors
    PQNode() : data(T()), priority(0) {}
    PQNode(T data, int priority) :
        value(data), priority(priority) {}


    // Assignment operator
    PQNode<T>& operator=(const PQNode<T>& other) {
        if (this != &other) {
            data = other.data;
            priority = other.priority;
        }
        return *this;
    }

    // Equality operator
    bool operator==(const PQNode<T>& other) const {
        return data == other.data
            && priority == other.priority;
    }

    // Operator overloading to compare PQNode objects
    bool operator<(const PQNode& other) const {
        return this->priority < other.priority;
    }

    bool operator>(const PQNode& other) const {
        return this->priority > other.priority;
    }
};
```

PQNode Class Interface

9.3 Priority Queues

Priority Queue Class Definition

The `PriorityQueue` class uses a customized `BinaryHeap` with a `MAX_HEAP` configuration. This ensures that the highest priority element is always at the root, making it ideal for scenarios where tasks with the highest priority need to be processed first.

```cpp
template <typename T>
class PriorityQueue {
public:
    PriorityQueue();
    ~PriorityQueue();

    // Inserts a new element into the priority queue
    void add(const T& data, int priority);

    // Removes the highest priority element
    T pop();

    // Returns the highest priority element
    T peek() const;

    // Checks if the priority queue is empty
    bool isEmpty() const;

    // Clears all elements in the priority queue
    void clear();

    // Prints all elements in the priority queue
    void print() const;
private:
    BinaryHeap<PQNode<T>> heap;
};

template <typename T>
PriorityQueue<T>::PriorityQueue()
    : heap(HeapType::MAX_HEAP) {} // Initialize max-heap
```
`PriorityQueue` Class Interface

Figure 9.11 shows the class diagram of the `PriorityQueue` and its relationship with `BinaryHeap` and `PQNode`.

9.3.3 Priority Queue Operations

The following sections describe the key operations of the `PriorityQueue` class, including insertion, removal, and peeking at the highest priority element.

Insertion

The add function inserts a new PQNode into the heap based on its priority, maintaining the heap property. This operation runs in $O(\log n)$ time due to the underlying heap structure.

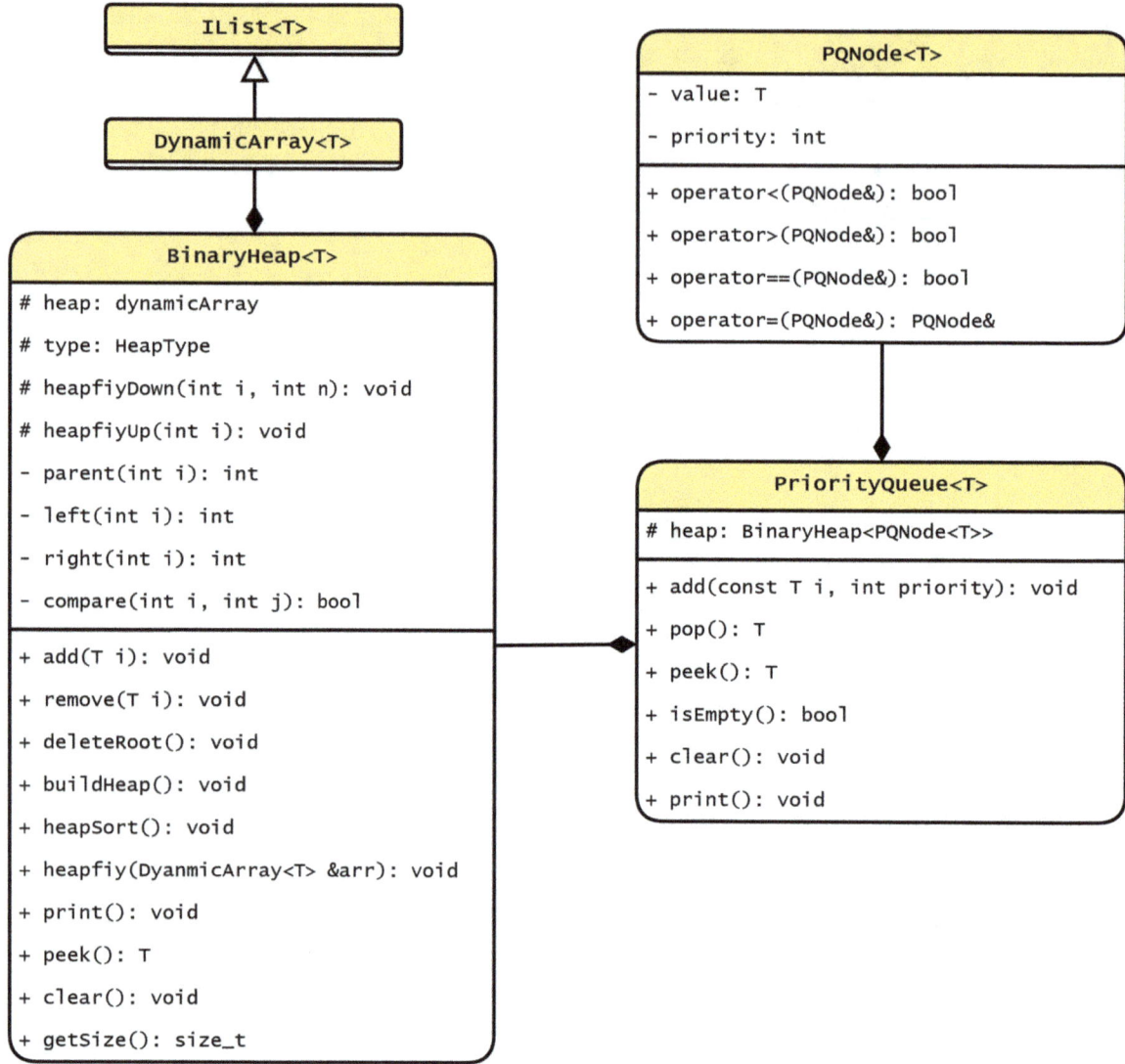

Figure 9.11: Class diagram of PriorityQueue showing its composition with BinaryHeap and its relationship with PQNode

9.3 Priority Queues

```cpp
template <typename T>
void PriorityQueue<T>::add(const T& data, int priority) {
    PQNode<T> node(data, priority);
    heap.add(node);
}
```

add Function: Adds an Element with Priority

Pop Operation

The `pop` function removes and returns the element with the highest priority, adjusting the heap to maintain the Max-Heap property. This operation is efficient with a time complexity of $O(\log n)$.

```cpp
template <typename T>
T PriorityQueue<T>::pop() {
    assert(!isEmpty() && "Priority queue is empty");
    T val = heap.peek().data;
    heap.deleteRoot();
    return val;
}
```

pop Function: Removes and Returns the Highest Priority Element

Peek Operation

The `peek` function retrieves the element with the highest priority without removing it, allowing you to inspect the top element of the priority queue efficiently. This operation runs in $O(1)$ time.

```cpp
template <typename T>
T PriorityQueue<T>::peek() const {

    assert(!isEmpty() && "Priority queue is empty");
    return heap.peek().data;
}
```

peek Function: Returns the Highest Priority Element Without Removing It

9.3.4 Performance Analysis

The efficiency of a priority queue implemented with a heap is closely related to the performance of the underlying heap operations:
- **Insertion:** $O(\log n)$ due to reordering the heap when adding new elements
- **Pop:** $O(\log n)$ as it involves removing the root and rebalancing the heap
- **Peek:** $O(1)$ as it simply accesses the root without modifying the heap

> **Note:** The use of a Max-Heap configuration allows the `PriorityQueue` to efficiently manage elements based on their priority, ensuring that the highest priority element is always quickly accessible.

This structure provides an efficient and scalable approach to managing elements based on priority, making it suitable for a variety of high-performance applications

9.4 Maps

9.4.1 Introduction to Maps

Maps, also known as dictionaries or associative arrays, are data structures that store key-value pairs. They provide an efficient way to associate data (**values**) with unique identifiers (**keys**). Maps are widely used in various applications, such as implementing databases, caching mechanisms, etc.

9.4.2 Key-Value Pairs

A **key-value pair** consists of a unique **key** and its associated **value**. The **key** acts as a unique identifier for the associated value. Keys are used to identify and access values quickly, making them essential for the efficient performance of maps. Keys must be unique within a map to ensure that each value can be accurately and efficiently retrieved. Examples of keys include
- Employee IDs
- Product codes
- Usernames

The **value** is the data associated with a specific key. When a key is provided, the map uses it to quickly locate and retrieve the corresponding value. Values can be any type of data, such as
- Names of employees
- Descriptions of products
- User profiles

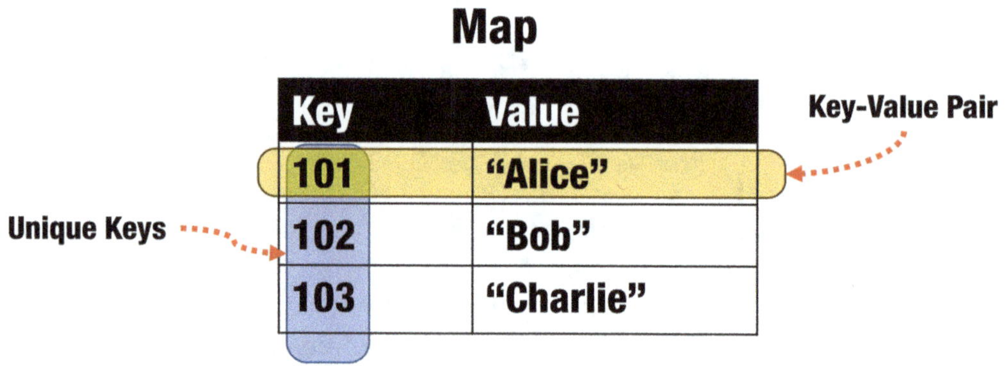

Map

Key	Value
101	"Alice"
102	"Bob"
103	"Charlie"

Unique Keys ⟶ (Key column)
Key-Value Pair ⟵ (101, "Alice" row)

Figure 9.12: Example of key-value pairs: each unique key (Employee ID) is associated with a value (Employee Name)

9.4 Maps

As shown in Figure 9.12, each unique key (Employee ID) is associated with a value (Employee Name). This demonstrates how maps store and retrieve data efficiently. For instance, keys 101, 102, and 103 are associated with values "Alice," "Bob," and "Charlie," respectively.

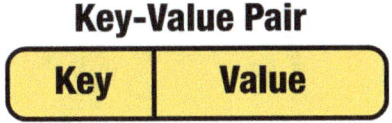

Figure 9.13: The structure of a key-value pair

Figure 9.13 illustrates the structure of a key-value pair. The separation of the key and value into distinct components allows maps to perform efficient lookups, updates, and deletions. This structure is fundamental in various applications, from databases to caching systems.

9.4.3 Map Structure

The primary operations supported by maps include insertion, deletion, and lookup of key-value pairs. The efficiency of these operations is crucial for the performance of applications that rely on maps.

As shown in Figure 9.14, the map structure consists of an array of buckets, each pointing to the head of a linked list. This approach, known as separate chaining, is used to handle collisions. When multiple keys hash to the same bucket, their key-value pairs are stored in the linked list associated with that bucket.

> ■ **Example 9.8** Key-Value Pairs in Map
> In this example (see Figure 9.14):
> - "Alice" with key 101 and "David" with key 111 are both stored in bucket 0.
> - "Bob" with key 102 is stored in bucket 3.
> - "Charlie" with key 103 is stored in bucket 4.
>
> ■

The array contains a fixed number of buckets, typically denoted by m. The array can be resized, but this requires rehashing to ensure keys are placed in their proper new locations.

9.4.4 Implementing a Map

We will build a simple map data structure in C++ using a `ChainedHashTable` for separate chaining to handle collisions. The `ChainedHashTable` class was implemented in Chapter 6 and will be used here as part of the `Map` implementation.

Pair Implementation

Let's start by defining the `Pair` structure that holds the key-value pairs. The `Pair` structure encapsulates a key and its corresponding value, providing constructors for initialization, operator overloading for comparisons, and implicit conversion for easy access.

274   Chapter 9. Specialized Data Structures and Techniques

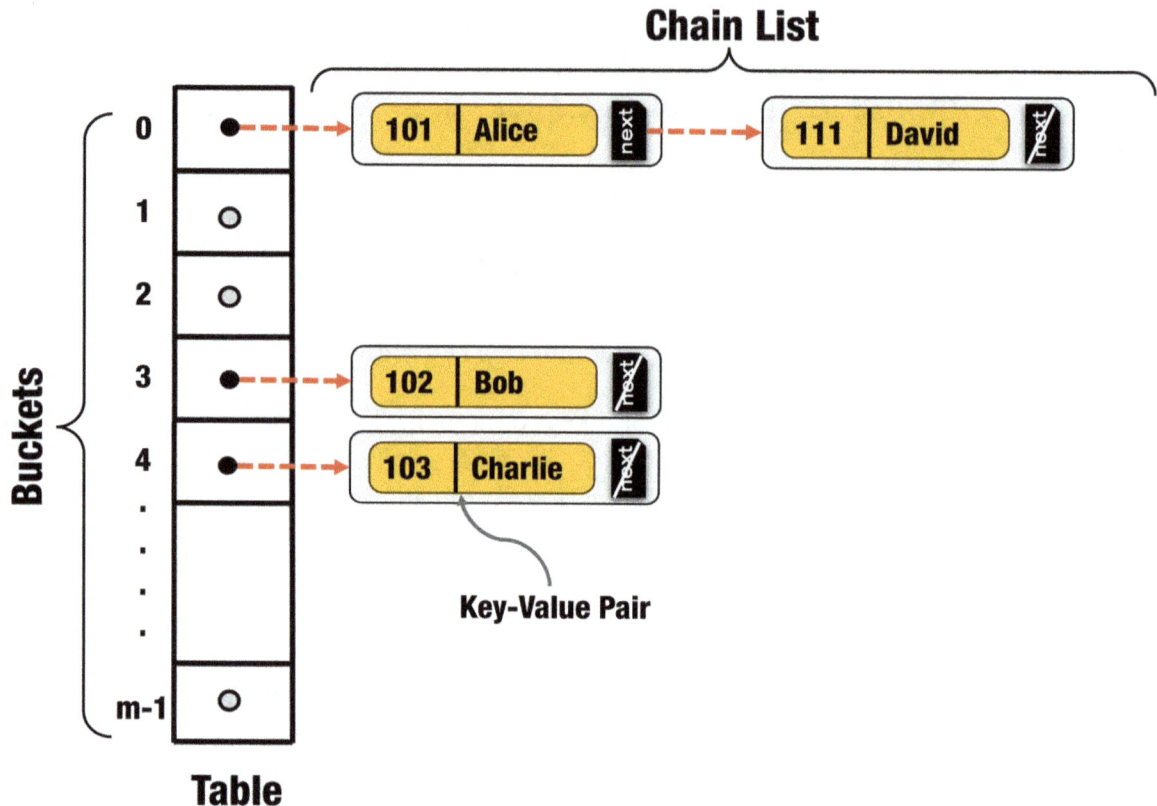

Figure 9.14: Structure of the map with array of buckets and linked lists for separate chaining

```
1  template <typename K, typename V>
2  struct Pair {
3      K key;
4      V value;
5  
6      // Constructors
7      Pair() : key(K()), value(V()) {}
8      Pair(K k, V v) : key(k), value(v) {}
9  
10     // Overloading equality operator for comparison
11     bool operator==(const Pair& other) const {
12         return key == other.key;
13     }
14  
15     // Implicit conversion to key type
16     operator K() const {
17         return key;
```

```
18      }
19 };
```
Pair Structure Definition

The `Pair` structure ensures that each key is unique and can be efficiently compared and stored within the `ChainedHashTable`.

Map Class Definition

Next, we define the `Map` class, which uses `ChainedHashTable` with templates to handle the `Pair` structure, allowing for flexible key-value pair storage. This class provides essential operations such as adding, removing, and retrieving key-value pairs.

```cpp
1  template <typename K, typename V>
2  class Map {
3  public:
4      Map(int buckets=64) : table(buckets) {}
5
6      // Add a key-value pair into the map
7      void add(K key, V value);
8
9      // Removes a key-value pair from the map
10     void remove(K key);
11
12     // Looks up the value associated with a key
13     V get(K key) const;
14
15     // Get all key-value pairs
16     DynamicArray<Pair<K, V>> getAll() const;
17
18     // Print the contents of the map
19     void print() const;
20
21     size_t getSize() const {
22         return table.getSize();
23     }
24 private:
25     ChainedHashTable<Pair<K, V>> table;
26 };
```
Map Class Interface

The `Map` class leverages the underlying `ChainedHashTable` for efficient management of key-value pairs, utilizing separate chaining to handle collisions.

The class diagram (refer to Figure 9.15) provides an overview of the structure and relationships within the Map class. In this implementation, the Map class is composed of a ChainedHashTable, a generic structure that implements the ISet interface. This allows it to store collections of Pair objects, where each Pair encapsulates a key-value relationship.

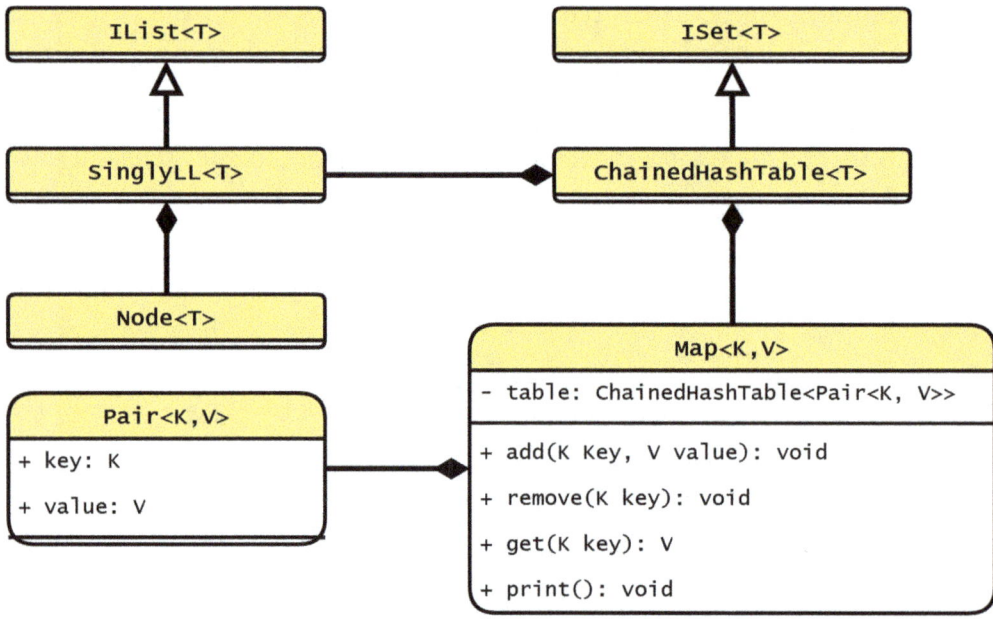

Figure 9.15: Class diagram of Map showing its relationship with ChainedHashTable, Pair, and ISet

Add Operation

Next, let's implement the add operation. This function adds a key-value pair to the map, handling collisions by appending the pair to the appropriate linked list.

```
1 template <typename K, typename V>
2 void Map<K, V>::add(K key, V value) {
3     table.add(Pair<K, V>(key, value));
4 }
```

add Function: Adds a Key-Value Pair

In this code, the add function creates a new Pair object with the given key and value and then calls the add method on the ChainedHashTable to insert it.

Deletion Operation

The deletion operation removes a key-value pair from the map. It involves finding the appropriate linked list using the hash function and then removing the pair from the linked list.

9.4 Maps

```
1  template <typename K, typename V>
2  void Map<K, V>::remove(K key) {
3      Pair<K, V> temp(key, V());
4      table.remove(temp);
5  }
```

remove Function: Removes a Key-Value Pair

In this code, the `remove` function creates a temporary `Pair` object with the given key and a default value and then calls the `remove` method on the `ChainedHashTable` to remove the pair.

Lookup Operation

The lookup operation retrieves the value associated with a given key. It uses the hash function to find the appropriate linked list and then searches for the key in that list.

```
1  template <typename K, typename V>
2  V Map<K, V>::get(K key) const {
3      Pair<K, V> temp(key, V());
4      if (table.contains(temp)) {
5          auto& bucket = table.get(temp);
6
7          for (size_t i = 0; i < bucket.getSize(); ++i) {
8              if (bucket.get(i).key == key) {
9                  return bucket.get(i).value;
10             }
11         }
12     }
13     throw std::runtime_error("Key not found");
14 }
```

get Function: Retrieves the Value Associated with a Key

In this code, the `get` function creates a temporary `Pair` object with the given key and a default value, checks if the `ChainedHashTable` contains the pair, and then iterates through the linked list at the appropriate bucket to find and return the value associated with the key. If the key is not found, an exception is thrown.

Display Operation

Finally, let's implement a function to print the contents of the map. This function iterates through each bucket and prints the key-value pairs.

```cpp
1  template <typename K, typename V>
2  void Map<K, V>::print() const {
3      table.print();
4  }
```
`print` Function: Displays the Contents of the `Map`

In this code, the `print` function calls the `print` method of the `ChainedHashTable`, which iterates through each bucket and prints the key-value pairs stored in that bucket.

Complete Example

Here is a complete example that demonstrates the usage of the `Map` class:

```cpp
1  int main() {
2      Map<int, string> map(10);
3
4      // Inserting key-value pairs
5      map.add(1, "One");
6      map.add(2, "Two");
7      map.add(3, "Three");
8
9      // Display the map
10     std::cout << "Map contents:\n";
11     map.print();
12
13     // Looking up a value
14     try {
15         std::cout << "Value for key 2: "
16                   << map.get(2) << "\n";
17     } catch (const std::runtime_error& e) {
18         std::cout << e.what() << "\n";
19     }
20
21     // Removing a key-value pair
22     map.remove(2);
23     std::cout << "Map after removing key 2:\n";
24     map.print();
25
26     return 0;
27 }
```
Map Usage Example

In the `main` function, we create a `Map` object with ten buckets, insert key-value pairs, print the map, look up a value, and remove a key-value pair.

9.5 A Space-Efficient Linked List

Performance Analysis

The performance of the map operations is crucial for many applications. Here is a brief analysis:

- **Insertion:** The average time complexity for insertion is $O(1)$ due to the efficient handling of collisions using separate chaining. However, in the worst case, it can degrade to $O(c)$, where c is the length of the longest chain.
- **Deletion:** The average time complexity for deletion is $O(1)$ for similar reasons. In the worst case, the time complexity can also degrade to $O(c)$.
- **Lookup:** The average time complexity for lookup is $O(1)$, making maps highly efficient for quick data retrieval. As with insertion and deletion, the worst-case time complexity is $O(c)$.

In conclusion, maps are versatile and efficient data structures that are widely used in various applications. By understanding their implementation and performance characteristics, you can make better decisions when designing systems that require efficient data storage and retrieval.

9.5 A Space-Efficient Linked List

A space-efficient linked list is a variation of traditional linked lists designed to reduce pointer overhead by storing multiple elements in each node. Instead of each node containing a single data value and pointers, each node contains an array of data values. This design minimizes the number of pointers, thereby reducing memory usage and potentially improving cache performance.

9.5.1 Structure of a Space-Efficient Linked List

In a space-efficient linked list, each node contains an array of data values and pointers to both the next and previous nodes. This structure reduces the number of pointers needed, as multiple data values are stored within each node.

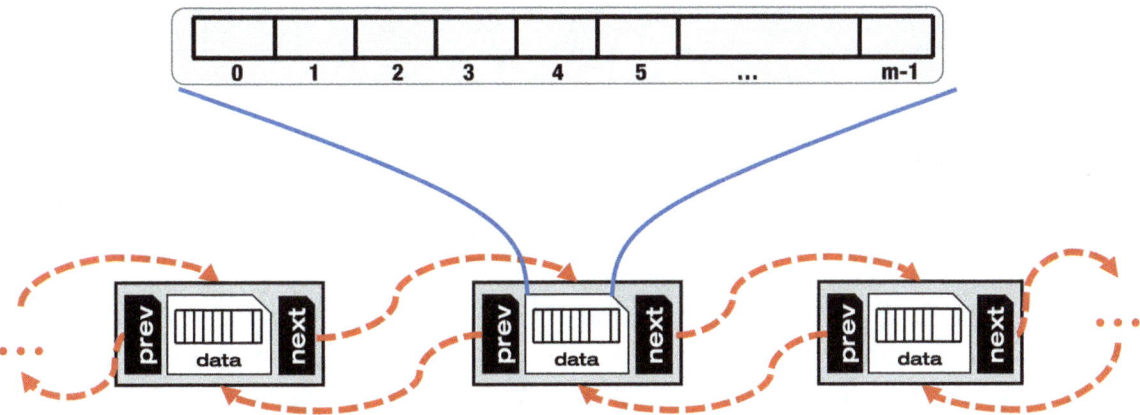

Figure 9.16: Structure of a space-efficient linked list node. Each node contains an array of data values and pointers to the next and previous nodes

As shown in Figure 9.16, each node stores an array of data values, effectively reducing the number of nodes and pointers compared to traditional linked lists. This compact design not only lowers memory usage but also improves cache locality, enhancing performance during traversal and manipulation.

Example: Pointer Complexity

To understand the benefits of a space-efficient linked list, let's compare the number of pointers needed for storing 1000 records in singly-linked lists, doubly-linked lists, and space-efficient linked lists with different array sizes.

In a singly-linked list, each node contains a single data value and a pointer to the next node. Therefore, for 1000 records, we need 1000 pointers. In a doubly-linked list, each node contains a single data value and pointers to both the next and previous nodes. Therefore, for 1000 records, we need 2000 pointers (1000 next pointers + 1000 previous pointers).

In a space-efficient linked list, each node contains an array of data values. Let's consider two scenarios: using an array size of $m = 50$ and $m = 200$. If we divide 1000 records into arrays of size 50, we will have 20 nodes, each containing 50 data values. The number of pointers needed is 40 (20 next pointers + 20 previous pointers). If we divide 1000 records into arrays of size 200, we will have 5 nodes, each containing 200 data values. The number of pointers needed is 10 (5 next pointers + 5 previous pointers).

Table 9.1: Comparison of Space Complexity for Different Linked Lists

Linked List Type	Pointers per Node	Total Number of Pointers	Additional Space Complexity
Singly-Linked List	1	1000	$O(n)$
Doubly-Linked List	2	2000	$O(2n) \approx O(n)$
Space-Efficient ($m = 50$)	2	40	$O(n/m)$
Space-Efficient ($m = 200$)	2	10	$O(n/m)$

As shown in Table 9.1, a singly-linked list with 1000 records requires 1000 pointers. A doubly-linked list with 1000 records requires 2000 pointers. A space-efficient linked list with an array size of $m = 50$ requires 40 pointers, significantly reducing the pointer overhead. A space-efficient linked list with an array size of $m = 200$ requires only 10 pointers, further reducing the pointer overhead.

It is important to note that the additional space complexity shown in the table is in addition to the space required for storing the data itself. By reducing the number of pointers through the use of space-efficient linked lists, we achieve lower memory overhead and potentially better cache performance, especially for large datasets. However, it's important to balance the node array size and the complexity of operations to suit the specific needs of the application.

9.5 A Space-Efficient Linked List

9.5.2 Node Definition

A node in a space-efficient linked list stores multiple data elements in an array within each node, reducing the number of pointers required. This section defines the `ListNode` class used in the implementation of a space-efficient linked list.

```cpp
template <typename T>
struct ListNode {
    T* dataArray;      // Array of data values
    size_t size;       // Number of elements in the array
    size_t capacity;   // Array Capacity
    ListNode* next;    // Pointer to the next node
    ListNode* prev;    // Pointer to the previous node

    ListNode(int arraySize);
    ~ListNode();
};
```

`ListNode` Structure Definition

In this implementation, each `ListNode` contains:
- `dataArray`: A dynamically allocated array of data values
- `size`: The current number of elements stored in the array
- `capacity`: The maximum number of elements the array can hold
- `next` and `prev`: Pointers to the next and previous nodes, respectively, allowing bidirectional traversal of the list

Constructor and Destructor for ListNode

The constructor initializes the node by allocating memory for the data array and setting the size and pointer fields appropriately. The destructor releases the memory allocated for the data array, ensuring proper resource management.

```cpp
template <typename T>
ListNode<T>::ListNode(int arraySize)
    : size(0), capacity(arraySize),
      next(nullptr), prev(nullptr) {
    dataArray = new T[arraySize];
}


template <typename T>
ListNode<T>::~ListNode() {
    delete[] dataArray;
}
```

Constructor and Destructor of `ListNode`

9.5.3 Implementation of Space-Efficient Linked List

The operations on a space-efficient linked list are similar to those on a traditional linked list, but they need to account for the fact that each node contains an array of data values.

Class Definition for SEList

We define the `SEList` class, which inherits from the `IList` interface and uses a dummy node to simplify edge cases, such as insertion and deletion at the boundaries.

```
1  template <typename T>
2  class SEList : public IList<T> {
3  public:
4      SEList(int arraySize);
5      ~SEList();
6
7      // Space-Efficient List-specific function
8      void printSubLists(const std::string& sep = "->") const;
9
10     // Abstract Interface methods implementation...
11
12 private:
13     ListNode<T>* dummy;
14     size_t nodeArraySize;
15 };
```

SEList Class Interface

The class diagram (refer to Figure 9.17) provides an overview of the structure and relationships within the `SEList` class. The `SEList` class inherits from the `IList` interface and is composed of multiple `ListNode` objects.

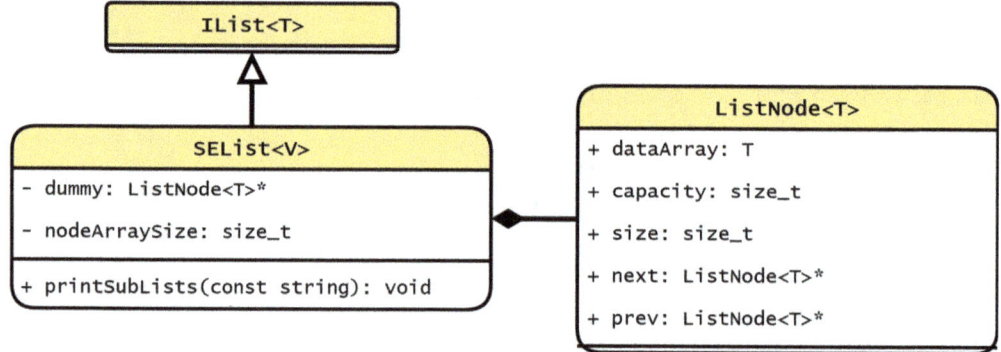

Figure 9.17: Class diagram of `SEList`, illustrating its inheritance from `IList` and its composition with `ListNode`

9.5 A Space-Efficient Linked List

Constructor and Destructor

The constructor initializes the list with a dummy node and sets the node array size. The destructor clears the list and deletes the dummy node, ensuring all allocated memory is properly released.

```cpp
template <typename T>
SEList<T>::SEList(int arraySize)
    : nodeArraySize(arraySize) {
    dummy = new ListNode<T>(arraySize);
    dummy->next = dummy;
    dummy->prev = dummy;
}

template <typename T>
SEList<T>::~SEList() {
    // Clear all nodes
    clear();
    // Delete the dummy node
    delete dummy;
}
```
Constructor and Destructor of SEList

Clear and Print Functions

The `clear` function removes all nodes from the list, resetting it to an empty state. The `print` function displays the elements of the list sequentially, while `printSubLists` provides a more structured view, showing the elements within each sublist separated by a custom delimiter.

```cpp
template <typename T>
void SEList<T>::clear() {
    ListNode<T>* curr = dummy->next;
    while (curr != dummy) {
        ListNode<T>* nextNode = curr->next;
        delete curr;
        curr = nextNode;
    }
    dummy->next = dummy;
    dummy->prev = dummy;
    this->size = 0;
}

template <typename T>
void SEList<T>::print() const {
```

```cpp
16        ListNode<T>* curr = dummy->next;
17        while (curr != dummy) {
18            for (int i = 0; i < curr->size; ++i) {
19                std::cout << curr->dataArray[i] << " ";
20            }
21            curr = curr->next;
22        }
23        std::cout << std::endl;
24 }
25
26 template <typename T>
27 void SEList<T>::printSubLists(const std::string& sep) const{
28        ListNode<T>* curr = dummy->next;
29
30        while (curr != dummy) {
31            std::cout << "[";
32            for (size_t i = 0; i < curr->size; ++i) {
33                std::cout << curr->dataArray[i];
34                if (i < curr->size - 1) {
35                    std::cout << ", ";
36                }
37            }
38            std::cout << "]";
39            if (curr->next != dummy) {
40                std::cout << sep;
41            }
42            curr = curr->next;
43        }
44        std::cout << std::endl;
45 }
```

`clear`, `print`, and `printSubLists` Functions: Managing and Displaying Elements

Accessing Operations

In a space-efficient linked list, elements are distributed across multiple nodes, each containing an array. When accessing an element, the list is viewed as a contiguous array, but the actual storage is split among nodes. For example, consider an array of size n divided into two nodes, each with an array size m.

As shown in Figure 9.18, Node 1 contains elements indexed from 0 to $m-1$, and Node 2 contains elements indexed from m to $2m-1$. To access the element at index 5, it is located in Node 2 at local index 1 (since $5-m=1$).

9.5 A Space-Efficient Linked List

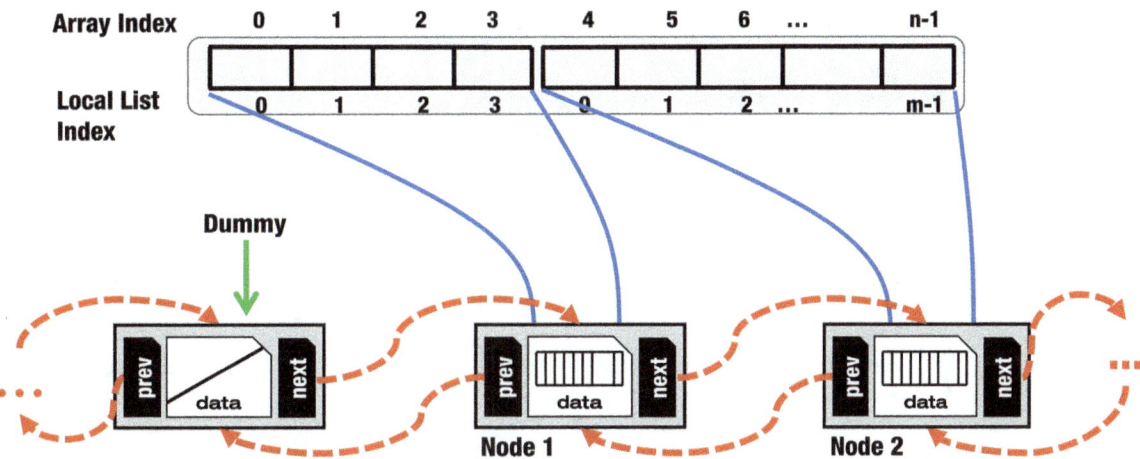

Figure 9.18: Illustration of array indexing in a space-efficient linked list

Array indexing is calculated by first navigating to the correct node and then using the local index within that node.

The `operator[]` function provides a convenient mechanism for accessing elements by their index. By overloading the `operator[]`, we can retrieve elements similarly to standard arrays. The `get` function leverages this operator to return the element at the specified index, ensuring consistent range checking to prevent out-of-bounds errors. Conversely, the `set` function identifies the appropriate node and the specific index within that node to update the value, maintaining the list structure's integrity.

```cpp
template <typename T>
T& SEList<T>::operator[](size_t index) {
    assert(index <= this->size && "Index out of range");

    ListNode<T>* curr = dummy->next;
    while (curr != dummy && index >= curr->size) {
        index -= curr->size;
        curr = curr->next;
    }
    return curr->dataArray[index];
}

template <typename T>
T SEList<T>::get(size_t index) const {
    return const_cast<SEList<T>&>(*this)[index];
}

template <typename T>
void SEList<T>::set(size_t index, const T item) {
```

```
20        assert(index <= this->size && "Index out of range");
21
22        ListNode<T>* curr = dummy->next;
23        while (curr != dummy && index >= curr->size) {
24            index -= curr->size;
25            curr = curr->next;
26        }
27        curr->dataArray[index] = item;
28 }
```

operator[], get, and set Functions: Accessing and Modifying Elements in the SEList

Lookup Operation

The indexOf function finds the index of the specified item in the list by traversing the list, checking each element in the node's array. If the item is found, it returns the index. If the item is not found, it returns −1.

```
1 template <typename T>
2 int SEList<T>::indexOf(const T item) const {
3     ListNode<T>* curr = dummy->next;
4     int currIndex = 0;
5
6     while (curr != dummy) {
7         for (size_t i = 0; i < curr->size; ++i) {
8             if (curr->dataArray[i] == item) {
9                 return currIndex + i;
10            }
11        }
12        currIndex += curr->size;
13        curr = curr->next;
14    }
15    return -1; // Item not found
16 }
```

indexOf Function: Finds the Index of an Item in the SEList

Insertion Operation

In traditional linked lists, inserting a node at a specific position involves navigating to the desired location and adjusting a few pointers. However, in a space-efficient linked list where each node contains an array of elements, the process becomes more complex due to the need to manage array boundaries and potentially shift elements. To simplify the shifting of all elements, we can opt to split the array if it is full. Figure 9.19 illustrates the steps involved in the insertAt operation.

9.5 A Space-Efficient Linked List

The `insertAt` function performs the following steps:
1. **Navigate to the Appropriate Node:** Traverse the list to find the node that contains the desired index.
2. **Handle Cases**
    - **Case 1: If the List Is Empty:** If the list is empty, insert into a new node.
    - **Case 2: If Inserting at the End:** If inserting at the end of the list, either append to the last node or create a new one.
    - **Case 3: Split the Node If Full:** If the node is full, split it into two nodes and adjust pointers accordingly.
    - **Case 4: Shift Elements and Insert:** If the node is not full, shift elements within the node to make room for the new element and insert it at the correct position.

```cpp
template <typename T>
void SEList<T>::insertAt(size_t index, const T item) {
    // Ensure the index is within valid range
    assert(index <= size && "Index out of range");

    // CASE 1: Inserting into an empty list
    if (size == 0) {
        ListNode<T>* newNode
            = new ListNode<T>(nodeArraySize);
        newNode->dataArray[0] = item;
        newNode->size = 1;
        newNode->next = dummy;
        newNode->prev = dummy;
        dummy->next = newNode;
        dummy->prev = newNode;
        ++this->size;
        return;
    }

    // Navigate to the appropriate node for insertion
    ListNode<T>* curr = dummy->next;
    size_t count = 0;

    while (curr != dummy && count + curr->size <= index) {
        count += curr->size;
        curr = curr->next;
    }

    // CASE 2: If inserting at the end of the list
    if (curr == dummy && count == index) {
        curr = dummy->prev;
```

288   Chapter 9. Specialized Data Structures and Techniques

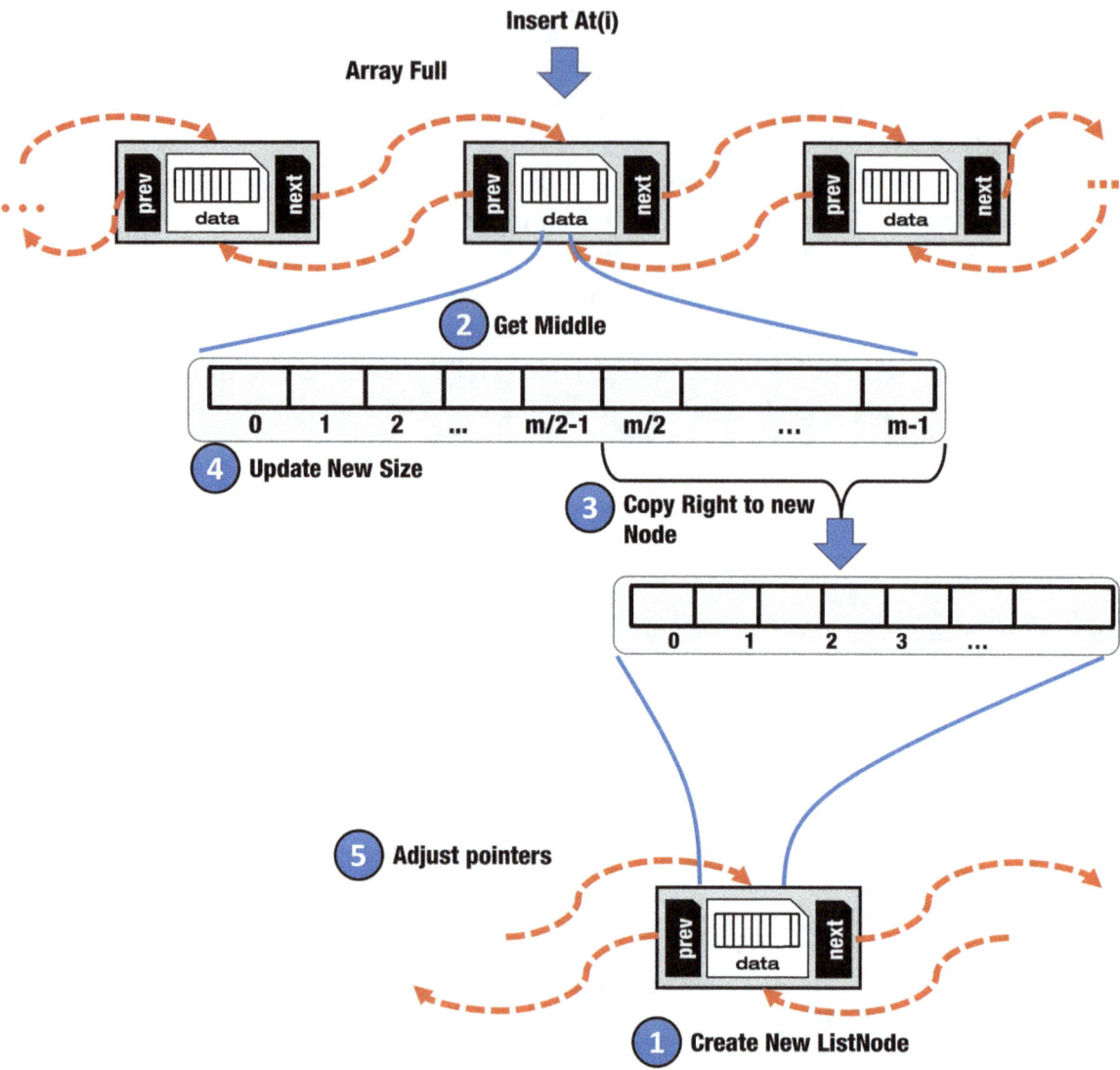

Figure 9.19: Illustration of the Insert At operation. If the node is full, the steps are as follows: (1) create a new `ListNode`, (2) calculate the middle point, (3) copy the right half to the new `ListNode`, (4) adjust the current `ListNode` size, and (5) adjust pointers

```
32
33          if (curr->size < curr->capacity) {
34              // Insert at the end of the last
35              // node if it has space
36              curr->dataArray[curr->size] = item;
37              ++curr->size;
38              ++this->size;
39          } else {
40              // Create a new node if the last node is full
```

9.5 A Space-Efficient Linked List

```
41              ListNode<T>* newNode
42                  = new ListNode<T>(nodeArraySize);
43              newNode->dataArray[0] = item;
44              newNode->size = 1;
45              newNode->prev = curr;
46              newNode->next = dummy;
47              curr->next = newNode;
48              dummy->prev = newNode;
49              ++this->size;
50          }
51          return;
52      } else {
53          assert(curr != dummy &&
54              "Unexpected dummy node encountered");
55      }
56
57      // CASE 3: If the node is full, splitting it
58
59      // Calculate the local index within the node
60      size_t localIndex = index - count;
61
62      if (curr->size == curr->capacity) {
63          // (1) Create a new ListNode
64          ListNode<T>* newNode =
65              new ListNode<T>(nodeArraySize);
66          // (2) Calculate the middle point
67          size_t mid = curr->capacity / 2;
68          // (3) Copy the right half to the new ListNode
69          std::copy(curr->dataArray + mid,
70              curr->dataArray + curr->size,
71              newNode->dataArray);
72
73          newNode->size = curr->size - mid;
74          // (4) Adjust the current ListNode size
75
76          curr->size = mid;
77
78          // (5) Adjust pointers
79          newNode->next = curr->next;
80          newNode->prev = curr;
81          if (curr->next != nullptr) {
82              curr->next->prev = newNode;
83          }
84          curr->next = newNode;
85
```

```
 86            // (6) Determine whether to insert in
 87            //     the new node or the current one
 88            if (localIndex >= mid) {
 89                curr = newNode;
 90                localIndex -= mid;
 91            }
 92        }
 93
 94        // CASE 4: If the node is not full
 95        // shift elements to free space for the new item
 96
 97        for (size_t i = curr->size; i > localIndex; --i) {
 98            curr->dataArray[i] = curr->dataArray[i - 1];
 99        }
100
101        // Insert the new item
102        curr->dataArray[localIndex] = item;
103        ++curr->size;
104        ++this->size;
105 }
```

insertAt Function: Inserts an Item at a Specific Index in the SEList

Removal Operation

The removeAt function removes an item at a specified index. It performs the following steps:
1. **Navigate to the Appropriate Node:** Traverse the list to find the node that contains the desired index.
2. **Shift Elements:** Shift elements within the node to fill the gap created by the removed element.
3. **Delete the Node If Empty:** If the node becomes empty after removal, delete it and adjust the pointers accordingly.

```
 1 template <typename T>
 2 void SEList<T>::removeAt(size_t index) {
 3     // Ensure the index is within valid range
 4     assert(index < this->size && "Index out of range");
 5
 6     ListNode<T>* curr = dummy->next;
 7     size_t count = 0;
 8
 9     // Navigate to the appropriate node
10     while (curr != dummy && count + curr->size <= index) {
11         count += curr->size;
12         curr = curr->next;
```

9.5 A Space-Efficient Linked List

```
13      }
14
15      // Ensure we have found a valid node
16      assert(curr != dummy &&
17          "Unexpected dummy node encountered");
18
19      // Calculate the local index within the node
20      size_t localIndex = index - count;
21
22      // Shift elements within the node
23      for (size_t i = localIndex; i < curr->size - 1; ++i) {
24          curr->dataArray[i] = curr->dataArray[i + 1];
25      }
26
27      --curr->size;
28      --this->size;
29
30      // Delete the node if it becomes empty
31      if (curr->size == 0) {
32          curr->prev->next = curr->next;
33          curr->next->prev = curr->prev;
34          delete curr;
35      }
36      // Optional: Handle merging of nodes if necessary
37  }
```

removeAt Function: Removes an Item at a Specific Index in the `SEList`

Push Front and Push Back

The `pushFront` and `pushBack` functions insert items at the beginning and end of the list, respectively. These operations are essential for efficiently managing elements in a space-efficient linked list, allowing for dynamic growth at both ends.

```
1  template <typename T>
2  void SEList<T>::pushFront(const T item) {
3      insertAt(0, item);
4  }
5
6  template <typename T>
7  void SEList<T>::pushBack(const T item) {
8      insertAt(size, item);
9  }
```

`pushFront` and `pushBack` Functions: Adds an Item to the Front or End of the `SEList`

Pop Front and Pop Back

The `popFront` and `popBack` functions remove items from the beginning and end of the list, respectively. These functions are crucial for manipulating the list from both ends, providing flexibility in managing the elements.

```
1  template <typename T>
2  T SEList<T>::popFront() {
3      assert(!this->isEmpty() && "List is empty");
4
5      T item = get(0);
6      removeAt(0);
7      return item;
8  }
9
10 template <typename T>
11 T SEList<T>::popBack() {
12     assert(!this->isEmpty() && "List is empty");
13
14     T item = get(size - 1);
15     removeAt(size - 1);
16     return item;
17 }
```

`popFront` and `popBack` Functions: Removes and Returns an Item from the Front or End of the `SEList`

Top Front and Top Back

The `topFront` and `topBack` return items at the beginning and end of the list without removing them. These functions are useful for peeking at the elements at both ends of the list, allowing access to the front and back elements efficiently.

```
1  template <typename T>
2  T SEList<T>::topFront() const {
3      assert(!this->isEmpty() && "List is empty");
4
5      return dummy->next->dataArray[0];
6  }
7
8  template <typename T>
9  T SEList<T>::topBack() const {
10     assert(!this->isEmpty() && "List is empty");
11
12     return get(this->size - 1);
```

9.5 A Space-Efficient Linked List

```
13 }
```

`topFront` and `topBack` Functions: Returns an Item from the Front or End Without Removing It

9.5.4 Performance Analysis

In an optimized linked list, each node holds an array of elements, which decreases the number of pointers required compared to conventional linked lists. This lowers memory usage and can enhance performance efficiency. Nonetheless, some operations, like inserting or deleting elements at particular positions, may become more complex due to the need to manage arrays within nodes.

- **Time Complexity**
  - **Insertion or Removal at Specific Location:** $O(n/m + m)$ – Navigating to the appropriate node takes $O(n/m)$ time, and shifting elements within the node takes $O(m)$ time. This combined time accounts for both traversal and adjustment within nodes.
  - **Access (Get, Set):** $O(n/m)$ – Accessing elements requires locating the correct node, which takes $O(n/m)$ time, as nodes store multiple elements, making access faster compared to traditional linked lists.
- **Space Complexity:** $O(n + n/m)$ – The number of pointers needed is reduced to $O(n/m)$, in addition to the space required for storing the data itself. In comparison, a traditional singly-linked list requires $2n$ pointers (one for each element and one for the next pointer), and a doubly-linked list requires $3n$ pointers (one for each element, one for the next pointer, and one for the previous pointer).

9.5.5 Advantages and Trade-Offs

The space-efficient linked list offers several advantages over traditional linked lists:
- **Reduced Pointer Overhead:** By storing multiple data values in each node, the number of pointers is significantly reduced, leading to lower memory overhead.
- **Improved Cache Performance:** Accessing an array of data values within a node can lead to better cache performance compared to accessing individual nodes scattered in memory.

However, there are also some trade-offs:
- **Complexity of Operations:** Insertion, deletion, and traversal operations become more complex due to the need to manage arrays within nodes.
- **Memory Allocation:** Nodes require dynamic memory allocation for their arrays, which can cause increased complexity in memory management.

In summary, a space-efficient linked list provides a balance between the flexibility of linked lists and the space efficiency of arrays. By understanding the structure and operations of this data structure, developers can make informed decisions about when and how to use it in their applications. The reduction in pointer overhead and improved cache performance make it a compelling choice for scenarios where space efficiency and performance are crucial, though it requires careful management of insertion and deletion operations.

9.6 Skip Lists

Skip lists are a probabilistic data structure that allows fast search, insertion, and deletion operations within an **ordered** sequence of elements. They are an alternative to balanced trees and are often easier to implement. Skip lists use a layered linked list structure, where each layer skips multiple elements to enable faster traversal.

9.6.1 Introduction to Skip Lists

Skip lists use multiple levels of linked lists to maintain order and allow for efficient search operations. The idea is to have multiple layers where each layer is a subset of the previous one, with the bottom layer containing all the elements in sorted order. Higher layers provide "shortcuts" to speed up the search process.

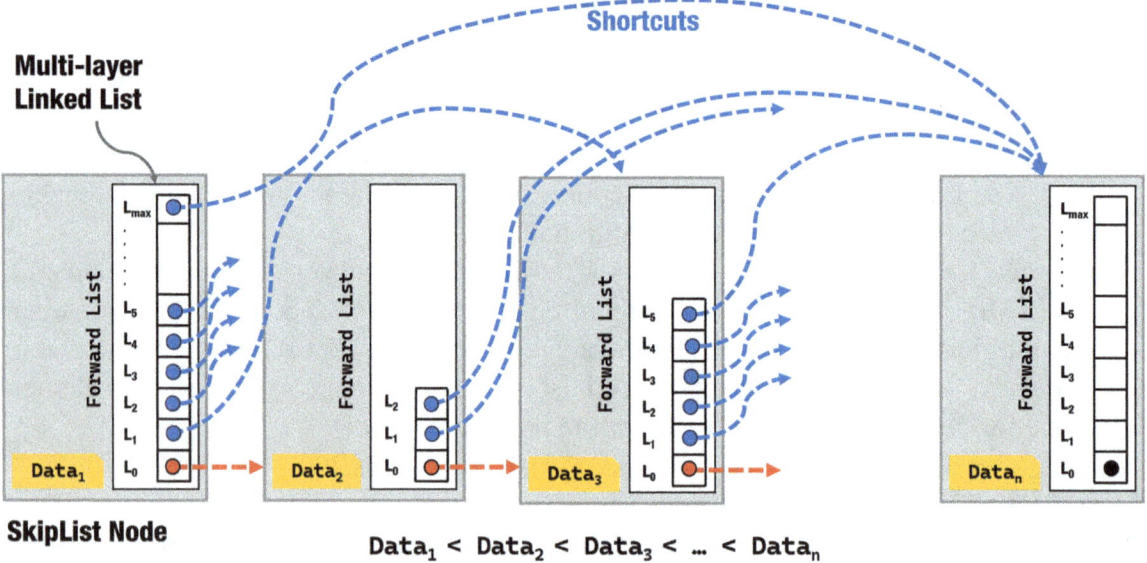

Figure 9.20: Structure of a skip list. The bottom layer contains all elements in sorted order, while higher layers provide shortcuts

As illustrated in Figure 9.20, a skip list consists of multiple levels. The lowest level contains all the elements, and each higher level acts as an express lane, skipping multiple elements of the lower level.

9.6.2 Skip List Structure and Rules

The structure and behavior of a skip list are governed by the following rules.

Levels and Nodes

The skip list consists of multiple levels of linked lists, and each node within these levels has specific characteristics:

9.6 Skip Lists

- **Multiple Levels:** The bottom level (level 0) contains all the elements in sorted order. Each higher level acts as an express lane that skips multiple elements.
- **Nodes:** Each node in a skip list contains a value and multiple forward pointers, one for each level (see Figure 9.21).
- **Number of Levels:** The number of levels for each node is determined randomly, typically using a geometric distribution with a fixed probability p. For example, with $p = 0.5$, the probability that a node appears in level i is p^i.
- **Maximum Level:** The maximum level of any node is capped by a predefined limit, which is usually logarithmic to the number of elements in the skip list.

> **Note:** The maximum number of levels in a skip list grows logarithmically with the number of elements n. Approximately half of the nodes are at level 1, a quarter at level 2, an eighth at level 3, and so forth. This distribution ensures that operations like search, insertion, and deletion can be performed in $O(\log n)$ time on average.

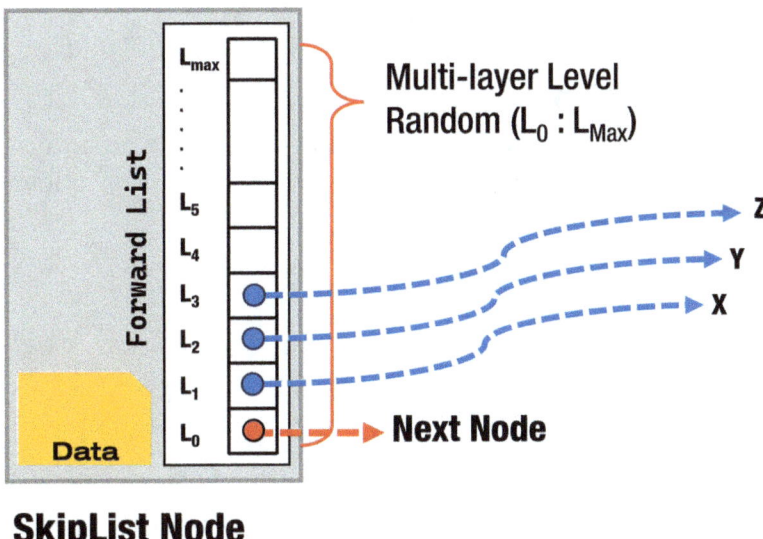

SkipList Node

Figure 9.21: Illustration of a skip list node. Each node contains a value and multiple forward pointers, with the number of forward pointers determined randomly. In this example, the node has forward pointers at levels L_0, L_1, L_2, and L_3. The pointer at level L_1 skips to Node X, the pointer at level L_2 skips to Node Y, and the pointer at level L_3 skips to Node Z. The data values maintain the order such that $\text{Data}(X) < \text{Data}(Y) < \text{Data}(Z)$

Insertion Rules

The following rules must be followed when inserting a new element into a skip list:
- **Insert at All Levels:** When inserting a new element, it is added to all levels from level 0 up to the randomly assigned level.
- **Maintain Order:** Each level must maintain the order of elements. The forward pointers of the nodes are updated to ensure that the new node is correctly placed at each level.

Search Rules

To search for an element in a skip list, the following rules are followed:
- **Start from the Top:** To search for an element, the process starts from the highest level and moves forward as long as the next element is less than the search value.
- **Drop Down a Level:** If moving forward is not possible (either the next element is greater than or equal to the search value, or the end of the level is reached), the search drops down to the next lower level and continues.
- **Reach the Target:** This process continues until the search either finds the target element or reaches level 0 and confirms the element is not present.

Deletion Rules

The following rules must be observed when deleting an element from a skip list:
- **Remove from All Levels:** When deleting an element, it is removed from all levels where it appears.
- **Update Pointers:** The forward pointers of the preceding nodes are updated to bypass the deleted node and maintain the skip list structure.

9.6.3 Node Structure Definition

First, we define the `SKNode` structure that contains a value and an array of forward pointers. The `forward` array stores pointers to nodes at different levels, allowing each node to participate in multiple layers of the skip list.

```cpp
template <typename T>
struct SKNode {
    T value;
    DynamicArray<SKNode*> forward;

    // Constructor
    SKNode(int level, T val) : value(val),
        forward(level + 1) {
      for (int i = 0; i <= level; ++i) {
            forward[i] = nullptr;
        }
    }
};
```

SKNode Structure Definition

9.6.4 Skip List Class Definition

Next, we define the `SkipList` class, which manages the nodes and provides the necessary operations for searching, insertion, and deletion. The `SkipList` class inherits from the `ISet` interface.

```cpp
1  template <typename T>
2  class SkipList : public ISet<T> {
3  public:
4      SkipList(int maxLevel, float probability);
5      ~SkipList();
6
7      // Inserts a value into the skip list
8      bool add(const T value);
9
10     // Removes a value from the skip list
11     bool remove(const T value);
12
13     // Searches for a value in the skip list
14     bool contains(const T value) const;
15
16     // Clears the skip list
17     void clear();
18
19     // Displays the contents of the skip list
20     void print() const;
21
22 private:
23     int maxLevel;
24     float probability;
25     SKNode<T>* head;
26
27     // To determine the random level
28     int randomLevel();
29 };
```

SkipList Class Interface

The class diagram (refer to Figure 9.22) provides an overview of the structure and relationships within the SkipList class. The SkipList class inherits from the ISet interface and is composed of multiple SKNode objects, each containing an array of forward pointers.

9.6.5 Implementing Operations
Constructor and Destructor
The constructor initializes the skip list with a maximum level and probability, setting up the head node and seeding the random number generator. The destructor cleans up allocated memory by deleting the head node.

Chapter 9. Specialized Data Structures and Techniques

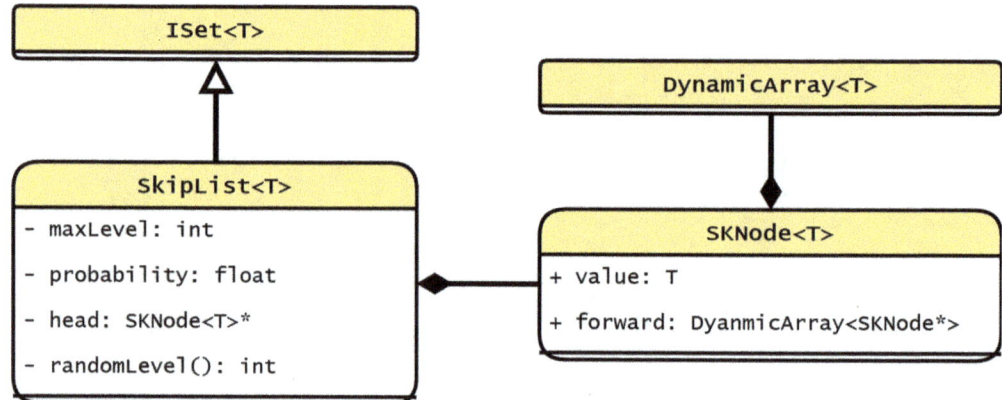

Figure 9.22: Class diagram of `SkipList` showing its inheritance from `ISet` and its composition with `SKNode`

```
1  template <typename T>
2  SkipList<T>::SkipList(int maxLevel, float probability)
3      : maxLevel(maxLevel), probability(probability) {
4      // Initialize head node with dummy value
5      head = new SKNode<T>(maxLevel, T());
6      // Seed the random number generator
7      srand(time(nullptr));
8  }
9
10 template <typename T>
11 SkipList<T>::~SkipList() {
12     clear();
13     delete head;
14 }
```

Constructor and Destructor for `SkipList`

Random Level Generation

The `randomLevel` function generates a random level for node insertion based on the specified probability. This function helps maintain the probabilistic balancing of the skip list.

```
1  template <typename T>
2  int SkipList<T>::randomLevel() {
3      int level = 0;
4      while ((rand() / double(RAND_MAX)) < probability
5              && level < maxLevel) {
6          level++;
```

9.6 Skip Lists

```
7    }
8    return level;
9 }
```

randomLevel Function: Generate Levels

Lookup Operation

Searching in a skip list involves traversing the express lanes at higher levels and dropping down to lower levels as needed. This process allows for efficient location of the target element.

The step-by-step lookup process is as follows:
1. **Start from the Top Level:** Begin the search at the highest level of the skip list.
2. **Traverse Forward:** Move forward in the current level as long as the next node's value is less than the target value.
3. **Drop Down a Level:** If moving forward is not possible, drop down to the next lower level and continue the search.
4. **Check the Bottom Level:** Once at the bottom level, check if the current node's forward pointer points to the target value.

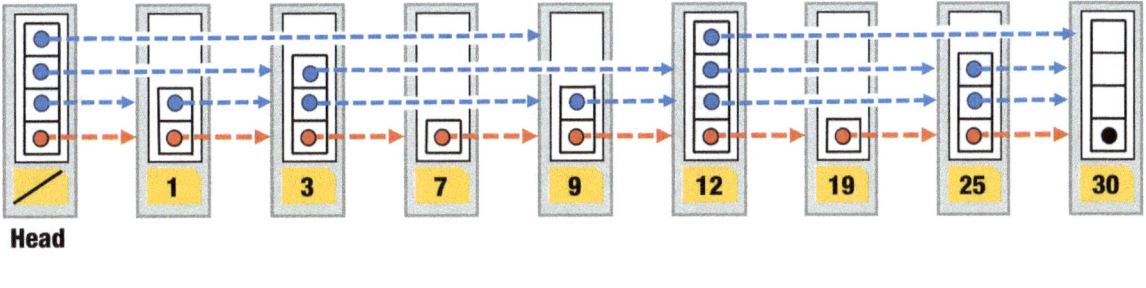

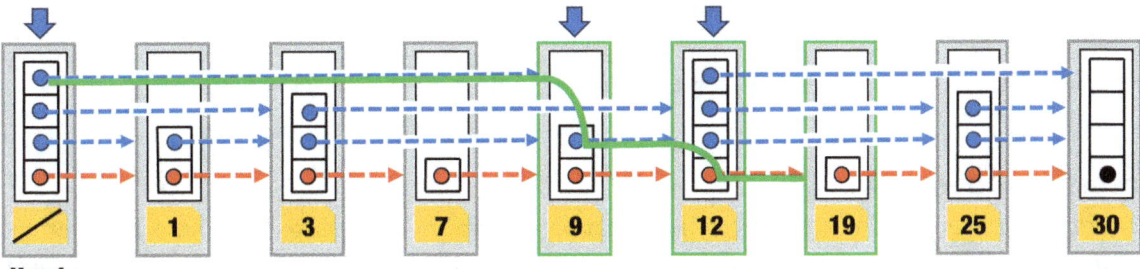

Figure 9.23: Example of skip list with element lookup. The element 19 is found by traversing the levels and moving forward

■ **Example 9.9 Lookup Operation**
Consider a skip list with levels 0 to 3 and the following elements: 1, 3, 7, 9, 12, 19, 25, 30. Let's go through an example where we search for an element (e.g., 19) in the existing skip list (see Figure 9.23).

- **Start from the Top Level:** At level 3, the head's `forward[3]` points to node 9, which is less than 19, so we skip to the node with value 9.
- **Traverse Forward:** Since there is no `forward[3]` from node 9, we drop down to level 2.
- **Drop Down a Level:** At level 2, node 9 does not have a `forward[2]` pointer, so we drop down to level 1.
- **Traverse Forward:** At level 1, node 9's `forward[1]` points to node 12, which is less than 19, so we skip to node 12.
- **Drop Down a Level:** At level 1, node 12's `forward[1]` points to node 25, which is greater than 19, so we drop down to level 0.
- **Check the Bottom Level:** Finally, at level 0, the `forward[0]` pointer from node 12 points to node 19, confirming the target value.

In this process, the element 19 is found by traversing the levels and moving forward, skipping unnecessary nodes.

∎

```
1  template <typename T>
2  bool SkipList<T>::contains(const T value) const {
3      SKNode<T>* curr = head;
4      for (int i = maxLevel; i >= 0; i--) {
5          while (curr->forward[i] != nullptr
6                  && curr->forward[i]->value < value) {
7              curr = curr->forward[i];
8          }
9      }
10     curr = curr->forward[0];
11     return curr != nullptr && curr->value == value;
12 }
```

contains Function: Lookup in Skip List

Insertion Operation

Inserting a new element into a skip list involves several critical steps to ensure the element is placed correctly across multiple levels, maintaining the skip list's efficiency and order. The process also includes checks to prevent duplicate entries.

The step-by-step insertion process is as follows:
1. **Navigate to the Insert Position:** Start at the highest level and traverse the skip list to find the appropriate position for the new element at each level.
2. **Handle Duplicate Check:** Before insertion, check if the value already exists in the skip list to prevent duplicates.

9.6 Skip Lists

3. **Determine the Level:** Use a random level assignment to determine the number of levels for the new node.
4. **Insert the Node:** Insert the new node by updating the forward pointers at each level where the node should appear.

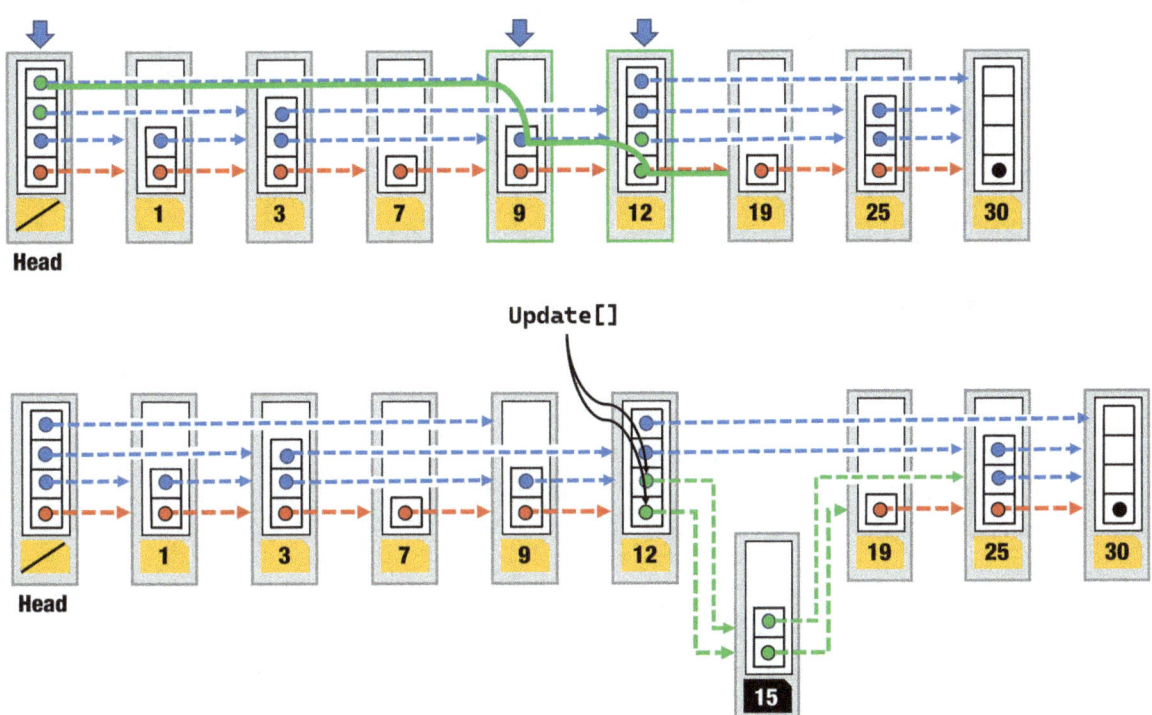

Figure 9.24: Example of skip list with element insertion. The new element 15 is added at levels 0 and 1, and the pointers are updated accordingly

> ### ■ Example 9.10 Skip List Operations
> Consider a skip list with levels 0 to 3 and the following elements: 1, 3, 7, 9, 12, 19, 25, 30. Let's go through an example where we insert a new element (e.g., 15) into the existing skip list (see Figure 9.24).
> 1. **Random Level Assignment:** Suppose the random level assigned to the new node with value 15 is 1.
> 2. **Find Insert Position:**
>   - Start at the highest level (level 3). The head's forward[3] points to node 9, which is less than 15, so we skip to the node with value 9.
>   - At level 3, there are no further forward pointers, so we drop down to level 2.
>   - At level 2, node 9 does not have a forward[2] pointer, so we drop down to level 1.

- At level 1, node 9's `forward[1]` points to node 12, which is less than 15, so we skip to node 12.
- Drop down to level 0. Node 12's `forward[0]` points to node 19, which is greater than 15, so the correct position for 15 is between nodes 12 and 19.

3. **Insert the Node:** Update the forward pointers at levels 0 and 1 to include the new node with value 15. At level 1, node 12's `forward[1]` now points to the new node 15, and node 15's `forward[1]` points to node 25. Similarly, at level 0, node 12's `forward[0]` points to the new node 15, and node 15's `forward[0]` points to node 19.

During this process, `update[i]` arrays are used to track the nodes where updates are needed for each level.

After insertion, the structure of the skip list is updated, and the forward pointers are adjusted to maintain the correct order. ∎

```cpp
template <typename T>
bool SkipList<T>::add(const T value) {
    DynamicArray<SKNode<T>*> update(maxLevel + 1);
    SKNode<T>* curr = head;

    // Find the position to insert
    for (int i = maxLevel; i >= 0; i--) {
        while (curr->forward[i] != nullptr
            && curr->forward[i]->value < value) {
            curr = curr->forward[i];
        }
        update[i] = curr;
    }
    curr = curr->forward[0];

    // If value already exists, return false
    if (curr != nullptr && curr->value == value) {
        return false;
    }

    // Determine the level for the new node
    int level = randomLevel();
    SKNode<T>* newNode = new SKNode<T>(level, value);

    // Insert the new node and update forward pointers
    for (int i = 0; i <= level; i++) {
        newNode->forward[i] = update[i]->forward[i];
        update[i]->forward[i] = newNode;
    }
```

9.6 Skip Lists

```
30        this->size++;
31        return true;
32 }
```
add Function: Insert in Skip List

Deletion Operation

Deletion in a skip list involves removing the element from all levels where it appears. This operation ensures that the skip list structure remains consistent after the element is removed.

The step-by-step deletion process is as follows:

1. **Find the Element:** Starting from the highest level, traverse the skip list to locate the node that precedes the element to be deleted at each level.
2. **Check for Existence:** Confirm that the element exists in the skip list before proceeding with the deletion.
3. **Update Pointers:** Adjust the forward pointers of the preceding nodes to bypass the node being deleted.
4. **Remove the Node:** Delete the node from memory to complete the deletion process and decrease the size of the list.

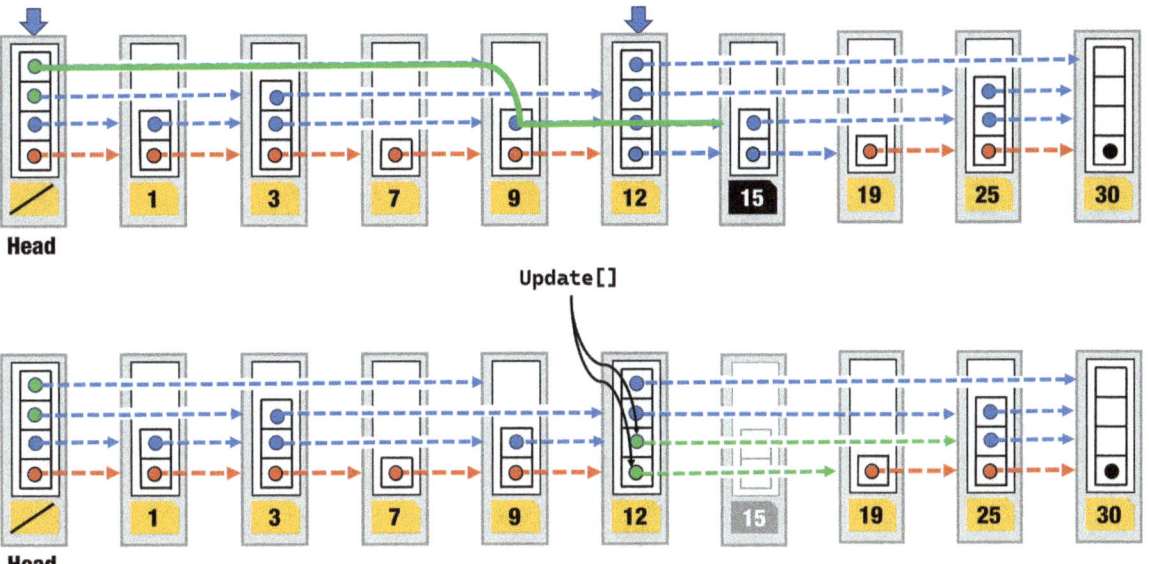

Figure 9.25: Example of skip list with element deletion. The element 15 is removed, and the pointers are updated accordingly

■ **Example 9.11 Deletion in a Skip List**

Consider a skip list with levels 0 to 3 and the following elements: 1, 3, 7, 9, 12, 15, 19, 21, 25, 30. Let's go through an example where we delete an element (e.g., 15) from the existing skip list (see Figure 9.25).

1. **Find the Element:**
   - Start at the highest level (level 3). Since the head's `forward[3]` points to node 9, which is less than 19, move to node 9.
   - At level 3, there are no further forward pointers, so we drop down to level 2.
   - At level 2, node 9 does not have a `forward[2]` pointer to node 15, so drop down to level 1.
   - At level 1, traverse through nodes 12 to find the position before 15.
   - Finally, at level 0, locate the node immediately before 15.
2. **Check for Existence:** Ensure that the element 15 exists in the list before proceeding.
3. **Update Pointers:** Adjust the forward pointers at each level to bypass the node containing 15.
4. **Remove the Node:** Delete the node from memory and update the size of the skip list.

After deletion, the structure of the skip list is updated, and the forward pointers are adjusted to maintain the correct order. ∎

```cpp
template <typename T>
bool SkipList<T>::remove(const T value) {
    DynamicArray<SKNode<T>*> update(maxLevel + 1);
    SKNode<T>* curr = head;

    // Find the position to remove
    for (int i = maxLevel; i >= 0; i--) {
        while (curr->forward[i] != nullptr
               && curr->forward[i]->value < value) {
            curr = curr->forward[i];
        }
        update[i] = curr;
    }

    curr = curr->forward[0];
    if (curr == nullptr || curr->value != value) {
        return false;  // Value not found
    }

    // Update forward pointers and delete the node
    for (int i = 0; i <= maxLevel; i++) {
        if (update[i]->forward[i] != curr) {
            break;
        }
        update[i]->forward[i] = curr->forward[i];
    }
```

```
27
28        delete curr;
29        this->size--;
30        return true;
31 }
```
remove Function: Delete in Skip List

Display Operation

Finally, let's implement a function to display the contents of the skip list. This function prints each level of the skip list, showing the values contained at that level in sequence.

```
1 template <typename T>
2 void SkipList<T>::print() const {
3     for (int i = maxLevel; i >= 0; i--) {
4         SKNode<T>* current = head->forward[i];
5         std::cout << "Level " << i << ": ";
6         while (current != nullptr) {
7             std::cout << current->value << " ";
8             current = current->forward[i];
9         }
10        std::cout << std::endl;
11    }
12 }
```
print Function: Display Skip List

In this code, the `print` function prints the values at each level of the skip list, starting from the highest level down to level 0. By iterating over the forward pointers at each level, it displays the sequence of nodes in the skip list, providing a clear visualization of its layered structure.

9.6.6 Performance Analysis

The performance of skip list operations is crucial for many applications. The average time complexity for insertion, deletion, and lookup operations in a skip list is $O(\log n)$. This efficiency is due to the random level assignment and the multiple levels that provide shortcuts, allowing for quick traversal and access.

Comparison with Other Data Structures

Skip lists offer several advantages over other data structures, such as balanced trees:
- **Simplicity:** Skip lists are easier to implement and understand compared to balanced trees.
- **Efficiency:** Skip lists offer similar average time complexity for search, insertion, and deletion operations as balanced trees.

- **Flexibility:** Skip lists can easily handle concurrent updates and searches, making them suitable for multithreaded applications.

In conclusion, skip lists are versatile and efficient data structures that offer an alternative to balanced binary search trees. Their simplicity, combined with $O(\log n)$ average time complexity for common operations, makes them an attractive choice for many real-world applications. By understanding their implementation and performance characteristics, you can make better decisions when designing systems that require efficient data storage and retrieval.

> **Note:**
> The performance of skip lists can be fine-tuned by adjusting the maximum level and probability parameters, allowing you to optimize the structure for specific application requirements.

9.7 Summary

This chapter presented a comprehensive examination of specialized data structures and techniques, offering insights into their implementation and applications. We started with an introduction to heaps, exploring both Max-Heaps and Min-Heaps, and their properties. We then moved on to the implementation details, including insertion, deletion, and heapification operations, highlighting their efficiency and performance benefits.

Following heaps, we delved into maps, focusing on their structure, key-value pairs, and operations. We provided a step-by-step guide to building a map data structure in C++, using a chained hash table for collision handling. The map section emphasized the importance of efficient insertion, deletion, and lookup operations.

Next, we explored space-efficient linked lists, which minimize pointer overhead by storing multiple elements in each node. The space-efficient linked list section included a detailed explanation of the node structure, implementation of operations, and performance analysis, showcasing the advantages and trade-offs of using space-efficient linked lists.

Finally, we introduced skip lists, a probabilistic data structure that allows fast search, insertion, and deletion operations. We discussed the skip list's layered structure and the rules governing its operation and provided a complete implementation in C++. The performance analysis section compared skip lists with other data structures, highlighting their simplicity, efficiency, and flexibility.

By the end of this chapter, readers will have a solid understanding of these specialized data structures, their implementation, and their practical applications. This knowledge will enable the design of more efficient algorithms and data management solutions in various computational scenarios.

Problems

Discussion

1. Discuss the advantages of using skip lists over balanced binary search trees. In what scenarios might a skip list be preferred?
2. Explain how separate chaining helps in resolving collisions in hash tables. Provide examples of real-world applications where this technique is used.
3. Describe the process of inserting an element into a skip list. How does the random level assignment affect the performance of the skip list?
4. Compare and contrast the use of maps and skip lists. What are the key differences in their implementations and use cases?
5. Discuss the impact of the probability p in the random level assignment of skip lists. How does changing p affect the performance and structure of the skip list?
6. Given a skip list with the following elements: 2, 4, 6, 8, 10, 12, 14, 16. Illustrate the process of inserting the element 9. Show the skip list structure before and after the insertion.

Multiple Choice Questions

1. Which of the following statements about skip lists is true?
   (a) Skip lists use a single linked list to store elements.
   (b) Skip lists guarantee $O(1)$ time complexity for insertion.
   (c) Skip lists are a probabilistic alternative to balanced binary search trees.
   (d) Skip lists do not support deletion operations.
2. The time complexity of searching for an element in a skip list is:
   (a) $O(1)$
   (b) $O(n)$
   (c) $O(\log n)$
   (d) $O(n \log n)$
3. In the context of maps, which of the following is true?
   (a) Maps can only store integer keys.
   (b) Maps do not support deletion of key-value pairs.
   (c) Maps associate unique keys with values for efficient retrieval.
   (d) Maps cannot handle collisions.
4. Which of the following best describes the role of a key in a map data structure?
   (a) It acts as a unique identifier for the associated value.
   (b) It stores the data value.
   (c) It determines the maximum size of the map.
   (d) It links to the next key-value pair in the map.
5. What is the primary advantage of using skip lists over traditional linked lists?
   (a) Skip lists are easier to implement.
   (b) Skip lists provide faster search operations due to multiple levels.

(c) Skip lists use less memory.
(d) Skip lists do not require random level assignments.
6. In a skip list, what happens when the randomly assigned level of a new node is higher than the current maximum level?
    (a) The new node is assigned to the bottom level only.
    (b) The new node is discarded.
    (c) The skip list is resized.
    (d) The maximum level of the skip list is increased to accommodate the new node.
7. Which of the following is NOT a typical application of maps?
    (a) Storing user profiles with unique IDs
    (b) Implementing a stack data structure
    (c) Creating a phone book with names and phone numbers
    (d) Managing configurations with settings and values
8. In a hash table, what is the primary purpose of a hash function?
    (a) To encrypt the data
    (b) To map keys to bucket indices
    (c) To sort the keys
    (d) To resize the hash table
9. Which of the following best describes the purpose of forward pointers in a skip list node?
    (a) They store the data values.
    (b) They link nodes at different levels, allowing efficient traversal.
    (c) They determine the node's position in the skip list.
    (d) They indicate the node's level.
10. What is the main reason for using separate chaining in hash tables?
    (a) To handle deletions efficiently
    (b) To manage collisions by linking all elements that hash to the same bucket
    (c) To minimize memory usage
    (d) To improve the speed of search operations
11. How is the maximum level of a node in a skip list typically determined?
    (a) By the number of elements in the skip list
    (b) By a fixed value set during initialization
    (c) Randomly, using a geometric distribution with a fixed probability p
    (d) By the depth of the binary tree equivalent
12. In a skip list, what is the expected height of the tallest node when n elements are inserted?
    (a) $O(1)$
    (b) $O(\log n)$
    (c) $O(n)$
    (d) $O(\sqrt{n})$
13. Which of the following is the most significant disadvantage of using skip lists?
    (a) Complexity in implementation
    (b) Higher memory overhead compared to binary search trees
    (c) Slower average-case performance compared to linked lists
    (d) Requirement for external libraries

9.7 Summary

14. When using separate chaining in a hash table, what happens to the time complexity of insertion when the load factor exceeds 1?
    (a) It remains $O(1)$.
    (b) It degrades to $O(n)$ in the worst case.
    (c) It changes to $O(\log n)$.
    (d) It changes to $O(\sqrt{n})$.
15. What is the amortized time complexity of resizing a dynamic array used in a hash table during rehashing?
    (a) $O(1)$
    (b) $O(\log n)$
    (c) $O(n)$
    (d) $O(n \log n)$
16. In a skip list, if a node with a high level is removed, what is the impact on the search efficiency of the skip list?
    (a) It improves.
    (b) It remains unchanged.
    (c) It temporarily degrades until the list balances itself through insertions.
    (d) It becomes unpredictable.
17. Which scenario could lead to the worst-case time complexity for searching in a skip list?
    (a) High variance in node levels
    (b) Extremely high probability value for level assignment
    (c) Skewed distribution of node levels causing many nodes at the lowest level
    (d) Uniform distribution of node levels
18. What is the primary benefit of using a geometric distribution for node level assignment in skip lists?
    (a) Simplifies implementation
    (b) Ensures balance by making high levels exponentially less frequent
    (c) Maximizes space efficiency
    (d) Guarantees a fixed maximum level
19. How does the expected number of pointers in a skip list node relate to the total number of nodes n?
    (a) $O(1)$
    (b) $O(\log n)$
    (c) $O(n)$
    (d) $O(n \log n)$
20. If the load factor of a hash table is kept constant by resizing, what is the amortized time complexity of insertion?
    (a) $O(1)$
    (b) $O(\log n)$
    (c) $O(n)$
    (d) $O(n \log n)$

21. How does the choice of hash function affect the performance of a hash table with separate chaining?
    (a) It has no impact on performance.
    (b) A poor hash function can cause many collisions, leading to $O(n)$ time complexity.
    (c) It affects only the space complexity.
    (d) It guarantees $O(1)$ performance if designed correctly.

Programming Problems

1. Implement a function in the priority queue class called `removeByData` that deletes a specified element from the priority queue, adjusting the heap as necessary to maintain order. Analyze the time complexity of your implementation and provide test cases to validate the function.
2. Implement the `getAll` function in the `Map` class. The function should return a `DynamicArray` containing all key-value pairs in the "Map." Consider how to efficiently traverse the internal data structure (a `ChainedHashTable`) to collect all the pairs. Discuss the time complexity of your implementation and provide test cases to validate the function.
3. Implement a skip list with a custom probability for level assignment and analyze its performance compared to the standard probability of 0.5.
4. Design a hash table that uses quadratic probing for collision resolution and compare its performance with separate chaining.
5. Modify the skip list implementation to support duplicate elements and ensure efficient search, insertion, and deletion operations.
6. Implement a multilevel hash table where each level has a different hash function and analyze its collision handling efficiency.
7. Develop a skip list with a maximum level determined dynamically based on the number of elements and analyze its impact on performance.
8. Implement a hash table with a custom rehashing strategy that minimizes downtime during resizing operations.
9. Implement a hash table with separate chaining that uses balanced binary trees instead of linked lists for collision handling and compare its performance.
10. Modify the priority queue implementation to handle elements with the same priority by maintaining their insertion order. Implement a system that tracks the insertion order using timestamps or sequence numbers, ensuring that elements with the same priority are dequeued in the order they were added.

10. Applications and Real-World Examples

Objective

In this chapter, we explore real-world case studies that demonstrate the effective use of data structures in solving practical, everyday problems. Through these examples, you will gain insights into how selecting the appropriate data structure can greatly enhance performance and efficiency, offering optimized solutions tailored to specific challenges. Here's what you will learn:

1. **Task Scheduling System:** Discover how to build a task scheduling system that efficiently manages tasks by assigning priorities and ensuring that the most critical tasks are processed first. This case study highlights the use of priority queues and heap structures to streamline task management.
2. **Social Network Friend Recommendations:** Explore the development of a friend recommendation system, which identifies potential friends based on mutual connections. This example demonstrates the application of graphs, maps, and priority queues to efficiently suggest new connections and enhance user engagement.
3. **Library Management System:** Discover how to design a library management system that manages book information, borrower details, and book loans efficiently.

Chapter 10. Applications and Real-World Examples

10.1 Task Scheduling System

Problem Description

In this case study, we need to design a task scheduling system for a software development team. The system should manage tasks, assign priorities, and ensure that high-priority tasks are addressed first. The system should support adding new tasks, removing completed tasks, retrieving the highest priority task, and clearing all tasks (Figure 10.1).

Figure 10.1: A cartoon representation of the task scheduling process, showcasing how tasks are prioritized and processed in the system for efficient management

Challenges

Designing such a system involves several challenges:
- **Priority Management:** Ensuring that high-priority tasks are always addressed first
- **Efficient Task Management:** Quickly adding, removing, and accessing tasks
- **Scalability:** Handling a large number of tasks efficiently

10.1.1 Solution and Analysis

The solution involves designing a task scheduling system that efficiently manages operations such as adding new tasks, removing completed tasks, and fetching the highest-priority task. This requires using data structures that provide fast access, insertion, and deletion capabilities.

10.1 Task Scheduling System

Data Structures Used

The task scheduling system is centered around the use of a **heap (priority queue)**. Implemented as a binary heap, the priority queue efficiently manages tasks according to their priority, allowing for fast insertion ($O(\log n)$) and extraction of the highest priority task ($O(\log n)$). Figure 10.2 illustrates the Max-Heap structure, where each node contains a Task object, and the task with the highest priority is always placed at the root.

Using a priority queue is ideal for task management as it dynamically maintains task order, ensuring efficient retrieval of the next task to be processed. Compared to other structures

- **Array:** An array requires $O(n)$ time for insertion and $O(n)$ time to find the highest-priority task, making it inefficient for frequent access and updates.

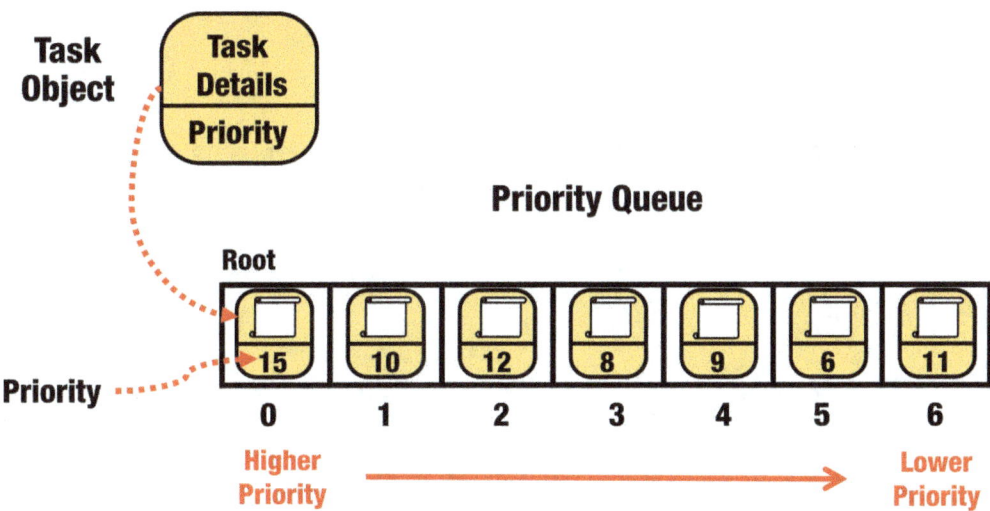

Figure 10.2: Priority queue representation using a Max-Heap structure. Each node contains a Task object with task details and priority, where tasks are arranged such that the highest priority task is at the root

- **Linked List:** A linked list, whether sorted or unsorted, also suffers from high insertion ($O(n)$) and search times, similar to arrays, making it unsuitable for real-time priority handling.
- **Map:** A map can store tasks with their priority as keys, but efficiently retrieving the highest-priority task in a sorted manner still requires additional overhead and does not provide the same level of performance as a priority queue.

The choice of a priority queue balances complexity and speed, optimizing both task addition and retrieval and making it the preferred data structure for managing tasks where priority handling is essential.

Class Design

The task scheduling system is built around two primary classes:
- **Task:** Encapsulates the information of each task, such as task ID, description, and priority
- **TaskManager:** Manages the tasks, including adding, removing, and fetching tasks based on priority using the Map and PriorityQueue

Additionally, we include the **TaskHandlerApp** class to provide an interactive interface for users to interact with the `TaskManager`. This class includes methods for displaying menus, handling user input, and performing task management operations.

10.1.2 Implementation

Let us discuss how the different components of the task scheduling system can be implemented.

Task Class

The `Task` class encapsulates the details of each task, including its ID, description, and priority level. The class also overloads the `==` and `«` operators to facilitate task comparison and output.

```cpp
class Task {
public:
    int Id;
    std::string description;
    int priority;

    // Default constructor
    Task()
        : Id(0), description(""), priority(0) {}

    // Parameterized constructor
    Task(int id, std::string desc, int prio)
        : Id(id), description(desc), priority(prio) {}

    // Overload == operator for Task comparison
    bool operator==(const Task& other) const {
        return Id == other.Id &&
               description == other.description &&
               priority == other.priority;
    }

    // Overload << operator for Task output
    friend std::ostream&
        operator<<(std::ostream& os, const Task& task) {
```

10.1 Task Scheduling System

```
25            os << "Task ID: " << task.Id
26               << ", Description: " << task.description
27               << ", Priority: " << task.priority;
28            return os;
29        }
30 };
```

Task Class Implementation

TaskManager Class

The `TaskManager` class is responsible for managing tasks within the system. It handles operations such as adding, removing, and fetching tasks using a `PriorityQueue`.

```
1 class TaskManager {
2 public:
3     // Default constructor
4     TaskManager();
5
6     // Adds a new task to the system
7     void addTask(const Task& task);
8
9     // Removes a completed task
10    void removeTask(int taskID);
11
12    // Fetches the highest-priority task
13    Task getNextTask() const;
14
15    // Displays all current tasks
16    void viewTasks() const;
17
18    // Checks if there are tasks
19    bool hasTasks() const;
20
21    // Clears all tasks from the system
22    void clearAllTasks();
23
24    // Returns the count of tasks
25    size_t getTaskCount() const;
26
27    // Completes and returns the highest priority task
28    Task completeHighestPriorityTask();
29 private:
```

```
30        PriorityQueue<Task> taskQueue;
31 };
```
TaskManager Class Definition

10.1.3 Method Implementations
Adding a Task
The `addTask` function inserts the task into the `taskQueue`, ensuring prioritized processing.

```
1 void TaskManager::addTask(const Task& task) {
2     taskQueue.add(task, task.priority);
3 }
```
addTask Function Implementation

Removing a Task
The `removeTask` function removes a task by its ID and then rebuilds the priority queue to ensure that the queue remains correctly ordered.

```
1  void TaskManager::removeTask(int taskID) {
2      PriorityQueue<Task> newQueue;
3
4      // Rebuild the queue without the task to remove
5      while (!taskQueue.isEmpty()) {
6          Task currentTask = taskQueue.pop();
7          if (currentTask.Id != taskID) {
8              newQueue.add(currentTask,
9                           currentTask.priority);
10         }
11     }
12     taskQueue = std::move(newQueue);
13 }
```
removeTask Function Implementation

Rebuilding the priority queue is necessary because the heap property (which ensures that the highest priority task is always at the root) can be disrupted when tasks are removed by their IDs. Unlike simple deletion, which occurs at the root, removing a specific element in a heap requires adjusting the entire structure to maintain the heap properties.

10.1 Task Scheduling System

The process of rebuilding the queue has a time complexity of $O(n \log n)$, where n is the number of tasks in the queue. This is because each task must be reinserted into a new heap after identifying which task to exclude. This approach, while straightforward, is not optimal due to its reliance on sequential processing and reinsertion.

Fetching the Highest-Priority Task

The `getNextTask` function retrieves the highest-priority task without removing it from the queue.

```cpp
Task TaskManager::getNextTask() const {
    if (taskQueue.isEmpty()) {
        throw std::runtime_error
            ("No tasks available");
    }
    return taskQueue.peek();
}
```

`getNextTask` Function Implementation

Other Utility Methods

```cpp
// Default constructor
TaskManager::TaskManager(): taskQueue() {}

void TaskManager::viewTasks() const {
    if (!taskQueue.isEmpty()) {
        taskQueue.print();
    } else {
        std::cout << "No tasks available."
            << std::endl;
    }
}

size_t TaskManager::getTaskCount() const {
    return tasksMap.getSize();
}

// Completing the Highest-Priority Task
Task TaskManager::completeHighestPriorityTask() {
    if (taskQueue.isEmpty()) {
        throw std::runtime_error
            ("No tasks available to complete.");
    }
    return taskQueue.pop();
```

```cpp
24 }
25
26 // Clearing All Tasks
27 void TaskManager::clearAllTasks() {
28     taskQueue.clear();
29 }
```
TaskManager Utility Methods Implementation

TaskHandlerApp Class

The `TaskHandlerApp` class provides a simple menu-driven interface for users to interact with the task management system.

```cpp
1 class TaskHandlerApp {
2 public:
3     TaskHandlerApp();
4     void run();
5
6 private:
7     TaskManager taskManager;
8
9     void displayMenu() const;
10    void handleAddTask();
11    void handleRemoveTask();
12    void handleDisplayTasks() const;
13    void handleCompleteHighestTask();
14    void handleGetNextTask() const;
15    void handleClearAllTasks();
16    void handleExit() const;
17
18    void printTaskCount() const;
19 };
```
TaskHandlerApp Class Definition

```cpp
1 TaskHandlerApp::TaskHandlerApp() : taskManager() {}
2
3 void TaskHandlerApp::displayMenu() const {
4     std::cout << "\n=== Task Manager Menu ===\n";
5     std::cout << "1. Add Task\n";
6     std::cout << "2. Remove Task\n";
7     std::cout << "3. Display Tasks\n";
8     std::cout << "4. Complete Highest Priority Task\n";
```

10.1 Task Scheduling System

```cpp
9        std::cout << "5. Get Next Highest Priority Task\n";
10       std::cout << "6. Exit\n";
11       std::cout << "Enter your choice: ";
12  }
13
14  void TaskHandlerApp::handleAddTask() {
15       int id, priority;
16       std::string description;
17       std::cout << "Enter Task ID: ";
18       std::cin >> id;
19       std::cin.ignore();
20       std::cout << "Enter Task Description: ";
21       std::getline(std::cin, description);
22       std::cout << "Enter Task Priority: ";
23       std::cin >> priority;
24       taskManager.addTask(Task(id, description, priority));
25  }
26
27  void TaskHandlerApp::handleRemoveTask() {
28       int id;
29       std::cout << "Enter Task ID to remove: ";
30       std::cin >> id;
31       taskManager.removeTask(id);
32  }
33
34  void TaskHandlerApp::handleDisplayTasks() const {
35       std::cout << "\n=== Current Tasks ===\n";
36       printTaskCount();
37       taskManager.viewTasks();
38  }
39
40  void TaskHandlerApp::handleCompleteHighestTask() {
41       try {
42           Task highestTask
43               = taskManager.completeHighestPriorityTask();
44           std::cout << "Completed task:\n"
45                     << highestTask << std::endl;
46       } catch (const std::runtime_error& e) {
47           std::cerr << "Error: " << e.what() << std::endl;
48       }
49  }
50
51  void TaskHandlerApp::handleGetNextTask() const {
52       try {
53           Task nextTask = taskManager.getNextTask();
```

```cpp
            std::cout << "Next highest-priority task:\n"
                      << nextTask << std::endl;
        } catch (const std::runtime_error& e) {
            std::cerr << "Error: " << e.what() << std::endl;
        }
    }

    void TaskHandlerApp::handleExit() const {
        std::cout << "Exiting Task Manager.\n";
    }

    void TaskHandlerApp::printTaskCount() const {
        std::cout << "Total number of tasks: "
                  << taskManager.getTaskCount() << std::endl;
    }

    void TaskHandlerApp::run() {
        int choice;
        do {
            displayMenu();
            std::cin >> choice;

            switch (choice) {
                case 1:
                    handleAddTask();
                    break;
                case 2:
                    handleRemoveTask();
                    break;
                case 3:
                    handleDisplayTasks();
                    break;
                case 4:
                    handleCompleteHighestTask();
                    break;
                case 5:
                    handleGetNextTask();
                    break;
                case 6:
                    handleExit();
                    break;
                default:
                    std::cout << "Invalid choice. "
                        <<"Please try again.\n";
                    break;
```

```
99              }
100         } while (choice != 6);
101     }
```

`TaskHandlerApp` Methods Implementation

10.1.4 Example Scenario

Scenario 1: Basic Task Management with `TaskManager`

Consider a scenario where the system manages the following tasks:
- Tasks: Task1 (ID: 1, Description: Complete homework, Priority: 5), Task2 (ID: 2, Description: Buy groceries, Priority: 10), Task3 (ID: 3, Description: Call plumber, Priority: 4)

In this scenario, Task2 is the highest-priority task, so it should be fetched and processed first.

Example 10.1 Scenario 1:
- **Step 1:** Add tasks Task1, Task2, and Task3 to the system.

```
1   TaskManager tm;
2   tm.addTask(Task(1, "Complete homework", 5));
3   tm.addTask(Task(2, "Buy groceries", 10));
4   tm.addTask(Task(3, "Call plumber", 4));
5   tm.viewTasks();
```

- **Step 2:** Fetch the highest-priority task (Task2).

```
1   Task highPriorityTask = tm.getNextTask();
2   std::cout << "Highest Priority Task: "
3           << highPriorityTask
4           << std::endl;
```

- **Step 3:** Complete the highest-priority task (Task2).

```
1   tm.completeHighestPriorityTask();
```

- **Step 4:** Fetch the next highest-priority task (Task1).

```
1   highPriorityTask = tm.getNextTask();
2   std::cout << "Next Highest Priority Task: "
3           << highPriorityTask
4           << std::endl;
```

Expected Console Output:

```
1   {Data: ID: 2, Description: Buy groceries, Priority: 10}
2   {Data: ID: 1, Description: Complete homework, Priority: 5}
3   {Data: ID: 3, Description: Call plumber, Priority: 4}
4
```

```
5 Highest Priority Task:
6     ID: 2, Description: Buy groceries, Priority: 10
7 Next Highest Priority Task:
8     ID: 1, Description: Complete homework, Priority: 5
```

Scenario 2: Running the `TaskHandlerApp`

In this scenario, the `TaskHandlerApp` is used to interact with the task scheduling system through a menu-driven interface.

■ **Example 10.2** Scenario 2:
- **Step 1:** Run the `TaskHandlerApp` and select options from the menu.

```
1    TaskHandlerApp app;
2    app.run();
```

- **Step 2:** Use the menu to add, remove, view, complete, and clear tasks as described in the previous scenario.

10.1.5 Performance Analysis

The primary data structure used in the current task scheduling system is a priority queue implemented as a binary heap. This structure is complemented by additional simple data structures for managing tasks:

- **Priority Queue (Heap-Based):** The `PriorityQueue` is implemented using a binary heap, which dynamically manages tasks based on their priority. This data structure is essential for ensuring that the highest-priority task is always accessible at the root of the heap.
  - **Complexity:** Insertion and deletion operations (pop) are $O(\log n)$, where n is the number of tasks in the queue. Accessing the highest-priority task (peek) is $O(1)$.
- **Dynamic Array:** Used internally within the priority queue to store tasks as heap elements. This structure supports efficient resizing and access operations.
  - **Complexity:** Insertion and access are $O(1)$ on average, but resizing the array during capacity expansion is $O(n)$.

Analysis of Key Operations

The performance of the main operations in the `TaskManager` class is closely tied to the efficiency of the priority queue and its underlying heap structure:
- **Adding a Task:** Involves inserting a new task into the priority queue
  - **Complexity:** $O(\log n)$, ensuring quick insertion while maintaining the heap property that keeps the highest-priority task at the root

- **Removing a Task:** Involves removing a specific task by its ID, requiring the entire priority queue to be rebuilt to maintain heap properties
    - **Complexity:** $O(n \log n)$, as each task must be reinserted into a new heap after removing the specified task. This process is the most time-consuming operation in the system and can be **optimized**.
- **Fetching the Highest-Priority Task:** Retrieves the task at the root of the priority queue without removing it
    - **Complexity:** $O(1)$, allowing instant access to the next task that needs attention

10.1.6 Optimization

Improving the performance of the task scheduling system involves revising the design and implementation of key functions within the `TaskManager` class. Below, we discuss several strategies for optimizing task handling, particularly focusing on improving task removal efficiency.

Using a Map for Efficient Removal

One major inefficiency in the current design is the complexity of removing tasks from the priority queue, which requires rebuilding the queue to maintain heap properties. This can be optimized using a `Map` (or hash map) to track the positions of tasks within the priority queue.
- **Direct Access:** Introducing a map to track task IDs and their positions within the heap can allow direct access and removal without rebuilding the entire queue. This approach reduces the time complexity of removal from $O(n \log n)$ to $O(\log n)$, as it eliminates the need to reinsert every task.
- **Efficient Deletion:** Once the task's position is found using the map, it can be swapped with the last element in the heap and removed, followed by re-heapifying to restore the priority order. This reduces the task removal complexity to $O(\log n)$, a significant improvement over the current $O(n \log n)$.
- **Complexity Impact:** This optimization balances the map's constant time access $O(1)$ with the heap's logarithmic adjustments $O(\log n)$, providing a much faster solution for task deletions without fully rebuilding the queue.

Optimizing Task Addition and Retrieval

Further improvements can be made to enhance overall performance:
- **Lazy Deletion:** Instead of immediately rebuilding the queue upon task removal, a lazy deletion strategy can mark tasks as removed without adjusting the heap immediately. Only when necessary (e.g., during retrieval), the queue is cleaned up, saving processing time during frequent deletions.
- **Balanced Use of Data Structures:** Combining the strengths of different data structures – such as using a sorted map to track priority or a balanced tree structure – can improve both the insertion and retrieval times under different scenarios.

10.2 Social Network Friend Recommendations

Problem Description

A social network requires a system to recommend friends to users based on mutual connections (Figure 10.3). The objective is to identify mutual friends efficiently and suggest new connections to enhance user engagement.

Challenges

Designing such a system involves several challenges:
- **Large Network Size:** The social network may consist of millions of users and connections, necessitating efficient data handling.
- **Efficient Friend Recommendations:** Quickly finding and suggesting friends based on mutual connections.
- **Scalability:** Handling a growing number of users and connections efficiently.

10.2.1 Solution and Analysis

To solve this problem, we need to design a friend recommendation system that efficiently handles various operations, such as finding mutual friends and suggesting new connections.

Figure 10.3: Social network friend recommendations: a visual representation of a social network where nodes represent users and edges represent friendships. The system aims to recommend friends based on the analysis of mutual connections

Data Structures Used

The system uses the following data structures to address the challenges, as illustrated in Figure 10.4:
- **Graph (Adjacency List):** Represents the social network, where nodes are users and edges signify friendships
- **Map:** Stores user details, enabling quick access to user information by user ID
- **Dynamic Array:** Manages dynamic collections of user recommendations efficiently

10.2 Social Network Friend Recommendations

- **Priority Queue:** Ranks potential friend recommendations based on the number of mutual connections, ensuring that the most relevant suggestions are prioritized

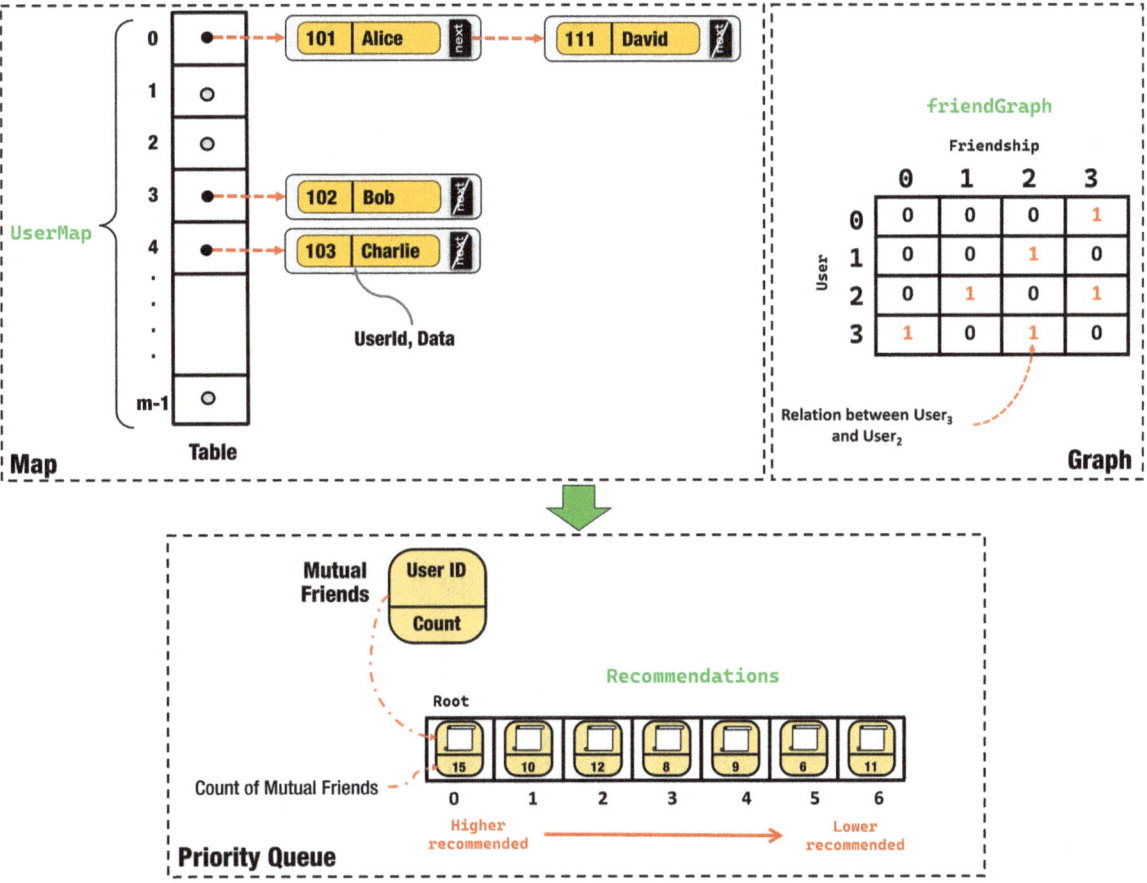

Figure 10.4: An integrated view of the friend recommendation system showing the use of a Map for storing user details, a Graph (Adjacency List) to represent user connections, and a Priority Queue to rank friend recommendations based on mutual connections

Class Design

The friend recommendation system is built around two primary classes:
- **User:** Encapsulates user information such as user ID and name
- **FriendManager:** Manages users and their relationships, including adding users, establishing friendships, and recommending friends based on mutual connections using the Map and GraphAdjList

Additionally, the **FriendsHandlerApp** class provides an interactive interface, allowing users to interact with the `FriendManager`. This class includes methods for displaying menus, handling user input, and executing friend recommendation operations.

10.2.2 Implementation

Below is an overview of the implementation of the different components of the friend recommendation system.

User Class

The `User` class encapsulates the details of each user, including the user ID and name. It includes necessary constructors, getter methods, and overloaded operators for equality and output.

```cpp
class User {
public:
    int userID;
    std::string name;

    User();
    User(int id, const std::string& userName);

    // Equality operator
    bool operator==(const User& other) const;

    int getUserID() const;
    std::string getName() const;
};
```

User Class Definition

FriendManager Class

The `FriendManager` class manages users and their relationships within the system. It handles operations such as adding users, establishing friendships, and generating friend recommendations based on mutual connections.

```cpp
class FriendManager {
public:
    // Constructors
    FriendManager();
    FriendManager(int initialGraphSize);

    void addUser(const User& user);
    User getUserByID(int userID) const;
    void addFriendship(int userId1, int userId2);
    DynamicArray<int> recommendFriends(int userID);
    void display() const;
    void displayRelationships() const;

private:
```

10.2 Social Network Friend Recommendations

```
15      // Map to store users by their IDs
16      Map<int, User> userMap;
17      // Graph to represent friendships
18      GraphAdjList<int> friendGraph;
19
20      // To check if a user exists in the map
21      bool userExists(int userID) const;
22 };
```
FriendManager Class Definition

10.2.3 Method Implementations

Adding a User

The `addUser` method adds a new user to the system and ensures that the user's information is stored in the `userMap`.

```
1 void FriendManager::addUser(const User& user) {
2     if (!userExists(user.getUserID())) {
3         userMap.add(user.getUserID(), user);
4         friendGraph.addVertex();
5     } else {
6         std::cerr << "User ID " << user.getUserID()
7             << " already exists." << std::endl;
8     }
9 }
```
Adding Users in FriendManager

Adding a Friendship

The `addFriendship` method establishes a bidirectional friendship between two users by adding edges in both directions within the graph.

```
1 void FriendManager::addFriendship(int userId1, int userId2){
2     if (!userExists(userId1) || !userExists(userId2)) {
3         std::cerr <<
4             "Error: One or both users do not exist."
5             << std::endl;
6         return;
7     }
8
9     try {
10        // Add edge in one direction
11        friendGraph.addEdge(userId1, userId2);
```

```
12            // Add edge in the opposite direction
13            friendGraph.addEdge(userId2, userId1);
14
15        } catch (const std::exception& e) {
16            std::cerr << "Graph Error: "
17                     << e.what() << std::endl;
18        }
19 }
```

Friend Recommendations Method

Recommending Friends

The `recommendFriends` function suggests friends based on mutual connections using a priority queue to rank potential friends. The function works as follows:

1. **Check User Existence:** The function begins by verifying whether the user exists in the system. If the user does not exist, it immediately returns an empty list of recommendations.
2. **Retrieve Direct Friends:** It fetches the direct friends of the user using the `outEdges` function, which returns all vertices directly connected to the user.
3. **Count Mutual Friends:** For each direct friend, the function retrieves their friends (i.e., friends of friends) and counts how often each friend appears, excluding the user and their direct friends from this count.
4. **Priority Queue for Sorting:** The mutual friends are sorted using a priority queue, where the number of mutual connections determines the priority. Friends with higher mutual counts are considered stronger recommendations.
5. **Return Recommendations:** The final list of recommended friends is extracted from the priority queue, ensuring that friends are ordered by the number of mutual connections.

```
1  DynamicArray<int> FriendManager::
2             recommendFriends(int userID) {
3      DynamicArray<int> recommendations;
4
5      // (1) Check if the user exists
6      if (!userExists(userID)) {
7          std::cerr << "User ID not found"
8                   << std::endl;
9          return recommendations;
10     }
11
12     // (2) Get the direct friends of the user
13     DynamicArray<int> directFriends
14            = friendGraph.outEdges(userID);
```

10.2 Social Network Friend Recommendations

```
15
16      // (3) Map to count mutual friends
17    Map<int, int> friendsOfFriendsCount;
18
19    // Iterate over each direct friend of the user
20    for (size_t i = 0; i < directFriends.getSize(); ++i) {
21      int friendID = directFriends[i];
22
23      // Get friends of each direct friend
24      DynamicArray<int> friendsOfFriend
25              = friendGraph.outEdges(friendID);
26
27      // Iterate over each friend of the direct friend
28      for(size_t j = 0;j < friendsOfFriend.getSize();++j){
29        int mutualFriendID = friendsOfFriend[j];
30
31        // Skip if the mutual friend is the user
32        //    itself or already a direct friend
33        if(mutualFriendID == userID ||
34            directFriends.indexOf(mutualFriendID)!= -1){
35          continue;
36        }
37
38        // If mutual friend is not already counted
39        //    add to the map with a count of 1
40        if(!friendsOfFriendsCount.contains(mutualFriendID)){
41            friendsOfFriendsCount.add(mutualFriendID, 1);
42        } else {
43          // If already counted, increment the count
44          int currentCount =
45              friendsOfFriendsCount.get(mutualFriendID);
46          friendsOfFriendsCount.add(mutualFriendID,
47            currentCount + 1);
48        }
49      }
50    }
51    // (4) Use a priority queue to sort friends
52    //   based on the number of mutual friends
53    PriorityQueue<int> pq;
54
55    // Add each mutual friend to the priority queue
56    // with their count as the priority
57
58    DynamicArray<Pair<int, int>> allMutualFriends =
59              friendsOfFriendsCount.getAll();
```

```cpp
60      for (size_t i = 0;i < allMutualFriends.getSize();++i){
61          pq.add(allMutualFriends[i].key,
62                      allMutualFriends[i].value);
63      }
64
65      // (5) Extract friends from the priority queue
66      // starting with the highest mutual count
67      while (!pq.isEmpty()) {
68          recommendations.pushBack(pq.pop());
69      }
70
71      // Return the list of recommended friends
72      return recommendations;
73 }
```

Get Recommendations

The `getRecommendations` function retrieves and displays friend recommendations for a specific user.

```cpp
1  void FriendManager::getRecommendations(int userID) {
2      std::cout << "\nFriend recommendations for "
3                  << getUserByID(userID).getName()
4                  << " (User ID " << userID << "):\n";
5      DynamicArray<int> recommendations =
6                          recommendFriends(userID);
7
8      if (recommendations.getSize() > 0) {
9        std::cout << "Recommended friends: ";
10       for (size_t i = 0; i < recommendations.getSize();++i){
11           try {
12               User recommendedUser =
13                       getUserByID(recommendations[i]);
14               std::cout << recommendedUser.getName() << " ";
15           } catch (const std::exception& e) {
16               std::cerr << "Error retrieving user details: "
17                           << e.what() << std::endl;
18           }
19       }
20       std::cout << std::endl;
21     } else {
22       std::cout << "No recommendations available for User "
23               << userID << "." << std::endl;
24     }
25 }
```

10.2 Social Network Friend Recommendations

Other Utility Methods

The utility methods in the `FriendManager` class facilitate additional operations like displaying user relationships, validating user existence, and managing user information.

```cpp
void FriendManager::displayRelationships() const {
  DynamicArray<Pair<int, User>> allUsers = userMap.getAll();
  for (size_t i = 0; i < allUsers.getSize(); ++i) {
    const User& user = allUsers[i].value;
    std::cout << user.getName() << " (User ID "
              << user.getUserID() << ") has friends: ";

    // Get the friends of the user from the graph
    DynamicArray<int> friends =
            friendGraph.outEdges(user.getUserID());

    if (friends.getSize() == 0) {
        std::cout << "No friends";
    } else {
      for (size_t j = 0; j < friends.getSize(); ++j) {
          int friendID = friends[j];

          // Ensure the friend ID is valid
          if (userExists(friendID)) {
            try {
               User friendUser = getUserByID(friendID);
               std::cout << friendUser.getName();
               if (j < friends.getSize() - 1) {
                  std::cout << ", ";
               }
            } catch (const std::exception& e) {
               std::cerr <<"Error retrieving user details: "
                   << e.what() << std::endl;
            }
          } else {
            std::cerr << "\nInvalid friend ID "
                      << friendID  << " for user "
                      << user.getUserID() << std::endl;
          }
      }
    }
    std::cout << std::endl;
  }
}
```

```cpp
41 bool FriendManager::userExists(int userID) const {
42     try {
43         userMap.get(userID);
44         return true;
45     } catch (const std::runtime_error&) {
46         return false;
47     }
48 }
49
50 void FriendManager::display() const {
51     DynamicArray<Pair<int, User>> allusers =
52                 userMap.getAll();
53     for (size_t i = 0; i < allusers.getSize(); ++i) {
54         std::cout << allusers[i] << std::endl;
55     }
56 }
57
58 User FriendManager::getUserByID(int userID) const {
59     try {
60         return userMap.get(userID);
61     } catch (const std::runtime_error& e) {
62         throw std::runtime_error("User not found");
63     }
64 }
65
66 // Stream output operator for User
67 std::ostream& operator<<(std::ostream& os,
68                 const User& user) {
69     os << "User ID: " << user.userID
70        << ", Name: " << user.name;
71     return os;
72 }
```

FriendsHandlerApp Class

The `FriendsHandlerApp` class provides a menu-driven interface for users to interact with the system, facilitating user input and executing friend recommendation operations.

```cpp
1 class FriendsHandlerApp {
2 public:
3     FriendsHandlerApp();
4
5     void displayMenu() const;
6     void handleAddUser();
7     void handleAddFriendship();
```

10.2 Social Network Friend Recommendations

```cpp
 8      void handleDisplayUsers() const;
 9      void handleDisplayRelationships();
10      void handleRecommendFriends() ;
11
12      void handleExit() const;
13      void run();
14
15 private:
16      FriendManager friendRel;
17 };
```

FriendsHandlerApp Class Definition

```cpp
 1 // Constructor
 2 FriendsHandlerApp::FriendsHandlerApp() :
 3     friendRel() {}
 4
 5 // Display the main menu
 6 void FriendsHandlerApp::displayMenu() const {
 7     std::cout << "\n== Friend Recommendation
 8                     System Menu ==\n";
 9     std::cout << "1. Add User\n";
10     std::cout << "2. Add Friendship\n";
11     std::cout << "3. Display Users\n";
12     std::cout << "4. Display Relationships\n";
13     std::cout << "5. Recommend Friends\n";
14     std::cout << "6. Exit\n";
15     std::cout << "Enter your choice: ";
16 }
17
18 // Handle adding a new user
19 void FriendsHandlerApp::handleAddUser() {
20     int id;
21     std::string name;
22     std::cout << "Enter User ID: ";
23     std::cin >> id;
24     std::cin.ignore();
25     std::cout << "Enter User Name: ";
26     std::getline(std::cin, name);
27     friendRel.addUser(User(id, name));
28 }
29
30 // Handle adding a friendship
```

```cpp
31  void FriendsHandlerApp::handleAddFriendship() {
32      int userId1, userId2;
33      std::cout << "Enter first User ID: ";
34      std::cin >> userId1;
35      std::cout << "Enter second User ID: ";
36      std::cin >> userId2;
37      friendRel.addFriendship(userId1, userId2);
38  }
39
40  // Handle displaying all users
41  void FriendsHandlerApp::handleDisplayUsers() const {
42      std::cout << "\n=== Current Users ===\n";
43      friendRel.display();
44  }
45
46  // Handle recommending friends
47  void FriendsHandlerApp::handleRecommendFriends() {
48      int userID;
49      std::cout << "Enter User ID to get
50                  friend recommendations: ";
51      std::cin >> userID;
52      friendRel.getRecommendations(userID);
53  }
54
55  // Handle displaying user relationships
56  void FriendsHandlerApp::handleDisplayRelationships() {
57      std::cout << "\n=== User Relationships ===\n";
58      friendRel.displayRelationships();
59  }
60
61  // Handle exiting the application
62  void FriendsHandlerApp::handleExit() const {
63      std::cout << "Exiting Friend
64                  Recommendation System.\n";
65  }
66
67  // Main application loop
68  void FriendsHandlerApp::run() {
69      int choice;
70      do {
71          displayMenu();
72          std::cin >> choice;
73
74          switch (choice) {
75              case 1:
```

10.2 Social Network Friend Recommendations

```
76                handleAddUser();
77                break;
78            case 2:
79                handleAddFriendship();
80                break;
81            case 3:
82                handleDisplayUsers();
83                break;
84            case 4:
85                handleDisplayRelationships();
86                break;
87            case 5:
88                handleRecommendFriends();
89                break;
90            case 6:
91                handleExit();
92                break;
93            default:
94                std::cout << "Invalid choice.
95                        Please try again.\n";
96                break;
97        }
98    } while (choice != 6);
99 }
```

FriendsHandlerApp Methods Implementation

10.2.4 Example Scenario

Consider a scenario where the system manages the following users and friendships:
- Users: User1 (ID: 1, Name: "Alice"), User2 (ID: 2, Name: "Bob"), User3 (ID: 3, Name: "Charlie"), User4 (ID: 4, Name: "Diana")
- Friendships: (1, 2), (1, 3), (2, 3), (3, 4)

Scenario 1: Basic Friend Recommendation with FriendManager
In this scenario, the system recommends friends based on mutual connections.

■ **Example 10.3** Scenario 1:
- **Step 1:** Add users to the system.

```
1    FriendManager frSystem;
2    frSystem.addUser(User(1, "Alice"));
3    frSystem.addUser(User(2, "Bob"));
4    frSystem.addUser(User(3, "Charlie"));
5    frSystem.addUser(User(4, "Diana"));
```

- **Step 2:** Establish friendships.

```
1    frSystem.addFriendship(1, 2);
2    frSystem.addFriendship(1, 3);
3    frSystem.addFriendship(2, 3);
4    frSystem.addFriendship(3, 4);
```

- **Step 3:** Recommend friends for a user (User 1).

```
1    frSystem.getRecommendations(1);
```

- **Expected Console Output:**

```
1    Friend recommendations for Alice (User ID 1):
2    Recommended friends: Diana
```

This example demonstrates how the system efficiently manages users and recommends friends using mutual connections. It ensures scalability and performance for large networks.

Scenario 2: Running the `FriendsHandlerApp`

In this scenario, the `FriendsHandlerApp` is used to interact with the friend recommendation system through a menu-driven interface.

■ **Example 10.4** Scenario 2:
- **Step 1:** Run the `FriendsHandlerApp` and select options from the menu.

```
1    FriendsHandlerApp app;
2    app.run();
```

- **Step 2:** Use the menu to add users, add friendships, display users and relationships, and get friend recommendations as described in the previous scenario.

This scenario illustrates how `FriendsHandlerApp` provides an intuitive interface for managing a social network, allowing users to interact with the system without needing to understand the underlying code.

10.2.5 Performance Analysis

The main data structures used in the current implementation include a map, a graph with adjacency lists, dynamic arrays, and a priority queue. Each plays a vital role in the system's overall performance:

- **Map (Hash Map):** The `Map` efficiently manages user information by storing user data indexed by user IDs.
  - **Complexity:** Average time for insertion, deletion, and access is $O(1)$; however, it can degrade to $O(n)$ in the worst case due to hash collisions.

10.2 Social Network Friend Recommendations

- **Graph (Adjacency List):** The `GraphAdjList` models the social network, with nodes representing users and edges representing friendships.
  - **Complexity:** Adding a vertex: $O(1)$; adding an edge: $O(1)$; retrieving edges: $O(V+E)$, where V is the number of vertices and E is the number of edges.
- **Dynamic Array:** Used for storing collections of users, recommendations, and friends, providing flexible and dynamic data handling.
  - **Complexity:** Average insertion and access: $O(1)$; resizing upon exceeding capacity: worst-case $O(n)$.
- **Priority Queue (Heap-Based):** Ranks friend recommendations by the number of mutual connections, utilizing a heap to efficiently manage priorities.
  - **Complexity:** Insertion: $O(\log n)$; deletion (pop): $O(\log n)$; peek: $O(1)$.

Analysis of Key Operations

The performance of the main operations in the `FriendManager` class is influenced by the underlying data structures:
- **Adding a User:** Involves adding the user to the map and a vertex in the graph. Complexity: $O(1)$ for both operations, making it highly efficient and scalable for large networks.
- **Adding a Friendship:** Involves checking user existence and adding edges in both directions in the graph. Complexity: Checking existence is $O(1)$, and adding edges is $O(1)$, resulting in a highly efficient overall complexity.
- **Recommending Friends:** Involves retrieving direct friends, counting mutual friends, and using a priority queue to rank recommendations. Complexity: Retrieving friends $O(V+E)$; counting mutual friends $O(k \times m)$, where k is the number of direct friends and m is the average number of friends per direct friend; and ranking with priority queue $O(n \log n)$, where n is the number of potential friends.

10.2.6 Optimization

Improving the friend recommendation system's performance requires refining the design and implementation of key functions within the `FriendManager` class. Below, we outline strategies to optimize data access and friend ranking.

Using Efficient Data Structures for Friend Management

The current system utilizes maps, dynamic arrays, and a priority queue to manage user data and recommend friends. However, there are opportunities to further optimize these operations by integrating more advanced data structures:
- **Balanced Trees for Faster Access:** Replacing the map with a balanced tree structure, such as AVL Tree, can enhance lookup, insertion, and deletion times. Balanced trees offer consistent $O(\log n)$ access time, improving worst-case performance compared to hash maps, which can degrade to $O(n)$ under certain conditions.
- **Skip Lists for Efficient Friend Recommendations:** Incorporating skip lists can improve the performance of mutual friend counting and sorting tasks. Skip lists offer $O(\log n)$ for search, insertion, and deletion, similar to balanced trees but simpler to

maintain in dynamic environments. This structure enhances performance in managing growing and frequently updated datasets.

Prioritizing Friend Recommendations with Optimized Priority Queues

The `PriorityQueue` plays a critical role in ranking friend recommendations based on mutual connections. Optimizing this component can significantly boost the recommendation process.

- **Optimized Heap Operations:** Using a d-ary heap (where each node has d children) reduces heap height, enhancing insertion and deletion from $O(\log n)$ to $O(\log_d n)$ for $d > 2$. This structural change improves efficiency in handling large datasets compared to the binary heap currently used.

These optimization strategies ensure that the friend recommendation system remains robust and efficient, even as the size and complexity of the social network grow.

10.3 Library Management System

Problem Description

Design a library management system that manages book information, borrower details, and book loans (Figure 10.5). The system should efficiently handle book searches, issue/return transactions, and borrower queries, ensuring smooth and organized operations within the library.

Figure 10.5: A conceptual illustration of a library management system

Challenges

Designing such a system involves several challenges:
- **Book Management:** Ensuring efficient storage, search, and retrieval of book information
- **Borrower Management:** Quickly accessing borrower details and loan history
- **Transaction Management:** Efficiently processing book issue and return transactions

10.3.1 Solution and Analysis

To solve these challenges, we need to design a library management system that effectively manages book and borrower data while processing transactions smoothly.

Data Structures Used

The system employs various data structures to handle different aspects of library management efficiently:
- **Map:** Manages book and borrower details, providing quick access and updates based on unique identifiers like book IDs and borrower IDs.
- **Queue:** Handles transaction requests, ensuring books are issued and returned in the correct order, particularly useful during peak times.
- **Priority Queue:** Manages overdue books and borrowers by prioritizing transactions based on due dates, ensuring overdue items are handled promptly.
- **Dynamic Array:** Manages borrower loan history, offering dynamic and flexible storage for all current and past loans. Dynamic arrays provide quick access to loan records and efficient resizing capabilities when more loans are added.

Class Design

The library management system is structured around three main classes:
- **Book:** Encapsulates information about each book, including book ID, title, author, and availability status
- **Borrower:** Manages borrower details such as borrower ID, name, and loan history using a dynamic array for efficient storage and access
- **LibraryManager:** Oversees book inventory, borrower data, and handles transactions like issuing and returning books using a combination of maps, priority queues, and dynamic arrays.

Additionally, the **LibraryHandlerApp** class offers an interactive interface for library staff to manage the system. It includes methods for displaying menus, handling input, and executing book and borrower operations.

10.3.2 Implementation

Below is an overview of the implementation of the different components of the library management system.

Book Class

The `Book` class encapsulates the details of each book, including its ID, title, author, and availability status. It includes constructors, getter methods, and overloaded operators for equality and output.

```cpp
class Book {
public:
    int bookID;
    std::string title;
    std::string author;
    bool isAvailable;

    Book();
    Book(int id, const std::string& bookTitle,
         const std::string& bookAuthor);

    // Equality operator
    bool operator==(const Book& other) const;

    int getBookID() const;
    std::string getTitle() const;
    std::string getAuthor() const;
    bool getAvailability() const;
    void setAvailability(bool status);

    // Overloaded stream output operator
    friend std::ostream& operator<<
            (std::ostream& os, const Book& book);
};

// Constructor
Book::Book() : bookID(0),
    title(""), author(""),
    isAvailable(true) {}
Book::Book(int id, const std::string& bookTitle,
           const std::string& bookAuthor)
    : bookID(id), title(bookTitle), author(bookAuthor),
      isAvailable(true) {}

// Equality operator
bool Book::operator==(const Book& other) const {
    return bookID == other.bookID;
}
```

10.3 Library Management System

```cpp
40
41 // Overloaded stream output operator
42 std::ostream& operator<<
43     (std::ostream& os, const Book& book) {
44     os << "Book ID: " << book.bookID
45         << ", Title: " << book.title
46         << ", Author: " << book.author
47         << ", Available: " <<(book.isAvailable ?"Yes":"No");
48     return os;
49 }
```

Book Class Definition

Borrower Class

The `Borrower` class manages information about each borrower, including their ID, name, and loan history, which is stored using a `DynamicArray` to allow efficient management of the borrower's loan records.

```cpp
1 class Borrower {
2 private:
3     int borrowerID;
4     std::string name;
5     // Dynamic array for managing loan history
6     DynamicArray<int> loanHistory;
7
8 public:
9     Borrower();
10    Borrower(int id, const std::string& borrowerName);
11
12    // Equality operator
13    bool operator==(const Borrower& other) const;
14
15    int getBorrowerID() const;
16    std::string getName() const;
17    void addLoan(int bookID);
18    void removeLoan(int bookID);
19    bool isOverdue() const;
20    void printLoans() const;
21
22    // Overloaded stream output operator
23    friend std::ostream& operator<<
24        (std::ostream& os, const Borrower& borrower);
25 };
26
```

10.3 Library Management System

```
6        Borrower added: 3, Alice
7        Book issued to John
8        Book returned: Clean Code
```

This example demonstrates how the library management system effectively handles book management, borrower interactions, and transactions, ensuring an organized and efficient library operation.

Scenario 2: Running the `LibraryHandlerApp`

In this scenario, the `LibraryHandlerApp` is used to interact with the library management system through a menu-driven interface.

- **Example 10.6** Scenario 2:
  - **Step 1:** Run the `LibraryHandlerApp` and select options from the menu.
  ```
  1        LibraryHandlerApp app;
  2        app.run();
  ```
  - **Step 2:** Use the menu to add books, register borrowers, issue/return books, and view inventory as described in the previous scenario.

This scenario illustrates how the `LibraryHandlerApp` provides an easy-to-use interface for managing a library, making the system accessible to users who may not be familiar with the underlying code.

10.3.5 Performance Analysis

The library management system leverages various data structures to efficiently manage books, borrowers, and transactions. Each data structure is critical to the system's performance:

- **Map:** The `Map` stores book and borrower details, providing fast access and updates based on unique identifiers such as book IDs and borrower IDs.
  - **Complexity:** Average time for insertion, deletion, and access is $O(1)$; however, it can degrade to $O(n)$ in the worst case due to hash collisions.
- **Dynamic Array:** Used for managing collections like borrower loan histories and book listings, providing flexible and efficient data handling.
  - **Complexity:** Average insertion and access time is $O(1)$, with resizing upon capacity being the worst-case $O(n)$.
- **Priority Queue (Heap-Based):** Manages overdue books, prioritizing based on due dates to ensure prompt handling of late returns.
  - **Complexity:** Insertion: $O(\log n)$; deletion (pop): $O(\log n)$; peek: $O(1)$.

Analysis of Key Operations

The performance of main operations in the `LibraryManager` class is influenced by the efficiency of the underlying data structures:

```cpp
27  // Overloaded stream output operator
28  std::ostream& operator<<(std::ostream& os,
29      const Borrower& borrower) {
30      os << "Borrower ID: "
31          << borrower.borrowerID
32          << ", Name: " << borrower.name
33          << ", Loans: ";
34      for (size_t i = 0;
35          i < borrower.loanHistory.getSize(); ++i) {
36          os << borrower.loanHistory.get(i) << " ";
37      }
38      return os;
39  }
```

Borrower Class Definition

LibraryManager Class

The `LibraryManager` class oversees all book and borrower operations within the library, including managing inventory, handling loans, and updating borrower information.

```cpp
1  class LibraryManager {
2  public:
3      LibraryManager();
4  
5      // Book and Borrower management
6      void addBook(const Book& book);
7      void addBorrower(const Borrower& borrower);
8      Book& getBookByID(int bookID);
9      Borrower& getBorrowerByID(int borrowerID);
10 
11     // Book issue and return functions
12     void issueBook(int bookID, int borrowerID);
13     void returnBook(int bookID, int borrowerID);
14 
15     // Display functions
16     void displayInventory() const;
17     void displayBorrowers() const;
18 
19     // New functions for handling overdue books
20     void addOverdueBook(int bookID, int daysOverdue);
21     void handleMostOverdueBook();
22 
23 private:
24     // Map for storing books
```

10.3 Library Management System

```
25      Map<int, Book> bookMap;
26      // Map for storing borrowers
27      Map<int, Borrower> borrowerMap;
28      // Priority Queue for managing overdue books
29      PriorityQueue<int> overdueQueue;
30
31      bool bookExists(int bookID) const;
32      bool borrowerExists(int borrowerID) const;
33 };
```

LibraryManager Class Definition

10.3.3 Method Implementations

Adding a Book

The `addBook` method adds a new book to the library's inventory and updates the system accordingly.

```
1 void LibraryManager::addBook(const Book& book) {
2     if (!bookExists(book.getBookID())) {
3         bookMap.add(book.getBookID(), book);
4         std::cout << "Book added: "
5                   << book.getTitle() << std::endl;
6     } else {
7         std::cerr << "Book ID " << book.getBookID()
8                   << " already exists." << std::endl;
9     }
10 }
```

Adding a Book in LibraryManager

Issuing a Book

The `issueBook` function handles the process of issuing a book to a borrower, updating the availability status of the book and the borrower's loan history.

```
1 void LibraryManager::issueBook(int bookID, int borrowerID) {
2     if (!bookExists(bookID) || !borrowerExists(borrowerID)) {
3         std::cerr << "Error: Book or Borrower not found."
4                   << std::endl;
5         return;
6     }
7
8     Book& book = bookMap.get(bookID);
9     if (!book.getAvailability()) {
```

```
10        std::cerr << "Book " << book.getTitle()
11            << " is currently unavailable." << std::endl;
12        return;
13    }
14
15    Borrower& borrower = borrowerMap.get(borrowerID);
16    borrower.addLoan(bookID);
17    book.setAvailability(false);
18    std::cout << "Book issued to "
19        << borrower.getName() << std::endl;
20 }
```

Issuing a Book in `LibraryManager`

Returning a Book

The `returnBook` function processes the return of a book, updating both the book's status and the borrower's loan history.

```
1 void LibraryManager::returnBook(int bookID, int borrowerID) {
2     if (!bookExists(bookID) ||
3                !borrowerExists(borrowerID)) {
4         std::cerr << "Error: Book or Borrower not found."
5             << std::endl;
6         return;
7     }
8
9     Book& book = bookMap.get(bookID);
10    Borrower& borrower = borrowerMap.get(borrowerID);
11
12    borrower.removeLoan(bookID);
13    book.setAvailability(true);
14    std::cout << "Book returned: " << book.getTitle()
15        << std::endl;
16 }
```

Returning a Book in `LibraryManager`

Handling Overdue Books

The `addOverdueBook` and `handleMostOverdueBook` functions manage overdue books by adding them to a priority queue and processing the most overdue book based on priority.

10.3 Library Management System

```cpp
// Adds an overdue book to the priority queue
void LibraryManager::
    addOverdueBook(int bookID, int daysOverdue) {
    if (!bookExists(bookID)) {
        std::cerr << "Book does not exist in the inventory."
            << std::endl;
        return;
    }
    overdueQueue.add(bookID, daysOverdue);
    std::cout << "Book ID: " << bookID
        << " added to the overdue queue with "
        << daysOverdue << " days overdue." << std::endl;
}

// Handles the most overdue book
void LibraryManager::handleMostOverdueBook() {
    if (overdueQueue.isEmpty()) {
        std::cout << "No overdue books to handle."
            << std::endl;
        return;
    }

    int mostOverdueBookID = overdueQueue.pop();
    Book& overdueBook = getBookByID(mostOverdueBookID);
    std::cout << "Handling the most overdue book: "
        << overdueBook.getTitle() << std::endl;
}
```

Handling Overdue Books in `LibraryManager`

Other Utility Methods

The utility methods within the `LibraryManager` class provide additional operations, including displaying all books, borrowers, and handling overdue items.

```cpp
// Display all books in the inventory
void LibraryManager::displayInventory() const {
    std::cout << "Library Inventory:\n";
    DynamicArray<Pair<int, Book>> books = bookMap.getAll();
    for (size_t i = 0; i < books.getSize(); ++i) {
        std::cout << books[i].value << std::endl;
    }
}

```

```cpp
10  // Display all borrowers
11  void LibraryManager::displayBorrowers() const {
12      std::cout << "Library Borrowers:\n";
13      DynamicArray<Pair<int, Borrower>>
14              borrowers = borrowerMap.getAll();
15      std::cout << "Total borrowers: "
16              << borrowers.getSize() << std::endl;
17      for (size_t i = 0; i < borrowers.getSize(); ++i) {
18          const Borrower& borrower = borrowers[i].value;
19          std::cout <<
20              "Borrower ID: " << borrower.getBorrowerID()
21              << ", Name: " << borrower.getName() << ", ";
22          borrower.printLoans();
23      }
24  }
25
26  // Check if a book exists in the map
27  bool LibraryManager::bookExists(int bookID) const {
28      try {
29          bookMap.get(bookID);
30          return true;
31      } catch (const std::runtime_error&) {
32          return false;
33      }
34  }
35
36  // Check if a borrower exists in the map
37  bool LibraryManager::borrowerExists(int borrowerID) const {
38      try {
39          borrowerMap.get(borrowerID);
40          return true;
41      } catch (const std::runtime_error&) {
42          return false;
43      }
44  }
```

Utility Methods in `LibraryManager`

LibraryHandlerApp Class

The `LibraryHandlerApp` class provides a user-friendly interface for library staff to manage the system, perform transactions, and handle book and borrower records.

10.3 Library Management System

```cpp
class LibraryHandlerApp {
public:
    LibraryHandlerApp();

    void displayMenu() const;
    void handleAddBook();
    void handleAddBorrower();
    void handleIssueBook();
    void handleReturnBook();
    void handleDisplayInventory() const;
    void handleDisplayBorrowers() const;
    void handleExit() const;
    void run();

private:
    LibraryManager libraryManager;
};
```

LibraryHandlerApp Class Definition

```cpp
#include "LibraryHandlerApp.h"
// Constructor
LibraryHandlerApp::LibraryHandlerApp()
        : libraryManager() {}

// Display the main menu
void LibraryHandlerApp::displayMenu() const {
    std::cout << "\n=== Library Management System ===\n";
    std::cout << "1. Add Book\n";
    std::cout << "2. Add Borrower\n";
    std::cout << "3. Issue Book\n";
    std::cout << "4. Return Book\n";
    std::cout << "5. Display Inventory\n";
    std::cout << "6. Display Borrowers\n";
    std::cout << "7. Exit\n";
    std::cout << "Enter your choice: ";
}

// Handle adding a new book
void LibraryHandlerApp::handleAddBook() {
    int id;
    std::string title, author;
    std::cout << "Enter Book ID: ";
```

```cpp
24         std::cin >> id;
25         std::cin.ignore();
26         std::cout << "Enter Book Title: ";
27         std::getline(std::cin, title);
28         std::cout << "Enter Book Author: ";
29         std::getline(std::cin, author);
30         libraryManager.addBook(Book(id, title, author));
31 }
32
33 // Handle adding a new borrower
34 void LibraryHandlerApp::handleAddBorrower() {
35     int id;
36     std::string name;
37     std::cout << "Enter Borrower ID: ";
38     std::cin >> id;
39     std::cin.ignore();
40     std::cout << "Enter Borrower Name: ";
41     std::getline(std::cin, name);
42     libraryManager.addBorrower(Borrower(id, name));
43 }
44
45 // Handle issuing a book to a borrower
46 void LibraryHandlerApp::handleIssueBook() {
47     int bookID, borrowerID;
48     std::cout << "Enter Book ID to issue: ";
49     std::cin >> bookID;
50     std::cout << "Enter Borrower ID: ";
51     std::cin >> borrowerID;
52     libraryManager.issueBook(bookID, borrowerID);
53 }
54
55 // Handle returning a book
56 void LibraryHandlerApp::handleReturnBook() {
57     int bookID, borrowerID;
58     std::cout << "Enter Book ID to return: ";
59     std::cin >> bookID;
60     std::cout << "Enter Borrower ID: ";
61     std::cin >> borrowerID;
62     libraryManager.returnBook(bookID, borrowerID);
63 }
64
65 // Display all books in the inventory
66 void LibraryHandlerApp::
67         handleDisplayInventory() const {
68     libraryManager.displayInventory();
```

10.3 Library Management System

```cpp
69 }
70
71 // Display all borrowers
72 void LibraryHandlerApp::
73         handleDisplayBorrowers() const {
74     libraryManager.displayBorrowers();
75 }
76
77 // Handle exiting the application
78 void LibraryHandlerApp::handleExit() const {
79     std::cout <<
80     "Exiting Library Management System.\n";
81 }
82
83 // Run the main application loop
84 void LibraryHandlerApp::run() {
85     int choice;
86     do {
87         displayMenu();
88         std::cin >> choice;
89
90         switch (choice) {
91             case 1:
92                 handleAddBook();
93                 break;
94             case 2:
95                 handleAddBorrower();
96                 break;
97             case 3:
98                 handleIssueBook();
99                 break;
100            case 4:
101                handleReturnBook();
102                break;
103            case 5:
104                handleDisplayInventory();
105                break;
106            case 6:
107                handleDisplayBorrowers();
108                break;
109            case 7:
110                handleExit();
111                break;
112            default:
113                std::cout << "Invalid choice.
```

```
114                    Please try again.\n";
115                    break;
116            }
117        } while (choice != 7);
118    }
```

Main Function of `LibraryHandlerApp`

10.3.4 Example Scenario

Consider a scenario where the system manages the following books and borrowers:
- Books: "1984" (ID: 1), "To Kill a Mockingbird" (ID: 2), "The Great Gatsby" (ID: 3)
- Borrowers: John (ID: 1), Mary (ID: 2), Alice (ID: 3)

Scenario 1: Basic Library Management with `LibraryManager`

In this scenario, the system handles book additions, borrower registration, and the process of issuing and returning books.

■ **Example 10.5** Scenario 1:
- **Step 1:** Add books to the system.

```
1    LibraryManager lm;
2    lm.addBook(Book(1,
3            "Clean Code", "Robert"));
4    lm.addBook(Book(2,
5            "The Programmer", "Andrew"));
6    lm.addBook(Book(3,
7            "Design Patterns", "Erich"));
```

- **Step 2:** Register borrowers.

```
1    lm.addBorrower(Borrower(1, "John"));
2    lm.addBorrower(Borrower(2, "Mary"));
3    lm.addBorrower(Borrower(3, "Alice"));
```

- **Step 3:** Issue a book to a borrower.

```
1    lm.issueBook(1, 1); // John borrows "Clean Code"
```

- **Step 4:** Return a book.

```
1    lm.returnBook(1, 1); // John returns "Clean Code"
```

- **Expected Console Output:**

```
1    Book added: Clean Code
2    Book added: The Programmer
3    Book added: Design Patterns
4    Borrower added: 1, John
5    Borrower added: 2, Mary
```

- **Adding a Book or Borrower:** Involves adding entries to the map, providing a fast and efficient $O(1)$ complexity on average, making the system scalable for large libraries.
- **Issuing a Book:** This operation checks the availability of the book and updates both the book's status and the borrower's loan history. Checking and updating both entities are $O(1)$ complexity, allowing quick processing of transactions.
- **Returning a Book:** Similar to issuing, this operation updates the book's status and removes it from the borrower's loan history. Both operations are executed in $O(1)$ time.
- **Handling Overdue Books:** Involves adding books to a priority queue based on overdue status and retrieving the most overdue book. Insertion and retrieval both have a complexity of $O(\log n)$, which efficiently prioritizes transactions.

10.3.6 Optimization

To further enhance the performance of the library management system, it is essential to optimize data handling, minimize processing times, and ensure scalability. Below are strategies for refining the key functions in the `LibraryManager` class.

Using Efficient Data Structures for Library Operations

While the current system effectively uses maps, dynamic arrays, and a priority queue, there is potential for further optimization by incorporating more advanced data structures:

- **Balanced Trees for Book and Borrower Management:** Replacing the map with balanced tree structures like AVL Trees can provide $O(\log n)$ access, insertion, and deletion times. This approach ensures consistent performance, particularly under high-load conditions that might degrade hash map performance.
- **Enhanced Borrower Loan Tracking with Skip Lists:** Implementing skip lists for managing borrower loan histories can improve search, insertion, and deletion times, maintaining $O(\log n)$ complexity while being more straightforward to handle dynamically compared to balanced trees.

10.4 Summary

In this chapter, we took a deep dive into the practical applications of various data structures through real-world case studies. Each case study highlighted the importance of selecting the appropriate data structure to solve specific computational problems efficiently. By examining these examples, you have seen firsthand how different data structures can be used to optimize performance and ensure effective data management.

10.5 Book Summary

This book has provided you with a thorough introduction to data structures and their applications in solving real-world computational problems. We started with fundamental data structures, such as arrays, linked lists, stacks, and queues, and progressively delved into

10.5 Book Summary

more complex structures, such as trees, heaps, graphs, and hash tables. Each chapter was designed to build a solid understanding of the theoretical concepts followed by practical implementations in C++.

By the end of this book, you will have a comprehensive understanding of data structures, their implementation in C++, and their practical applications. This knowledge will enable you to design efficient algorithms and systems, making informed decisions about data structure selection and usage in your projects.

Your journey through this book has equipped you with the skills to tackle a wide range of computational problems. Whether you're optimizing performance, managing large volumes of data, or ensuring real-time processing, you now have the tools and insights to succeed. Keep experimenting, keep learning, and continue to explore the fascinating world of data structures.

Problems

Programming Problems

Figure 10.6: Scrambler ride reservation

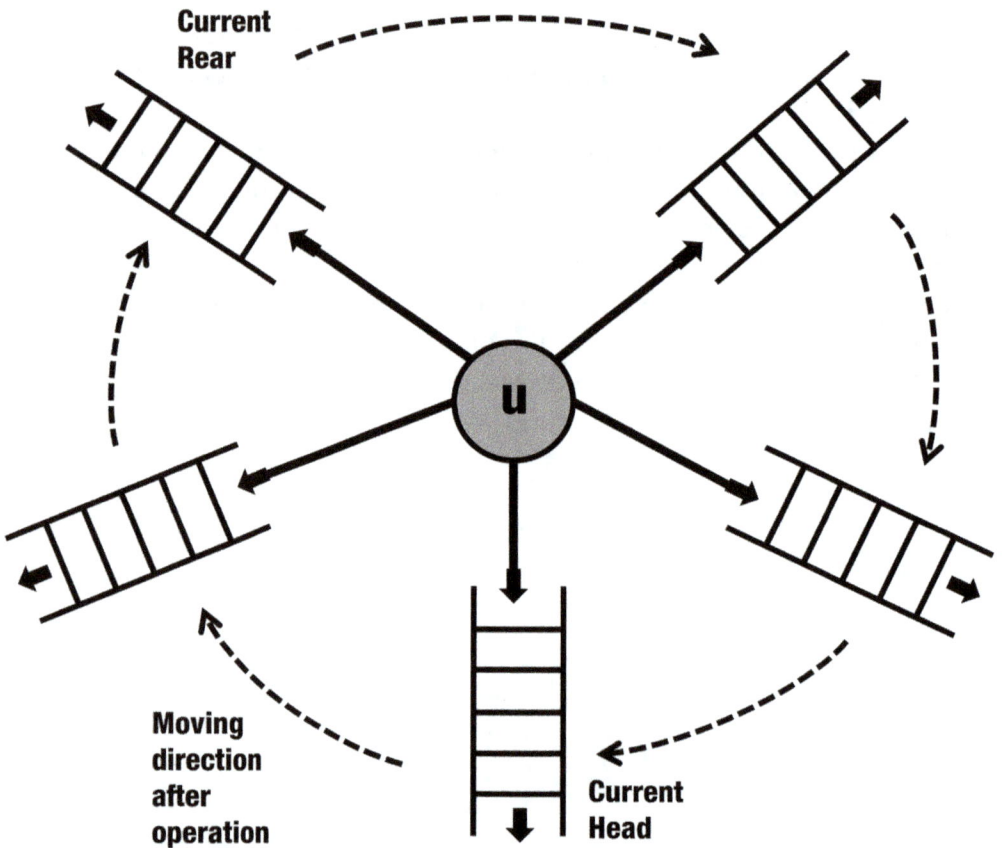

Figure 10.7: Scrambler ride reservation

1. **Scrambler Ride Reservation System**

   You are tasked with designing a reservation system for a Scrambler ride at an amusement park (Figure 10.6). The Scrambler ride consists of N arms, each with K chairs, for a total of $N \times K$ chairs (see Figure 10.7). Your system must ensure that reservations for chairs are balanced across all arms of the ride to maintain its operational stability. The system must handle reservations, cancelations, and check for ride availability efficiently.

   (a) **Data Structure Selection**

   i. What data structure would you use to manage the $N \times K$ chairs and why?

   ii. How would you ensure that reservations are balanced across all arms?

   (b) **Implementation**

   i. Write a class definition for the Scrambler ride reservation system. Include methods for reserving a chair, canceling a reservation, and checking availability.

   ii. Implement the method `reserveChair()` to add a reservation to a chair, ensuring even distribution across the arms.

10.5 Book Summary

(c) **Class Design**
   i. Design a class `ScramblerRide` that includes properties for the number of arms, number of chairs per arm, and methods for managing reservations.
   ii. Explain how your class design ensures operational stability of the ride.

(d) **Testing**
   i. Write test cases to validate the functionality of your reservation system.
   ii. How would you test for edge cases such as all chairs being reserved or attempting to cancel a nonexistent reservation?

2. **Online Examination System**

   Create an online examination system that manages exam schedules, question banks, and student submissions. The system should handle exam creation, question randomization, and automated grading.

   (a) **Data Structure Selection**
      i. What data structure would you use to manage the question bank and why?
      ii. How would you handle the randomization of questions for each exam?

   (b) **Implementation**
      i. Write a class definition for the online examination system. Include methods for creating exams, randomizing questions, and grading submissions.
      ii. Implement the method `createExam()` that selects a random subset of questions from the question bank.

   (c) **Class Design**
      i. Design a class `OnlineExamSystem` that includes properties for exam schedules, question bank, and student submissions.
      ii. Explain how your class design ensures efficient management of exams and submissions.

   (d) **Testing**
      i. Write test cases to validate the functionality of your examination system.
      ii. How would you test the system's ability to handle multiple exams and large numbers of submissions?

3. **Airline Reservation System**

   Create an airline reservation system that manages flight schedules, bookings, and passenger information. The system should handle booking requests efficiently and provide quick updates on flight availability.

   (a) **Data Structure Selection**
      i. What data structure would you use to manage flight schedules and bookings, and why?
      ii. How would you handle efficient search and updates of flight availability?

(b) **Implementation**
  i. Write a class definition for the airline reservation system. Include methods for booking a flight, canceling a booking, and checking flight availability.
  ii. Implement the method `bookFlight()` to add a booking for a flight, ensuring quick updates to availability.

(c) **Class Design**
  i. Design a class `AirlineReservationSystem` that includes properties for flight schedules, bookings, and passenger information.
  ii. Explain how your class design ensures efficient management of bookings and availability.

(d) **Testing**
  i. Write test cases to validate the functionality of your reservation system.
  ii. How would you test the system's ability to handle multiple bookings and flight cancelations?

4. **Real-World Case Study: Ecommerce Inventory Management**

Create an inventory management system for an ecommerce platform. The system should track product availability, manage orders, and handle restocking efficiently.

(a) **Data Structure Selection**
  i. What data structure would you use to manage the inventory of millions of products and why?
  ii. How would you handle frequent updates and quick access for users?

(b) **Implementation**
  i. Write a class definition for the ecommerce inventory management system. Include methods for adding products, updating product information, and searching for products.
  ii. Implement the method `addProduct()` to add a new product to the inventory.

(c) **Class Design**
  i. Design a class `EcommerceInventory` that includes properties for product information, inventory levels, and search functionality.
  ii. Explain how your class design ensures efficient management of a large and dynamic inventory.

(d) **Testing**
  i. Write test cases to validate the functionality of your inventory management system.
  ii. How would you test the system's ability to handle a large number of products and frequent updates?

Index

A

Abstraction 16
Accessing
    array 44
    double-linked list 89
    linked list 78
    space-efficient 284
Adaptability 41, 130
Algorithm analysis 8
    efficiency
      space, 9
      time, 9
      time, running time, 9
    evaluation 9
      lower bounds, 9
      optimality, 9
      performance, 10
    growth orders 9, 10
      average-case, 10
      best-case, 10
      worst-case, 10
Algorithms 2, 6
    programming *vs.* problems 6
    types of problems 8
    combinatorial logic, 8
    geometrical computation, 8
    graph theory, 8
    numerical analysis, 8
    searching, 8
    sorting, 8
    string manipulation, 8
Appending
    dynamic array 46
Array 34, 90, 313
    advantages 40
    dynamically allocated arrays 35
    fixed capacity 40
    heap-based 37
    limitations 40, 41, 132
    resizable 41
    stack-based 37
    stack *vs.* heap 36
    static arrays 34
Array-based queue 103
Array-based stack 100
Associative arrays 272

B

Best practices
    linked lists 92
    templates 20
Binary search tree (BST) 179
    deletion 183
    find max 185
    find min 185
    insertion 180
    searching 181
Binary trees 166
    arrays 168
    complete 167
    depth 171, 172
    destruction 173
    full 166
    height 171, 173
    linked lists 170
    perfect 167
    properties 166
    representation 168
    size 171, 172
    traversal 174
    types 166

C

Choosing data structures
    array 40, 121
    graph 243, 244
    linked-list 93, 121
Classes
    `AVLTree` 196
    `BinaryHeap` 253, 264
    `BinarySearchTree` 186
    `BinaryTree` 171
    `BinaryTreeArray` 169
    `BTreeNode` 170
    `ChainedHashTable` 147
    `DequeArray` 115
    `DequeLL` 119
    `DLList` 81
    `DNode` 80
    `DynamicArray` 42
    `GraphAdjList` 227, 242
    `GraphAdjMatrix` 218
    `IGraph` 213
    `LinearHashTable` 150
    `ListNode` 281
    `Map` 275
    `Node` 63
    `Pair` 273
    `PQNode` 268
    `PriorityQueue` 269
    `QueueArray` 105
    `QueueLL` 113
    `SEList` 282
    `SinglyLL` 64
    `SinglyLLTailed` 71
    `SkipList` 297
    `SKNode` 296
    `StackArray` 101
    `StackLL` 103
    `Vertex` 227
Code reusability 19
Cohesion and coupling 16
Comparison
    algorithms *vs.* data structure 3
    graph 243
    hash table 146, 158
    space-efficient 280
    tree traversal methods 179
Compile-time polymorphism 19
Consistency 16
Constant-time 40, 41

D

Data access 130
Data structures 2, 3, 5
    composite 5, 6
      linear, 6
      non-linear, 6

INDEX 359

generic 19
interfaces 21
primitive 5
Deque 114
advantages 120
circular increment 115
circular representation 115
dequeue 121
dequeue front 114
dequeue rear 114
empty 115
enqueue 121
enqueue front 114
enqueue rear 114
front 114
front index 115
full 115
insert 121
linked list-based 119
performance 121
rear 114
rear index 115
remove 121
Design flexibility 19
Design patterns 16
Design strategies 7
Dictionaries 272
Direct addressing 132
Double hashing 146
Dummy node 80
Dynamic arrays 41
advantages 41
limitations 41
resize rules 47

E

Efficient memory usage 41
Encapsulation 16
Enums
`HeapType` 264
Example

binary search tree
insertion, 180
searching, 181
chaining 141
double hashing 144
graphs
adjacency matrix, 225
hash functions 134–136, 138, 139
hashing usage 131
heaps
deletion, 257
heapify, 260
insertion, 255
max-heap, 251
min-heap, 253
removing, 259
heap sort 262
key-value pairs 273
linear probing 143
map 278
probing 141
quadratic probing 144
singly-linked list 64
skip lists
insertion, 301
lookup, 299
removal, 303
traversal
in-order, 178
level-order, 179
post-order, 178
pre-order, 178

F

First In, First Out (FIFO) 103, 239
Functions
`add` 26, 149, 155, 256, 276, 302
`addEdge` 222, 232
`addVertex` 220, 229
`balanceTree` 198
`BFS` 239

```
buildHeap .................... 260
clear .... 23, 26, 30, 79, 90, 173, 283
compare ...................... 265
contains ........ 26, 149, 155, 300
deleteAVL .................... 200
deleteNode ................... 183
deleteRoot ................... 257
deleteSubTree ................ 173
depth ..................... 30, 172
dequeue ...................... 109
dequeueFront ............ 117, 118
dequeueRear .................. 118
DFS ...................... 237, 241
DFSUtil ...................... 237
edgeCount ............... 223, 233
enqueue ...................... 109
enqueueFront ............ 117, 118
enqueueRear .................. 118
find ...................... 30, 182
findMax ...................... 185
findMin ...................... 185
get ......... 23, 44, 78, 89, 277, 285
getBalance ................... 197
getDegree .................... 217
getInDegree .................. 235
getOutDegree ................. 235
getRoot ....................... 30
getSize ............. 23, 26, 30, 172
hasEdge ................. 223, 232
heapify ...................... 260
heapifyDown ........ 257, 263, 265
heapifyUp ............... 256, 265
heapSort ..................... 262
height .................... 30, 173
inEdges ................. 224, 234
indexOf .................. 23, 286
inOrderTraversal ............. 176
insert ............... 30, 180, 199
insertAVL .................... 199
insertAt 23, 45, 49, 76, 86, 110, 287
insertNode ................... 180
isConnected .................. 240
isEmpty ............... 23, 26, 30
```

```
jumpTo ........................ 85
leftRightRotate .............. 195
leftRotate ................... 193
levelOrderTraversal ...... 177
operator[] ..... 23, 45, 78, 89, 285
optimizedHeapifyDown ..... 263
outEdges ................ 224, 234
pathExists ................... 241
peek ......................... 261
pop .......................... 271
popBack ...... 23, 47, 69, 75, 83, 292
popFront ........ 23, 47, 69, 84, 292
postOrderTraversal ........ 176
preOrderTraversal ......... 176
print .. 23, 26, 79, 89, 196, 223, 233,
        278, 283, 305
printSubLists ................ 283
pushBack . 23, 46, 47, 67, 73, 82, 291
pushFront ....... 23, 47, 66, 84, 291
randomLevel ................. 298
remove ... 26, 30, 150, 156, 183, 200,
        259, 276, 304
removeAt 23, 46, 49, 77, 88, 111, 290
removeEdge .............. 222, 232
removeVertex ........... 221, 230
resize ............... 48, 108, 157
rightLeftRotate ............. 195
rightRotate ................. 194
searchNode ................... 182
set ................. 23, 45, 89, 285
topBack ................. 23, 292
topFront ................ 23, 292
traverse ...................... 30
updateHeight ................ 197
vertexCount .................. 217
```

G

Generic programming 19
Graphs 208
   adjacency list 227
   adjacency matrix 217

applications	211
bfs	239
bipartiteness	209
connectedness	209
connectivity	240
cycle	209
definition	208
degree	209, 217, 224
density	210
dfs	236
edges	209, 236
incidence matrix	236
interface	213
path	209, 241
performance	243
planarity	209
representation	212
space complexity	243
terminology	209
time complexity	243

traversal
  bfs, 238
  depth-first, 236

vs. trees	212
types	209
vertices	209
weight	209

H

Hash functions	133
collisions	139
compound data types	138
criteria	139
data types	135
deterministic	139
floating point numbers	137
minimal collisions	139
multiplicative	133
random values	139
strings	135
uniform distribution	139
usage	133
Hashing	130
Hash table	130
applications	131
chaining	140, 273

    add, 149
    advantages, 145
    analysis, 145
    disadvantages, 145
    lookup, 149
    remove, 150

comparison	146
double hashing	144
linear probing	150

    add, 155
    lookup, 154
    remove, 156
    resize, 157

load factor	146
open addressing	141
performance	144, 158
probing	145

    linear, 142
    quadratic, 144
    variants, 142

resize	158
Heapification	255
Heaps	250
batch insertions	264
binary heaps	253
customization	264, 266
deletion	257
heapify	260
heap sort	262
insertion	255
Max-Heap	251
Min-Heap	251, 252
optimization	263
peek	261
performance	263
properties	251
remove	259
time complexity	263

I

Implementation
- array-based queue 105
- array-based stack 101
- AVL trees 196
- binary search tree 186
- binary trees 169
  - traversal, 175
- deque 115
- doubly-linked list 82
- dynamic array 42
- graphs
  - adjacency list, 227
  - adjacency matrix, 218
  - bfs, 239
  - dfs, 237
- hash table 147
  - chaining, 147
  - linear probing, 150
- linked list-based deque 119
- linked list-based queue 113
- linked list-based stack 103
- priority queue 267
- skip lists 297

Insertion
- array 39
- chaining 149
- doubly-linked list 85
- dynamic array 45
- linear probing 155
- linked list 76
- queue 110

Interface 16
- benefits 16
- definition
  - `IList`, 22
  - `ISet`, 25
  - `ITree`, 29
- dynamic array 42
- graphs 213
- implementation 20
- interface *vs.* implementation 17
- pure virtual functions 18
- standardization 20
- virtual functions 18

Interoperability 16

K

Key-value pairs 272

L

Last In, First Out (LIFO) 100, 236
Linear probing 146
Linked list 58, 90, 313
- advantages 90
- circular doubly-linked list 80, 93
- disadvantages 91
- doubly-linked list 80, 93
  - anatomy, 80
  - dummy node, 80
  - traversing, 89
- limitations 132
- singly-linked list 63, 92
  - anatomy, 63
  - without tail, 64
  - with tail, 71
- space-efficient 279, 282
  - performance, 293
- tail 73
- traversing 79

Lists 21
- interface 21

M

Map 272, 313
- add operation 276
- deletion operation 276
- display 277
- implementation 273
- keys 272

INDEX

list-based 132
lookup operation 277
performance 279
structure 273
values 272
Memory
    dynamic allocation 41
    heap 34, 35, 63
    stack 34, 35, 63
Memory management 62
    linked list 79

N

Node definition 281

O

Object-oriented programming 16
Open addressing 141
Operations
    array 44
    deque 117, 120
    doubly-linked list 82
    heaps 255
    priority queues 269
    queue 109
    singly-linked list 66
    skip lists 297
Optimization
    copy 48
    doubly-linked lists 85, 92
    dynamic arrays 48
    heaps 263

P

Performance analysis
    array 37
    arrays *vs.* linked lists 90, 130
    AVL trees 201

binary search tree 186
deque 121
graph 243
hash table 144
heaps 263
linked lists 91
map 279
priority queues 271
queue 121
skip lists 305
space-efficient linked list 293
stack 121
Pointer 34, 58
    arrays 36
    complexity 280
    heap-based arrays 36
    linked lists 63
    linked objects 60
    next 92
    objects 58, 60
    previous 92
    stack-based arrays 36
    tail 91
Priority queues 267
    add 270
    peek 271
    performance 271
    pop 271
    time complexity 271
Probing 141

Q

Quadratic probing 146
Queue 103
    array-based 103
    array-based deque 115
    circular 104
    dequeue 103, 104, 121
    double-ended 114
    empty 104
    enqueue 103, 104, 121

front 103, 104, 107–109
full 104
insert 121
linked list-based 113
performance 121
rear 103, 104, 107, 108
remove 121
resize 107

R

Removal
    array 39
    chaining 150
    doubly-linked list 85
    dynamic array 45
    linear probing 156
    linked list 76
    queue 110
Reusability 16

S

Sets 24
    interface 25
Singly-linked list................. 63
Skip lists........................ 294
    comparison 305
    deletion 296, 303
    display 305
    insertion 295, 300
    introduction 294
    levels 294, 295
    lookup operation 299
    node 294, 296
    performance 305
    random level 298
    rules 294
    search 296
    structure 294
Software design................... 16

Space complexity
    graphs 243
    hash function 133
    hash table 145, 146
    heaps 263
    space-efficient........... 280, 293
Stack 100
    array-based 100
    linked list-based 102
    performance 121
    pop 100, 121
    push 100, 121
    top 100

T

Templates 19
    interface design 20
    type abstraction 19
Testability 17
Time complexity
    array 40, 91
    AVL trees 201
    balanced binary trees 187
    binary search tree 186
    deque 121
    graphs 243
    hash table
      chaining, 145
      probing, 145
    heaps 263
    linked list 91
    priority queues 271
    queueu 121
    space-efficient 293
    stack 121
Trade-offs
    space-efficient linked list...... 293
Traversal
    breadth-first 174
      level-order, 174, 177
    depth-first 174

INDEX

    in-order, 174, 176
    post-order, 174, 176
    pre-order, 174, 175
  level-order 174
Trees 26
  AVL trees 190
    balanced, 191
    balance factor, 197
    balancing, 198
    deletion, 200
    height, 197
    implementation, 196
    insertion, 199
    introduction, 190
    operations, 197
    performance analysis, 201
    properties, 190
    rotations, 191
    unbalanced, 191
  balanced binary trees 187
    skewed, 188
    sparse, 188
  balanced trees 27
  binary 166

binary search trees 28, 179
  operations, 180
  properties, 180
binary trees 27
interface 28
rotations
  left rotation, 191
  left-right rotation, 194
  right-left rotation, 195
  right rotation, 193
self-balancing 188
structure 27
  depth, 27
  edge, 27
  height, 27
  internal node, 27
  leaf, 27
  node, 27
  root, 27
  subtree, 27
terminology 27
types 27
unbalanced binary trees 187

GPSR Compliance

The European Union's (EU) General Product Safety Regulation (GPSR) is a set of rules that requires consumer products to be safe and our obligations to ensure this.

If you have any concerns about our products, you can contact us on

ProductSafety@springernature.com

In case Publisher is established outside the EU, the EU authorized representative is:

Springer Nature Customer Service Center GmbH
Europaplatz 3
69115 Heidelberg, Germany

www.ingramcontent.com/pod-product-compliance
Lightning Source LLC
LaVergne TN
LVHW080135260326
834688LV00042B/1173